LVIV'S UNCERTAIN DESTINATION

A City and Its Train Terminal from Franz Joseph I to Brezhnev

ANDRIY ZAYARNYUK

Lviv's Uncertain Destination

A City and Its Train Terminal from Franz Joseph I to Brezhnev

UNIVERSITY OF TORONTO PRESS
Toronto Buffalo London

Toronto Buffalo London
utorontopress.com

ISBN 978-1-4875-0519-6 (cloth)
ISBN 978-1-4875-3173-7 (EPUB)
ISBN 978-1-4875-3172-0 (PDF)

Library and Archives Canada Cataloguing in Publication

Title: Lviv's uncertain destination : a city and its train terminal from Franz Joseph I to Brezhnev / Andriy Zayarnyuk.
Names: Zayarnyuk, Andriy, 1975- author.
Description: Includes bibliographical references and index.
Identifiers: Canadiana 2019018664X | ISBN 9781487505196 (hardcover)
Subjects: LCSH: Railroad stations – Ukraine – L′viv – History – 20th century. | LCSH: L′viv (Ukraine) – History – 20th century.
Classification: LCC DK508.95.L86 Z39 2020 | DDC 947.7/9 – dc23

This book has been published with the help of a grant from the Federation for the Humanities and Social Sciences, through the Awards to Scholarly Publications Program, using funds provided by the Social Sciences and Humanities Research Council of Canada.

University of Toronto Press acknowledges the financial assistance to its publishing program of the Canada Council for the Arts and the Ontario Arts Council, an agency of the Government of Ontario.

Canada Council for the Arts   Conseil des Arts du Canada

Funded by the Government of Canada   Financé par le gouvernement du Canada

Contents

Figures and Tables

Figures

Tables

Acknowledgments

This book owes many debts to people who supported my work on this project for many years, patiently read my drafts, and generously shared their knowledge and time. Andriy Orel was the manuscript's first and enthusiastic reader. Sean Patterson went through the whole manuscript, and his comments improved its readability extensively. Alan Rutkowski edited the language and gave very encouraging feedback. Freelancer Barry Norris meticulously copy edited the manuscript's final version. Jakub Beneš and John-Paul Himka commented on selected chapters, Oksana Vynnyk and Serhy Yekelchyk kindly shared some sources with me. Klavdiia Tatar and Antony Tomlin did an excellent job as research assistants. Oleksandr Avramchuk helped me in Warsaw. Editor Richard Ratzlaff, formerly with the University of Toronto Press, found excellent peer reviewers for the manuscript. Stephen Shapiro, who inherited the manuscript from Richard, guided me expertly through the rest of the publication process. Iryna Kotlobulatova generously shared with me her knowledge of Lviv's history, as well as postcards and photographs. Oleksandr Korobov, David Lee Preston of Philadelphia, Volodymyr Rumiantsev, and Harrie Teunissen kindly gave permission to use items from their personal collections as illustrations. The Holocaust Research Project (www.HolocaustResearchProject.org) team gave permission to use their map of the Lviv ghetto.

The book's final version benefited immensely from the discussion at the conference "Recovering Forgotten History: The Image of East-Central Europe in English-Language Academic and Text Books." Spasimir Domaradzki, Yaroslav Hrytsak, and Maciej Janowski furnished excellent detailed reviews. Finally, I would like to thank two anonymous peer reviewers of my manuscript. Their comments helped me to write a better book. I alone am responsible for all the remaining shortcomings and errors.

Institutional support for this project was indispensable. The book became possible because my research was generously funded by the University of Winnipeg and the Social Sciences and Humanities Research Council of Canada. The University of Winnipeg deserves special mention for being such a great workplace. The Harvard Ukrainian Research Institute awarded me a Eugene and Daymel Shklar Fellowship to work on the book in 2015, while a visit to Jerusalem was at the invitation of the Galicia Research Group with the Israel Institute for Advanced Studies at the Hebrew University of Jerusalem. I would also like to thank the Center for Urban History of East Central Europe; my research benefited from their library and two great projects: "Urban Maps Digital" and "Urban Image Database."

From year to year my colleagues from the Canadian Association of Slavists had to endure a torrent of Lviv train terminal papers – thank you all for your patience! My final thanks go to Winnipeg, Lviv's sister city, with its multitude of railway tracks, two splendid train terminals, extensive train yards, and busy depots. I wrote this book there.

Note on Transliteration and Names

Names of people and places have been transliterated from the Cyrillic alphabet according to a modified Library of Congress scheme. Modifications include dropping the apostrophe that marks a soft sign (Horodotska instead of Horodots'ka) and ending surnames with "-y" instead of "-yi" or "-ii." These adaptations have not been made in the bibliography. Generally, places in present-day Ukraine are transliterated from Ukrainian; for places in present-day Poland, Polish names are used. Normally, other versions of place names are provided in parentheses on the first use. Since Lviv's streets in the first half of the twentieth century were better known by their Polish names, I provide these in brackets every time a street name is used for the first time in any given paragraph. If the current Ukrainian name is a recent invention, I use a historical one, either in its Polish or internationally used version, with the current name in parentheses. For some geographic and personal names, established usage in the English language has been followed (Galicia, Nicholas II). For personal names with several available versions, I tried to follow either people's self-identification or their ethnicity – using Ukrainian versions for ethnic Ukrainians, Russian for ethnic Russians, and so on. When ethnicity and national loyalty most likely did not coincide, but an explicit statement from the person in question is missing, the reader will see two version of the same name – for example, Viitovych (Wójtowicz). Jewish names from Soviet documents are transliterated from Cyrillic.

Archives, Manuscript Depositories, and Related Abbreviations

Most archives and manuscript depositories used in this book have their holdings divided into collections composed of individual files. Post-Soviet collections also include an intermediary stage of "registers," into which collections are subdivided. Collections, registers, and files have unique numbers, while archives and depositories are denoted by their abbreviated names. Below the reader will find a list explaining those abbreviations, English translations and geographic locations.

AAN	Archive of Modern Records (*Archiwum Akt Nowych*), Warsaw.
AGAD	Main Archive of Ancient Records (*Archiwum Główne Akt Dawnych*), Warsaw.
ANK	National Archive in Krakow (*Archiwum Narodowe w Krakowie*), Krakow.
BJ	Manuscript Section of the Jagiellonian Library (*Sekcja Rękopisów Biblioteki Jagiellońskiej*), Krakow.
BN	Manuscript Collection of the Polish National Library (*Zakład Rękopisów Biblioteki Narodowej*), Warsaw.
d.	file (*delo*).
DAKO	State Archive of the Kyiv Oblast (*Derzhavnyi arkhiv Kyïvs'koï oblasti*), Kyiv.
DALO	State Archive of the Lviv Oblast (*Derzhavnyi arkhiv L'vivs'koï oblasti*), Lviv.
f.	collection (*fond*).
LNB	Manuscript Collection of the Lviv National Vasyl Stefanyk Scientific Library of Ukraine (*L'vivs'ka natsional'na naukova biblioteka Ukraïny imeni V. Stefanyka*), Lviv.

MILZ	Museum of the History of the Lviv Railroad (*Muzei istoriï L'vivs'koï zaliznytsi*), Lviv.
TsDAHO	Central State Archives of Public Organizations of Ukraine (*Tsentral'nyi derzhavnyi arkhiv hromads'kykh orhanizatsii Ukraïny*), Kyiv.
TsDAVO	Central State Archives of Supreme Bodies of Power and Government of Ukraine (*Tsentral'nyi derzhavnyi arkhiv vyshchykh orhaniv vlady ta upravlinnia Ukraïny*), Kyiv.
TsDIAuL	Central State Historical Archive of Ukraine in Lviv (*Tsentral'nyi derzhavnyi arkhiv Ukraïny u Lvovi*), Lviv.
Op.	register (*opys, opis'*).
Rkps. Ossolin.	*Manuscript Division of the Ossolineum Library (Dział Rękopisów Zakładu Narodowego im. Ossolińskich), Wroclaw.*
RGIA	Russian State Historical Archive (*Rossiiskii gosudarstvennyi istoricheskii arkhiv*), Saint Petersburg.
RGAE	Russian State Archive of Economy (*Rossiiskii gosudarstvennyi arkhiv ekonomiki*), Moscow.
RGASPI	Russian State Archive for Social and Political History (*Rossiiskii gosudarstvennyi arkhiv sotsial'no-politicheskoi istorii*), Moscow.
RGVIA	Russian State Military-Historical Archive (*Rossiiskii gosudarstvennyi voenno-istoricheskii arkhiv*), Moscow.
Spr.	file (*sprava*).
Sygn.	file number (*sygnatura*).
Yad Vashem	Yad Vashem Archives, Jerusalem.
Zesp.	collection (*zespół*).

Abbreviations for Political Parties, State Offices, Associations, and Railway Divisions and Departments

CC	Central Committee
CM	Council of Ministers
CPSU	Communist Party of the Soviet Union
CPU	Communist Party of Ukraine
KPP	Communist Party of Poland (*Komunistyczna Partia Polski*)
KPZU	Communist Party of Western Ukraine (*Komunistychna partiia Zakhidnoï Ukraïny*)
KPW	Railway Military Preparation (*Kolejowe Przysposobienie Wojskowe*)
MGB	Ministry of State Security (*Ministerstvo Gosudarstvennoi Bezopasnosti*)
MPS	Ministry of Communications (USSR) (*Ministerstvo Putei Soobshcheniia*)
Narkomat	People's Commissariat
NKVD	People's Commissariat of Internal Affairs (*Narodnyi Kommisariat Vnutrennikh Del*)
NKPS	People's Commissariat of Communications (*Narodnyi Kommisariat Putei Soobshcheniia*)
Obkom	Oblast Committee of the Communist Party
OUN	Organization of Ukrainian Nationalists
PKP	Polish State Railways (*Polskie Koleje Państwowe*)
PPS	Polish Socialist Party (*Polska Partia Socjalistyczna*)
PPSD	Polish Social Democratic Party of Galicia and Silezia (*Polska Partia Socjalno-Demokratyczna Galicji i Śląska*)
Sovnarkom	*Council of People's Commissars*
UPA	Ukrainian Insurgent Army (*Ukraïns'ka Povstans'ka Armiia*)
USDP	Ukrainian Social Democratic Party
USVR	Department of Construction-Rebuilding Works (*Upravleniie stroitel'no-vosstanovitel'nykh rabot*)

USVZ Department of Construction and Rebuilding of Plants (*Upravleniie stroitel'stva i vosstanovleniia zavodov*)
ZKP Union of Polish Railwaymen (*Związek Kolejarzy Polskich*)
ZZK Trade Union of Railway Workers (*Związek Zawodowy Kolejarzy*)

LVIV'S UNCERTAIN DESTINATION

A City and Its Train Terminal from Franz Joseph I to Brezhnev

Introduction

Lviv's distinctive cityscape is hard to imagine without the unmistakable silhouette of its main railway terminal.[1] Built in 1904 when Lviv – German and Yiddish: Lemberg; Polish: Lwów; Russian: Lvov; also known as Leopol in French and Leopolis in Latin – was part of Austria-Hungary, the terminal was seen as a wonder of modern civilization by locals and foreigners alike. An American journalist who visited "the beautiful city" of Lviv during his stint in the Russian Army in the First World War, believed that, "among its imposing buildings there is none finer than the gigantic railway station, whose classical lines and symmetrical proportions speak of the masterhand."[2] A Russian officer who also came to Lviv with the Russian occupational forces, noted in his diary: "What a train terminal! I have nothing to compare it with, since I have not seen terminals like that in Russia."[3]

Lively air connections and dense road traffic notwithstanding, the terminal still serves Lviv's multitudinous visitors as the main access point to the city. The city still takes pride in this survivor of the twentieth century and living testament to its complicated recent history. By comparison, in the old empire's capital of Vienna – a metropolis with ten times Lviv's population prior to the First World War – not a single imperial-era train terminal survived the twentieth century. Although not the most important difference between the two cities, the story of their train terminals points to the diverging trajectories that various parts of the Habsburg Empire followed in the aftermath of its breakup, and to the material consequences of this divergence.

This book tells Lviv's history by following the fate of the city's main train terminal through the turbulent twentieth century: from the last decades of the Habsburg Empire to the last decades of the Soviet Union. Never fully demolished, the terminal building has remained in the same location and fulfilled the same function even as it witnessed changing political regimes. In addition to its life under Austrian imperial (1900–18), national Polish (1918–39), and Soviet (1939–91) rule, the terminal weathered both World Wars, including the Russian imperial (1914–15) and Nazi (1941–44) occupations, not to mention "local wars" that raged through the city after the end of both global wars.

This book is based on the assumption that historical investigation into a single material structure can yield unique insights, inaccessible to research with a broader scope. The Lviv terminal has experienced a range of modern political regimes: the dynastic Habsburg Empire, the national Polish state with clear authoritarian tendencies, the wartime Nazi occupation, and the Soviet dictatorship. Through them all, the terminal remained one of the most important city structures for strategic, economic, and policing reasons. Excavating the imprints of these political regimes on the material building and people in it, this book also tackles the differences between these political regimes at the level of their everyday operations and in a particular peripheral city.

Walter Benjamin's *Arcades Project* served as the main methodological inspiration for this book.[4] A meticulous archaeology of city life, Benjamin's unfinished project traces the changes of material forms and their perceptions in order to explore capitalism's social imagery. It also shows how central are materiality and perception for urban capitalist modernity. Following Benjamin's approach, this book explores social and political imaginations in their material and aesthetic dimensions, while connecting them with the more conventional domains of social enquiry, such as those pertaining to the economy, social class, and state. Unlike Benjamin's project, the present book does not focus on modernity in a capital city; rather, it examines the historical actualizations of possibilities, not merely their potential dream-like presence, and it takes a more conventional historical approach by following chronologically unfolding events, so as to grasp the nature of the changes experienced by people and material objects in their interrelation.

Since its founding in the middle of the twelfth century, Lviv has been one of Eastern Europe's most important and interesting urban centres. Lviv's founder Danylo Romanovych, a Rus' prince and since 1253 the king of Rus', named the city after his son Leon (Lev in Ukrainian). Lviv became the capital of the Rus' lands of Halych and Volhynia, and together with the rest of Halych land was annexed by the Polish king Casimir the Great in the 1340s. Under Casimir, Lviv became a royal city, enjoying self-government according to the Magdeburg law, and saw an influx of German-speaking colonists from the west. An important trade centre on the route connecting the Baltic Sea region with the Balkans and Black Sea, during the Polish-Lithuanian Commonwealth the city was also a gateway from the Polish crown's core lands to its Ukrainian acquisitions. A booming multi-ethnic metropolis, by the beginning of the seventeenth century Lviv had become the third-largest city of the Polish-Lithuanian Commonwealth. From the fourteenth century until well into the nineteenth, Lviv was the largest city on the territory of present-day Ukraine. The city's fortunes changed with those of the Commonwealth. The great Cossack rebellion of 1648 opened a period of war that stalled Lviv's growth, and the eighteenth century opened with the devastation caused by the Great Northern War. Only after the partitions of Poland at the end of the eighteenth century did the city resume its growth in the new political framework of the nineteenth-century Habsburg Empire.

In the first half of the twentieth century, Lviv experienced a kaleidoscopic change of states. The Russian Empire governed the city in 1914–15, the Western Ukrainian People's Republic was proclaimed in the city in November 1918, and by the end of the same month the city ended up in the new independent Poland. The Soviet Union annexed the city in September 1939, and in June 1941 Nazi Germany came. The return of the Red Army in July 1944 ended three decades of the violent redrawing of state borders. The front rolled through the city twice in both the First and Second World Wars, but the latter war brought not only combat but also genocide and forced resettlement, the cataclysm of the Holocaust, and the forced resettlement of the city's Polish majority. The physical city survived, but many Lvivites believed it was no longer the same city. After the Second World War, Lviv became an important urban centre of Soviet Ukraine, with a very non-Russian, non-Soviet past. In 1991 the Ukrainian Soviet Socialist Republic declared its independence, and the city found itself in independent Ukraine.

This book uses the Lviv's main train terminal as a key to accessing the city's painful twentieth-century history. The terminal allows us to relate that history afresh, shifting the narrative point of view away from governing states, city administrations, bounded ethnic and social groups, and milestone political events. Focusing on an individual building helps to bypass the "city as organism" metaphor that has informed much urban history. This book looks at a city's microcosm, using a fragment to understand the whole and to excavate the city buried beneath layers of narratives, each claiming it for their own and legitimizing existing political regimes.

The focus on Lviv should help overcome a certain insularity of chronologically and nationally organized subfields in the region's historiography. Historians working on the Habsburg and Russian Empires rarely venture into inter-war Poland, and even more rarely into the USSR's post-war period. Using Lviv's terminal, this book explores how very dissimilar political regimes all used essentially the same object to fulfil similar functions. Although there has been a long and insightful historical discussion of differences between the political systems of a dynastic empire, a nationalizing state, and a Soviet socialist state, strikingly few works go beyond comparing the formal political structures, dominant ideologies, and state policies of these regimes. This study is interested not in the political regimes themselves, but in the ways they filled, organized, and ordered social space, as well as in the human experiences generated in that space.

On the rare occasions when existing historical scholarship trespasses chronological and state borders, it tends to focus on violence and war in the studies of both the larger Eastern European region[5] and the city of Lviv in particular.[6] Without diminishing the importance of studying mass violence, I argue that this tendency limits our ability to imagine and conceptualize the effect of major political changes on the level of mundane peacetime daily practices. This book focuses on everyday "normalcy," for which most people longed, especially during the most extreme violence, and to which they tried to return at the first available opportunity.

As a fixture of everyday city life, the railway terminal exemplifies the connection between the urban mundane and larger political, economic, and cultural formations that structure the humdrum rhythms of the everyday. Social and cultural histories of the railway have been instrumental in bettering our understanding of modernity.[7] Although trains and the larger railway network loom large in this book, it is not a study of railway history per se. I use a single and very particular railway structure to shed light on the larger dimensions of the local experience. The terminal was not exceptional as a node in the larger regional, national, and international networks – many other urban sites, institutions, and enterprises, even the city itself, played analogous roles in those larger networks. The terminal, however, can function as a vantage point from which to study the city's links to larger contexts.

This is not the first book to venture into a less visible dimension of states and political institutions to explore the everyday consequences of their operations. The growing literature on the subject is largely situated within the "modernity paradigm." Instead of seeing Eastern European history as an aberration from the Western path of development, these new studies emphasize the common origins of Eastern and Western Europe in the Enlightenment and their shared experiences of industrialization and metropolitanism.[8] In one of the key texts on the emergence of the modernity paradigm in Soviet studies, Stephen

Kotkin compares the Soviet experience "to a mirror in which various elements of the modernity found outside the USSR are displayed in alternately undeveloped, exaggerated, and familiar forms."[9] The bulk of literature that has appeared in the modernity paradigm, however, tends to focus on the familiar and the similar. Some recent studies emphasize continuities that stretch across apparent political disruptions, mostly via the techniques states use to survey, classify, and shape their populations.[10] Michael David-Fox points out that, although extremely productive, the historiography of Soviet modernity also comes dangerously close to being an all-encompassing platitude. He observes that "discussions of Russian and Soviet modernity thus focused first and foremost on elements of comparability rather than on the distinguishing contours of a Soviet system that diverged quite radically from other modern states."[11] Among other things, in this book I seek to identify and explain divergences. Without denying similarities, borrowings, and cross-fertilization, I take seriously Soviet (or Nazi) claims to being an alternative.

Modern power, however, operates not only through authority, knowledge, and discourse, but also through mundane, seemingly innocuous material objects and spheres. This book explores the workings of modern power through "everyday material politics," or the relationships between the infrastructure of urban life, its uses and political formations.[12] My focus on material forms helps to overcome the analytical separation between "social" and "cultural," and between "political" and "economic." Analytical abstraction is a powerful tool, but it tends to tear apart historical reality. Singling out certain dimensions of social life, we tend to forget that they form inseparable facets of actual human experience.[13] Classifications and concepts often acquire a life of their own, and are treated as an ontologically existing reality. This study heeds the plea of those historians who maintain that, since most social objects are both economic units and cultural sites, the corresponding analytical approaches "should ideally be undertaken *together*."[14] Instead of analytically defining and scrutinizing discrete domains of human experience, I draw on William Sewell's proposed solution to the conundrum by combining the "social," the "cultural," and the "political." I attempt to scrutinize practices as shaped by a particular power in their "material instantiations."[15] Lviv's main railway terminal provides a series of such material instantiations.

The terminal, however, is not merely a material object; it is part of the cityscape, and as such allows for the exploration not only of materiality, but also of spatiality as integral parts of human experience.[16] I address the spatiality of the terminal on several levels: the organization of its inner space; its location in the region's largest city; and its effect on the development and organization of the city space. Space and spatiality function in historiography as extremely open-ended metaphors, referring to a wide range of concepts and traditions.[17] This book looks at the terminal's spatiality following Henri Lefebvre's "social space" approach, not only as a space of representation, an interplay of symbols and messages, but also as a practice, embedded in everyday routines and strategies.[18]

Although a particular space itself, and an important strategic point in the imperial and nation-state's spaces that railway lines helped to create, the terminal was also a nodal point in a global railway network with specific rules and rhythms. Most important, at least for this book, the terminal was also, and remains, an inseparable part of the urban fabric in Lviv, a city that has gained increasing attention from the region's historians. This attention has resulted in an immense wealth of literature, to which this brief introduction cannot do full justice. Therefore the remarks below provide only a very schematic general overview.

Western historians neglected the city during the Cold War, discussing it only in the context of Soviet "nationality" problems.[19] In Soviet Ukraine and communist Poland, the history of twentieth-century Lviv had to conform to the official narrative that hailed communist ideology and celebrated Soviet achievement. The closer to the present, the tighter became censorship controls and strictures of ideological orthodoxy. The most valuable part of that historiography was the publication of primary sources.[20] After the Soviet Union collapsed, partly because of the prominent role the city played during *perestroika* and subsequent Ukrainian nation building, Lviv promptly found itself in the scholarly limelight. Arguably, in much of that literature, Lviv was present as a stage set, but not the actual object of investigation. A number of excellent works, however, have appeared on the city's architectural history, but these tend to concentrate on the Austrian period, and concern themselves with the question of style and architectural detail in a purely artistic context.[21] Markian Prokopovych's monograph, notwithstanding its flaws, is probably the only attempt to move beyond architecture per se and to situate architectural changes in the social and political landscape of the Habsburg reforms.[22]

Non-architectural histories of the city also tend to celebrate the multicultural "golden age" of the Habsburg Empire. Paradoxically, this emphasis on multiculturalism has only reinforced the national focus of historical studies. Scholars think about cultures first of all as national;[23] even studies of the city's demography are preoccupied with ethnic divisions and the numerical strength of different national and linguistic communities.[24] It is no accident that initially only Polish historians wrote about the city's most "Polish" period – the inter-war years – and covered the tragedy of the city during the Second World War, but focusing on the experiences and suffering of the city's Polish community.[25] Although these histories do not claim to be methodologically innovative, they are properly researched, and try to maintain balance in their interpretation while introducing plenty of factual material.[26]

Not only a large regional centre, but also a modern city that has gone through cataclysmic and traumatic political changes, Lviv has developed a rich tradition of antiquarian and memoir literature. Although it does not qualify as academic history, this tradition is extremely valuable for any historical enquiry into the city's past. No matter how good, academic history cannot replace Iryna Kotlobulatova's albums of postcards and historical photographs, Yuri Biriuliov's invaluable guidebook, Józef Wittlin and Stanisław Lem's memoirs, or Ilko Lemko's account of everyday life in Lviv, which relies heavily on personal experiences.[27]

Until recently, Ukrainian scholarship on Lviv's post-Habsburg history remained quite modest. Characteristically, the first monograph on Soviet Lviv's everyday life was published in Polish in Poland, although written by a Lviv-based scholar.[28] Ukrainian historians, however, now have produced excellent works on the city's Soviet past. In particular, Halyna Bondar's detailed reconstruction of the experiences of rural migrants to Soviet Lviv stands out as an example of rigorous and rich scholarship combining historical and anthropological methods.[29] Lviv-based historians have also collectively produced a valuable three-volume reference text, a synthetic academic history of the city.[30]

Lviv's Soviet period has also attracted the attention of Western scholars. Tarik Cyril Amar begins his study with the destruction of the old multinational Lviv in the Second World War. According to him, nationalism played an even more important role in this process than did war. Although openly nationalist movements and regimes contributed to the city's reshaping, Amar argues that the effort to integrate Lviv into Soviet Ukraine proved to be crucial for the creation of a nationally homogeneous "Ukrainian Lviv."[31] William Jay Risch picks up the story where Amar leaves off, focusing on the 1960s and 1970s. Risch also pays attention to the "national question," but sees it as a field of contestation, where boundaries were probed by intellectuals and by the population at large. Even more important, he draws attention to the rich layers of urban culture that had little to do with national projects and identities. He stresses the importance of the city's borderland location and its very non-Soviet, non-Russian history for the formation of lively sub- and countercultures.[32]

A major lacuna in the historiography of Lviv for decades was its wartime experience, especially the Holocaust.[33] This situation, however, has changed of late. Christoph Mick's account of the city's transformation in the longer continuum of violence, from the outbreak of the First World War until the end of the Second, shows how changing and escalating patterns of violence transformed Lvivy.[34] Kai Struve has provided us with the most detailed account to date of the violence and murder of Jews in Lviv in the summer of 1941 in his study on the wave of anti-Jewish pogroms that swept across Western Ukraine.[35] Ola Hnatiuk's recent book, structured as a study of several Lviv families, uncovers complex motivations behind people's choices, demonstrating a complex intertwining of the individual fates of Jews, Poles, and Ukrainians.[36]

Almost all of these diverse historical works on twentieth-century Lviv share a common problem: they treat the city merely as a territory. In most, "Lviv" could easily be replaced with "Western Ukraine" or any other name for the region without much change in their arguments or narrative structure.[37] What is missing in these works is some essential "city-ness": the distinct nature of this large urban settlement, its unique spatiality or "synoecism," which, as Edward Soja argues, must not "remain simply a useful add-on, a flashy new interpretive approach," but should "*take precedence* in writing about the city."[38] This book accordingly takes "synoecism" seriously, seeing it as a fundamental fact of urban life. It also assumes that, to know the city, one has to take its unique spatial and social constellation seriously.

Another problem with the historiography of Lviv is its preoccupation with national communities, national activism, national conflict, and the concomitant reification of nationality and ethnic difference. This preoccupation is so overwhelming that even books focusing on criticizing and condemning nationalism assign it a pivotal role in the city's twentieth-century history. These books also describe and explain historical events or changes as the doing of national groups. Although nationalism has been an important force in Lviv's modern history, I argue it has not been the only force, or even the most important one. I draw attention to the most basic and habitually neglected fact that, throughout the twentieth century, the majority of Lviv's population were wage workers, under both capitalism and socialism, in the dynastic Habsburg Empire and in the "nationalizing"[39] Polish state. I assume that, for the people of twentieth-century Lviv, this experience was far more fundamental than either ethnicity or language.

When it comes to the various twentieth-century political regimes that controlled the city, clashing ideologies and spectacular armed conflicts doubtless affected the lives of Lvivites. Equally important, however – which existing studies fail to address – were the differences between those regimes' mundane operations: how they organized everyday economic activities and social interactions, those microtechnologies of power that, in a modern city, work not only in but also through the city's space. How can we discern those spatial practices in the modern city? A conventional approach would be to map the city and to analyse distributions and variations across this map – basically, to repeat the algorithms and use techniques of the governments trying to control and shape the city's space. In this book, I try to do justice to the experience of ordinary people navigating their urban space. That pedestrian experience is centred on the city's concrete material fragments: a dwelling, a workplace, a neighbourhood, or familiar and favourite streets. The study follows those experiences, focusing on a fragment of the city's built environment and those who interacted with it most often. The narrative tries to capture those ordinary experiences without expecting to do so fully, since fleetingness is in their nature, and their wholeness is very different from the comprehensiveness of knowledge deployed by political powers. Hence the book's shifting focus, one that oscillates between the terminal and its neighbourhoods, the railway and the city, workers and passengers.

This investigation has two chronological brackets, although they are not impermeable. The first bracket is relatively obvious: the initial years of the twentieth century, when Lviv's new train terminal was built. The second bracket is more arbitrary: the investigation ends in 1980, the year of the Moscow Olympic games. This unconventional caesura helps to avoid the teleology implicit in historical narratives that end with a clear-cut political rupture. Nineteen-eighty was the heyday of the Brezhnev era, when, to paraphrase the title of Alexey Yurchak's famous book, everything still seemed to be forever.

The book's narrative is structured chronologically. Chapter 1 deals with the terminal's pre-history and provides a brief overview of nineteenth-century Lviv's railway lines and stations. Chapter 2 looks at the construction of the new terminal and scrutinizes the building's various contexts. Chapter 3 explores the terminal's effect on the fabric of the city, paying particular attention to how it shaped the city's neighbourhoods, society, and politics. Chapter 4 describes the terminal during the First World War, the experiences and effect of occupation and military governance, and the damages inflicted on the terminal and the city. Chapter 5 surveys the inter-war period of the terminal's history, focusing on the changes enacted by the nationalizing Polish state. Chapter 6 follows the terminal through the Second World War, with its concomitant Soviet and Nazi occupations – experiences that proved to be most damaging to the terminal and to the city, reshaping both more radically than any other event in the city's twentieth-century history. Chapter 7 focuses on the Soviet reconstruction of the terminal and that undertaking's practical and symbolic dimensions. Chapters 8 and 9 describe the terminal's life in the post-war Soviet era, detailing its transformation and operations in a self-professed socialist state that strived to become an alternative to everything the city had experienced before. That unique Soviet space in Lviv is now irretrievably lost, together with its Polish and Austrian predecessors.

Chapter One

City Gates of the Steam Age

In 1900 Lviv enjoyed capital status within the Kingdom of Galicia and Lodomeria with the Grand Duchy of Krakow and the Duchies of Auschwitz and Zator – Galicia, for short. This factitious nineteenth-century kingdom was about to vanish in the first storms of the new century.[1] The Habsburgs invented Galicia and Lodomeria in 1772 as a name for their most recent annexation, arbitrarily carved from the dying Polish-Lithuanian Commonwealth. The regal name referred to the medieval Rus' duchies of Halych and Volodymyr, which a Hungarian king happened to rule briefly in the twelfth century. Unlike the phony medieval title used to legitimize Vienna's conquest, nineteenth-century Galicia was a very real entity, a unique historical experience that could be discerned in the landscape, buildings, and people long after the province disappeared from Europe's political map in 1918.

Although Lviv was the capital of the largest Habsburg province in the nineteenth century, after the First World War it had to content itself to rule much smaller administrative units. Twice a Ukrainian state was proclaimed in the city, but neither attempt lasted long, and even local Ukrainians believed their nation's capital was elsewhere. Even while the city held the title of a "royal capital city" in the nineteenth century, it was scorned not only by Vienna, the imperial capital, but also by the much larger and more dynamic cities of Prague and Budapest. As an overwhelmingly agrarian and barely literate region, Galicia was often seen as the epitome of poverty and ignorance. For much of the nineteenth century to the centres of Western European modernity Galicia remained a mysterious and virtually unknown land, not unlike Dracula's Transylvania. As one compendium of the nineteenth-century West's geographic knowledge explained, before a major railway crossed it, "Galicia was hardly accessible, and it was less frequently referred to than many a less important country in distant Asia."[2] It took some time, however, for the railway, a symbol and sign of the dawn of the industrial age, to reach Lviv.

Provincial and backward and separated from the rest of the empire by the Carpathian Mountains, the landlocked Kingdom of Galicia was also a stage for the Habsburg projects of civilizing the empire's own East[3] and for the provincial elites' home-brewed dreams of modernization. Since their invention, iron roads and steam engines had been part and parcel of those visions. As early as 1830, the year passengers first boarded the Liverpool-Manchester train, opening the "Railway Age," Vienna's Rothschilds and Professor Franz Riepl entertained the vision of an ambitious railway project to connect Austria's Russian border via Lviv with Vienna and Trieste, the empire's main seaport.[4] Perhaps overreaching at the time, the Rothschilds' railway visions for Galicia came to naught. Only a section of the railway, from Vienna to Brno, the capital of Moravia, was built in 1837–39 – Austria's first and continental Europe's longest steam railway.[5] Another decade would pass before the first railway track was laid in Galicia. In 1847, Krakow, which had been annexed the year before and was now the province's second-largest city, obtained a train terminal and regular railway service. Krakow and Warsaw, old Poland's two capital cities, were now connected by railway with each other, and through Vienna with the wider European railway network, but there was still no railway connection to Lviv. Even the service between Krakow and Vienna had to cross the empire's border twice, and ran through rapidly industrializing Prussian Silesia.

As is often the case with Eastern European modernizations, international tensions provided a missing catalyst to help the railway reach Lviv. The Crimean War shattered the Austrian-Russian friendship that dated back to the Congress of Vienna in 1815. As recently as 1849, Russia's Nicholas I had sent his troops through Galicia to help Franz Joseph I suppress the Hungarian Revolution. In 1854, however, instead of reciprocating Russian support, Austria showed hostility with an ultimatum demanding the Russians withdraw from the Danube. Nicholas I famously turned Franz Joseph's portrait on his cabinet to face the wall, and jotted "*Du Undankbarer!* (you, ungrateful one)" on its back.[6] Chances were good that the next time Russian troops moved through Galicia, it would be as an enemy. To defend Galicia, it had to be integrated better into the rest of the Habsburg Empire. With these considerations, large-scale railway construction began on Galicia's first and most important latitudinal line. Thousands of soldiers worked as navvies, and by 1856 Krakow was linked with Vienna via a wholly domestic line.[7] This time, the line would also extend to East Galicia and Lviv.

It took until 1861 for the railway from Krakow to reach Lviv, arriving, symbolically, from the west. This was quite late by the standards of industrializing Western Europe, but not by those of the rest of the continent. Only ten years earlier, Saint Petersburg was connected by rail with Moscow and the first train reached Madrid, while Rome saw its first train in 1856. On the territory of present-day Ukraine, Lviv was the first city to obtain a regular railway service (the British built a short military railway in Crimea in 1855 during the war). When the railway reached Lviv in 1861, Romania, Serbia, and present-day Bulgaria were still waiting for their first trains.

The railway that connected Lviv with Krakow, and with the empire's capital, was a private enterprise, a consortium created mainly by Galicia's large aristocratic landowners. It was named after the archduke Karl Ludwig, the emperor's younger brother, who had been assigned to the Viceroy's Office and lived in Lviv from 1853 to 1855. The state guaranteed the new enterprise a fixed minimal revenue; in exchange, it reserved the right to purchase the enterprise at any time after a period of thirty years.[8] The consortium was to continue its railway to Brody, on the border with the Russian Empire (Figure 1.1). Indeed the Russian border was the end point of all previous Galician railway projects, including one in 1842 that had entertained the possibility of using horses rather than steam to pull the rail cars.[9] Strategic reservations in the aftermath of the Crimean War did not change the final destination. Consequently, from the very beginning, the railway station in Lviv was conceived as an en route station, not the real end, or terminus, of the line. Since an en route station's buildings are located along the track, not across its endpoint, the precise location of the Lviv station on the railway tracks was not predetermined. This helped to spark a major public controversy around the planned terminal's location within the city, the echoes of which would reverberate for nearly half a century.

The first Austrian census of 1857 recorded the population of Lviv at 81,084, nearly a fourfold increase since 1772, when Austria first acquired the city.[10] Lviv could not compete with large European metropolises, but it was approximately the same size as Kyiv (Russian: Kiev), only slightly smaller than Odesa (Russian: Odessa), and significantly larger than Kharkiv (Russian: Kharkov), which was only approaching the sixty thousand mark. About the same size as Lviv were Buffalo in the United States, Strasbourg in France, and Danzig (modern-day Gdańsk, Poland) in Prussia. Frankfurt-am-Main, Germany, was slightly smaller, while Montreal was slightly larger. Lviv was thus among Europe's hundred largest cities, and the fifth-largest in the Austrian Empire, whose population in Europe at the time was second only to Russia's.

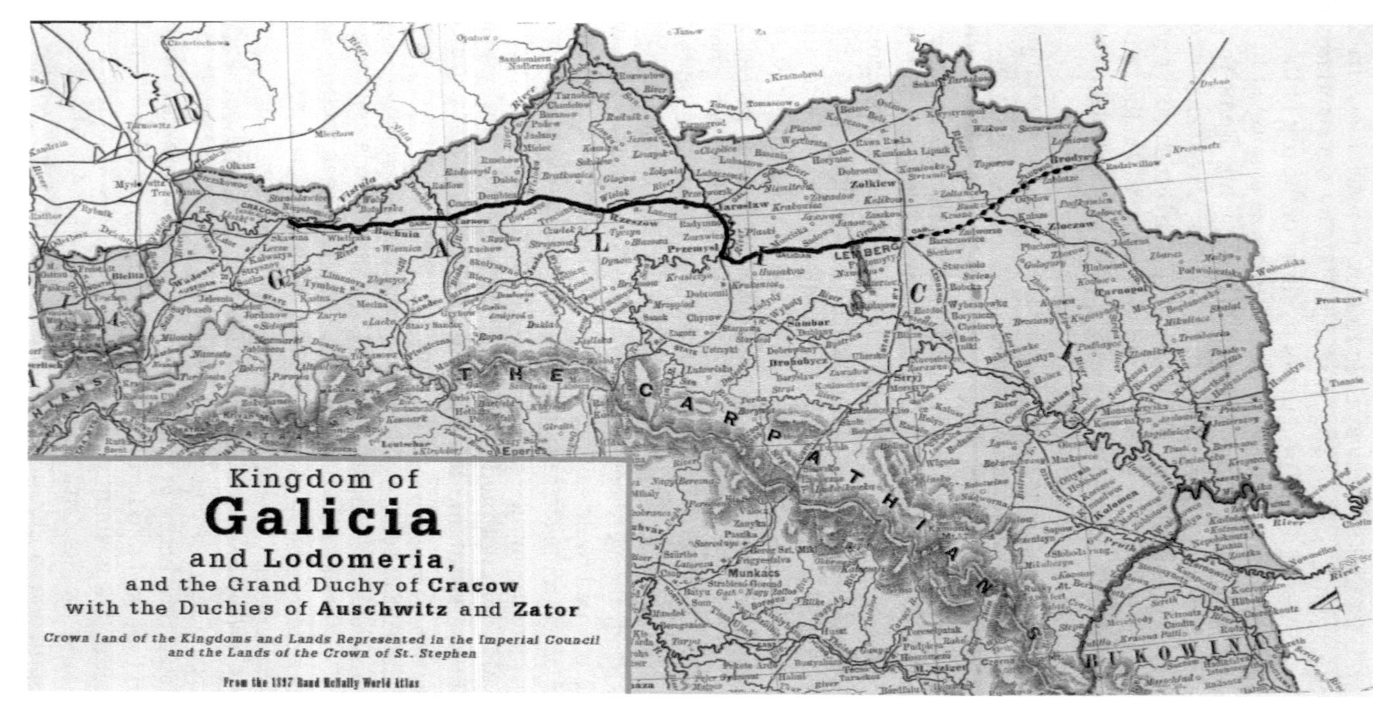

Figure 1.1. The Karl Ludwig Railway line connecting Krakow and Lviv in 1861, with the eastward extensions finished in 1869. Source: "Galicia 1897"; Wikimedia Commons.

Moreover, the pace of Lviv's population growth in the first half of the nineteenth century was faster than of London, Paris, Vienna, Berlin, Saint Petersburg, or Moscow.[11] This speed was all the more remarkable in the absence of industrialization, and was mostly due to the city's newly acquired administrative and cultural prominence.

In the first half of the nineteenth century, the size of Lviv's population multiplied, and the degree of comfort enjoyed by the city's middle and upper classes rose. The provincial administration and city authorities created wide paved promenades, razed the old city walls, and built square apartment blocks in their place. They introduced parks and assigned a vast stretch of parkland on the city outskirts as Lviv's new cemetery. They also erected impressive representative buildings for state offices and public institutions.[12] While the city lacked modern industry, it obtained modern amenities. A city sewage system was extended and improved, and new sanitation regulations were introduced.[13] A centralized gasworks was built simultaneously with the railway from Krakow. In 1858 Lviv received gas lighting for its streets before Moscow and Warsaw managed to do so (Saint Petersburg bypassed the gas stage altogether). Besides numerous governmental offices, Lviv also had a modern university, an up-to-date large public library, a large theatre building (the Skarbek Theatre), and several publishing houses. Krakow, physically and numerically smaller than Lviv, was a rival intellectual and cultural centre to the west, but one had to travel north as far as Warsaw or Vilnius and south as far as Budapest to find comparable islands of nineteenth-century urbanity. To the east, Lviv had virtually no competition. Both Kyiv and Kharkiv had universities, but lagged behind Lviv in terms of publishing, cultural institutions, and urban amenities. The streets of Kyiv waited for gas lighting until the 1870s and modern sewers until the 1890s.

Moreover, alongside the arrival of the first train to Lviv, a constitution and parliament were reintroduced in the Habsburg Empire. Unlike during the revolutionary upheaval of 1848–49, this time they were to stay for good. The province of Galicia obtained its own elected Diet and a degree of self-government, which by 1873 had become far more extensive than that of any other province in the Austrian part of the Dual (Austro-Hungarian) Monarchy. In 1861 Lviv also obtained its own representation, in the form of a city council. Self-government and a separate city statute were granted the city in 1870, finalizing the structure and jurisdiction of municipal authorities for the rest of the Austrian period.

Had the city received municipal self-government before 1861, the location of the train station might have been different. In the 1850s, however, the mayor and members of the city board were still appointed by the governor. They allowed the railway to choose the site for the station at will. The railway chose the marshy meadows on the city's western outskirts, north of the road leading from Lviv to the town of Horodok (Polish: Gródek) and therefore called Horodotska Street (Polish: Gródecka) within the city boundaries. The city board's only concern was the irrigation scheme for the site. The railway planned to drain excess water from the swampy station terrain into the Poltva River, which passed through the city centre. When the city board objected to this plan, the railway redirected irrigation canals away from the city, towards the village of Bilohorshcha (Polish: Białohorszcze) and its ponds.[14]

Once the foundations for the station were laid, the city's "high society" – the station's most likely users – realized that the site was 2.5 kilometres away from the city centre, a considerable distance that was seen as a major impediment to its use. Moreover, other grand public buildings were located in the well-ordered city centre that had emerged by the mid-nineteenth century, and it was thought that the station would add beauty and convenience to that area. In those public demands, however, there was blissful ignorance of a future of ever-increasing traffic and crowds, smoke, noise, and proliferating warehouses. Neither did it show much understanding of the needs and nature of the railway.

The railway consortium had barely raised the capital necessary for the construction, and any major change could turn into a financial disaster, jeopardizing the whole enterprise. The closer to the city centre the more expensive was the land. Moreover, Lviv was to become a major railway hub, with the land needed not only for tracks, but also for yards, depots, workshops, and warehouses. These considerations, as well as a suitably flat surface – quite rare in Lviv – determined the station's location. The tracks would reach the station site from the west and encircle the city to the north, bypassing major hills. Having made a semicircle, the tracks would cross the city boundary a second time, where a smaller station would be located. These were grounds barely touched not only by urban development but even by agriculture. Much of the land in the northern part of the city belonged to the army and was used as training grounds, which made appropriation much easier.

It is not by accident that this same branch of the main line, as well as the location of both stations, was closely outlined twenty years earlier in a study for the proposed Galician railway. Although the actual tracks laid in 1861 made an even wider circle than the line originally proposed in 1842, the site of the main station coincided with remarkable precision.[15] It proves that the location of the station was essentially determined by topographical and engineering considerations. The station was to sit exactly on the main Eastern European watershed separating the waters flowing into the Baltic from the Black Sea. Creeks from the northern and eastern part of the site flowed into the Poltva, the city's main rivulet, and with it to the Buh (Polish: Bug), the Vistula, and the Baltic Sea. The southern and western slopes belonged to the Dnister River's tributaries and thus to the Black Sea basin.

Since municipal self-government was coming into being, the wishes of the public could not simply be discarded. Although the station's location was sealed, the railway gave serious consideration to the city's suggestions to move the passenger terminal itself closer to the city centre (Figure 1.2). As a condition of moving its terminal east, the railway demanded monetary reimbursement from the city for the already laid foundation and permission to drain canal water towards the Poltva and the city centre, with the work on the canals to be partly covered by the city. The city board found these conditions unacceptable, however, and the terminal remained on its present site.[16] The city and the railway also agreed that, once the tracks were laid farther east, another station would be built in the city's northern suburbs, closer to the city centre. In the meantime, throughout the 1860s, the tracks barely touched the city, and the main train station remained on the edge of the city map.

In 1869 the Karl Ludwig Railway finished its line connecting Lviv with Brody. When the first train departed for Brody, it passed through the recently finished northern city station: Pidzamche (Polish: Podzamcze). Literally translated as "under the castle," the name was used for the suburbs located beneath the northern slopes of Castle Hill (Figure 1.3). Although the new station was closer to the city centre than the first one, it was separated from the centre by the hills, and located in Zamarstyniv (Polish: Zamarstynów), the poorest part of the city's poorest Third or Zhovkva (Polish: Żółkiew) ward.

From the very beginning Pidzamche station was built as a smaller suburban pavilion servicing only some trains. By the time the terminal was finished, another railway had appeared in Lviv. In 1866 it connected Lviv with Chernivtsi (better known then by its German name, Czernowitz), the capital of the small province of Bukovina, located between Galicia and Romania. Because of budgetary considerations and for the sake of efficiency, the Chernivtsi terminal was situated next to Karl Ludwig station, easing the transfer of passengers and goods from one railway to another and enabling joint use of the supporting infrastructure. The building of the Chernivtsi terminal sealed the fate of Pidzamche station, which had access only to the trains moving along the latitudinal east-west tracks. The junction that gave access to all Lviv's tracks was at the site of the 1861 station (Figure 1.3).

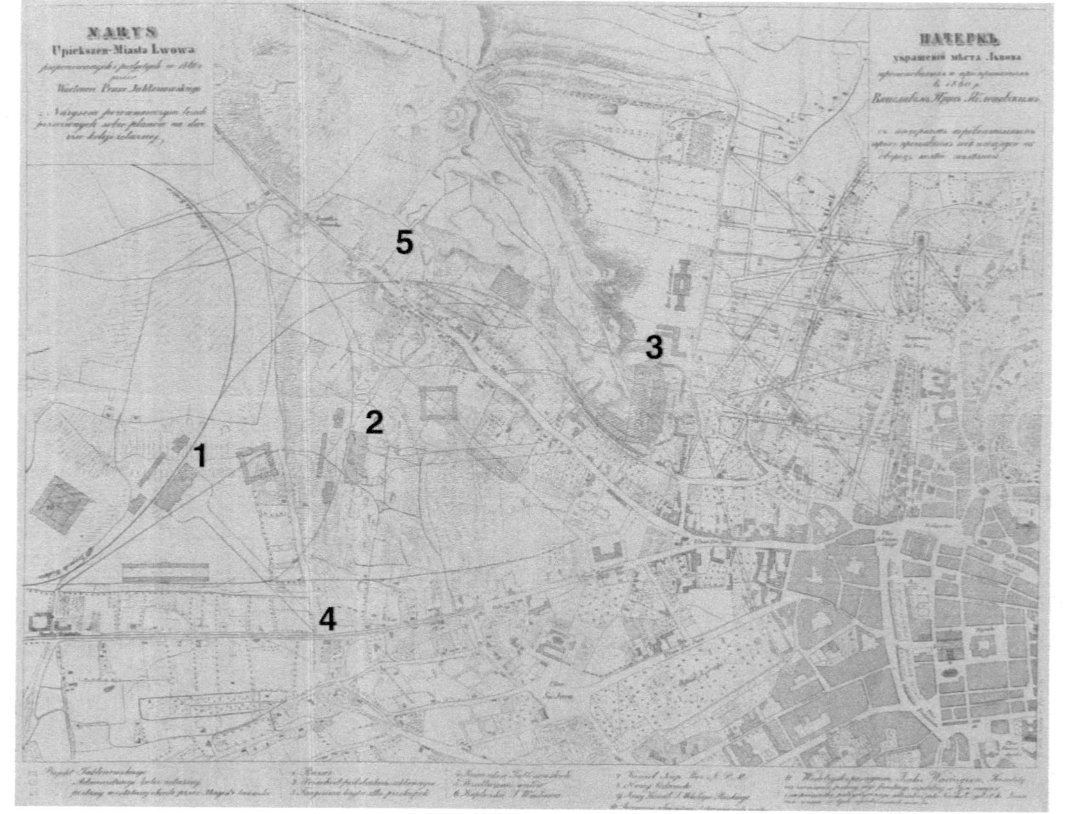

Figure 1.2. Proposed locations of Lviv's first terminal, 1861. Source: Viacheslav Pruss Iablonovskii, *Nacherk ukrashenii mista L'vova* (Lviv, 1860); from the collection of the Austrian National Library, AB 125 (2) KAR MAG.

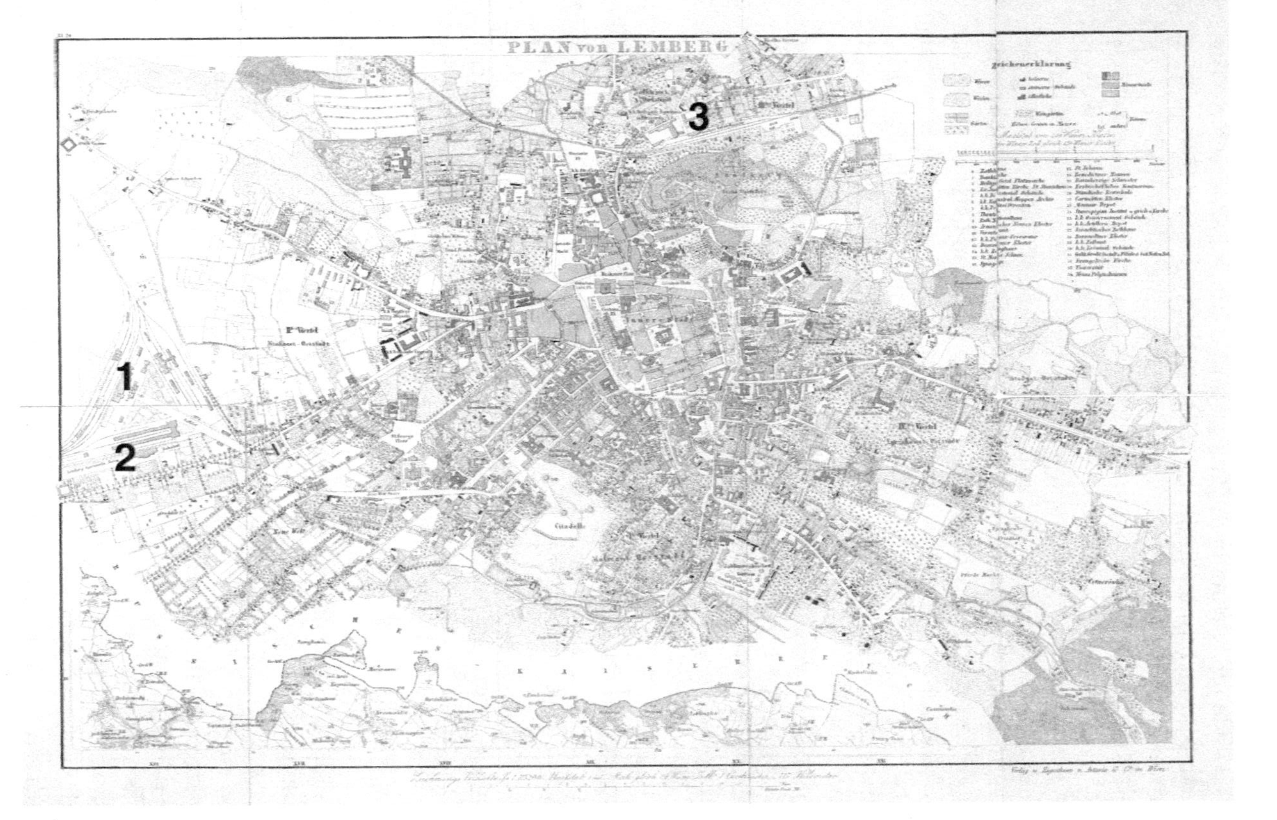

Figure 1.3. City plan showing Lviv's first three train stations. Source: *Plan von Lemberg* (Vienna: Artaria, 1878); Center for Urban History of East Central Europe, Lviv.

Lviv's first train terminal was designed in a version of the "Round Arches Style" (*Rundbogenstil*) (Figure 1.4). This was a late Romanesque revival style referencing both classical and medieval architecture. The Chernivtsi train terminal built in 1866 was a more austere, Biedermeier interpretation of the same style (Figure 1.5). The Chernivtsi railway constructed all its stations stylistically as exact replicas of its main terminal in Lviv, the only difference being their size. *Rundbogenstil* was an attempt to create a German national style, maintaining historical references but suitable to the early industrial age. The style spread all over the German-speaking lands of Central Europe and shaped the first generation of many railway terminals, including those in Leipzig, Munich, and Tübingen. For Lviv, *Rundbogenstil* was the style of the imperial capital. Lviv's grandest public building at the time was the Invalids' Home, designed by the prominent Viennese architect Theophil Hansen (Figure 1.6). The Ruthenian (Ukrainian) National Home also displayed a more modest version of the same style. Both were finished in the early 1860s, built nearly simultaneously with the city's first two grand train terminals. All four buildings demonstrated that Vienna served as the unquestionable authority on architectural taste, and the model to imitate. *Rundbogenstil* was an architectural sewing together of the empire that had been fractured by the 1848 revolution. Although the Invalids' Home incorporated a chapel designed by Hansen in a Byzantine style, there was hardly any reference to local specificity in Lviv's first two train terminals. Unlike the Karl Ludwig terminal, the Chernivtsi terminal was an actual end of the route, but it was still built alongside the tracks, primarily because building a structure parallel to the tracks was much easier and cheaper than spanning them. Just as there was little originality in both buildings' exteriors, there was no ingenuity in the terminals' organization of interior space. Both were later called "barrack-like," and consisted of a multitude of rooms aligned in enfilades running their entire length, with long narrow corridors connected the rooms.[17]

For a while the two terminals competed with each other for the title of the city's main gateway, and the Karl Ludwig emerged the winner. It connected Galicia's two largest cities, and served as Lviv's link to the imperial capital and to the Russian Empire, which was far more important as a trading partner and passenger destination than was Romania, to which the Chernivtsi railway led. The latter was of great significance for the Galicia's southeast, linking its centres – Stanislau (Ukrainian: Stanislaviv; Polish: Stanisławów; today Ivano-Frankivsk) and Kolomyia (Polish: Kołomyja) – with the provincial capital.

Figure 1.4. The main terminal of the Karl Ludwig Railway, Lviv, 1861. Source: Ihor Kotlobulatov collection, courtesy of Ihor Kotlobulatov.

Figure 1.5. Chernivtsi station, Lviv, from Horodotska Street, 1866. Source: "Aufnahmsgebäude in Lemberg von der Strassenseite." *Lviv-Chernivtsi Railway Album* (Lviv, ca. 1868).

Figure 1.6. Invalids' Home, designed by Theophil Hansen (1863); postcard from 1901. Source: Ihor Kotlobulatov collection, courtesy of Ihor Kotlobulatov.

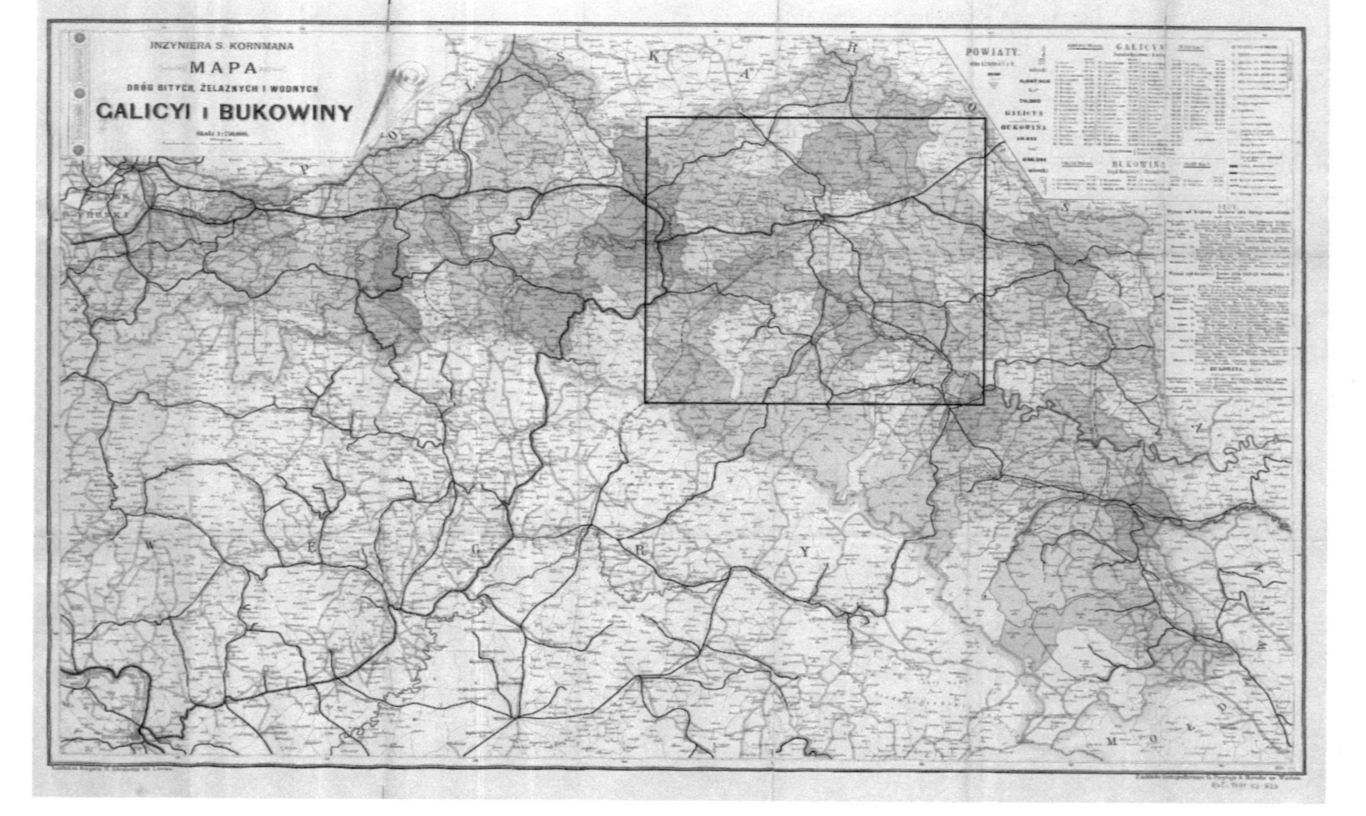
INZYNIERA S. KORNMANA
MAPA
DRÓG BITYCH, ŻELAZNYCH I WODNYCH
GALICYI I BUKOWINY
POWIATY
GALICYA
BUKOWINA

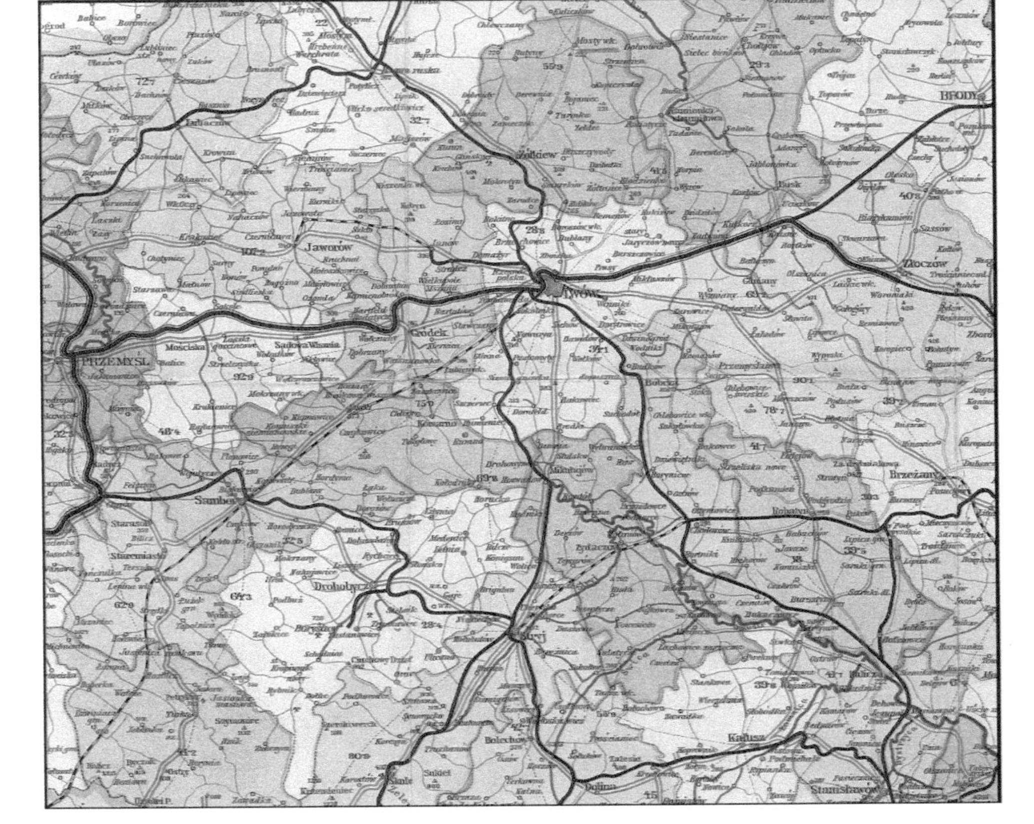

Figure 1.7. Galicia's transportation network in 1898, with a close-up of the Lviv junction. Source: S. Kornman, *Map of Galicia* and *Bukovina's Highways, Railways and Waterways* (Lviv: H. Altenberg, 1898).

By 1870 Galicia had 1.13 kilometres of railway track per 100 square kilometres of the province's area, and 1,627 kilometres of track per 10,000 population.[18] In terms of area penetration, this was better than, Portugal's 0.74 or even Spain's 1.02, but below Italy's 2.77 and Germany's 3.13, not to mention Britain's 7.70. Much of the railway construction in Galicia in the 1870s and 1880s bypassed Lviv, and belonged to the 800-kilometre-long Transversal railway, which ran alongside the Carpathian Mountains. Lviv, however, continued to sprout new lines as well, becoming connected with Stryi to the south in 1873 – in 1887 the line would continue to the mountains and the empire's Hungarian part – and in 1887 another line opened to the north, running through Zhovkva and Rava Ruska (Polish: Rawa Ruska) to Belzec (Polish: Bełżec). In 1898 a line opened to Janów (today Ivano-Frankove), which eventually would continue to Iavoriv (Polish: Jaworów). By the end of the nineteenth century, Lviv had become a major railway hub, with six lines converging at the Lviv junction (Figure 1.7). Three more would be added by the beginning of the First World War.

By the end of the nineteenth century, most of these lines had a single owner. In 1884 the state-owned *kaiserlich-königliche Staatsbahnen* (Imperial-Royal State Railways) was established, and this entity built most of the Galician railways in the 1880s. In 1889 the state acquired the Galician Chernivtsi Railway, and in 1892 the Karl Ludwig Railway.[19] Some local railways survived as privately owned companies, but even they were managed by the state railway. In 1884 two directorates of the state railways were created in Galicia, in Krakow and Lviv, and in 1894 a third one was created in Stanislau (Stanisławów, Ivano-Frankivsk) for the southern part of the province. Nationalization of the railway, however, sealed the fate of the Chernivtsi terminal in Lviv. To keep two large passenger terminals within five minutes' walk from each other made no economic sense. Trains from the direction of Chernivtsi could be easily redirected to the Karl Ludwig terminal and vice versa. The Lviv directorate accordingly turned the Chernivtsi terminal into the centre of the station's freight complex, while the 1861 terminal became the passenger station for all of Lviv's railway lines.

Lviv entered the twentieth century as one of the largest railway hubs in East-Central Europe. A total of forty pairs of passenger trains arrived and departed daily from Lviv's main railway station in 1903, compared with only eighteen a day in Kyiv.[20] Railway lines running from Lviv west, south, and east crossed the province's borders, forming sections of international railway corridors. Only the northern lines all ended on the Austrian side of the Austro-Russian border. Lviv also became the physical centre of the dense and extensive Galician railway network, a large segment of which was managed from the city. The city's "railwayization" was part and parcel of the transformation Lviv underwent in the second half of the nineteenth century. This transformation occurred simultaneously with a demographic explosion, the introduction and strengthening of municipal self-government, and the construction of major infrastructure projects and grand civic buildings. As Galicia's most important railway junction, Lviv was obliged to develop extensive infrastructure to support the railway, including passenger terminals and freight docks, the depots in which locomotives were serviced, and train yards in which trains were assembled, turntables, coal warehouses, water pumps, and ever-multiplying tracks. By the beginning of the twentieth century, they all had become an integral part of the city's landscape.

Chapter Two

The Shape of Things to Come

The longevity of Europe's first-generation railway terminals proved much shorter than the average human lifespan. As a rule, after a couple of decades, the terminals were demolished and replaced with new structures. The London station that was opened in 1836 was replaced with a new one in 1844. Vienna's first railway station, built in 1838, was replaced in 1865. The first Anhalter station in Berlin was completed in 1841 and demolished in 1875. The development of the railway network, together with technological change, which placed new demands on station infrastructure, was a part of the story. An equally important factor was the nature of capitalist urban space, with its incessant transformations that both absorb and maximize surplus value.[1] Finally, there were changing aesthetic tastes. At the end of the nineteenth century, the dominant architectural styles began to change more frequently and profoundly than ever before in concert with the increasing capitalization of urban space that encouraged demolition and rebuilding.

Lviv, despite its semi-peripheral location within European capitalism,[2] was not immune to these influences. The state purchased the Karl Ludwig Railway in 1893 and the reconstruction of Lviv's main station became new management's top priority. At first the Lviv railway directorate tried to expand existing platforms and add tracks, but soon realized that only a completely new structure would solve the mounting problems with budding freight and passenger traffic.[3]

The new terminal opened on 26 March 1904 in a carefully prepared spectacle. The rituals enacted and the speeches delivered during the opening give us the official interpretations of the new building and the context for its appearance. The celebration took place on a Saturday morning, on the square in front of the new terminal. The magnificent, wide, and half-transparent arch of the main entrance was decorated with a golden curtain that allowed a glance into the main vestibule, where a portable wooden altar stood by the back wall under a stained-glass depiction of Archangel Michael. On the square, several dozen uniformed railwaymen formed a semicircle.

The two most important guests at the ceremony were Heinrich von Wittek, the Austrian minister of railways, and Andrzej Potocki, viceroy of Galicia. The railway band welcomed them with a march, "A Thousand of the Brave," a popular Polish patriotic song dedicated to the heroes of the 1830 uprising against the Russian Empire, with lyrics from a poem by a German, Julius Mosen; another German had written the music.[4] The march signified not only the Polish patriotic tradition, but also its acceptance in German-speaking lands. Once the two guests took their place of honour in front of the altar, the ceremony started. The "Lute" choir sang "Lauda anima," a hymn by the Viennese court composer Matthäus Stegmayer, and a Christian service followed. Since the province had two large Catholic denominations – the Roman Catholic Church of the Latin rite and the Greek Catholic, or Uniate, Church of the Byzantine rite – two liturgies were served. The Roman Catholic archbishop Józef Bilczewski officiated in the Latin liturgy, the Greek Catholic archbishop Andrei Sheptytsky in the Byzantine liturgy. When the time came for speeches, Archbishop Bilczewski was the first to address the assembly. Roman Catholicism was not only Lviv's largest Christian confession, but also the faith of the Habsburg dynasty and of the province's political and economic ruling class. At the turn of the century some began to see Roman Catholicism also as an integral part of Polish national identity.[5] Bilczewski was followed by Godzimir Małachowski, Lviv's mayor. Both speakers acted as hosts, praised the state and Imperial-Royal State Railways, and stressed the contributions of Minister Wittek and the Lviv railway director Ludwik (Ludwig) Wierzbicki. Małachowski ended his speech with a cheer to the emperor, which was followed by the Austrian state anthem.[6]

The opening speeches had a dialogical dimension. As guest speaker, Wittek answered the hosts, returning Bilczewski's compliments and praising him for giving his blessing to the construction. Wittek assured the audience that the government worked to "implement the Highest intentions of the Most Illustrious Emperor and Lord, whose truly fatherly care unceasingly watches over the well-being of His peoples."[7] The minister also announced promotions and awarded decorations to railway officials and local entrepreneurs. "The Lute" choir responded with a Felix Mendelssohn cantata, bringing to the two-hour-long ceremony to an end. Afterwards all guests of honour were given a tour of the new facility.[8] Wittek's visit to the city continued until Monday, and included business meetings, official dinners, and audiences, and was widely covered in local press. Imperial ministers – with the exception of those hailing from Galicia – were rare guests in Lviv, and therefore perceived as celestials whose social status approached that of the emperor's own family.

The political message of the ceremony was similar to that conveyed during the emperor's first visit to autonomous Galicia.[9] Local elites were content with the empire and showed their loyalty and gratitude. The rhetoric of the hosts' speeches and the selection of music conveyed the compatibility of Polish and Austrian patriotism. Wittek, in turn, on behalf of the central government, assured Galicians that Vienna treated the province respectfully and fairly. He also signalled Vienna's commitment to stimulate Galicia's economic and cultural development.

When compared to other public ceremonies taking place in Lviv at the time, the opening of the terminal was somewhat atypical. A liberal city daily quipped that the scene of the ceremony was "filled with sunlight and ... empty."[10] Another popular daily jestingly observed that, "for maintaining order two pedestrian and one mounted policemen sufficed, [police] commissars ... for lack of other tasks, tried to copy two motionless Caryatides at the main entrance."[11] Both accounts point to the rather dry and overly official character of the ceremony and the absence of the "wider public." Indeed the audience was rather exclusive. All the guests arrived at the ceremony in carriages, not by foot.[12] Among them we find the speaker and the presidium of the provincial Diet, members of the city council, the senates of the university and the polytechnic, generals, and senior officers.[13] There was also a complete set of officials from the Lviv railway directorate and numerous officials from the Viceroy's Office.

It is hardly surprising that the newspaper of the socialist railwaymen's union attacked the ceremony bitterly. The newspaper disparaged railway director Wierzbicki for the "grand pomp and pride" with which he tried to "crown his 'blessed' rule, imprinted in the railwaymen's memory by the brutal trampling of their civic rights." The union also ridiculed the program of the minister's visit: "After numerous toasts, solemn breakfasts and dinners, Mister Minister with an overfilled stomach left for a tour of Galicia to continue accepting further 'obeisances.'"[14] For the province's socialists, Wittek exemplified the old civil service, with its court connections and integration into the aristocratic social milieu. Their ideal was a more transparent and less subservient civil service, responsible to the body of citizens and dedicated to the protection of labour. Indeed the schedule of Wittek's business visit was full of gastronomic events and entertainment, which today we would call "business dinners." Moreover, Wittek managed to visit all important local railway projects: the planned bridge where the railway crossed Zhovkivska (Żółkiewska) Street, one of the busiest city arteries; the tracks of the new Lviv–Pidhaitsi (Podhajce) line; and the site of a new city station, Lychakiv (Łyczaków), planned on that line. Finally, on his way to Vienna he was to inspect a new line being laid through Sambir (Sambór) and the Carpathians to Hungary.[15]

Nonetheless the urban middle-class public kept its distance from the ceremony. The attitude of the middle class was related to the terminal's peculiarities as a public building. In its size and decor the terminal matched or even surpassed the city's other monumental buildings. Unlike them it was also mundane: a public utility and an industrial enterprise. Although the terminal drew crowds larger than any museum, theatre, or school, it was assigned no formal educational role. Its crowds were of a transitory nature, coming only to leave, and rarely for the sake of the building itself. Other grand public buildings belonged to the city or the province via their associations and corporations, but the train terminal belonged to the state railway. As a result, Lviv's public could not own it in the same way it owned the city theatre, council, or monuments.

The opening ceremony was corporate and bureaucratic, but also thoroughly religious in character. It was described as a "blessing" in the popular evening newspaper, analogous to the Church's blessing of houses and fields.[16] And indeed an actual blessing of the building did take place. The two archbishops, referred to as the "Princes of the Church," were the only guests, besides the minister and the viceroy, to be greeted by a march by the railway orchestra.[17] The Church claimed the terminal, this "cathedral of the modern age,"[18] precisely as a symbol of progress and the machine age, ritualistically and discursively reaffirming the Church's leading role in society no matter how modern. The opening showcased not only the alliance between the Church and provincial elites, but also their ability to cope with the challenges of the new century.

Despite the presence of two liturgies representing two rites, the ceremony was far from all-inclusive. Lviv's second-largest confession, Judaism, was excluded and never mentioned. This was in stark contrast to the emperor's visit in 1880, when he stopped at two of the city's numerous synagogues.[19] One explanation for this omission is that the 1904 ceremony took place in a single location, where the archbishops would have been forced to share a Christian altar with a Jewish rabbi – an unimaginable scenario for the time. Additionally the province's ruling class was staunchly Catholic, and Wittek himself was an ally of Vienna's antisemitic Christian Socialists. Whatever the reasons, the ceremony was a reminder that tolerance towards the Jews was not synonymous with unconditional acceptance and inclusion.

Did the physical space of the building reflect the same hierarchies, ideologies, and ambivalences as the ceremony that opened it to the public? The overall architectural style of a building often provides a master code for its interpretation. Guidebooks usually describe the terminal as the second structure in Lviv built in the Secession (*Sezession*) style,[20] a Habsburg version of Art Nouveau that took its name from a group of artists in Vienna who separated themselves from the dominant academic art in 1897. The honour of being Lviv's first structure in the Secession style went to the Mikolasch Passage, a shopping arcade finished in 1901. Some authors, however, characterize the terminal as second-hand Viennese historicism, predating Secession.[21] Art historian Marta Rymar argues that the terminal forms a "neo-Baroque whole," and terminal's façade is "historicist in its crucial part," while the Secession elements are present in the interior and on the platforms.[22] If we accept Rymar's interpretation, stylistically the building becomes little different from other grand public buildings constructed in booming *fin-de-siècle* Lviv, starting with the neo-Renaissance polytechnic and Diet (1877–81) and ending with an eclectic city theatre (1900). According to this interpretation, the terminal's main reference was Vienna and the monumental historicist architecture of the imperial capital's new main boulevard, the Ringstraße, embodying the sensibilities of a triumphant bourgeoisie.[23]

The terminal's façade indeed contains strong elements of historical styles. At the same time, the building's original appearance was anything but neo-Baroque. The second storey, which solidifies the façade and adds volume to the structure, is a post–Second World War addition of Stalin's architects (Figure 2.1). The original 1904 building was divided vertically, not horizontally. Instead of an avant-corps attached to the bulk of the main structure – a plausible interpretation of today's building – the original terminal had three autonomous pavilions that served as entry points to a large and visible, exhibition-like structure (Figure 2.2). An observer standing in front of the building in 1904 could see the slanting roof of the connecting galleries rising and merging with the glass roof of the train sheds. The galleries, with their large windows and delicate masonry, were arcade-like. The roof of the galleries was made of shiny asbestos tiles, reflecting sunglow and blending with the glass roof of the train shed (Figure 2.3).

The meaning of the "Secession" term used to describe the style of the terminal in 1904 had not yet been finalized. One of the building's creators, Lviv's railway director Wierzbicki, a professional architect himself,

Figure 2.1. Lviv's main terminal, present-day view. Source: Johnny, "Holovnyi zaliznychnyi vokzal stantsiï L'viv," 26 January 2011; Wikimedia Commons, used under a CC BY-3.0 licence.

Figure 2.2. Postcard of Lviv's main terminal in 1904. Source: *Lwów, Dworzec kolejowy* [1905]; Biblioteka Narodowa, Warsaw, Pocz. 1006.

Figure 2.3. Postcard of Lviv's main terminal. Source: *Lwów, Główny Dworzec kolejowy* (Krakow: J.K., 1916); Biblioteka Narodowa, Warsaw, Pocz. 1062.

interpreted "Secession" as a utilitarian style, a sacrifice of "architectural considerations" for the sake of "common and public need."[24] Other architectural experts did not subscribe to such an eccentric view. They saw Secession in the building's style, not in the lack thereof. Because of the historicist elements, some called it a "moderate Secession," or a "mixture of the Renaissance with Secession."[25] As was often the case with early Secession, the style in its pure form was to be found in the interior – in the ornaments, furniture, and metalwork – not in elevations.[26] Contemporaries did notice historicist elements of the façade, but saw them as referring to the Renaissance, not the Baroque.[27] They knew that the cityscape inherited from the early modern period in Lviv was largely Baroque, with the Renaissance playing second fiddle.[28] The city's nineteenth-century architecture, however, favoured neo-Renaissance. Baroque referred to the Counterreformation, the Habsburgs, and the demise of the Polish-Lithuanian Commonwealth. By contrast the Renaissance stood for the Commonwealth's "golden age" of toleration and prosperity under the Jagellonian dynasty.

For many contemporaries the style of the building was simply "modern," exemplifying a "harmony between beauty and convenience."[29] Aesthetically, for them "modernity" was a departure from the dominant and familiar historicism. The terminal's "modernity," however, was larger than the building's style; it was also about its function, expectation, emotions, and global trends. Minister Wittek praised the new building for matching the latest – which was synonymous with the best – available models.[30] Years later Lvivites still remembered that their terminal was up to Western European standards.[31] Even during the construction stage, the site became a major attraction. Józef Wittlin, a brilliant writer but less well known in the West than his friend Joseph Roth, claimed that he "remembered exactly" how the terminal was being built. As a child he visited the construction site with his nanny to watch. Rumours circulated that the building was a "wonder of architecture and technology" well before it was finished.[32]

The terminal signified modernity, but there was no shortage of claims as to whose modernity it was. Although nationalism is a usual suspect when it comes to such claims, the building itself had no explicitly national symbols. Historians also commonly point to locality or to the city as an important alternative to national identity.[33] Indeed the city was present prominently in the opening's rhetoric. The terminal's practical importance to landlocked Lviv is difficult to overestimate. The very first newspaper reports about the terminal refer to the pride city people should feel about it and its unforgettable place in the cityscape.[34] At the opening ceremony the mayor compared the train sheds to ancient city gates. The new terminal was to "usher a new, happier era in the history of our city, contribute to its development, attract as many guests as possible, and testify to the world about our maturity and independence."[35] Today the city's coat of arms is in the terminal's centrepiece, winged by sculptures usually understood as personifications of the railway and of Lviv (Figure 2.4). This commonly accepted interpretation[36] makes the scene both tautological and narcissistic: the spirit of Lviv[37] rests on a lion – the city's symbol – and is upholding yet another lion on the city's coat of arms.

In contrast, the original composition was different and the allegory more complex. Instead of a lion, the 1904 shield of the centrepiece featured a double-headed eagle and was topped with an imperial crown: the coat of arms of Cisleithania, the "Austrian" part of Austria-Hungary. The original specifications of the competition committee for this sculpture defined it as an allegory of communication, stipulating that the Austrian eagle should be interwoven with it.[38] In the original composition, two figures were supporting or embracing Austria – just as the actual railway linked and united the state. The female figure, with her winged wheel and rope, represented the connecting and binding side of communication, while the male one stood for communication's strength and power. The lion's pose in this composition suggested submission, and might have referred to the taming of nature or the wilderness by communication. If indeed the lion derived from the coat of arms – of either Lviv or the Ruthenian Palatinate, which was taken over by Austria to become a core part of the new province – its taming would have pointed to the railway and to the empire's civilizing mission in its eastern borderlands.

Cisleithania's coat of arms was not the only imperial sign on the building. A large cartouche directly beneath the centrepiece stated unambiguously in Latin, "*Imperatori Francisco Josepho I*," indicating that the terminal was dedicated to the emperor (Figure 2.5). Latin was the language of monuments, taught in gymnasia and used on public buildings, but in the local context avoiding German was also important. Although, in the middle of the nineteenth century, Lviv could have been taken for a German city, by the beginning of the twentieth the politically and culturally dominant Polish community emphasized the city's distinct Polish-ness.[39]

The imperial frame of reference was not limited to the terminal's centrepiece. Massive iron eagles crowned the arches of two wide train sheds spanning the tracks (Figure 2.6). The eagles, sitting on the "gates of the modern city," welcomed travellers, reminding them that this part of the Earth's surface belonged to Austria-Hungary, and that railway

Figure 2.4. Centrepiece of the terminal's present-day façade. Source: Serhiy Tereshchenko, courtesy of Serhiy Tereshchenko.

Figure 2.5. Original centrepiece of the façade of the terminal's central pavilion (indicated by the white box). Source: *Lwów, Główny Dworzec kolejowy* ([Budapest]): W.L. Bp., [ca. 1910]); Biblioteka Narodowa, Warsaw, Pocz. 1050.

tracks were among the imperial sinews that maintained the unity of the state. Ironically, however, neither passengers from their train cars with side windows nor pedestrian observers inside the train sheds were likely to notice these eagles. Not all the symbols placed in the public space succeeded equally in conveying their message. A finely wrought imperial eagle and initials were also on the doors of the terminal's left pavilion, the entrance to the "Emperor's Rooms," a space reserved for the monarch and his family. The original architect's drawing for the terminal's façade envisioned two more massive eagles that were to sit on two pylons flanking the central pavilion, copying the obelisks of the Schönbrunn Palace, the emperor's residence near Vienna (Figure 2.7). The design was modified during construction, however, and these eagles never materialized.

Figure 2.6. Imperial eagles on the terminal's train sheds. Source: Oleksandr Korobov collection, courtesy of Oleksandr Korobov.

Figure 2.7. Two planned eagles on the station's façade. Source: "Nowy dworzec kolei państwowej we Lwowie," *Architect* 5, no. 7 (1904): 105.

Observers immediately noticed that the overall shape of the terminal, from an aerial perspective, was bird-like (Figure 2.8).[40] If this was indeed the architect's intentional reference, the shape could have alluded not just to a generic bird or to the bird-like speed of a train journey, but also to an imperial eagle with its wings spread. Hardly any other station in the Habsburg realm was so thoroughly imbued with imperial symbolism. A report to a Warsaw-based Polish magazine complimented the newly built terminal as the largest "in Austria," even though the same could be said about the lands of partitioned Poland.[41] The empire served as a natural geographic framework for comparisons even in the case of Polish patriots. The Lviv Secession style had a strong local colour, but came to the city from Vienna. As Pieter Judson observed, local "grand public buildings ... designed to project their municipality's greatness and their town's distinctive achievements ... also accomplished the opposite of their intended effect, contributing to a powerful visual sense of imperial commonality and even uniformity throughout Austria-Hungary."[42]

Despite this overabundance of imperial connotations, Lviv journalists hailed the new terminal as "ours." The Lviv railway director was praised, for "he did not allow a standard design from the ministry's bureaus to be imposed upon him; he presented our projects, commissioned our engineers, entrepreneurs and industrialists, so that we could say loudly and boldly to everyone: 'this is our terminal!'"[43] Others specified that "ours" meant Polish: the building allegedly "followed plans elaborated by Polish engineers, [and] was finished by Polish professional forces with the participation of all the province's major enterprises."[44] The opening ceremony also emphasized the local contribution, although "ours" was interpreted there as Galician: the mayor's speech referred to "exclusively the province's own forces."[45] Railway director Wierzbicki himself claimed that, until then, "in Lviv, public buildings had been

Figure 2.8. Bird's-eye view of the terminal. Source: Edmund Libanski, 1928; Ihor Kotlobulatov collection, courtesy of Ihor Kotlobulatov.

built by invited foreigners; I decided that a different approach would do us good."[46] His was a tall tale. By 1900 the city had a dozen important buildings designed by local architects connected to the Department of Architecture at the Lviv polytechnic. Indeed the design competition announced for the city theatre in 1895 had stipulated that entries would be accepted only from architects of "Polish and Ruthenian nationality."[47] Art historian Mieczysław Gębarowicz believed that Lviv's own school of architects should be credited with making out of Lviv "one of the most beautiful museums" of turn-of-the-century architecture.[48]

"Ours" referred not only to designs, but chiefly to the actual execution of the project. Local commentators emphasized that only Galician firms received construction-related contracts worth some 12 million crowns, and that "the whole capital assigned to the construction of the Lviv terminal would stay in Galicia."[49] Here, however, a qualification is in order. An expensive (600,000 crowns) and technologically sophisticated part of the building – the metal frames of the train sheds – was subcontracted by the Galician Zieleniewski firm to the Vitkovice steel mill in Moravia, an iconic enterprise of Habsburg heavy industry and a pioneer of the puddling method of steel making in the empire. The rails of the train tracks and iron truss of the pavilions' roof were also made elsewhere. One journalist calculated that only two-thirds of the terminal's cost stayed in the province, while the rest was eventually subcontracted to the outside.[50]

Even the remaining 8 million crowns was a significant sum for the cash-strapped province. But the effect of the construction went far beyond capital gain. It served as a test for reinforced concrete and helped to launch its large-scale production and application in Galicia. A decorative bridge had been built of reinforced concrete in Lviv as early as 1894, but the province had to wait another ten years before Michael Finkelstein, Ivan Levynsky, Jan Sosnowski, and Alfred Zachariewicz – a Jew, a Ruthenian, and two Poles – purchased François Hennebique's patent for monolithic reinforced concrete elements. They were able to do so because the terminal provided the first opportunity to make money on this new technology in Lviv. Levynsky, Sosnowski, and Zachariewicz – co-owners of the city's largest construction firm – founded a factory producing reinforced concrete, while Finkelstein managed a reinforced concrete design bureau. Both were located next to the terminal on Na Błonie (Zaliznychna) Street. The terminal proved that reinforced concrete was a reliable and economic solution, and secured a steady stream of railway commissions for the newly founded firm. A congress of Polish technicians that took place in Lviv in 1904 recognized the city as the "cradle of reinforced concrete on Polish lands."[51]

Reinforced concrete was not the only technical innovation in the new terminal. For the first time in Galicia, asbestos tiles were used for roofing.[52] As well, the terminal restaurant featured a most contemporary kitchen, with a centrally located – island-style – main cooking range, and separate ones for coffee, soup, and so on. Underground vents carried away smoke and steam. Dishwashers and pantries were equally modern.[53] There was electric light in the tunnels, restaurants, arrivals hall, and on the platforms. Electric elevators were used to move baggage between the platforms and the ground floor, while an electric engine synchronized all seventy-eight terminal clocks. Electric current was supplied by a separate power plant. Finally, there was a modern central-heating system that operated on low-pressure steam.[54] These technological innovations were part and parcel of the terminal's "modernity."

The province of Galicia was present in the terminal not only in the form of unmarked construction material and invisible local labour, but also in its display of symbols. Coats of arms of larger Galician cities were placed above the windows of the galleries that linked the terminal's pavilions (Figure 2.9).[55] Although Polish newspapers often conflated people and things from the province (*krajowe*) with Polish-ness, these were not synonymous. A "nationally aware" Ruthenian visitor would be at home in the terminal's symbolic environment. The largest material reference to the province in the terminal was the figure of the Archangel Michael on the stained-glass window of the main vestibule (Figure 2.10). (As one Galician newspaper complained, the stained-glass window was also one of those parts of the terminal that came from elsewhere: St Michael "unfortunately" was made in Innsbruck.)[56] St Michael was Galicia's patron, but he was also the ancient patron of Rus', honoured more in the province's eastern part, former Russia Rubra (Red Rus'). Even local Polish magnates acknowledged that Lviv was "an old capital of Rus'," while Galicia was "the name awkwardly invented a hundred years ago."[57] St Michael's stained glass was in blue and yellow, which the Ukrainian national movement had adopted as its distinguishing colours back in 1848. By 1900 signboards with the names of stations on the platforms, as well as office signs on Galician railways, were in three languages: German, Polish, and Ukrainian (Yiddish was officially considered a German dialect). Moreover, Ukrainian signs were in the most recent phonetic orthography, which accentuated differences between Ukrainian and Russian and for Russian travellers served as visual proof that Ukrainian was a distinct language.[58] While the terminal was still under construction, students from the Lviv Ukrainian gymnasium – returning home to the countryside

Figure 2.9. Coats of arms of Galician cities. Source: Polish National Digital Archive, 41-774-2.

Figure 2.10. The terminal's main vestibule, 1904. Source: Oleksandr Korobov collection, courtesy of Oleksandr Korobov.

for Christmas vacation – organized what today might be termed a patriotic flash-mob, speaking to ticket cashiers only in Ukrainian. As one student later recalled, all were served – however grudgingly – and received their discount student tickets.[59]

Finally, during construction, the terminal's central dome was made taller. Originally envisioned as a Baroque or Second Empire dome, it began to resemble the domes of local Greek Catholic churches. Modified by railway director Wierzbicki, the dome came to resemble the octagonal elliptical or pear-shaped dome with copula that became a trademark of the reinvented Byzantine tradition and local "Greek Catholic" style. Together with the Jewish synagogues, they gave the city a certain "Eastern" appearance. Ludwik Wierzbicki was an architect by education, and while in the railway service he maintained a keen interest in the local vernacular architecture. An ethnic Pole, he attended the school in Drohobych (Drohobycz) run by Greek Catholic Basilian Fathers, and he was among the first to study and popularize local Ruthenian cultural tradition.[60] Wierzbicki authored the first codification of local Ukrainian vernacular art.[61] Architect Julian Zachariewicz, Wierzbicki's friend[62] and for many years a fellow railway employee, used a church with similarly shaped domes to illustrate the local architectural tradition for the 1898 volume on Galicia in the famous series *Austro-Hungarian Monarchy in Word and Picture.*[63] All of this suggests that the revised shape of the terminal's dome was not accidental. Another ethnic Pole, Tadeusz Obmiński, designed the terminal's third-class premises and eventually became the most prolific architect working in Lviv's "Ukrainian national style." When the new terminal was being built, the new style evoking folk traditions was making its first inroads into Lviv, and was seen as the latest fashion. The portable altar used during the opening ceremony was carved in the vernacular "Carpathian" style. The same style was used in the terminal's third-class restaurant and waiting hall.

Although the opening ceremony, as noted, excluded Judaism, the religion of one-third of Lviv's city dwellers, there were numerous Jewish entrepreneurs and craftsmen in the "Polish" firms involved in the terminal's construction, particularly among the upholsterers, carpenters, smiths, and glassworkers.[64] Among these Jewish craftsmen were the Fleck brothers, parlour painters, who did the terminal's interiors. One of the brothers, Maurice Fleck, was the father of Ludwik Fleck, a famous physician and biologist, best known as the philosopher of science who inspired Thomas Kuhn's *Structure of the Scientific Revolution*. Jewish employment in the railway service, including at the Lviv station, was not a novel occurrence. A memoirist recalled that Galician railways readily employed Jews, and many of them worked in positions that involved interaction with passengers.[65] The Christian Socialist Reichsrat deputy Ernst Schneider even accused Wierzbicki of favouritism towards Jews, claiming that their number among officials of the Lviv directorate alone increased from thirty-one in 1896 to fifty-two in 1900. At the Lviv main station, eighteen of its fifty-eight officials were Jewish.[66]

Jewish culture was not explicitly referenced in the station's designs, but just like our hypothetical Ruthenian, its Jewish guests could find in the terminal familiar "native" motifs. Contemporary art historians believed that Jewish vernacular architecture in Galicia had been influenced by its Christian counterpart, with the same masters using the same techniques and templates for both.[67] Indeed Wierzbicki had studied not only Ruthenian but also Jewish Galician architecture.[68] Floral and geometric ornaments in the terminal resembled both Christian and local Jewish folk art. Breaking with "historic" Western styles, Secession architecture drew inspiration from non-Western sources, including the ancient civilizations of the Near East.[69] In the case of Lviv, this more general all-European fascination with the "Oriental" style encountered local "Eastern" groups, Ukrainians and Jews, who appropriated and used "Eastern" motifs to emphasize their distinct cultural heritage. The most visibly Jewish building in Lviv at the time was the Beth Hulim Jewish hospital (1898–1901), designed by Kazimierz Mokłowski, a socialist who believed that the modern arts should draw inspiration from folk art.[70] The architect designed his Jewish hospital in the Moorish Revival style, which by the end of the nineteenth century was widely used as the basis for a modern Jewish national style.[71] The hospital's prominent and distinctly "oriental" dome contributed to Lviv's architectural "Easternization."

At the beginning of the twentieth century, multiplying "Byzantine" and "Oriental" references reinforced the image of Lviv as one of the most "Eastern" cities of both the Habsburg Empire and the historic Polish-Lithuanian Commonwealth. Moreover, these references pointed to the Jewish and Ruthenian cultural presence. Despite consolidating nationalisms, leftist intellectuals as well as ruling and artistic elites acknowledged and celebrated the city's ethnic diversity. In the words of a Polish aristocrat, Lviv "reconciled and harnessed to the joint work those Ruthenians, Jews and Latinites, without whom all its efforts [to develop] would have been wasted."[72]

Despite all the local input, the empire's contribution to the terminal was not limited to the overall aesthetic and political framework: the project could not have been accomplished without investments from Vienna. In 1901 the city, assisted by the province, had barely managed to finish the construction of its grand new theatre and was deeply in debt.

The budget for the theatre, a monumental structure built on the Lviv's central boulevard over the vaulted Poltva river, was only one-tenth the amount needed for the new terminal.[73] Luckily for Galicia, the Austrian Ministry of Railways was under Wittek, who was known for his ambitious and generously funded railway projects. The opposition later would use these projects against him in a parliamentary debate that led to his dismissal in 1905.

Large railway projects needed approval from the Austrian premier. Luckily Minister-President Ernest von Koerber believed that the solution to mounting national and social tensions in the empire was economic growth achieved via technical modernization and regional investment – in infrastructure in particular. Among other things, the Habsburg Empire was a pioneer in "pre-Keynesian" state intervention to stimulate the economy.[74] The government also needed consent from the Austro-Hungarian State Bank, which was to supply the funds. Leon Biliński, the bank's chairman, was not only a Pole from Galicia, but also a former president of the Austrian state railways. He had worked with Wittek since the beginning of the 1890s and was a good friend of Koerber's.[75] Wittek and Wierzbicki had also known each other for many years, having worked together on the Austrian railways. The financial side of the project, like the allegorical dressing of the building, was an intertwining of the imperial and the regional – in this case, of interests and personal networks.

The discharge of funds did not conform fully, however, to the rules of transparency and fair competition. Personal connections and favours remained important in the world of Austrian governance. Galician firms received all the contracts, as Wierzbicki confessed, "only because of my personal interventions, sometimes with risks to my position."[76] During the opening ceremony, Archbishop Bilczewski also thanked the minister for "having a deserved trust in our honorable Railway Director, leaving him a greater freedom of action."[77] Nevertheless there were proper requests for tenders, submissions were weighed against each other, and the budgets were calculated diligently down to the penny.[78] When strings were pulled and personal connections used, it was for public benefit, not personal enrichment; political considerations and probable social outcomes were to override purely monetary calculations.

The symbols on the terminal's façade were silent about one more element that helped to convince the imperial government in Vienna to shower the Galician economy with money. (Twelve million crowns, the cost of the terminal's construction, was roughly equal to half of the annual revenue of the province's self-government.)[79] That element was

Lviv's working class. Although the ministry approved the project's budget in 1901, finding investors with sufficient capital ready to commit to a long-term investment with moderate returns could have taken forever. The completion of the city theatre, however, ended the construction boom of the two preceding decades, which had been sustained by large-scale civic infrastructure projects and the construction of public edifices. By 1901, with the city budget depleted and no new projects being launched, unemployment struck city construction workers, the largest group of the Lviv proletariat.[80] The unemployment bureau, created by the city in 1899, characterized 1901 as the year "of trial by fire."[81]

Frustrations came to a head on 29 April 1901 when violence broke out on Strzelecki (today, Danylo Halytsky) Square, a food market and unofficial labour exchange. The crowd consisted of "workers, who were paid by the day, women, woodcutters, [and] construction workers."[82] The incident began with shouts, followed by attacks on the bread booths. The authorities were startled because "the movement started completely spontaneously, without any agitation."[83] The only policeman on the square was struck by a stone and fled. The agitated crowd broke store window displays and plundered and vandalized fancy coffee houses. The disturbance had become a large urban riot, of the type Vienna frequently experienced at that time.[84] Social Democrats mediated, and with their help the crowd elected a deputation to send to city hall. The mayor could not offer much, and the deputation proceeded to the Viceroy's Office. Viceroy Leon Piniński responded by blaming Vienna for the delays with the construction of the new terminal, which would have eased unemployment – the central government had told the province to find private investments.[85]

Quite unusually, in this case, Lviv's main liberal daily sided with the local authorities. The newspaper defended the city council from accusations that it had spent its large investment credit too soon: the theatre, water mains, sewers, gas, and electrical lines were essential to the city and provided employment for workers. The paper stressed that the terminal was the face of the empire, not merely of Lviv: "For a year and half, the main terminal in Lviv, through which the lightning-fast trains of the Vienna–Kyiv–Odesa and courier Berlin–Istanbul trains pass, looks like a barrack for American trappers in Patagonia, while travelling Europe discovers with astonishment that this is a terminal of k. k. Austrian state railway."[86] The "unaligned Socialist" Ernest Breiter – parliamentary deputy, editor, and most frequent contributor to his own newspaper, the *Monitor* – loved conspiracy theories and scandals. He believed that the Lviv disturbances were no mere "hunger riot" but must have been organized. Breiter concluded that the Polish Club in the parliament and the viceroy were behind this "terror from below" as a means of putting additional pressure on the cabinet.[87] Although it is doubtful that the province's political elites organized the disturbances, they indeed made good use of them. Public opinion in Lviv firmly linked delays in railway investments with the April riot.[88] The government in Vienna then decided to ease political and social tensions and help Lviv. During the May Day demonstration, the architect Kazimierz Mokłowski announced to the workers that the government had approved the credits and, as a result, large-scale works would be launched.[89]

On 1 October 1901 the foundation stone for the new terminal was laid and construction works started. Minister Wittek came for this ceremony as well. A foundational act written in Polish, Ukrainian, and German was sealed in a capsule and placed in a special opening in the foundation stone. Wittek himself put the first trowel of lime over the stone, and struck it with a golden hammer.[90] Once the ceremony was over, Wittek went to the "railway reading room," organized for workers by the railway administration, and praised Wierzbicki's model tutelage over the workers.[91]

The construction of the new terminal did not end the social unrest, however. In May and June 1902, construction workers went on strike and together with the unemployed held demonstrations. At the new terminal's construction site, those in favour of the strike clashed with strike breakers and police. Navvies, bricklayers, and masons took part in the walkout; building materials and three overturned freight cars were repurposed as barricades.[92] On 2 June nearly five thousand construction workers in Lviv went on strike and paraded through the city streets. Cavalry were deployed against the protesters, leaving four workers dead on the streets and more than two hundred wounded. Forty gendarmes and policemen were also wounded. The burial of the workers turned into an even greater demonstration, in which, according to the Socialists, eighteen thousand people took part.[93] For the first time since 1848, Lviv saw actual fighting, the use of firearms by the military, and the dead bodies of protesters. This street violence had nothing to do with ethnic tensions or nationalist aspirations.

Even in largely agrarian Galicia, by the beginning of the twentieth century, urban social problems and industrial class conflict had taken on foremost importance. The rituals enacted around the new terminal were not only about modern technologies, the relationships between empire and province, or municipal self-government and urban identity. To a large extent those rituals were a symbolic affirmation of the existing social order threatened by powerful new social currents. Archbishop Bilczewski was among the first to discern and address the danger of social antagonism in a capitalist city. At the opening of the new terminal, he stressed that, while "even on a much smaller construction nearly always some human life is sacrificed. Here, among thousands of workers employed for several years, not a single one has suffered serious harm."[94] Benevolent employers helped to reduce the risk of social explosion, as did good government – Bilczewski also expressed thanks for the credits discharged "in the moments of great lack of work."[95] Clearly the Church endorsed both employer paternalism and state interventionism as proper instruments to deal with the social question.

The symbols of the new terminal maintained a silence about class conflict, but did not ignore social change. Although many disagreed with the archbishop's vision of a happy future in which the Church has managed to harness progress, the terminal's builders shared his belief in humankind's forward march. The signs of progress were evident everywhere, even in such "backwater" provinces as Galicia. Here, against the backdrop of a predominantly agricultural economy, the railway was an especially powerful symbol of the advance of modern civilization, seen as a harbinger of improvements and prosperity. The two sculptural allegories of "trade" and "industry" that embellished the main pavilion visualized these hopes (Figure 2.11).

The male figure was one of the first plastic representations of modern industry and industrial work in Galician fine arts. Classical attire does not hide the living flesh and muscles of a worker, while the pose and facial expression convey intelligence and mental effort. The hammer and anvil are traditional smithy tools, symbols of craftsmanship and the Greek god Hephaestus. The cogwheel stands for mechanics and engineering in general. Thus the figure alludes not only to workers, but also to technicians and engineers, representing industry as an amalgam of physical labour and intellectual effort. The figure is holding a crafted piece with the tongs. His pose indicates full investment in his work and the satisfaction it brings.

The allegory of trade is a female figure surrounded by the symbols of trade and communication. She is arriving in a boat, symbolizing the importance of transportation for trade. Her paddle is also a version of the caduceus – Hermes' winged serpent rod representing commerce and negotiation. A symbolic engine serves as a vehicle of commerce and harbinger of peace.[96] The owl on the boat's prow symbolizes wisdom and maturity. In her right hand the figure holds a jar, which stands for the goods the railway carries, while the weigh scale points to exchange, trade's most important element.

Although thematically appropriate, the two sculptures were dissonant with the overall style of the terminal. Their execution was too traditional, dressing contemporary themes in classical rags. The socialist Mokłowski would have preferred something more powerful, resembling dynamic and disturbing depictions of industrial labour from the chisel of the famous Belgian sculptor Constantin Meunier.[97] Mokłowski had similar reservations about the murals of the main vestibule and their "dirty clay colours," poorly fitting the colourful polychrome of the interior.[98] They depicted the story of technical progress and linked it with the province. There was the invention of the locomotive by Stephenson and the "contemporary most modern engine." There were allegories of Galicia's industries and vernacular ornaments.[99] Depicting the history of the railway, the murals also featured its "industrious pioneers"[100] in Galicia, especially Wierzbicki,[101] who was also an ardent advocate for the industrialization of Galicia.[102]

The praise Wierzbicki received from the press and officialdom contrasted with the conspicuous neglect of Władysław Sadłowski, the architect who drafted the first (1899) and the second (1900) projects of the building. Once the construction started, Wierzbicki removed Sadłowski from overseeing it and contested the latter's claims to authorship. Wierzbicki claimed that the design of the terminal was the collective undertaking of a group of railway engineers and architects and that Sadłowski was commissioned for only one part of the project. Moreover, Sadłowski worked on that part in the railway bureau, while his design was later modified during the construction phase. Wierzbicki, just like railway administrators all over Europe, preferred centralized goal-oriented overseeing, and relied on engineers more than on architects. In his grand reconstruction of Paris, Georges-Eugène Haussmann used this management model as well.[103] Financial considerations also played a role. Even in the case of much richer railways and mammoth train stations, such as St Pancras in London, companies were wary of high bills and would thwart an architect's ambitious designs, sometimes removing him altogether from overseeing the project.[104]

All the more surprising was Sadłowski's eventual victory over a powerful state railway, a victory he owed to the Galician Union of Artists. A recently founded association, the union delegated a special commission to investigate the case, and its resolution of 30 April 1904 confirmed Sadłowski's authorship.[105] He was helped by Galicia's economic underdevelopment. A trifling park of industrial machinery was serviced by a tiny corps of industrial engineers. The gap between architects and engineers was not as wide as in more developed parts of the world. Architecture was the largest department at the Lviv polytechnic, and it had strong ties with local industry. Julian Zachariewicz, who chaired the local architecture department, served two terms as the polytechnic's

Figure 2.11. Sculptural allegories of "trade" and "industry" near the main entrance. Source: Serhii Tereshchenko, courtesy of Serhii Tereshchenko.

president and owned a large construction business of his own. Moreover, in the 1860s he had served as a director of the Karl Ludwig Railway. Wierzbicki himself was an architect, not an engineer, by training. This uniquely strong position of local architects allowed them successfully to challenge Wierzbicki and protect their authorship rights, which were of vital importance to them as a group. The terminal was the young architect Sadłowski's first large project and became a ticket to a successful career in architecture. History has requited Sadłowski's injury: present-day guidebooks list Sadłowski as the building's architect, while Wierzbicki is usually omitted.

Władysław Sadłowski was also Wierzbicki's cousin, and received his commission without open competition because Wierzbicki was trying to save the railway's funds. Born in 1869, Sadłowski was thirty-five years younger than Wierzbicki, thus belonging to the next generation of Galician professionals. Sadłowski was of the generation exposed to socialist ideas during their gymnasium and university education. The founders of the first Galician socialist parties were his peers. Sadłowski was a good friend of Jędrzej Moraczewski, a railway engineer and one of the leaders of the Polish Social Democratic Party of Galicia and Silesia. Later, Moraczewski would serve as the first prime minister of independent Poland in 1918.[106] Sadłowski's socialist sympathies aligned well with his aesthetic preferences at the time. He belonged to the Arts and Crafts movement, whose socialist founder, William Morris, tried to elevate the work of a craftsman to that of an artist, returning beauty to manmade objects. Fine arts was to merge with industry and turn society into a better place to live.[107] Kazimierz Mokłowski transplanted these ideas to Galicia, directing artists to folk culture, in which art was inseparable from craft. He was among the first to comment on the new terminal, commending the chosen style because there was "a harmony of the new art with the new social content, both form and content had grown out of the shared cultural background, which the nineteenth century gave to humankind."[108]

Although fine detail and craftsmanship could be found largely in the passengers' building, it was the train sheds that most impressed contemporaries. In 1904 only one shed was finished, with a second soon to follow, and Mokłowski admired it even more than the folk art imitations: "There are no adornments, but thanks to the relation between the whole mass and constitutive details, this shed is simply charming as a complete expression of fugacity and lightness."[109] The new space, open and transparent, carried with it a promise of a new society. London's Crystal Palace, the archetype of all glass and iron shells, is also a metaphor for the future socialist society in Nikolay Chernyshevsky's *What Is to Be Done*, a work well known among Lviv socialists.[110] Fyodor Dostoevsky attacks the Crystal Palace as a symbol of socialism in his *Notes from Underground*,[111] while Walter Benjamin noticed that, for early socialist Charles Fourier, Parisian arcades served as "the architectural cannon of the phalanstery."[112] It is probably no accident that the first modern structure of vaulted glass and wrought iron in Lviv, the Mikolasch passage shopping arcade, was the favourite hangout of local socialists. Socialist intellectuals congregated daily in the passage's café – named, not surprisingly, "The Crystal Palace" – while the union of metalworkers leased a hall there that was used for various socialist and trade union events.[113]

One did not have to be young and socialist to embrace new architecture and modern technology. Wierzbicki was very fond of the terminal's modern designs, while Bilczewski believed progress and modern technologies could be reconciled with Catholicism, augmenting the latter. During his stint as the president of the Austrian railways, Leon Biliński, the president of the state bank in Vienna and a conservative only slightly younger than Wierzbicki, went to London, arguably still the centre of modernity, for a railway congress. While there Biliński attended a banquet in the Crystal Palace and a reception with Queen Victoria. He remembered the trip afterwards as the "greatest journey of my life."[114] Wiktor Chajes, "a Pole of Mosaic faith" born in 1879, a banker, and since 1913 a city councillor, in the 1890s studied in the trade academy in Berlin. While no socialist, he "loved the grandeur of Berlin." Chajes spent his evenings with Mokłowski, who studied architecture in Charlottenburg, Berlin's wealthy satellite, and "dreamt about Paris, London and most of all about ... Lviv. Not about the Lviv of then, but about a new one, in which I shall be a great merchant or banker, and shall turn it into a great city of modern people and attitudes."[115] For all those admirers of modernity and modern cities, the terminal was Lviv's wide stride in the direction of their dreams.

Modernity and that unfathomable spirit of a great city could not be conveyed through symbols, summoned with speeches, or inculcated through instruction. In their material manifestation, they were about great numbers of real people, sharing in multiple ways the same limited space. The ability to accommodate and handle these people was a fundamental feature of modernity. The terminal was modern because it performed its most direct function successfully.

The terminal was not just a whim of the Lviv railway director, or an edifice meant to impress travellers, or a means to keep workers employed. Essentially the new terminal appeared because the city had physically outgrown the old one. Although Lviv's growth was not as spectacular as that of Europe's new industrial centres and great capitals, it was impressive. By 1900 its population had doubled since 1860, reaching 159,877. A substantial increase of 25 per cent during the last decade of the nineteenth century was surpassed in the first decade of the twentieth by a 29 per cent increase. By 1910 the number of inhabitants reached 206,113.[116]

Passenger traffic through the train terminal increased at an even faster rate. By the early twentieth century, the railway in Galicia ceased to be a luxury accessible only to the wealthy. New railway lines kept sprouting, while passenger and freight traffic showed no signs of slowing down. Georges Bataille once compared museums to a city's lungs, through which crowds flow on weekends, coming out purified and recharged.[117] A train station could qualify as the city's heart: rhythmically pumping masses of people, day and night, weekend and weekday. Not only the building of the new Lviv terminal, but also its passenger and baggage ticket counters, were open twenty-four hours.[118] Seventy-six passenger and 80 freight trains passed through the station every twenty-four hours, and in the event of military mobilization the total number was expected to increase to 186.[119] Such heavy traffic created crowds of passengers. This was a practical problem for the railway officials, but also a source of phantasmal concern for the public. The layout and interior design of the new terminal answered both of these.

The main difference between the new and the old terminals was not in scale or opulence. The replaced building had also been monumental and picturesque. Its frontage was even wider than that of the new terminal, while its Romantic style had been a welcome addition to the cityscape. The real problem with the old building was its interior organization of space and poor access to the multiplying train platforms. Its long corridors offered office space aplenty but very little room for movement.[120] In the new terminal, tracks and their adjoining platforms were raised to the level of the terminal's second floor. Access to them was via ground-level tunnels, with stairs connecting the tunnels to platforms. There were seven tunnels, each serving a distinct function. The flow of passengers and items was divided and channelled into separate circuits. Two wing tunnels – one reserved for the imperial postal service and another for express packages – bypassed passengers' premises altogether and led to the platforms from the square in front of the building. Two more tunnels led from the platforms into the terminal, one reserved for arriving passengers and another for their baggage. The remaining three led from the terminal to the platforms. First- and second-class passengers had exclusive use of one of them, the third class used another, and the final tunnel was reserved for baggage loading (Figure 2.12).

A peculiar feature of this terminal was the lack of a "concourse" where people could mingle upon arrival or before departure. Its main vestibule was not much larger than its restaurants or arrivals hall. Immediately

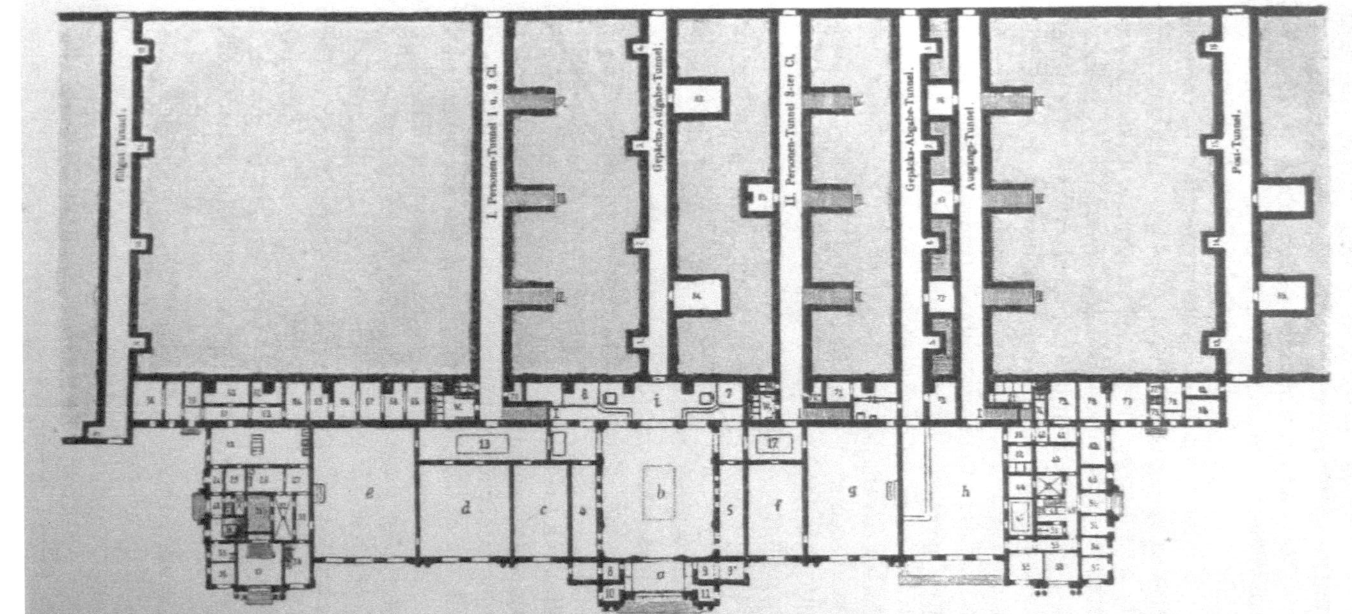

Abb. 180. Aufnahmsgebäude Lemberg. (Bahngeschoß) a Vorhalle. — b Empfangshalle. — c Wartesaal I. Kl. — d Wartesaal II. Kl. — e Restauration I. und II. Kl. — f Wartesaal III. Kl. — g Restauration III. Kl. — h Ausgangshalle. — i Gepäcksaufgabe.

Figure 2.12. Layout of the new terminal. Source: Hermann Strach, ed., *Geschichte Der Eisenbahnen der Österreichisch-Ungarischen Monarchie*, Band 6, vol. 2 (Vienna: Karl Prochaska, 1908), 183.

upon entering the vestibule, passengers would divide into separate streams: first- and second-class ticket windows were to the left, third class to the right. Posts and banisters preceded ticket windows, splitting the flow of passengers into trickles and directing them to individual counters (Figure 2.13).

Having purchased their tickets, passengers continued to the waiting halls and restaurants. Passengers of each class had their own waiting hall. There were only two restaurants, though, and first and second class had to share one – first-class passengers were so rare, in fact, that a separate restaurant for them would not have survived. The premises for the first and second class were to the left side of the main vestibule, while those for the third class were on the right. Entrances to those clearly separated zones at the back of the vestibule followed the lines of their respective ticket windows. Heading for their waiting rooms, passengers with tickets could drop their baggage at the baggage desk by the vestibule's back wall.

For the first- and second-class rooms, Alfred Zachariewicz used an international bourgeois Art Nouveau design, while Tadeusz Obmiński used an Art Nouveau rereading of vernacular motifs for the third class area (Figure 2.14). Although Mokłowski complained that Obmiński's vernacular motifs were quite superficial, mixed with Secession, and designed somewhat sloppily. Still, he was "inclined to boundless lenience, since those lilies, stars, diamonds and merlons of the Polish people earned the distinction to decorate these halls, from which so many people would still leave for *'Hamerica'* forever, and where these folk adornments will serve for them as a native parting song."[121] Indeed it was the first time vernacular motifs had made their way into such a monumental public building. Moreover, while these motifs were later seen as "national," originally their social and class connotations were far more important. Plebeian masses entered not only politics but also public buildings, monumental art, and society's self-perception.

This hierarchy of waiting spaces (and aesthetic styles) did not end with first class. It was topped with the most exclusive of spaces: the "Emperor's Rooms," reserved for the emperor and members of his family in the highly unlikely event of their visit to Lviv. Franz Joseph I died in 1916, however, without seeing Lviv's new terminal, although he did visit the city in 1903, while the terminal's construction was entering its final stage. Instead the temporary terminal on the other side of the tracks was used for his arrival, with the emperor having to pass through the long corridor and cut through construction decorated to hide the worksite.[122] The exchange the old emperor had with the mayor of Lviv was very telling of that time's agendas and concerns. Franz Joseph enquired "if gentlemen

Figure 2.13. Ticket counters in the main vestibule. Source: Ihor Kotlobulatov collection, courtesy of Ihor Kotlobulatov.

First-Class Waiting Room

Second-Class Restaurant

Third-Class Waiting Room

Second-Class Waiting Room

Third-Class Restaurant

Figure 2.14. The new terminal's waiting rooms and restaurants. Source: T.C., "Nowy dworzec lwowski," *Tygodnik ilustrowany*, no. 13 (1904), 246; the photograph of the second-class waiting room is from the Oleksandr Korobov collection, courtesy of Oleksandr Korobov.

conduct now any large works?" The mayor told him about "important and expensive work on sewers, which had great importance for city sanitation." The emperor also asked whether the city had finished work on its new water supply, and when found that it was completed, asked about water quality. The mayor assured him that the water was great, everyone drank it eagerly, and "*Giesshübler* [the maker of famous mineral water] suffered a heavy loss." The emperor laughed, remarking that "drinking clear and good water" was indeed healthy.[123]

Had the emperor ever come to the new terminal, he would have arrived by a separate track reserved for those occasions, and used a separate entrance without having to descend into tunnels. His rooms consisted of a parlour, two rooms, and two bathrooms.[124] A report from an American journalist accredited with the Russian Army who visited Lviv in 1914 gives some idea about the furnishing of this space: "We found ourselves in a suite equal in every way to the Emperor's private apartments in his own palace. Heavy carpets, richly tapestried walls, daintily concealed electric lights, and rich and heavy furniture, completed as luxurious an apartment as any potentate could desire."[125] A slightly less luxurious residence was reserved in the same left pavilion for visiting railway dignitaries, although those had to enter their rooms from inside the terminal.[126]

The terminal's space reflected the social hierarchies of *fin-de-siècle* Galicia. The policing function of the new terminal, however, was not limited to the hierarchical organization of space. The principles of spatial organization used in the 1904 terminal remain relevant, and are known today as "functional transparency."[127] In 1904 the terminal was praised not only for its transparency – the ability to guide passengers flawlessly through its "modern labyrinth" – but also for the "mastery of crowd," and "segregation of travellers" embedded in it.[128] The building could direct passengers and control them because its spatial arrangements endowed material structure with certain autonomy. The terminal, whose design carried an imprint of socialist dreams, worked as a self-regulating space of "liberal governmentality."[129]

In *The Practice of Everyday Life*, Michel de Certeau devotes a whole chapter to "Railway Navigation and Incarceration," emphasizing the nearly complete loss of control over movement experienced by the train passenger. Certeau writes of the insularity and immobility of a compartment where "rest and dreams reign" supreme.[130] For him the train station serves as a threshold: crossing from the fully controlled space of railway cars to the spontaneous life of city streets, the passenger must pass through the noise and movement of the terminal. In reality the passenger's freedom of movement was severely curtailed immediately upon entering the terminal. An environment very much unlike that of city streets also began there. The organization, design, and logic of the terminal space kept the traveller within invisible bounds, responding to prompts from the space and modifying his behaviour accordingly. Unsurprisingly the liberal newspaper identified illiterate Galician peasants as the main potential threat to the system: unable to read signs identifying tunnels and trains, they could bring havoc to the whole well-thought-out system.[131]

This spatial self-policing required very little human intervention, but it did not eliminate it altogether. The public had to learn new rules, and the new terminal subjected passengers to a new discipline tied to the railway schedule. To get to the platforms, visitors without travel documents had to purchase special platform tickets, and the railway authorities warned that "the enforcement of this will be significantly increased." City excise inspectors checked arriving baggage in the arrivals hall on a massive table divided into ten sections. Baggage had to be checked in at least fifteen minutes before departure, otherwise it would follow with the next train.[132] The right pavilion was filled with offices for operating the terminal and enforcing the regulations. Customs officials, police, a post office, and a quarantine room for ill passengers – furnished with a separate entrance – were located on the first floor, while railway officials and a central telegraph station with fifteen machines were on the second.[133] Entering the terminal, passengers partly surrendered their personal autonomy and property rights and full control of their bodies.

The legibility of the pathways charted throughout the terminal, as well as the abundance of translucent glass, should be not be confused with absolute transparency. Even the Crystal Palace was much darker inside than usually imagined.[134] The interior of the terminal was dim; light was dampened by beams and the soft glow of stained-glass windows. The tunnels were continuously lit with electricity, but waiting rooms used gaslight at night. There was enough light to ensure the disappearance of blind spots and dark corners, but its dimness was a reminder that the terminal was neither a street nor a dwelling, but rather a special place akin to the sacred space of monumental temples.[135]

A winged head sits on top of the gate-like entrance to the terminal – a reference to the city's medieval gates, triumphal arches, and gate-like train sheds (Figure 2.15). It is often interpreted as the head of Mercury, the god of trade and speed, who appears in railway architecture and design more frequently than any other deity. Marta Rymar, however, identifies this head as that of Hypnos. The present-day winged head is a 1920s substitute for the original, which was damaged in the First World War. The substitute probably does indeed refer to Mercury, but could be a misreading of the original allegory depicting Hypnos. The original head resembled the famous bronze head of Hypnos from the British Museum collection, which, in turn, served as an inspiration for several works of *fin-de-siècle* art, including Fernand Khnopff's "The Head of Hypnos," first shown to the public in 1900 (the year Sigmund Freud's *The Interpretation of Dreams* also appeared). In Greek myth Hypnos dwells in a dark cave, with drug-inducing plants at its entrance. The arched gate of the terminal was its main entrance facing the city, and had an intricate Secession-style floral ornament, which some observers praised as a much greater achievement than the more traditional allegorical sculptures on the terminal's façade. For them the gate was "simply a masterpiece of its kind"[136] (Figure 2.16).

Behind the gate was the dim interior of the terminal. Besides guiding and splitting the crowd, it was supposed to induce tranquillity.

Figure 2.15. The winged head over the main entrance today. Source: Serhii Tereshchenko, courtesy of Serhii Tereshchenko.

Waiting halls, restaurants and platforms were divested of descriptive and allegorical representations that could challenge the mind and invite questions. Instead, art nouveau ornaments invited viewers to endlessly follow their lines without offering any decipherable references. Discouraging contact with fellow travellers, the terminal's lighting and ornaments created an oneiric atmosphere. It helped to quell the anxiety induced first by crowds and anticipation, and later by noise, smell and the close physical presence of engines.

The wings of Hypnos also stood for speed, but not of Mercury's kind: speed in the realm of Hypnos was one of dreams. To achieve its breath-taking velocity, the railway had created an environment of its own: the railway space. The terminal was Lviv's entry point into

Figure 2.16. The terminal's main entrance. Source: Ihor Kotlobulatov collection, courtesy of Ihor Kotlobulatov.

Figure 2.17. The train shed interior, Lviv. Source: Ihor Kotlobulatov collection, courtesy of Ihor Kotlobulatov.

that space, where natural light, rhythms, and perspectives no longer applied. This unfamiliar railway space accompanied travellers all the way to their destination. The station's façade, with its familiar historicist elements and sculptural allegories, masked the profound strangeness of the railway space. Ultimately the terminal's design helped passengers accomplish the transition from the metaphors and allusions of the city's civic architecture to the bare mechanical truth of steam engines and railway tracks.

The new Lviv terminal belonged to the last wave of stations with great train sheds and a clear dual structure, with passengers' buildings and train sheds, while linked, kept separate. With the arrival of twentieth-century modernist terminals, this duality disappeared. The age of grand train sheds ended in 1915 with the eight enormous sheds of the new Leipzig station.[137] The architectural and technological origins of glass-covered train sheds were in early nineteenth-century glasshouses.[138] Like glasshouses, they enclosed and cultivated the environment at odds with the regular masonry of city streets. While glasshouses allowed urban dwellers to encounter and enjoy nature in artificially created islands of greenery, train sheds enclosed the railway's industrial underbelly, and gave the public safe access to the machines, whose usefulness did not cancel their monstrosity.

The façade the terminal turned towards the city was picturesque. Although architectural styles changed, throughout the nineteenth century picturesqueness was seen as the main source of beauty in masonry buildings.[139] Lviv's terminal façade thus conformed to the aesthetic taste of the city's middle class, which was used to the dominant picturesque historicism. But the train sheds subverted this middle-class certainty. They were no longer a separate and merely functional element – the domain of engineers rather than architects – but an aesthetic experience that broke with the sensibilities projected by the terminal's façade. In a way the sheds were Secession in its purest, most radical departure from nineteenth-century historicist masonry architecture. In the train sheds, distinctions between walls and ceiling vanished, and constructive elements were exposed as bare ribs blended with the decorative Secession metalwork of the platforms and halls (Figure 2.17). The sheds, praised by Mokłowski, instilled astonishment and barely contained terror, as things Edmund Burke defined as the "sublime," in distinction to the "beautiful."[140] The experience the sheds provided, moreover, was not merely aesthetic. They were the stage for close encounters with the most potent technology of the time. Their airiness and delicacy could also be read as a metaphor for the fragility of the social and political order that contained the powerful forces modernity had unleashed.

Chapter Three

Steel, Stone, Sweat, and Imagination

Galicia's period of railway expansion did not end with the construction of the new terminal in Lviv. Investments in Galician railways, approved in 1901, had not been fully spent even by 1905.[1] The expansion was not confined to new lines covering the province: Lviv felt the effects of it as railway tracks guided the city's spatial development, determined the location of industrial zones, and influenced the quality of housing. These features were common to large nineteenth-century cities that shared the experience of "the railroad invasion."[2] In social terms the railway enabled the emergence of a strong working class in Lviv, created a culture of passengerhood as an integral part of urban experience, and fed the social imagination.

Train yards, depots, turntables, workshops, and warehouses mushroomed in the vicinity of the terminal. The railway was devouring suburban space and transforming it into industrial railway space. Although the terminal itself was a compact structure, by 1904 the area occupied by sprawling railway infrastructure equalled dozens of medieval and early modern Lvivs. Railway infrastructure served as a magnet attracting commercial and industrial enterprises. Virtually every sizable Lviv enterprise required a warehouse in the vicinity of the station for its shipping and receiving needs. Granaries and oil reservoirs, cold storage facilities and coal sheds, storage for industrial machinery and perishable foods, all rushed towards the railway tracks. Larger enterprises were themselves located by the station. Industry, in turn, shaped nearby neighbourhoods. The Krakow ward (near the main railway station) and the Zhovkva ward (centred on Pidzamche station) became the city's working-class areas, which anxious bourgeois observers associated with poverty, dilapidation, disease, and crime. The very same neighbourhoods in the first decades of the twentieth century turned into strongholds of Lviv's vibrant and largely socialist labour movement.

By Lviv standards any enterprise with more than fifty employees was considered large.[3] The workshops of the Karl Ludwig Railway, employing 650 to 700 workers in 1890 and located near the main terminal, were the city's largest enterprise. By 1906 the number of workers there reached 800, not counting officials and foremen.[4] On Lviv's scale this was a gigantic enterprise. Moreover, the workers of the railway workshops and train depots in Lviv resembled most closely the classical industrial proletariat. Zygmunt Żuławski, later to become a socialist trade union leader in independent Poland, recalled a tour his gymnasium teacher organized in the 1890s to the railway workshops in Nowy Sącz, "where more than 1,000 laborers worked. I was carried away by the work itself, its organization, workers' postures."[5] Żuławski claimed that this experience decided his conversion to socialism. It was only logical that the railway workers' union dominated organized labour in both Galicia and Lviv.

Railway workers' associations in Lviv predated socialism. As early as 1869, workers of the Lviv railway workshops had founded the "Society of Brotherly Help."[6] By the mid-1890s, Galicia's railway workers had joined the first all-Austrian union of railway workers. In 1897 that union, together with its Galician subsidiaries, was dissolved. It reconstituted itself in 1898 as a federation of provincial Associations of Legal and Trade Defence, including the Galician association.[7] By the end of 1899, the federation had close to 400 members in Galicia.[8] In 1900 it started publishing its own newspaper *Kolejarz* (The Railwayman). For practical purposes membership in the new union was coterminous with party membership.[9] In 1899, on the third day of deliberations of the Fifth Congress of the Polish Social Democratic Party of Galicia and Silesia, the party changed its name and became the First Trade Union Congress of Galicia and Silesia, without altering the composition of its delegates.[10] Its own newspaper and party support helped the railway union to increase its province-wide membership to 2,956 by 1902, making it the largest socialist labour organization in Galicia.[11] In 1907 the union, weakened by a split, still had more members than the next two largest unions in the province combined. Its members accounted for more than 21 per cent of the total membership in Galicia's socialist unions. By 1912 its membership increased to 4,607 and its share in the unionized pro-socialist workforce to 27.4 per cent.[12] On the eve of the First World War it remained the largest socialist union in Galicia.[13] Kazimierz Kaczanowski, who had joined the socialist movement in the 1890s as a student, chaired the executive of the railway union from 1903 on and served as the main editor of *Kolejarz*.[14] After the creation of independent Poland, he led its largest railway workers' union until his death in 1937. The print run of the railway workers' newspaper in Galicia was higher than that of *Naprzód*, the main Galician Social Democratic daily – 4,000 against 2,800 copies in 1903.[15]

In 1913 14 per cent of all Galician wage workers were unionized.[16] Galicia, that archetype of under-industrialization and underdevelopment, while well below Britain and Denmark in union membership, was almost on par with Belgium and Germany (15–16 per cent) and ahead of Norway, France, and Italy.[17] Moreover, in Galicia organized labour was overwhelmingly socialist. In 1902 Lviv's socialist unions claimed a combined membership of 5,900; the second largest was the pro-clerical nationalist Polish Union of Christian Workers, with 1,300 members.[18] By 1914 socialist unions overwhelmingly dominated Galicia's organized labour, with non-socialist unions accounting for less than 10 per cent of all organized workers.[19]

When the Social Democratic Party of Galicia renamed itself the Polish Social Democratic Party of Galicia, Krakow became the seat of its executive. Lviv, with its numerous Jewish and Ukrainian socialists, was too multi-ethnic for the taste of party leader Ignacy Daszyński. Nevertheless, as the province's capital and its largest city, Lviv played an important role in Galician politics. In comparison with Krakow, Lviv was a more democratic city. Although Lviv's more democratic politics is often associated with the rise of the chauvinistic Polish "National Democracy," before the First World War Lviv was also seen as more "progressive," liberal, and leftist than Krakow.[20] Moreover, in Lviv, the Galician socialists' electoral performance was staggeringly successful not only by Galician but also by imperial standards.

As early as 1897, following the limited enfranchisement of male wage labour – for whom a separate fifth "curia" without property qualifications was created – a socialist deputy was elected to the parliament from Lviv. In 1900, from the same curia, Lviv elected Ernest Teodor Breiter,[21] who defined himself as an "unaligned," or non-party socialist with anarchist tendencies. His father, originally from Moravia, was the wealthy owner of a local brick factory, which provided bricks for the new Lviv train terminal.[22] In 1900 authorities tried to bring Breiter down by appealing to the railwaymen's corporate solidarity. Their counter-candidate was a local railway official.[23] The strategy failed. By 1900 Lviv's railway workers were mostly under socialist influences.

With the introduction of universal male suffrage for parliamentary elections in 1907, socialist deputies were elected in three of the city's seven electoral districts. Social Democratic candidates Józef Hudec and Herman Diamand won the Seventh and Third districts (roughly corresponding to the Krakow and Zhovkva (Żółkiew) wards), while

Ernest Breiter won the Second, bordering the latter two (Figure 3.1). By comparison, in Vienna, on the cusp of becoming "Red," socialists won only ten of thirty districts.[24] Moreover, since ruling elites tried to manipulate the outcome through gerrymandering electoral boundaries, the number of voters in the three socialist districts (13,051 votes altogether), was higher than in the remaining four (9,087 votes). Socialist candidates won 39.4 per cent of the total vote in the city.[25] All three socialist candidates were re-elected in the same districts in 1911.

The three districts in which socialist candidates regularly won elections were home to the majority of the city's railway employees. Lviv candidates, who busily analysed the sociological profiles of their districts, singled out railway workers and officials as a separate group unique among other blue- and white-collar workers.[26] Pre-election agitation and debates often took place in the railway workers' milieu.[27] A former state official who had overseen public meetings before an election recalled his terror when faced by thousands of organized railway workers, marching in files of six, armed with iron bars and singing "The Red Banner"[28] – the unofficial anthem of Galician, and later Polish, socialists, for which both the lyrics and music were written in Lviv in 1881.[29]

The railway not only populated but also physically created Lviv's working-class neighbourhoods, which expanded simultaneously with the urban railway space. While, in the 1870s and 1880s, buildings had stood only on the major transportation arteries, in the first two decades of the twentieth century, a dense network of streets and apartment blocks filled the space (Figure 3.2). A reconstruction of the railway workers' neighbourhoods on the basis of a 1913 address book shows that Horodotska (Gródecka) and its side streets were home to the bulk of the city's numerous railway workers and officials (Figure 3.3). Horodotska,[30] the longest of several radial streets connecting the city centre to the suburbs, also connected the city centre with the main train terminal. The street and its environs also housed numerous pubs and inns,[31] where drinking was often accompanied by heated political debates and the occasional brawl with political overtones.[32]

In such neighbourhoods, a railway worker was a common presence and represented an inspiring career option. In his "youthful dreams," Bronisław Łotocki, a fatherless grandchild of a butcher's helper, who lived next to Pidzamche station, saw himself as a railway worker: "The railway bewitched me, crossing each other, tangles of tracks leading to far away countries, a measured and melodious clatter of the machine."[33] For many boys from the Horodotska neighbourhood the dreams were similar. Some of them knew "all the makes of machines and train cars," and composed "fictional timetables for a fictional state."[34]

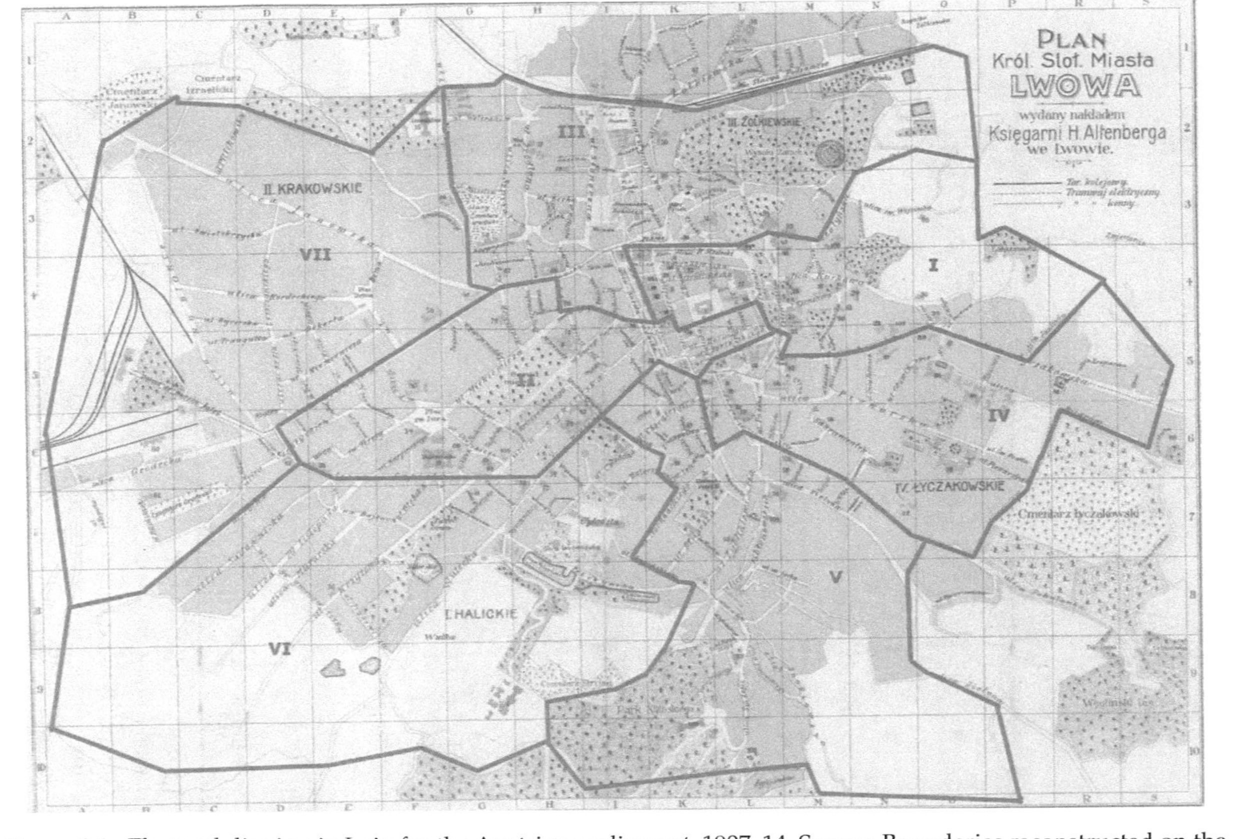

Figure 3.1. Electoral districts in Lviv for the Austrian parliament, 1907–14. Source: Boundaries reconstructed on the basis of information in *Gazeta Lwowska*, no. 112, 16 May 1907, 2.

Figure 3.2. Fragments of Lviv plans from 1892 and 1905, showing railway station neighbourhoods. Source: Józef Chowaniec, *Najnowszy dokładny plan królewskiego stołecznego miasta Lwowa* (Lviv: księgarnia Hermana Altenberga, 1892); *Plan miasta Lwowa* (Lviv: Atlas, 1922).

The neighbourhood by the main terminal, dominated by railway workers, was a more respectable one. Much poorer and dangerous areas for a middle-class passerby started north of it, in the vicinity of Janowska (today Shevchenko) Street, which "distinguished itself by the Polish-Ruthenian-Jewish mixture, with the sombre types fast to reach for a knife during a tavern brawl."[35] Even more notorious were the Klepariv (Kleparów) and Zamarstyniv (Zamarstynów) neighbourhoods of the Zhovkva ward. Mortality rates in those neighbourhoods were also higher than the city average.[36] Even police agents were not safe there, and could be attacked by robbers near the train tracks.[37]

Figure 3.3. Addresses of railway employees, 1913. Source: Map by Andriy Zayarnyuk, based on Franciszek Reichman, ed., *Księga adresowa król. stoł. miasta Lwowa: rocznik siedemnasty 1913* (Lviv: Narodowa, 1912).

The Krakow ward was not only a neighbourhood where railway workers lived; it was also the epicentre of their associational life. The provincial headquarters of the railway union and its newspaper offices were also there, on Horodotska (Gródecka) and Sheptytskys (Szeptyckis) streets.[38] For over a decade after the new terminal was finished, the central office was located at Horodotska 95–99,[39] buildings on a wide intersection from which a short boulevard was the only access to the terminal. Union infrastructure sustained neighbourhood life and vice versa. Leading union activists lived on neighbouring streets.[40] The city section of the union ran an "entertainment circle," with a dance hall in nearby Sheptytskys Street.[41] Engine drivers had their own club two blocks down from the provincial headquarters.[42] The large courtyard of the union headquarters was used for rallies that could not be accommodated indoors.[43] Eventually the union's bureaus, newspaper, clubs, dance halls, and reading rooms were also joined by a cooperative store[44] and a cooperative bakery with the cheapest bread in town.[45]

Lively associational life attracted city-wide socialist institutions to the neighbourhood. Although socialists claimed the city's central boulevards during May Day parades, demonstrations, and strikes, much of their day-to-day work took place in the working-class neighbourhoods by the train station. The Lviv branch of the Adam Mickiewicz People's University, a socialist educational initiative for workers, was initially located at the Solarnia (today Kropyvnytsky) Square, which joins Sheptytskyks (Szeptyckis) and Horodotska (Gródecka). The university offered weekly lectures that were open to the public and included talks by prominent socialist leaders.[46] The City Health Insurance Fund for workers was located at Na Błonie (Zaliznychna) Street, running from Horodotska to the railway workshops. This location was initially also used for the offices of socialist deputy Józef Hudec, who chaired the Fund.[47] Dense overlapping of union, communal, and socialist infrastructure turned the neighbourhood of the train station into a bastion of the socialist and workers' movement. Other socialist organizations and activists also often used the premises of the railway union. The women's circle in 1907, for example, had a meeting there with a simple agenda: "A woman and socialism."[48] On the other hand, larger railway workers' meetings took place in rented halls to accommodate the participants. One was in the Jewish artisans' society *Yad Haruzim* – which was also used for Ukrainian theatre performances – in the largely Jewish neighbourhood at the southern edge of the Zhovkva ward. Frequent use of this building testifies to the internationalist character of the railway union.[49]

When railway workers marched to show their power, they used Horodotska (Gródecka), the street that connected the heart of the railway neighbourhoods with the city centre. On 11 August 1907, for example, delegates of the railway workers of the Lviv railway directorate met at the terminal, then marched to their union offices and held their meeting in the courtyard there – its long, shared balconies, like those of most working-class apartment buildings, filled with workers. Once the meeting was over, the delegates, accompanied by a crowd of local railway workers, marched down Horodotska to the city centre and the railway directorate's headquarters.[50]

Although parliamentary politic and elections (and preparations for them) were of crucial importance to the Galician socialists, they did not neglect workers' everyday concerns and struggles. The railway workers' employer was the local administration of state railways: the Lviv railway directorate. Socialists and the railway administration had already clashed during the founding moment of the Galician socialist party, the first May Day celebration in 1890, when the administration threatened to lay off without forewarning any employee absent from work that day.[51] The administration was recruited from those with a gymnasium education,[52] while senior railway officials were normally either engineers or financiers. Heinrich von Wittek belonged to the latter, Ludwik Wierzbicki to the former. Sometimes railway officials also had an education in law.[53] Engineers had a secure, steady, and well-paid career on Galician railways. One of them, Bolesław Wasilewski, graduated from the Lviv polytechnic in 1880 and entered the railway service the same year. Four years later his salary was 700 gulden; by 1900, in Lviv, he was earning 2,700.[54] By comparison an engine driver, the railway's best-paid worker, made 1,350 gulden after twenty years of work; a stoker's salary on the same engine would be capped at 800 and that of a qualified metalworker's at 750. And this was after a substantial raise railway workers received in 1907.[55] Female ticket clerks had a starting salary of 420 gulden and could see that increased to 660 after ten years of work.[56] These were the salaries of those lucky enough to secure a permanent position. Almost half the railway workforce was paid by the day and deprived of benefits and promotion.

The main weapon of the workers in their struggle with the administration was direct action on the job. A partial workshop strike of 300 workers had already occurred in 1894.[57] By 1918 dozens of railway workers' strikes had taken place in Lviv, but none of them was general. The only time the whole railway went on strike in the Habsburg monarchy was in 1904, in its Hungarian part.[58] This strike paralysed the state and forced the government to develop contingency plans, which included provisions for a possible takeover of the railway by the military. Equally important, the government indicated a willingness to negotiate with the union to prevent future strikes. As a result, during the November 1905 general strike in Cisleithania, Social Democrats and union leaders decided to exempt railway workers from participation (together with postal, health care, power, gas, and water supply workers) as providers of essential services.[59]

Direct action was not the only instrument used by organized labour in its struggles. Many workers' concerns related to workplace routines and conditions. For those working in workshops and depots, at the stations, or on the tracks, accidents were a very real possibility. Accidents had haunted the railway since the first ride of Stephenson's "Rocket."[60] Although the railway was a dangerous place because of the very nature of its operations, the union justly claimed that its drive for profit, and concomitant attempt to save on workers' health and safety, exacerbated the dangers, turning Galician railways into "a factory of corpses and cripples." In response to charges of excessive spending, the railway administration overworked workers and overclocked machines.[61]

The union criticized the administration and protected workers, offering them legal aid in the case of workplace accidents.[62] The union's very name – the Council for Legal Defence – reflected the importance of legal action. Socialist lawyers provided free legal counsel to union members in work-related cases.[63] In 1902 the Galician union handled 919 lawsuits against the railway administration, and passed 614 more to the Czech union, since it could not physically take care of all of them. More than one-third, 351 cases, involved accidents, 47 of which were fatal.[64] These legal battles were possible only because the foundational principle of the Austrian constitutional state was recognized to be the rule of law – indeed E.P. Thompson's "unqualified human good" that could be used to the benefit of the weak and exploited.[65] Arguably health was more important for workers than for the middle class since the body's physical powers were their only source of sustenance. *Krankenkasse* (municipal health insurance funds) were seen as workers' institutions. In Lviv this fund had been controlled by the Social Democrats since its inception.[66]

The railway workers' union also tried to improve the physical environment of the workplace. Despite the new terminal, most railway employees worked in much older and often inadequate buildings. Premises of the railway workshops dated back to the 1860s. By the 1900s they were overcrowded, drafty, and full of structural problems that posed a serious safety hazard. In 1904 there were six serious railway workshop incidents in February alone.[67] The union claimed that, since the railway was a state enterprise, state labour inspectors turned a blind eye to health and safety violations that would not have been tolerated in private enterprises.[68] Whether because of union pressure or of its own accord, the railway administration did a major overhaul of its workshops, depots, and other auxiliary structures between 1909 and 1913. In 1910 even the union newspaper, highly critical of the administration, acknowledged that the new conductors' dorms were "without worms, with high ceilings, bright, spacious and healthy, pleasant to enter."[69] The workplace was becoming safer and healthier.

The union also scrutinized the organization of work, especially relations between superiors and subordinates. The majority of the union's complaints were directed against negligent and unprofessional managers and foremen.[70] The thrust of the union campaign was against the arbitrary power of supervisors, and in favour of clearly defined rules and procedures. Very early on the union defined its main enemy, the Austrian state railway, as the "mammoth machinery of capital, favouritism, and connections."[71] Transparent rules were supposed to uproot abuse of power by unscrupulous individuals. The union argued that promotion should depend on performance and seniority instead of bribes and the whims of superiors. Activists branded railway managers who abused their subordinates as "caciques," a reference to the Spanish and Latin American system of *caciquismo*: bosses who believed their authority extended to all aspects of workers' social and political lives, and who did not feel bound by regulations. Impersonal universal rules and procedures were the alternative favoured by the union, and its intervention was sometimes successful.[72]

The abuse of power in the railway hierarchy often had a gender component. While in the 1880s there were only 12 women working for the Austrian railways, by 1900 481 women were employed, mostly as ticket clerks and secretaries.[73] These white-collar workers often had even less power vis-à-vis their superiors than did manual workers in the workshops and depots. The union newspaper often reported cases of sexual harassment and rape.[74] In the railway bureau, sexual relations between superiors and female bureau workers were allegedly common, going hand in hand with completely unequal power relations. Railway women attracted public attention as some of the first female white-collar workers in Galicia. The main protagonist of a highly popular novel by Artur Gruszecki, *Kolejarze* (railway workers), works as a clerk in a railway bureau. Feeling defenceless against her superiors, she joins the labour movement. But politics make her position even more precarious, and a lecherous boss pursues her with unwelcome sexual advances.[75] The union defended the rights and dignity of working women and believed that the same recipe of transparency and enforced rules would eradicate such abuse.

In their struggle against the railway administration, union activists defended not only their own narrow corporate interests, but also the larger public good. The "satraps," "caciques," and "mafias" of the superiors unmasked by the unions were also involved in the theft, fraud, and large-scale embezzlement of state funds.[76] In a string of scandals, union activists uncovered ties between railway officials, corrupt city councillors, and gangs of thieves.[77] The most sensational scandal of the pre-war years involved alleged fraud by Inspector Popowicz, the deputy chief of the Lviv directorate's first department.[78] Socialists accused senior officials of running their own private enterprises at the expense of the state railway.[79] Although socialists served as watchdogs for the general public, they often paid dearly for that service because, as a rule, the courts rejected their allegations as unproven.[80]

Finally, there were the workers' lives outside the workplace. Although remuneration of railway workers was better than in many other trades, in a large and expensive city their salaries barely allowed them to meet basic needs.[81] Throughout the 1900s the cost of living in Lviv continued to increase, with soaring real estate prices and rents mostly to blame.[82] As the city's growth brought "gentrification" to some parts of the railway neighbourhoods, railway workers started moving to suburban villages in search of more affordable accommodation. A new arrangement emerged where women and children lived in the countryside, while male workers shared cheap rooms in the city, living on "dry bread with a bit of butter or buttermilk."[83] Behind the new terminal and depot, the new suburb of Levandivka (Lewandówka) appeared, populated primarily by railway workers. The trend worried the union – the flight of workers from the city weakened Lviv's socialist constituency – and in 1904 it began to demand housing projects for railway workers.[84]

The railway had a long tradition dating back to 1861 of providing housing for its employees. A sizable land plot on the corner of Horodotska (Gródecka) and Na Błonie (Zaliznychna) was allocated to Victorian-style cottages buried in verdure (Figure 3.4). By the turn of the century, with soaring real estate prices, this type of housing was no longer sustainable. From the 1900s onwards, railway housing took the form of massive apartment blocks. In 1909 a pair of four-storey buildings with 192 apartments, the largest the city had yet seen, appeared on Horodotska across the street from the platforms of the former Chernivtsi terminal (Figure 3.5). These lonely giants towered above a sea of one- and two-storey buildings. Their construction became possible via a 1907 city ordinance accompanied by the repeal of an old law limiting buildings to three stories on certain streets.[85] These large rectangular buildings had both wide tree-lined thoroughfares and long courtyards

Figure 3.4. Remains of the original railway village from 1861, walled off by newer apartment blocks. Source: Biblioteka Narodowa, Warsaw, Pocz. 2311.

Figure 3.5. Railway workers' buildings on Horodotska Street, present-day view. Source: Aeou, "Budynky No.165-167 na vulytsi Horodots'kii u L'vovi," 10 January 2012; https://commons.wikimedia.org/wiki/File:165-167_Horodotska_Street_(01).jpg, used under a CC BY-3.0 licence.

large enough to serve as mini-parks. Railway buildings on Horodotska and Hlyboka (Głęboka) shared a similar neo-Gothic design, a style at odds with the Secession/neo-Renaissance design of both the new terminal and the neighbourhood. Moreover, the buildings' architecture communicated a very different ideological message.

In 1909 the railway administration also completed a building for its senior officials, away from busy Horodotska (Gródecka), with its warehouses, tracks, and workers. It was at Hlyboka (Głęboka) Street 14, in the middle of the newly developed area south of the polytechnic known as the "New World" (Figure 3.6).[86] This was a lavish area of modern, upscale apartments and villas, well connected to the station, while at the same time safely shielded by working-class neighbourhoods from the discomforts of railway infrastructure. Early on, complaints accumulated that, although buildings on Horodotska were meant for poorer

Figure 3.6. Railway employees' building at Hlyboka Street 14, present-day view. Source: Posterr, "Zhytlovyi budynok. Lviv. Hlyboka 14"; Wikimedia Commons, used under a CC BY-SA-4.0 licence.

workers with families, many officials had obtained residences there too. Seeking modern convenience at cheap rates, these officials sometimes even merged two units into one. The union was outraged because competition for these apartments was high: five hundred applications for thirty-two apartments in 1910 alone.[87] While sporadic conflicts with middle-class occupants continued,[88] the workers and their union eventually came to see this apartment complex as their own.[89]

While responding to the demands of organized labour, the railway administration did not renounce its own interests and agenda. The very same administration created and supported splinter unions,[90] and tried to envelop workers within a cocoon of paternalistic initiatives and institutions as alternatives to socialist ones. There was, for example, a school next to the terminal with regular classes for children and evening classes for railway employees. Its premises were used for cultural events sponsored by the administration, while teachers conducted anti-union agitation during evening classes.[91] The management also founded and funded a loyal "Railway Reading Club."[92] The administration created a camp for employees' children, which prompted the creation of a union camp (both in the Carpathians).[93] Likewise, two competing kindergartens were established.[94]

In the struggle against socialists and organized labour, the railway administration found political allies among nationalist and clerical politicians. In 1903 they jointly created "Self-Help," an alternative non-socialist union.[95] Although at one point "Self-Help" claimed 865 members throughout Galicia, its fortunes suffered a serious blow in 1910, when, with its support, the Polish parliamentary club voted against new railway legislation tabled by the socialists,[96] who claimed that, after the vote, only nine active members remained in the Lviv "Self-Help" branch.[97] The administration also periodically allowed nationalists and clericals to use the luxurious first-class waiting room of the new terminal for their events.[98] At the same time it blocked the use of railway-owned premises by the socialist union.[99] The most visible offensive against socialist influences, however, took place in the architectural environment of the city's streets.

Józef Bilczewski, Lviv's Roman Catholic archbishop from 1901 to 1923, led the anti-socialist offensive. Already in his 1901 inaugural speech, Bilczewski had attacked socialism as the "new religion" of the dissatisfied, based on hatred and "self-love."[100] Later that same year, at the blessing of the foundation stone of the new terminal, Bilczewski claimed that scientific and technological progress, the most obvious and exciting part of modernity, was fully compatible with Church doctrine and could be used to the Church's benefit: "The railway is the most useful instrument of Christian civilization. It delivers the truth of the Gospel and the fruits of science all over the world, draws people close to each other and brings close that moment, when inhabitants of the Earth, on all its territory, will live as in one house and the whole of humankind, brought up on the truths of the Catholic faith ... will unite in one large family."[101] In a voluminous pastoral letter, "On the Social Question," Bilczewski presented socialism as an unfortunate outcome of existing social problems, not a solution to them.[102] It was "the greatest of all heresies that ever appeared in the world;"[103] and "the greatest enemy of society."[104] In combatting socialism, Bilczewski allotted a special role to Catholic unions and societies. He also mentioned the architectural environment: "I consider the construction of churches and chapels as one of the most important means of the revival of society's spirit."[105]

In Bilczewski's own backyard, Lviv's vast new neighbourhoods around the main terminal had no churches. There was only the old Roman Catholic Church of St Anne, at the corner of Janowska (Shevchenko) and Horodotska (Gródecka). The church dated back to the sixteenth century, and was still in the vicinity of the old city centre. There was also a small monastery founded in 1897, with the church finished in 1901, in the middle of Janowska Street. South of Janowska and west of St Anne, the city had no churches. The only city church that could be seen from the train terminal was the Greek Catholic cathedral of St George, on top of the hill overlooking the flats between Horodotska and Janowska.

Bilczewski made missionary work in the railway neighbourhoods his foremost priority. St Elizabeth Church was the material embodiment of his effort. The site chosen for this church was Solarnia (Kropyvnytsky) Square on Horodotska (Gródecka), in the geographic centre of the railway workers' neighbourhoods and associations. The square, filled with lumber warehouses and bulk goods shops, was the site of the socialist Mickiewicz People's University. St Elizabeth was to become the largest of Lviv's churches. One of the conditions of its design was the ability to host 2,200 parishioners.[106] The building of St Elizabeth's was also a costly project that required the support of the rich and powerful. The emperor donated the land, while Archduke Franz Ferdinand agreed to serve as the construction's patron. The viceroy, the Diet's speaker, and the city council donated funds as well.[107] The railway administration also contributed large sums. Cooperation became even closer under Stanisław Rybicki, who succeeded Wierzbicki in 1905 as Lviv railway director.[108] It is not surprising that Rybicki was immortalized in one of the church's side altars. Petro Viitovych (Piotr Wójtowicz), who had sculpted allegories of trade and industry on the terminal's façade, finished the altar dedicated to St Joseph in 1917. In it he depicted Rybicki's return to the city liberated from Russian troops in 1915 and his welcome by Bilczewski.[109] Immortality in art, however, proved elusive: the altar was destroyed during the Soviet period.

St Elizabeth's was supposed to serve the religious needs of railway workers and be built by them, and the union complained that the administration was forcing workers to contribute sizable "voluntary" donations.[110] Nonetheless the project took much longer than expected. Bilczewski blessed the beginning of work on the church's foundations in 1904 and the foundation stone of the actual building in 1905.[111] Instead of 1907, as planned, the construction ended only in 1911. The work on the interior continued during the First World War and well afterward.[112] Once finished, the neo-Gothic church with its eighty-eight-metre-high spear tower became the tallest city building – and still is, if one counts only roofed buildings, not TV towers (Figure 3.7). Its Gothic silhouette was not accidental: Bilczewski himself stipulated in the terms of the design competition that the church had to be either in Romanesque or Gothic style.[113] Gothic, however, was the style most foreign to the Eastern Christian tradition. The spires of the new church eclipsed the domes of St George, the spiritual centre of Galicia's Greek Catholics, and emphasized the city's Polish-ness, as did the neo-Gothic winner of the 1908 competition for the new city hall design,[114] although, luckily for the city's architecture, the latter never materialized.

The use of Gothic style, however, was not only about city's Polish-ness. In this particular context, Gothic signified conservatism and anti-Enlightenment. The name of the church's patron evoked the memory of Empress Elizabeth, Franz Joseph's wife, who was loved by the Galician common folk, and the church was to serve as a memorial to her.[115] The fact that Empress Elizabeth had been assassinated in 1898 by an anarchist also mattered, pointing to the danger and immorality of social radicalism. The Gothic style of the new church was also an explicit rejection of Viennese Secession, with its "eastern," pre-Christian, and progressivist references. (Secession was the style of the grand Workers' Home in Favoriten, Vienna's working-class suburb. Hubert Gessner, Otto Wagner's pupil and an unofficial "party architect" of Austrian Social Democrats, designed it in 1901.[116]) The church, while honouring the murdered empress, had to be named after a saint, not after the emperor's wife. There were a number of St Elizabeths to choose from, but Bilczewski selected a medieval Hungarian princess "to secure for the new parish, composed predominantly of poorer people, the patronage of that great servant of God, who, despite being

Figure 3.7. St Elizabeth Church. Source: Ihor Kotlobulatov collection, courtesy of Ihor Kotlobulatov.

of royal blood, fell in love with the poor, and completely dedicated herself to their service, and while alive was called the mother of the poor."[117] At the opening of the church, Bilczewski reiterated: "In our times the social question trumps all other concerns. And St Elizabeth is precisely the most social saint."[118] Indeed, a social saint was a proper choice for the neighbourhood, which was unmistakably working class. Upon completion, the new church became a centre of anti-socialist activity. The "White Banner" – white was associated with purity in the Catholic tradition and with the eagle on the Polish coat of arms – was founded by the parish priest, held its meetings in the parish hall, and joined the "Catholic Union of Workers," the only alternative to socialist unions in Lviv.[119]

St Elizabeth's was the pinnacle of a much grander plan. Simultaneously with the construction of the church, Bilczewski built the Catholic Home (1908–11), another fortress of Catholicism with Gothic and Romanesque elements on Horodotska (Gródecka), between the St Anne and St Elizabeth churches (Figure 3.8). The Gothic style of the railway housing also symbolically aligned it with Bilczewski's crusade of building edifices in that style in working-class neighbourhoods. As well, the archbishop supplemented monumental construction with a ubiquitous, less immense marking of city space. Gypsum statues of St Mary, connected with the very Roman Catholic but also very Polish Marian cult, were its signifying marker. In 1912 such a St Mary statue was blessed at the main terminal.[120] Apparently St Michael in the main vestibule was not sufficiently Roman Catholic and Polish. The statue of St Mary also appeared at the back of the union offices, accessible from Kubasiewicz (Alla Horska) Street.

Bilczewski continued his offensive against the godless space of railway neighbourhoods even after his death in 1923. It was his will to be buried in the Ianivsky (Janowski) cemetery, opened in 1883[121] side by side the new Jewish cemetery and far less prestigious than the exclusively Christian Lychakiv (Łyczaków) cemetery, opened at the end of the eighteenth century. Ianivsky served as the city's "poor quarter" in afterlife.[122] Bilczewski was the first person from the Roman Catholic hierarchy to be buried there. Staying with his working-class flock after death, Bilczewski was also claiming the cemetery for the Catholic Church. Besides being in "dangerous" proximity to the Jewish cemetery, there was another reason for Bilczewski to worry about the cemetery's Catholic character. On 2 June 1904 Lviv socialists unveiled memorials to the workers massacred during the 1902 demonstrations.[123] The commemorations started in the new Jewish cemetery, at the graves of the massacre's Jewish victims.

The material resources of the railway workers were no match for those at the disposal of the Catholic Church, state railway, and governmental

Figure 3.8. The Catholic Home, Lviv. Source: Marek Münz, [Ulica Gródecka we Lwowie, ca.1915]; Biblioteka Narodowa, Warsaw. F. 7814/II.

authorities. Before the First World War labour did not contribute a single monumental building to Lviv's cityscape. Nevertheless, as early as 1907, the railway union in Lviv started raising funds for a building of its own.[124] The building would materialize only at the end of the 1930s, behind the railway housing project on Horodotska (Gródecka). Its slender, unadorned, and decisively modernist Bauhaus design stood in stark contrast with Bilczewski's massive Gothic (Figure 3.9).

Even before 1914 the railway labour movement had won several impressive victories. Galician railway workers had unionized before railway workers in the Russian Empire, who made their first attempt to do so only during the 1905 revolution.[125] Galicia, as part of Cisleithania, had more progressive social legislation – second only to German legislation – than its rapidly industrializing Russian neighbour.[126] The rule of law and a constitution helped to channel class conflict into legal and parliamentary arenas. Begrudgingly and resentfully, the railway

Figure 3.9. The building of the railway workers' union. Source: Fedor Koniukhov, http://photos.wikimapia.org/p/00/03/10/06/71_full.jpg, used under a CC BY-SA-3.0 licence.

administration nonetheless accepted self-organization of the workers and negotiated with them. In 1909 the socialist union leader Kazimierz Kaczanowski boasted during a meeting at the Jad Charuzim hall: "At present the organization has great influence in the Railway Board, we have reached the point when all the governmental reforms introduced by the government come first to our representatives and without their approval, no changes can happen in the life of railway workers."[127]

Archbishop Bilczewski emphasized both Catholicism and Polish-ness for a reason. The world of Lviv's socialism at the beginning of the twentieth century was remarkably internationalist. There were three national Social Democratic parties – Polish, Ukrainian, and Jewish – as well as factions and sympathetic political organizations. Historiography usually portrays the relationships among them as one of growing national antagonisms.[128] In Lviv, however, ground-level cooperation among all three parties continued at least until 1914. A leader of Lviv's branch of the Polish Social Democratic Party of Galicia and Silesia was also a leader of the Ukrainian Social Democratic Party. Moreover, by and large, city unions were not divided by nationality. The headquarters of the railway union itself was internationalist. One of the leading Ukrainian Social Democrats, Teofil Melen, worked there together with Kaczanowski.[129] Socialist leaflets were often in Polish, Ukrainian, and Yiddish, as were the speeches during major socialist rallies and demonstrations. Indeed the railway union consistently emphasized internationalism: "Wise railwaymen will not be allowed to sever them from the united ranks with phrases of false patriotism."[130] Demonstrations of socialist labour regularly crossed ethnic and religious boundaries, with the 1904 commemoration of the 1902 massacre, linking Jewish and Christian cemeteries, exemplifying the internationalist approach.

At the same time, Social Democrats supported national self-determination – and in Galicia, Polish, Ukrainian, and Jewish "self-determination" did not have to be mutually exclusive. Both Polish and Ukrainian Social Democrats agreed that in an ideal future both Poland and Ukraine would be independent countries in which socialists would dominate national politics. During the May Day demonstration in 1904, socialist activists carried placards saying "Long live the free, independent Ukrainian republic" and "Long live independent Poland."[131] Those independent nation-states, however, were located in the same future, after the social revolution that would end the rule of capital. In theory these parties were committed simultaneously to socialist revolution and national independence; in practice they fought for political democracy, social welfare, and national equality, actively using the imperial political framework to achieve these ends.

While Social Democrats resisted the temptations of a narrow nationalism, resisting the national public sphere proved to be much harder. That sphere was not so much about identification with the nation as about public and associational life. The socialists could not afford severance from it, since the struggle for hegemony took place in the nationally organized public sphere.[132] Seemingly innocuous things such as sports and theatre provided the most fertile ground for integration. In 1903 the railway union advised its members to avoid the Polish gymnastic society Sokol, which was under the influence of radical nationalists, and promised an alternative.[133] Workers' sport clubs were indeed created, but they shared facilities with others, competed in tournaments, and joined leagues. In 1908 Sokol moved into the railway neighbourhood, obtaining large modern facilities at Kętrzyński (Fedkovych) Street 30, between the union headquarters and the railway housing project on Horodotska (Gródecka).

The integration of socialists into national communities was not painless: every step in that direction encountered significant resistance from more internationalist socialist activists. The joint Galician socialist party decided to become "Polish" during the Fifth Congress in 1897. The hall of the Congress's sessions was decorated with the slogan, "Proletarians of all countries unite," in Polish, Ukrainian, and Yiddish. Ukrainian poet Taras Shevchenko's portrait, with blue and yellow ribbons, hung next to Adam Mickiewicz and Juliusz Słowacki.[134] Kornel Żelaszkiewicz, who represented Lviv's construction workers, voted against the motion to change party's name; so did Kazimierz Kaczanowski and many others.[135] The situation would repeat itself in the 1900s and 1910s. Support for Józef Piłsudski's faction of the Polish Socialist Party in the Russian Empire, recognition of Jewish national rights, and Polish paramilitary formations on the eve of the First World War repeatedly divided the Polish Social Democratic Party of Galicia and Silesia's leading activists.

One national conflict among Galician socialists involved railway workers. In 1910 Ukrainian Social Democrats started their own railway paper, *Zeliznychnyk* (The Railwayman), in Chernivtsi. The executive of the railway union, supported by the Polish Social Democratic Party, welcomed the Ukrainian initiative, offering to pick up its publication and support it financially.[136] In Lviv, however, the Ukrainian paper became merely a monthly supplement to the Polish bi-weekly. To sweeten the pill, the union appointed Teofil Melen, a Ukrainian, as the editor of both papers. Eventually, in 1912, the Ukrainian paper stopped altogether.[137] The official explanation given was the small number of subscribers (about three hundred) and the paper's financial problems.

Younger Ukrainian socialists, however, saw this as yet another case of Polish duplicity and the inability to form an equal partnership. Even though tensions accrued and cracks multiplied, they were not irreparable. On the ground in Lviv, Polish, Jewish, and Ukrainian socialists negotiated compromises and cooperated, especially when the lives and rights of local workers were at stake.[138]

Although not at the forefront of theoretical Marxist discussions, Lviv's socialist intellectuals forged strong connections with the workers and with the city. In a way their activity prefigured an answer to late twentieth-century debates about the danger of divorcing formal politics from the neighbourhood-based, informal life of social classes.[139] The railway workers' neighbourhood became a political unit to be mobilized for political and social struggles. A network of institutions, support centres, and union activists in the neighbourhoods where railway workers lived transformed them into spaces dominated by the labour movement. This domination, however, was fiercely contested in its multiple dimensions, including the material. Working-class space could not be neatly demarcated and separated from the largely middle-class urban public space or from the national public spheres and civil societies. On the other hand, the latter were not able merely to swallow and digest the former.

This heterogeneity of urban space was a characteristic feature of large modern cities. Lvivites knew perfectly well that their city was no *Weltstadt*, or "world city." The closest truly world city to Lviv in the nineteenth century was Vienna.[140] Warsaw was much livelier and larger than Lviv, but did not qualify as a cosmopolitan metropolis. In the 1900s many also looked towards Berlin as a new standard of urban modernity.[141]

The railway enabled such comparisons. Ever-increasing numbers of people routinely travelled between large and small cities. Train terminals often decided the traveller's first impressions. In 1912 Warsaw-Vienna Railway's terminal in Warsaw "appeared as an anachronism in comparison with Lviv's. [It was] small, crammed, with narrow passages, rather inconvenient."[142] Berlin, on the other hand, offered a terminal experience much grander than that of Lviv.[143] Still, just as people from Lviv looked up to larger cities, arrivals from small Galician towns saw Lviv as a true metropolis.[144] Even Krakow, the second-largest Galician city, looked like "a small provincial town" compared to Lviv.[145] Alexander Granach, the future Hollywood actor, came to Lviv from Horodenka. He found that "the noise and confusion were immense. Hundreds of people were getting on and off trains, pushing, calling to porters with trucks and luggage, engines breathed, puffed, blew, squealed, whistled, screamed. People rushed busily in all directions."[146] For Granach the train terminal had more of a great city character than the city itself.

Comparisons with Galicia's eastern neighbour were also inevitable. Early twentieth-century Lviv was a Mecca of Ukrainian nationalism. For Ukrainian travellers from the Russian Empire, a visit to Lviv was akin to a pilgrimage. Those modern pilgrims as a rule arrived by train. One of them, the historian Dmytro Doroshenko, came to Lviv for the first time in 1904. Years later he recalled the joy of openly purchasing a Ukrainian newspaper at a station kiosk and of seeing station boards in Ukrainian. In the Russian Empire, the Ukrainian language was still suppressed.[147] A year before, another Ukrainian intellectual from the Russian Empire, Serhiy Iefremov, visited Galicia for the first time. He too recalled his delight in seeing, in the border town of Brody, for the first time in his life, simple official signs in Ukrainian, such as "do not spit on the train cars' floor": "I felt as if I broke out from the constraining, suffocating cage into a wide, free ... world."[148]

The famous Jewish writer Sholem Aleikhem (Solomon Rabinovich), who stopped in the city after leaving the Russian Empire for America in the wake of the 1905 pogroms, described Lviv later in his novel *Motl, the Cantor's Son*. Notwithstanding its general ironic tone, Jewish emigrants from the Russian Empire in the novel also exalt in the freedoms found in Lviv. The city is "clean, airy, pretty – a sight for sore eyes ... On Saturdays the Jews promenade in their fur hats and no one says a word. It's a free country. And the people! Pure gold!"[149]

Even though Austria was freer, travellers agreed that Russian trains were more comfortable. Russian train cars were usually in better shape than their Austrian counterparts, and double windows were better soundproofed.[150] Dmytro Doroshenko noticed that Austrian train cars were more crammed, while the time to board a car was much shorter.[151] This last difference would persist throughout the Soviet period. In the Russian Empire, with its vast expanses, long-distance trains were brought to the platform earlier to provide plenty of boarding time. Wheel sets were checked while the train was at the platform. In Central Europe, where the rail traffic was denser, trains would come for boarding just before departure.

There were other complaints about Galician trains. They could be chilly in winter and sizzling hot in summer,[152] sometimes making travel unbearable.[153] Some cars were newer, which also meant cleaner and more comfortable.[154] A well-disposed conductor or stationmaster could provide help getting into one of those.[155] Galician railway was not immune to petty corruption, and it was not uncommon for passengers, instead of purchasing tickets, to pay a smaller fare into the conductor's private pocket.[156]

Frequent train passengers who compared cities and railway systems were as a rule well-to-do people. Spatial mobility was largely determined by financial means. For these affluent people, Krakow and Vienna were the most common destinations. Spa towns famous for their curative facilities, such as Karlovy Vary (German: Karlsbad) in Bohemia, were also popular – Lviv had a sufficient number of wealthy citizens to maintain a sizable colony there.[157] By the beginning of the twentieth century, Lviv's middle class also discovered vacation destinations closer to home. The railway, which offered direct connections from Lviv to several picturesque regions of the Carpathians, facilitated the discovery.[158] Resort areas developed there, and soon became covered with guest houses and summer cottages. Railway employees facilitated and actively participated in this kind of tourism. There were railway camps for children; senior managers owned villas near high-ranking state officials, industrialists, and professors;[159] and poorer railway employees partook in special vacation trips, often by charter trains.[160]

Railway employees enjoyed ticket discounts and were also frequent users of rail. Those living on small stations and outposts were compensated for the lack of local community with ready access to trains and high spatial mobility. Railway workers called the network of lines and small stations the "space" (*przestrzeń*) in contradistinction to the railway infrastructure of large junctions such as Lviv. That "space" helped to maintain connections with other railway workers.[161] They were the "locals" of the railway, whose assistance was invaluable to travellers in the age before telephone booths.[162]

For most people the railway trip itself was an experience beyond the scope of the usual. It fascinated children and adults alike.[163] There were also those for whom train journeys were repulsive. One of them was Romanticist independentist activist Zofia Romaniczówna, born in 1842 and quite conservative in her attitudes. Her dislike of trains extended to industrial labour, to the "stifling atmosphere of a factory which squeezed one's chest, strangling physically and morally."[164] On the other hand, Zygmunt Żuławski, the future leader of Poland's socialist unions, who was fascinated by the scenes of industrial labour in railway workshops, was also "madly" impressed by his first train journey, "not able to take [my] eyes off the window even for a second."[165] It is probably not an accident that in both these cases the railway journey is paired with industrial labour. In Galicia both were equally novel and intertwined.

Train journeys were also about encounters with old acquaintances and strangers. On the train to Vienna, a member of parliament would converse with a fellow socialist MP, and then the whole compartment would turn into "something like a club." All would share a roasted chicken and a bottle of wine brought by the Greek Catholic priest.[166] Prior to 1914 restaurant train cars were rare and could be found only on some trains, even in the Russian Empire, famous for its distances.[167] Hence restaurants at large railway stations were even of greater importance. Restaurants were excellent both in Lviv and in smaller provincial towns.[168] In Lviv, as in many other cities, tourist guides listed the train station restaurant as among the best in the city.[169]

The restaurants served not only travellers on their journey, but also those in the terminal. With the increased traffic and new luggage regulations, people would come to the terminal in advance and entertain themselves with reading "railway" fiction and newspapers from the terminal's bookstands.[170] The terminal was the first place to receive fresh news from other cities in the form of daily papers. In summer 1914, eager for news, people all over Galicia rushed to the stations, purchasing newspapers thrown from trains right onto the platforms.[171] In 1907, sitting in the Lviv terminal, the city's leading socialist and by virtue of being MP, a "frequent traveller," Herman Diamand sent a postcard to his wife, who was at home, also in Lviv, reporting that his three-hour wait was "quite pleasant here, I see acquaintances and we chat."[172] As Diamand's correspondence makes clear, delays were frequent.[173] For local celebrities like Diamand, encounters at the terminal also involved strangers seeking favours[174] or proposing business deals.[175]

Finally, terminals provided plenty of opportunities for observing people. Observers tended to be higher on the social ladder, while those observed, lower. In one of countless letters to his wife, Diamand describes the station in Przemyśl between two and four a.m.: "a picture typical of the province: railway employees sleeping in the corners, a half-lit waiting room, women, children and sacks, all the intelligentsia of Przemyśl in the restaurant. At one table army officials with some woman, officials pretend to be officers and the woman pretends to be a lady. The second table, taken by two students, very critical under the influence of vodka ... then unter-officers telling their stories ... A collection of people unhappy about the city, about themselves, and their positions."[176]

Although a small station was a window into the life of one town's demi-monde, in the Lviv terminal one could observe the whole province, including peasants. Of course, peasants were a common sight in Lviv. Peasant women were a permanent feature of its central square, trading their goods next to city hall. Those city peasants, however, rarely came on trains. Even those who lived near a major railway junction and daily observed passing express trains could spend their entire lives without ever setting foot in Lviv.[177] The peasants one encountered at the main train terminal were often in the middle of the longest and most transformative journey of their lives. The building that housed the union's headquarters, where the street from the terminal entered Horodotska (Gródecka), also accommodated the main office of the Cunard Line, selling ship fares to Canada and the United States.[178] Huge white steamships called to passersby from signboards and to readers from ads in newspapers of all political persuasions.

An anonymous reporter for Lviv's socialist daily, which published a series of feuilletons on the city's nocturnal life, depicts in one of them the terminal at night. Four chandeliers with electric bulbs throw a dim light on the grand hall. There is a canteen with an aged waitress and a salesman who has spread his wares out on a small table. Besides napping passengers, there are the city poor, who use the waiting hall as a free night shelter. Third-class passengers wear peasant wool coats, Jewish kaftans, or regular urban dress remarkable only for its pitiable condition. There are some "gentlemen" too, careful to keep their distance from the rest of the crowd. A bell and a railwayman announce departures and arrivals. A whole peasant family encamps by one wall, near the exit door. A railway official tries to get rid of them several times, but the peasants refuse to move and he gives up. A family from the Carpathian Mountains on its way to America wait for an agent who has the tickets for the rest of their journey and a booked accommodation. At midnight some of the bulbs are switched off, making the hall darker and quieter. The peasant family stands helpless and undecided about what to do next. Eventually their agent shows up, the adults wake up the children, and the "whole caravan" leaves the terminal.[179]

In the 1860s and 1870s, railway travel in Lviv was still a privilege of the wealthy. Even in Britain, the cradle of railway "passengerhood," only first and second class existed at first, and only later were third-class cars added, initially only to some trains. The Midland Railway, for example, added third-class cars only in 1872, after nearly thirty years of operation.[180] By the time the new terminal was built in Lviv, however, railway travel was no longer a luxury. In 1897 Austrian railways moved nearly 41 million passengers, 37 million of them in third class;[181] only a minuscule quarter of a million travelled first class. In Lviv first class "was completely out of reach of common mortals below His Excellence or Baczewski [a rich owner of Lviv's most famous distillery]."[182] For third-class passengers, a train journey into a wider world was often eye-opening. Herman Lieberman, a future socialist MP, made his first train trip to Vienna to attend university there. During the trip, he had to share cheap accommodation with fifty other complete strangers in Budapest. His first sighting of a black person in the very same room was an indelible experience for an adolescent from the lower middle class.[183] Galician peasant emigrants also recalled the overwhelming impressions that large cities made on them.[184]

Anti-emigration sentiment in East-Central Europe fuelled panicky discourse about slowing down or stopping emigration.[185] Nonetheless emigrants faced real dangers, not only because of the uncertainties of the journey, but also because of con men and swindlers. Railway officials, conductors, and keepers of station restaurants collaborated with networks of immigration agents for a commission. Some cheated peasants, charging for nebulous services such as alleged telephone conversations with the emperor.[186] Government spies posed another threat. The peasant lad Jan Sudoł first tried to leave for America in 1902. An undercover agent did not believe his story about a seasonal job in the Silesian mines, and took him and his four buddies from the train. They were all approaching conscription age and their emigration was seen as draft evasion. The police confiscated their money, put them on a train home, then mailed the remaining funds.[187] Sudoł tried again the next year, this time successfully, taking a longer route via Hungary, which was less watched by the police, and travelling without money. Even though the station in Vienna was swarming with "agents who recognized immediately those travelling to America by physiognomy," he managed to avoid them. From Vienna Sudoł telegraphed his family and received 200 gulden to pay his agent and the ship fare.[188]

It was not only the design and décor of the Lviv terminal that stirred people's emotions. When people described it as "the most beautiful, majestic and most modern, truly monumental building,"[189] grander than even the city theatre,[190] they invariably recalled very personal experiences and associated emotions. Józef Wittlin conveys this intimate connection between the terminal and personal memory in his own account: "as Siamese sisters, attached to each other, entrance sheds ... half-round and very harmoniously shaped ... Many stations I have entered on this tormenting travel called life. Not one, however, maybe with the exception of Gare du Nord in Paris, has awakened in me such an excitation, such a 'metaphysical thrill.'"[191] These memories could go back to childhood. For the girl from a provincial town, the terminal was a major attraction, both the "enormous glass hall, in which voices hummed and rumbled, travellers' calls spread out, numbered porters bustled about, burdened with luggage" and "the vast terminal's vestibule, always swarmed with the stirred-up crowd." Only "the view of the flowered lawn before the terminal relaxed, and the plume of a tall fountain soothed excitement."[192]

The terminal offered not only noise and tumult; it had a greenhouse nearby, from which flowers were sold to those greeting arrivals.[193] Between departures the waiting room was a quiet place, where one was simultaneously with people and alone. Stefan Banach, one of the twentieth century's most important mathematicians, liked to work in cafés and restaurants; he also "sometimes went on purpose to the train station, where the buffet was open all night, and in that difficult place developed his concepts."[194] Wittlin used the terminal as a refuge from maths and physics in his school. Skipping lessons, he stayed in the second-class waiting hall and read detective novels under the portrait of Archduke Karl Ludwig.[195] In his recollections this was "not a waiting hall but a true salon, full of chandeliers, mirrors, gilding, and soft upholstery with scented leather couches and settees. It also smelled of a distant world, an allure of foreign land. People waited here not only for train departure, but as if for the happiness itself, to which terminal cashiers back then did not sell tickets."[196] The Lviv writer Stefan Grabiński, sometimes called the Hitchcock of Polish prose,[197] describes the magnetism of the train terminal in his novella "Perpetual Passenger." The protagonist is addicted to the space of a terminal and scenes unravelling there. "The quiet of the hall ... broken from time to time by the dry cough of a consumptive, the heavy, traversing gait of a bored passenger, or the murmur of well-behaved children by the window asking something of their parents"[198] excite him, as do the scrutinizing eyes of railway officials. The protagonist crosses social and gender boundaries, striking up conversations with passengers, and thriving on the "railroad fever" of others, but never embarks on a train journey of his own.[199]

Grabiński was not the only Galician writer fascinated by the railway, and the terminal was but one among many exotic railway sites and sightings. Railways and trains are ubiquitous in Ivan Franko's works. There are songs of praise in Franko's poetry to "a mighty, thunderous and ferocious" "iron horse," for whose speed "the Earth is cramped" and who "has united into one family all the lands and all peoples."[200] There are also much darker images, as in "droning train cars" full of "children's weeping, women's mournful moan, // heavy sigh and bitter curse," platforms where "people are crammed like herring" – Franko's portrayal of Galician peasants leaving for Brazil.[201] Finally, one of Franko's novellas describes a locomotive, a complex, fascinating, powerful, and profoundly strange thing waiting in a depot to be awakened to life by a small army of specialized workers: engineers and stokers, shunters, conductors, and mechanics.[202] Nineteenth- and early twentieth-century Galician writers were in no way unique in their fascination with trains. But for a provincial literature of a single "backward" region, the range of attitudes and connotations is astonishingly wide.

Grabiński's work, among other things, captures a certain unity to the railway space, those "lines of rails, stations and terminals sunk in the sleepy boredom of waiting, the nervousness of the crowds of travellers, the uniform rhythm of incoming and departing trains."[203] In Grabiński's imagination that space lives life and produces ghosts of its own, akin to other, more traditional, liminal spaces and elemental forces. It is a space of modern urbanity – uncanny, inflicting strange ailments and desires on people – a space of machinery that cannot be controlled, of deadly but fascinating speeds. Grabiński's heroes are "driven to the railway" through its inexplicable powers.[204] Grabiński shows that the railway was much larger than its narrow utilitarian function: "The job of the railway was not to transport people from place to place with the object of communication, but motion in and for itself, the conquest of space."[205] From being a servant of humankind, the railway in his texts becomes a master of human beings. Strikingly, Grabiński's fantasies correlate with real events reported in the daily chronicle of newspapers. His mad engine driver had a real-life prototype who threw out his stoker and rode the locomotive between Lviv and Shchyrets (Szczerzec) until stopped by gendarmes.[206] Even Grabiński's "perpetual passenger" can be recognized in the contemporary traveller's description of the terminal "always filled with people, these are not travellers, but town dwellers that come to the trains to observe both those arriving and those passing by."[207] When Grabiński died in 1936 in poverty, he was buried at the Ianivsky (Janowski) cemetery, next to the railway space he grasped so well.[208]

Chapter Four

Inter Arma

The First World War did not take Galicia by surprise. Tensions between Russia and the Central Powers had been felt there since at least the end of the 1880s, when war with Russia was discussed as a distinct possibility.[1] In 1908, after the annexation of Bosnia-Herzegovina, Herman Diamand thought that war was "almost certain."[2] The Balkan wars of 1912–13 broadened and deepened this anticipation of a great war. Galicia's political parties started to announce their position in the possible conflict with Russia, while radical organizations and activists launched paramilitary formations and combat training.[3]

The news of Archduke Franz Ferdinand's assassination provoked a wave of panic in Lviv. Vacations were cancelled and trains jam-packed: "inhumanely squeezed passengers looked like a crowd escaping into the unknown from some spectre of destruction."[4] Galicians in Western Europe were astonished that local publics virtually ignored the assassination.[5] Although many in Lviv saw that the country was heading for war, no one had a premonition about the kind of war awaiting them. Just as in the rest of Europe, Lvivites "at the café tables were arguing that, given technological advances, the war could not last longer than two to three weeks, after which peace, quiet and prosperity would return."[6] The railway network carried the news of war across Europe, and declarations of war were announced at train stations, since they were among the most attended sites in local communities. Railway employees at Galician stations hung posters with the emperor's address on war to "his peoples"[7] where they could be read by the largest crowds these stations had ever seen.

In Karel Čapek's 1920 play, *R.U.R*, the timetable – this "most perfect product of human soul" and necessary accessory of business offices – survives an uprising of robots and the near-extinction of humankind, arousing false hopes: "If the timetable is operating again, then human laws are operating again, and God's laws are operating again and the laws of the universe are operating again and everything is operating that should be operating."[8] The railway timetable was the first thing to break down when the war began.

The first "sieges" of the war were of trains and train terminals. Foreign nationals, including middle- and upper-class Galicians, rushed home from all over Europe. Days were spent in front of "literally besieged" terminals and in nightmarishly slow and packed trains.[9] Many Lvivites returned home only to realize that they had to leave. The rapid advance of Russian troops in August 1914 prompted a mass evacuation of an estimated forty to fifty thousand people, up to a quarter of Lviv's population.[10] Two factors aggravated the situation of the evacuees. First, the mobilization made extensive use of the railway network. Trains with conscripts, with their right-of-way, jammed the network and stalled passenger traffic. Second, the authorities in Lviv, concerned with the population's morale, announced the abandonment of Lviv too late for an orderly evacuation.

The well-thought-out order of the Lviv terminal collapsed together with the railway timetable. The terminal was "filled with a restive crowd," ticket offices were closed, and the public stormed platforms and trains.[11] Witnesses recalled that law-abiding "legalists" found themselves at a disadvantage, while assertiveness, energy, and physical strength ruled.[12] The terminal was the epicentre of a social earthquake: "In the last days of August, the basic physiognomy of the city had changed. Trams stopped running, fiacres were hiding somewhere, stores were closed while crowds of people were moving in the direction of the main terminal."[13] While most of the city seemed deserted, a sea of people pounded against the terminal and filled all the access ways.[14] "The trains were coming to the platform already tightly stuffed with people somewhere in depots, or before the platform, [and] no one could get into a car either with pleas or with threats."[15] People boarded cars through the windows, no one asked for tickets, and railway officials themselves declined the fares passengers offered.[16]

The panic started on August 28, when Russian patrols were spotted near the city,[17] and reached its peak on August 31.[18] The night before, the gold from the state bank had left the city.[19] Senior officials of the Viceroy's Office received a sudden order to evacuate that night. A special viceroy's train left the city at midnight for Krynica, a resort village in the province's western mountains, which became the Viceroy Office's first temporary seat.[20] Even on that exclusive train, "true hell, complete havoc, shouts, swearing, crush and rush" reigned supreme.[21]

Boarding a train was only the beginning of the evacuees' ordeal. Many trains were requisitioned by the army en route, and had to detrain their passengers at way stations. Some never made it to the second leg of their journey.[22] Even senior officials from the viceroy's train feared being left behind. In Krynica, one department head became so overwhelmed by anxiety that he moved to a hotel across from the train station and spent days by the window watching trains.[23] The train that finally picked up the Viceroy's Office staff from Krynica "consisted, except for a small salon car for the Viceroy, of freight cars, terribly dirty, evidently used by the military to transport horses."[24] Its journey to Biała, on the border of Galicia and Austrian Silesia, slightly over two hundred kilometres away, took fifty-four hours without food or the possibility of leaving the train because of a quarantine.[25] Senior officials from the Lviv railway directorate also left on August 31.[26] Workshop personnel left only at the very last minute on September 2. Since there was not enough room on the train, the majority of the workers stayed.[27] The movement branch of the railway service was "militarized" – that is, subordinated to the military and placed under military law. The bulk of the officials in the movement branch evacuated, sometimes leaving their families behind.[28]

The Russian army entered Lviv on September 3. Because of its rapid advance, the Austrian evacuation was not very thorough. The retreating army blew up some bridges and derailed the remaining rolling stock, but the damage was generally superficial. The infrastructure of the Lviv junction was left intact. Moreover, the Russians discovered a spectacular supply cache, far exceeding the railway's immediate needs; a reserve of thirty-two thousand tons of coal alone was pillaged. Since the Austrians had destroyed all the documentation, the rightful owners of the goods could not be established,[29] and remaining city dwellers helped themselves to these supplies during the brief interregnum. With the collapse of the state authorities, private property rights collapsed as well. Some state property, such as firewood, was officially distributed among Lviv's population to help it survive the winter of 1914–15.[30]

During the war, survival needs trumped property rights, especially if the property belonged to abstract entities such as a state. The war undermined the very foundations of the constitutional order. The law was replaced with courts martial as the Habsburg Empire experienced unprecedented militarization.[31] Thousands of Ruthenians all over the province were interned and tens of thousands arbitrarily executed as alleged spies and traitors.[32] The Russian occupation of Galicia came with its own military rule and its own ethnic and social profiling. Russian authorities targeted Ukrainian activists, political elites connected with the Habsburg court and government, and Jews as an inherently unreliable ethnic group. Lviv's Jews feared a pogrom, something they had not experienced under Austria.[33]

Lviv experienced its first twentieth-century deportations. Metropolitan Sheptytsky, a spiritual leader of Galician Ukrainians; Ernst Breiter, an independent socialist and Austrian parliament deputy; and Jakób Diamand, the head of the city's Jewish community were among those deported by the Russians.[34] Not only prominent citizens were deported. A visitor to the terminal in November 1914 saw a crowd of "retired old Austrian military men" who "are being deported, even though they have not fought at all and are unable to carry arms."[35] The last wave of deportations came in June 1915, during the Russian retreat, and carried away Tadeusz Rutowski, Lviv's mayor.

The Russian occupation encountered little active resistance among the local population. For a large city to survive, a state administration, even a foreign one, was a necessity. Work was also a necessity, even if it meant work for the invader. Russians found Lviv's railway workshops "excellently equipped" but deserted. In Stanislau (Stanisławów, Ivano-Frankivsk), however, the workers not only stayed, but, according to Russian officials, "wished, if their former compensation packages are preserved, to switch over to the Russian service in their entirety, together with the head of the workshops engineer Schmitt."[36] Similar requests were repeated in other Galician localities once the front rolled farther west.[37] Even in Lviv, workshop workers who stayed behind eventually returned to work in November-December 1914 for the sake of survival.[38]

Although some local railway employees were accepted into the Russian service, the railway under the occupation was Russian in both name and personnel. Administrative units of the Russian state railway were individual "railroads." The railway of the occupied Galicia was organized as "Galician Railroads," with the administrative centre in Lviv. A temporary statute for Galician Railroads was approved in October 1914. Although the organizational structure of Galician Railroads was identical to that of other Russian railroads, it had considerable autonomy and offered above-average salaries.[39] Because of its location in the front zone, Galician Railroads was subordinated to the military authorities, not to the Ministry of Communications, "until the end of the military action."[40] Klavdii Nemeshaev volunteered for the position of the Railroads' head (*nachal'nik*), and was duly appointed.

Nemeshaev was a legendary person in the Russian railway service. He was a graduate of the Saint Petersburg Institute of the Engineers of Routes of Communications. After twenty-five years of railway service, Nemeshaev was appointed head of the recently nationalized South-Western Railroad in 1896. During the next ten years in his office in Kyiv, he turned a deficient and nearly bankrupt railroad into one of Russia's best. Nemeshaev was the Russian counterpart of Ludwik Wierzbicki. Both worked at the same time on adjacent, recently nationalized railways divided by the state border. Both excelled in their jobs. In 1905–06 Nemeshaev briefly served as minister of communications. In 1912 he returned to Saint Petersburg as a member of the State Council, only to leave this essentially honorary position for Lviv in 1914.[41]

The top management of Galician Railroads came from South-Western, but relations between the two were complicated. The new head of South-Western was Vadim Shmit, who resented the fame of his illustrious predecessor and tried to maintain a distance between the two railway administrations.[42] In-fighting at the court and among the ministries in Saint Petersburg only escalated with the outbreak of the war. Shmit "remained a loyal executor of [Minister Sergei] Rukhlov's orders," while Rukhlov tried to maintain as much independence from the military as possible.[43] Unlike Shmit, Nemeshaev in 1914 was an independent figure, unconstrained by career considerations and court intrigues, and saw "no need to account for the Ministry of Communications."[44] Colonel Boris Stelletsky supervised Galician Railroads as a representative from the Department of Military Communications of the South-Western fronts.[45]

Initially the Russians assessed the railway economy they inherited from the Austrians as excellent. The railways had a great throughput capacity, were well organized, and had novelties such as an electrical blocking system and electric signalization.[46] Since the Austrians had retreated in a hurry, the damage to the network was superficial.[47] Nonetheless tracks and bridges had to be repaired, and military engineers saw Galicia as a testing ground for this kind of work.[48] While Russian engineers praised the Galician railway economy, they also used the rebuilding of the Galician network as a demonstration of their own technical prowess and the maturity of Russian railroading. A photographic album prepared on this occasion showcased their ability to resuscitate the paralysed infrastructure of modern civilization.[49] Galician Railroads served as evidence that Russia was capable of a civilizing mission not only in the East but also in the West.

Russians both revived old Austrian lines and laid down new ones. To ensure an uninterrupted supply of troops, the Railroads, together with the army, decided to use the existing "European" track gauge (1,435 millimetres) instead of changing it to the broader Russian gauge (1,520 millimetres), concluding that "altering all or even the main railway lines of Galicia is currently impossible."[50] European gauge was not completely foreign to Russia – the Warsaw-Vienna Railroad, for example, used European gauge on its Russian stretch. At the same time the Russians recognized that connecting "at least the city of Lviv, which is the centre of Galicia, and the main base of quartermaster and artillery resources, via broad gauge track with the network of South-Western Railroads seems to be an urgent necessity."[51] The problem was that altering the already existing and "most heavily operated lines" – from Lviv to the former border – presented "nearly insurmountable obstacles" because of the interruptions it would cause.[52]

Nemeshaev found the following solution. A new broad-gauge line would be built from Volodymyr-Volynskyi to Sokal, while the local Austrian line from Sokal to Lviv would be regauged. On the Lviv–Brody line, a single Russian-gauge track would be added to the existing one – the roadbed there was wide enough – without interrupting movement on the old track.[53] Eventually the same would be done with the Krasne–Pidvolochysk section. In the last phase, the broad track would appear between Pidzamche and the main station in Lviv.[54] The Russian army was especially interested in lines from the north that would provide the shortest access to the front.[55] These lines were built quickly. Volodymyr-Volynskyi–Sokal was finished by November 1914,[56] While regauging the Sokal–Lviv section had to wait until spring 1915.[57] The first train on the Russian gauge came to Lviv from Sokal on 19 April 1915.[58] The broad-gauge station was still six kilometres from the city, in the suburban village of Dubliany.

Although the construction of broad-gauge tracks helped the Russian war effort, they were also endowed with greater strategic and ideological significance. In March 1915, Major-General Vladimir Feldt, a military engineer who had built military railways in Volhynia before the war, argued that "[w]hatever turn historical events take in the future, at present it has become sufficiently clear that Galicia will be annexed to Russia. In the future, therefore, we shall have only this goal, only this task – to retain forever the part of the primordially Russian land that was once torn away from us. The best way of securing Galicia is to link its railroads to the network of Russian railroads, and this linking should be made with the help of our broad track."[59]

Even before the war, the Russian government had planned for massive railway construction in Volhynia and Podolia – two Ukrainian regions of the Russian Empire on the border with Galicia similarly crucial for strategic and ideological regions. Strategically, the two regions constituted the Russian Empire's base for military operations against the Habsburgs; ideologically they were the bulwark of the struggle against Ukrainian "separatism" and Polish influences. On the eve of the war, the Russian government planned to integrate these regions further with the help of new railways.[60] Economic considerations also played a role, both before and during the war. In 1915 the Podolian railway proposed building the Shepetivka–Ternopil (Tarnopol) and Shepetivka–Zbarazh (Zbaraż) lines,[61] expecting that, "after the state and political unification of Galicia with Russia, close economic convergence will follow unavoidably."[62] Local capital, commercially interested in these lines, appealed to state interests, promising to connect Galicia with central Russia, the Caucasus, and Siberia.[63]

In spring 1915 the regauging of Galician lines accelerated. Military engineers argued that leaving Galician track on the narrower European gauge was a mistake, and a smoother short-term transition stalled the Russians' long-term logistical capacity. The Russians also learned from the Germans, who were changing Russian track to the narrower gauge immediately upon occupation.[64] Technically, regauging was not overly complicated: in the fall of 1914 Russian railway detachments worked at a pace of eight kilometres a day. The only challenges were stations and junctions, where tracks had to be integrated with switching mechanisms and signalization, and the shortage of labour. By March 1915 only 75 per cent of the broad-gauge track from Lviv to Brody was completed. Two thousand navvies were brought from Russia to finish the job,[65] and on 10 May the first train from Brody arrived at Lviv's Pidzamche station on the Russian gauge.[66]

Lviv was indispensable to the logistical support of the Russian army. The Russian gauge would not help much if it was not integrated into Lviv's junction with it capacious yards, warehouses, and converging lines. At first, Pidzamche, with its eastward lines, was considered for the Russian-gauge station. The problem was that Pidzamche was located on a narrow strip between the hill of High Castle and a densely built-over residential area, while the broad-gauge station in Lviv needed spacious reloading facilities for changing between gauges.[67] On 26 February 1915, military and civilian authorities agreed that the most convenient site was on Janowska (Shevchenko) Street, by the existing Klepariv station. The terrain was flat and there were no apartment buildings, while the water, power, warehouses, and barracks of Lviv-Main (the city's central station) could be used for both stations. Janowska Street also had spacious warehouses by the cemetery capable of taking in fifty thousand tons of goods.[68] Moreover, there was already an existing tram connection with the city centre. The proposed station was named Lviv-Russian. A separate broad track had to connect it with the regauged eastern and northern lines;[69] work was to start immediately and finish in four months. In the meantime a temporary reloading station was organized at Pidzamche,[70] while another was in Dubliany (Dublany), the end station of the broad-gauge Sokal line.[71]

When in April 1915 Emperor Nicholas II visited Lviv, Pidzamche was still being regauged. The emperor's visit intended to confirm that Lviv was not merely a temporary occupied border city, but a Russian city returning to its rightful owners. Crowds greeted the emperor, and the liturgy was served in the crammed Russian Orthodox "garrison church," converted from a military dressage ring. The emperor's visit convinced at least one person – namely, Nicholas II himself – that Galicia was indeed Russian. In his diary the emperor notes that in Galicia "the appearance of villages and people strongly resembled Little Russia,"[72] while Lviv "makes a very good impression; it reminds one of Warsaw, with a smaller appearance, but with a Russian population on the streets."[73] Nicholas II probably did not realize how many Russian employees had come to Lviv to administer the territory and run its essential services, such as the railway.

Nicholas II had a special train reserved for royal railway trips, with the engine made at the Putilov iron works in Saint Petersburg and capable of running at ninety kilometres an hour.[74] The train also carried the emperor's enormous entourage, which included, among many others, four chefs and five kitchen assistants, five waiters, and a barber.[75] The train had the highest priority: all other movement on the line would be stopped to yield the right of way, which allowed the train to maintain an average of seventy kilometres an hour near Saint Petersburg. But in Volhynia, the train slowed down to forty-eight, and on the recently regauged former border it managed a meagre thirty.[76] Since there was no broad gauge directly to Lviv, Nicholas II employed an automobile for the last leg of his journey, between Brody and Lviv.[77] The emperor had an opportunity to experience travel on Galician Railroads from Lviv to Sambir, and on his return from Lviv. But these were on the old Austrian track.[78]

The engines that carried Nicholas II in Galicia ran on oil.[79] Changing an engine from coal to oil was not technically difficult. Oil-fuelled engines were used on Galicia's busiest railway lines starting in 1910 – the outcome of a 1908 railway ministry decision. Justified as a technological advancement and a response to the crisis of overproduction in the Galician oil industry, the decision led to mammoth investment in infrastructure, with oil reservoirs and refuelling facilities at Galicia's main stations.[80] These investments helped to raise the price of oil, which, coupled with greater transportation and storage expenses, made the use of oil in locomotives unprofitable and led to the experiment's abandonment.[81] In 1914 Galician Railroads (together with Russia's other western railroads) used coal from the Dąbrowa basin. But in early 1915 the basin was lost to the German army, and the choking railway network could not bring sufficient quantities from the east. Since local oil was abundant, in January 1915 the ministry recommended that Galician Railroads switch from coal to oil. The greatest problems were refuelling and the lack of infrastructure – only large stations had oil tanks. In the end Galician Railroads changed only thirty engines to oil, and only on main routes at that.[82]

When Nicholas II came to Lviv, Nemeshaev was no longer the head of railroads in Galicia. Decorated by the emperor for his services in Galicia, he resigned on 7 March 1915, and the statute of Galician Railroads was abolished.[83] A consensus was emerging that the Galician network should be merged with South-Western.[84] Vadim Shmit managed the former Galician Railroads under the army's supervision.[85]

By spring 1915 Galician Railroads was a large operation staffed mostly by people from the Russian Empire. While the management came from South-Western, rank-and-file employees came from "from virtually every Russian railroad."[86] A majority of those working at the Lviv-Main station were from Southern Railroad, with its centre in Kharkiv.[87] In the zone of the front, the railway was ethnically more Russian than railways in the Russian rear. An accelerated ethnicization of loyalty and political reliability during the war[88] influenced the selection of railway personnel. Poles had been treated with suspicion long before the war and barred from positions with access to sensitive military information.[89] During the war the list of restricted positions expanded.[90] In spring 1915 Jews were forbidden from entering the war zone as providers of auxiliary services and suppliers of goods. The prohibition extended to ethnic Germans, including the descendants of eighteenth-century colonists.[91]

There were also restrictions on *inorodtsy*, or non-European, non-Slavs, who were forbidden to work in the area of active operations.[92] Front railroads depleted rear railroads of "Russian" (or Eastern Slavic) workers. In December 1916 the Tashkent Railroad reported that "there are almost no Russian workers, even permanent, [left]."[93] Eastern Slavs were transferred to the front zone. The railroad's appetite for workers in the front zone was great, and its officials kept asking for permission to employ *inorodtsy* and even prisoners of war (POWs) on auxiliary jobs.[94] The need for labour proved to be greater than fears of the *inorodtsy* or POWS, and eventually both categories were widely used.[95]

Galician Railroads poached both personnel and machines from the rear,[96] but the latter usually tried to dump its old and worn-out engines.[97]

In a grand scheme, involving many intermediaries, the Russians also managed to exchange some Austrian engines and rolling stock that had been evacuated to Romania for cavalry horses.[98] By 1 March 1915 Galician Railroads was operating 396 engines and over 9,000 cars of various types.[99] The length of track under its control increased from 1,037 kilometres in November 1914 to 1,915 kilometres by March 1915. During the same period, Galician Railroads' personnel increased from 3,296 officials and 3,469 workers to 7,400 and 7,700, respectively.[100]

Nemeshaev estimated that monthly exploitation costs would amount to 500,000 rubles,[101] but actual expenses increased to more than a million rubles by January 1915. No one expected wartime operation to be profitable, but Nemeshaev's Galician Railroads proved to be far more expensive than other Russian railroads. Salaries accounted for the lion's share of the costs.[102] Nemeshaev had fixed salaries high to offset the hardship of living in the front zone and in a foreign land. To save money the management tried to replace temporary with regular employees, but "feared that the majority of those taken into permanent employment will be the dregs from other railroads and an element little suited to the work."[103]

Maintaining discipline and order was no mean task. Large stations were controlled by both the railroad and the military. Lviv-Main, for example, had a military commandant and seven assistants,[104] although the commandant felt this was insufficient.[105] The station resumed regular passenger and luggage operations on 31 December 1914, reorienting itself towards the Russian Empire.[106] Twice a day packs of periodicals arrived from the empire's large centres and were distributed to establishments in the city.[107] The semblance of normality was fragile, however, and wartime limitations were never completely lifted.

Although integration was the official goal, practical security considerations kept Galicia apart from the rest of the empire. Special permits were needed to enter the province.[108] Villagers from Podolia traded in Galicia illegally, moving back and forth as stowaways in freight cars.[109] Periodicals from Saint Petersburg (now renamed Petrograd) arrived after a delay of up to three weeks.[110] The steady stream of looted and purchased contraband that flowed from Lviv to Russia proper underlined the tentative nature of this territorial acquisition.[111] Despite tight military control, things tended to mysteriously disappear on Galician Railroads. Sealed oil tanks from Groznyi arrived in Lviv, each short up to four hundred kilograms.[112] In March 1915 eighteen *puds* (almost 300 kilograms) of linen for the 165th Regiment – a gift from the wives of workers at Sava Morozov's factory in Orekhovo-Zuevo – were allegedly stolen at Lviv station. Ensign Evreinov claimed that he had checked them as his baggage with a station official in Lviv, who convinced him that no receipt was needed.[113] The railroad management stressed that station officials were few and their whereabouts easy to follow, so none of them was involved.[114] Suspiciously the ensign returned to his regiment after two days' delay, allegedly spent waiting for lost baggage. Whoever pulled off this con job made use of the confusion that reigned in spring 1915 at the Russian Lviv-Main station. In May 1915 the officer assigned to the station's postal office asked for permission to provide information to military men lost at the station and looking for their regiments. The request was denied since the information was confidential.[115]

A pre-war epitome of punctuality and reliability, the railway fell victim to the havoc of war. In Lviv the epicentre of confusion was its main train terminal.[116] Simple routine tasks, such as a census of rolling stock, took months to complete.[117] Conflicts between railway officials and army officers were commonplace.[118] Military discipline loosened as well. In March at the Lviv station, a group of officers from the transportation department hijacked personal train car No. 1, which belonged to Nikolay von Mekk, Empress Alexandra's special envoy.[119]

Confusion and chaos did not preclude wartime travellers to Lviv from appreciating the grandeur of its main train terminal, and often used it as an indication of the city's character and importance. For Stanley Washburn, the "huge Imperial station" opened onto "the most beautiful city," whose "broad streets, numerous parks, and shops are equal to those of most of the big capitals of Europe."[120] The Russian officer Iosif Il'in, who believed that Russian terminals were no match for Lviv's, was equally impressed with the city: "Magnificent stores, wonderful sidewalks – as good as those on Nevsky [Prospect in Saint Petersburg]."[121] For the Russian-born, Jewish S. Ansky (Shloyme Zanvl Rappoport), too, Lviv was a "cultivated European city," in which "the largest and most glorious structure was the train terminal, one of the most beautiful in Europe."[122]

The beauty and glory of the terminal were in striking contrast to its wartime uses. Already in fall 1914 the benches and tables had been removed from the station's restaurants and waiting rooms, which were turned into hospital spaces and surgery rooms for emergency operations.[123] The station also served as an evacuation centre for wounded soldiers and was filled with them, "the air, laden with anaesthetics, disinfectants, and the subtle smell of dried blood and unwashed humanity."[124] In spring 1915, even before the Russians retreated, chaos returned to the terminal, and the barely established railway connections were on the brink of collapse. Ansky's express train to Lviv was delayed for eight hours,[125] while Il'in had to wait in Lviv for thirty-two hours before he could board an eastbound train. It took his train seven hours to cover the eighty-kilometre distance from Lviv to Brody.[126]

Galician Railroads had experienced its first serious bottlenecks in the winter of 1914–15. The main problem was with transfer stations, where people and freight were moved between the Russian and European gauges.[127] Much of the traffic consisted of transported troops: in February 1915 alone, 32,049 soldiers of lower ranks were sent through Lviv in 870 cars.[128] As fighting intensified, the number increased to 56,853 in March.[129] The speed with which troops were moved was well below the benchmark,[130] however, and backlogs accumulated.[131] In January 1915 Galician Railroads was operating 802 engines and 20,251 cars per length of track below the Russian norm.[132] Troops often had to move to the front on foot, with marching companies going through Lviv "in a solid stream."[133] The railroads also moved the wounded from the front to hospitals. Galician Railroads had thirty sanitary trains, which sufficed in the winter, but not in spring 1915, when the fighting picked up.[134] The Russian Eighth Army alone had suffered eighteen thousand wounded and ill, eight thousand of them needing immediate evacuation.[135] The railroads also moved POWs. Conditions for them were usually bearable, but cars were overcrowded and POWs spent days without hot meals.[136] People were the railroads' priority;[137] the situation with freight was much worse. In January 1915 General Aleksei Brusilov complained that freight from Lviv took eight to ten days to arrive at Sanok and suffered en route from "colossal pilfering."[138] When the general complained about four hundred train cars with food for his starving troops being stuck in Lviv for two days, the answer was that in Lviv three days was a normal waiting time for army food supplies.[139]

The fall of Przemyśl on 22 March 1915 and the emperor's visit to Galicia in April marked the high point for the Russians in this war. The railways prepared for an offensive in the Carpathians and made estimates of engines and cars needed to support the operation.[140] They ought to have been preparing for retreat instead. On 1 May 1915 a joint Austro-German offensive was launched in Galicia. Conversion to the Russian gauge stopped the same day.[141] The same units that repaired tracks and bridges were now destroying their own work, derailing engines and blowing up tunnels. The same photographic album that celebrates the prowess of Russian technical genius in fall 1914 is equally proud of the destruction accomplished during the retreat.[142] The destruction could be quite inventive, with track-scraping machines created to accelerate the process.[143]

In June 1915 Galician Railroads stopped accepting any freight, except for weapons, munitions, kerosene, and barbed wire.[144] The wholesale evacuation of Russian officials began. Before leaving, railway officials dismantled and sent east all portable equipment. The stations were then left to the army railway brigades for mining and blasting.[145]

The Lviv railway junction was scheduled for destruction on 7 June 1915. Major General Mikhail Kolobov, commander of the Second Transamurian railway brigade, was in charge.[146] Russian demolition was far more thorough than the damage the Austrians had done in 1914. All the track beds were blasted on several levels, as were all three turntables in the station's depots, water mains and oil pump, and an airplane hangar. Ansky believed, mistakenly, that the Russians had blown up the terminal itself.[147] Indeed the plan was to destroy the whole station, together with the terminal and workshops, but luckily for the terminal, Kolobov's brigade ran out of the explosive pyroxylin: they estimated that at least sixty-four tons would be needed, but only nineteen were available. As a result, the station was not destroyed "to the desirable extent."[148]

The retreat from Lviv in 1915 was not the end of the Russian Galician Railroads, which still employed twelve thousand people in August 1915.[149] Even after it was officially dissolved on 21 August,[150] Galician Railroads kept paying salaries and pensions and compensating property losses.[151] Former Austrian citizens working on Galician Railroads suffered most, since they were forbidden to work in the Russian Empire proper.[152] Shmit tried to make an exemption for them, arguing that "Austrian subjects serving on the Galician Railroads had proven their loyalty with their deeds" and "deserve an especially caring and attentive attitude."[153] Chief of Military Communications of the South-Western Front Ivan Pavsky suggested sending Galicians to the railroads in the rear.[154] A temporary permit allowed them to work on South-Western but in unskilled occupations only.[155] That permit, however, was soon rescinded and in September 1915 the chief of army communications decided that on no condition could Austrian citizens be employed on the railroad. On 18 September Shmit ordered a mass discharge of all Galicians.[156] Eventually the secondees were sent back to their home railroads,[157] while permanent employees – those who gave in to the Russian government's effort to create a "lasting settled cadre of Russian officials in this land"[158] – were simply discharged. By January 1916 only 188 people were left on pay.[159]

Half a year later, during the Brusilov offensive, once the length of Austrian track under Russian control reached 1,500 kilometres, the autonomous Galician Railroads was resurrected.[160] In less than a year, in summer 1917, another evacuation of fifteen thousand employees followed.[161] The story of the Russian Galician Railroads after 1915, however, is not directly connected to Lviv.

The Austrians returned to Lviv in June 1915 to stay until the end of the war. Another exodus from the city took place on the eve of the Austrians' return. Alongside deportees and the evacuated were voluntary refugees who had worked with the Russian authorities and feared repercussions. The architect Alfred Zachariewicz, who had worked on the terminal from 1901 to 1904 but during the Russian occupation enterprise had worked for Galician Railroads, was in this category. He left his wife behind in Lviv,[162] and came back in 1918, but neither his business nor his psyche would recover from the traumatic wartime experience.[163] During the evacuation, the station was bombed by the Austrian air force, while its tunnels served as a bomb shelter, passing this test of durability with distinction.[164]

Russian officials had been billeted in the abandoned apartments of their Austrian counterparts. According to an eyewitness, furniture and other articles, down to "silk wallpapers" and "parquet floor," were taken from the places where Russian officials and officers had been quartered.[165] Upon his return, a manager of the Austrian state bank found his apartment reduced to bare walls.[166] Magnificent, and finished just before the war, the new offices of the railway directorate was on the same street and in a similar condition.[167]

The Lviv directorate spent the occupation period in Brno, returning to Lviv in August 1915.[168] Numerous Galician railway officials were suspected of collaboration, and some were tried.[169] Wierzbicki's successor Stanisław Rybicki was also under investigation for the poorly organized evacuation and the employment of suspicious individuals. One of those was the brother of the famous colonel Alfred Redl, who had sold secrets of the Austrian general staff to the Russians before the war. He remained in Lviv during the occupation, and although he did not provide a full account of his whereabouts, Rybicki took him back in 1915.[170] Numerous railway employees of the lower ranks who had worked under the Russians were accepted back into the Austrian service after clearance from the fairly lenient "rehabilitation commissions."[171] The army, however, insisted on the dismissal of Rybicki. He was sent into retirement, even though he was only fifty-nine.[172] Karl von Stelzer, the former director in Stanislau (Stanisławów, Ivano-Frankivsk), took his place.[173]

The "rehabilitation commissions" showed that "collaboration" with the Russians had been too extensive to follow all the leads and punish all the guilty.[174] Those who had cooperated with the Russians closely had left with them anyway. One of them was Jarosław Więckowski, from the railway construction department. He had worked on the designs for the new Lviv-Russian station, and was seen carrying Russian colours during Nicholas II's visit to the city. He agitated other railway workers in Lviv to return to work and betrayed the location of a cache with valuables hidden by senior officials in the railway headquarters before the evacuation.[175] In the main terminal itself, a foreman from the depots, Sigmund Mozer, allegedly worked eagerly for the Russians "as if he was a station master," while the first Russian train to enter Lviv was driven by local worker Michał Ładyga.[176] Wartime investigations of the railway directorate in Lviv also revisited numerous cases of embezzlement and abuse from before the war. Pre-war charges against senior officials by the socialist union, then deemed as unproven by the courts, were essentially confirmed. Wartime investigations pointed to a system of protection and personal favours that shielded officials from outside charges. With war at hand and questions about the loyalty of local officials, this system became a threat to the state.[177]

While combing the railway service for unreliable elements, the Austrians paid salaries and compensation to all railway employees who had remained in occupied territory and had not collaborated with the enemy. Moreover, the time spent under the occupation counted towards their service increments and retirement. Later, in the inter-war period, railway workers fondly recalled the "feeling of the legal order" and "humanitarian consideration of the employees' interests" experienced under old Austria even during the war.[178]

The damage of the Russian occupation was not limited to social trust but extended to buildings. American journalist John Reed, best known for his account of the Bolshevik Revolution, *Ten Days That Shook the World*, was not as impressed by the Lviv terminal as other visitors from both West and East. Unlike them he saw the terminal during the Russian retreat "choked with troops running and calling, with soldiers asleep on the filthy floor, with stupefied refugees wandering vaguely about."[179] Although the building survived the retreat, it was "befouled to such an extent, that a long time would be needed before it could be brought to order."[180] The filth and excrement Russian troops left behind in public buildings were a common motif in Austrian and German accounts.[181] This was interpreted as yet another proof of the civilizational boundary separating Russia from Europe.

Repair of the damaged railway lines and the supply of troops, not cleaning up, were the main priorities of the Austrian railway. With the removal of Rybicki, both tasks were successfully solved, and cooperation with the army was smooth. At the same time the distrust of locals persisted. Austrian authorities suspected Ukrainians, as well as Poles – indeed, all Galician Slavs were "unreliable."[182]

Even after the front rolled farther east, neither Lviv nor its train terminal returned to their pre-war life. The army had an upper hand over the railway's civilian administration. The mobility of residents was limited, and special permits were required even for short trips within the same district. To move between the front zone and the rear, one needed a passport.[183] With military needs taking precedence, the railway was physically unable to resume smooth civilian operations. Obtaining a ticket was challenging, even if one arrived at the station well in advance.[184] In 1917 trains were overfilled, and station restaurants no longer served patrons without a ration card.[185] The local aristocrat Aleksander Raczyński had to stand in a train car from Przemyśl to Lviv in November 1917.[186] That year even members of parliament stood in crowded corridors[187] or would take turns on a shared seat all the way from Vienna to Lviv.[188] In December 1917 it could take twelve hours for a passenger train to cover 120 kilometres.[189] Rarely did a train arrive on time during the war:[190] in January 1918 one train from Lviv to Vienna was nineteen hours late.[191] Cars were no longer properly maintained and sometimes lacked heating.[192] During the Russian offensives of June 1916 and July 1917, regular passenger movement was completely suspended. The stoppage caused great anxiety among Lvivites whose memories of 1914 were still fresh.[193] The situation with freight was no better.[194] Delivery delays affected the city economy and disrupted its services.[195] The terminal square was often empty, and even arriving aristocrats had to walk to the city centre ferrying their luggage on their backs.[196] There were no fiacres, and porters were too expensive.

The collapse of the old social order was especially visible on trains and in stations, the most public of public spaces. The upper classes complained about the arrogant *nouveaux riches* who made fortunes on speculation and travelled first or second class. Antisemitism was on the rise, and the Christian public was eager to identify speculators and draft dodgers as Jewish. In his diary Raczyński noted an incident with "several arrogant Jews with second-class tickets, sitting and behaving intolerably."[197] The frustration and fears generated by the collapse of the pre-war world were offloaded onto Jews, the perennial "Other" to European Christendom.

The city's poor had to resort to theft to survive. Children stole regularly, since they were unlikely to suffer serious consequences if caught. They would steal from train cars, carts carrying goods from stations, and from the stations themselves.[198] Coal, needed for heating and cooking, was by far the most popular commodity to steal – or to "catch crows," in the jargon of the street urchins.[199] Coal was taken from train cars and from railway storage pits.

Remarkably, the railway union was still active. In 1914 only the movement service was subjected to military discipline and regulations, while the rest of the railway service lived under peacetime arrangements. Job action remained possible. Moreover, because mobilization railway workers were almost irreplaceable, lockouts became virtually impossible. As well, socialist deputies intervened on behalf of the railway workers in the parliament.[200] Just as before the war, organized protest often went hand in hand with old-fashioned urban riots. When in January 1918 Austria-Hungary was engulfed by a massive strike brought on by food shortages, close to a thousand railway workers in Lviv participated.[201] During the strike, a "women's riot" took place. A teenage participant recalled being instructed by older women to throw stones at the windows of the city council. As darkness fell and the police and military descended upon the rioters, children would break street lamps to make escape easier.[202]

By all accounts the largest job action in Lviv that year was organized for a national cause. On 2 February street demonstrations by Poles ignited in protest against the Brest-Litovsk Treaty that Austria had signed with the newly independent Ukraine.[203] (One of the treaty's secret provisions was a separate Ukrainian province in the Habsburg Empire that would encompass Eastern Galicia and the transfer of some contested Ukrainian-Polish border territories to Ukraine.) After a gymnasium student was killed by the police, the city went on general strike on 18 February. Lviv came to standstill; the railway and telegraph were paralysed.[204]

During the inter-war period, when nationalist narratives became dominant, the memory of the February strike eclipsed all others.[205] In reality the ground for it was prepared by the all-Austrian strike in January. When in April 1918 workers of Lviv's railway workshops went on strike again, their demands were purely social. The authorities answered with the "militarization" of all railway service, outlawing strikes under the threat of court martial.[206] The number of participants and the territorial range of the 1918 strikes far surpassed those of 1904–06 in both Galicia and the empire at large. Although a reaction to war, starvation, and the depreciation of real salaries, they were also inspired by the Russian Revolution of 1917, in which Galician deportees, refugees, and POWs took direct part.

The Russian Revolution also enabled the deportees to return. Mayor Rutowski, Deputy Breiter, and Metropolitan Sheptytsky came back. Sheptytsky's return was the reverse of Vladimir Lenin's famous itinerary from 1917, with Sweden as an intermediate stop.[207] While Sheptytsky was physically absent from the local scene, a new cohort of Ukrainian activists in uniform had come of age. For them the war proved the bankruptcy of parliamentary politics and Austrian imperial legalism. The war accustomed them to violent solutions and provided a perfect opportunity to redraw state boundaries. They were convinced that the new world would consist of national states destined to replace shattered empires. The empires themselves, with their extensive wartime ethnic profiling, strengthened this vision. When the Habsburg Empire fell, it did so to the accompaniment of national revolutions.

Early in the morning of 1 November 1918, Ukrainian troops from the Austrian regiments stationed in the city and led by young Ukrainian officers took over the train terminal along with the city council, main post office, police headquarters, army barracks, state bank, and a slaughterhouse. The Western Ukrainian People's Republic was proclaimed without a single shot fired. Lviv was its first capital. In the afternoon, Polish military organizations in the city decided to resist the Ukrainian "coup" with arms. Fighting began. The centre of the Polish insurrection was in the "New World" and its adjacent neighbourhoods. Polish insurgents had already tried to take the terminal, strategically the most important site in the city, linking Lviv with the newly proclaimed Polish state in Western Galicia. The terminal and the workshops were deserted, engines stayed silent in depots, and the Ukrainian outpost at the terminal covered approaches with machine-gun fire.[208]

From the very first day the belligerents had to deal both with each other and with those who showed no desire to fight. Disarmed Ukrainian soldiers, who came by train from Przemyśl, had to be dispersed with fire from the Ukrainian outpost. Part of the Ukrainian garrison deserted with them, leaving only twenty soldiers to defend the station.[209] On 2 November the Polish insurgents managed to get into Chernivtsi terminal from Horodotska (Gródecka) Street and requisition the weapons stored there.[210] Ukrainian troops sent from the city centre to relieve the terminal could not get past St Elizabeth Church. Under the cover of a single armoured engine, Poles advanced on the terminal from Riasne (Rzęsna Polska) and Klepariv station.[211] Kazimierz Bartel, a polytechnic professor and future minister of communications and prime minister of Poland, was on that engine. As the last Austrian military commandant of the terminal, he knew the station intimately. The remaining Ukrainian troops left at night for Pidzamche station, and the Poles seized the terminal on the morning of 3 November.

On the same day, Ukrainian reinforcements arrived from Chernivtsi. Having disembarked at the city's southern outskirts, one company of arrivals reached the main station and entered the terminal through its sheds. From time to time the fighting was interrupted by trains arriving with returning or wounded soldiers of the imperial army, which added to the confusion. Moreover, using fires as a pretext, railway workers from the immediate neighbourhoods looted warehouses with supplies, including alcohol. "Old railwaymen got so drunk that the ground was covered with their bodies."[212] Ukrainian and Polish officers were forced to arrange a truce to introduce some semblance of order, protect the remaining supplies, and let the civilians out. The Poles carried the day, and the Ukrainians abandoned the terminal. The last and equally unsuccessful Ukrainian attempt to recover the station took place on 4 November.[213] After that the station remained firmly in Polish hands until the Ukrainians abandoned the city on 21 November. Bronisław Pieracki, minister of the interior in inter-war Poland, became the station's first Polish commandant.[214]

The loss of the main train station largely determined the outcome of the fighting in Lviv. The station became the backbone of the defence of the Polish-controlled northwestern neighbourhoods. It gave the Poles a vital link with Krakow, much needed supplies, and repair facilities in the workshops. Besides weapons and munitions, there were also field kitchens, uniforms, food, even cattle brought to the city slaughterhouse, all of which helped Polish forces persevere until the arrival of reinforcements.[215]

The massive pillaging by civilians, mostly railway workers and their families, in November 1918 was glossed over by Polish inter-war narratives. Central to the Polish inter-war mythology of Lviv was the self-sacrifice of the local citizenry who defended the city's Polish-ness. Presented as both staunch socialists and impeccable Polish patriots, Lviv's railway workers played a prominent role in that narrative.[216] The plunder of warehouses for private gain and individual survival during the days crucial to the success of the Polish insurgency in Lviv was not compatible with that narrative – indeed, a socialist deputy later recalled that he had to force a railwaymen to work for the new Polish state at gunpoint.[217]

After Ukrainian troops left Lviv, its Jewish population suffered through the city's first modern pogrom. The Polish military formed the core of the perpetrators "punishing" Jews for their neutrality in the Polish-Ukrainian conflict and alleged assistance to the Ukrainians. The mob broke into apartments, stole property, humiliated, beat, shot, and raped. It is estimated that between 41 and 150 Jews were killed.[218] The pogrom also did not square well with the heroic narrative of a just and noble armed struggle.

The war did not end with the Ukrainian retreat. For the following six months, the city was besieged by Ukrainian troops, with the railway line to Krakow as Lviv's only supply line. The city suffered from artillery bombardment and disruptions of its water supplies. The relatively brief Ukrainian-Polish war proved to be more damaging to the city's built environment than the much longer and bloodier war between powerful continental empires. The same was true of the city's societal bonds. The war divided society by ethnicity, sowing hatred and suspicion. Much of the damage came not from the conflict itself but from how it was conceptualized, represented, and used afterwards.

During the siege of Lviv, the supposedly uncompromisingly Polish railway workers of the city obtained martyrs of their own. In December 1918, before Christmas, news of a Ukrainian atrocity shook the city. Nine "railwaymen" went to the forest on the Lviv's northern outskirts to bring home some fir trees and never came back. Later their bodies were found, and the murder was blamed on Ukrainian troops. Although the victims lived in the railway neighbourhood, not all of them worked for the railway; moreover, there were two Ukrainians among them – one worked at the warehouse and the other in the railway workshops. No evidence surfaced, however, linking these murders with Ukrainian troops. Instead rumours named deserters, and even Polish troops, as possible perpetrators. Nevertheless on Christmas day 1918 the remains were solemnly interned in the Ianivsky (Janowski) cemetery.[219]

In the besieged city, the neighbourhood around the train terminal was the one that suffered from artillery bombardment, the conspicuous Gothic spires of St Elizabeth Church helping to provide targets for the guns. On 9 March 1919 a grenade was thrown into the church, killing several faithful.[220] A Polish field hospital operated in one of the terminal's waiting rooms,[221] while tunnels were used as bomb shelters.[222] Still, the terminal received occasional trains from Krakow; on one of them was a Warsaw correspondent who described an eerie place, barely lit with gas lanterns, the electrical light of the terminal providing the only bright spot in the city.[223]

The terminal sustained the most serious damage on 5 March when a shell hit the munitions warehouse near Chernivtsi terminal, producing a massive blast. Five railway workers were killed on the spot and an estimated eight hundred thousand rifle cartridges and fifteen thousand shells of recently replenished munitions exploded. Shards and shrapnel peppered the terminal for hours.[224] Panic engulfed the city. In later narratives, "railway workers were the first to rush to the defence of the endangered outpost, and localized the explosion." They were "railwaymen-heroes, the pride of the Polish railroading."[225] At the time, however, rumours of treason circulated,[226] and Ukrainian railway workers were identified as the most likely culprits.[227] Once the detonations stopped, people from the neighbourhoods rushed to the warehouses for another round of pillaging.[228]

The city population was far from being united around the national cause. The upper classes expected a socialist coup any day. In their fears, railway workers figured as one of the most unreliable social groups. Thirty-five train cars sent to Lviv with food supplies were robbed on the way, allegedly by railway workers, "so that not a single kilogram got to the city." When a supply train finally arrived from Lublin, "the railwaymen stole all the food and the city did not get even a single kilo; even the cars themselves were hidden."[229]

Most people in working-class neighbourhoods – even the younger generation, immortalized in post-war narratives as "Lviv eaglets" who sacrificed their lives for Poland – tried to stay away from fighting, remaining uncommitted to the national cause. Bronisław Łotocki recalled teenagers from his apartment building: Polish, Ruthenian, and Jewish, they banded together as the Iarychiv gang, thirty teenagers strong. Apparently, in November 1918, even those among them who went to a "Ruthenian school" did not know much about mysterious "Ukrainians" who had taken Lviv. Nevertheless gang members would easily approach Ukrainian soldiers at Pidzamche station in Ukrainian to get some free soup.[230]

Community leaders of besieged Polish Lviv, however, took nationality seriously. A Committee of National Defence was created, with retired railway director Stanisław Rybicki and right-leaning socialist Artur Hausner were among its members.[231] The railway was at the forefront of the committee's concerns. In March 1919, after the train station explosion, the committee claimed there was a Ukrainian-Zionist conspiracy in the city. Allegedly the committee was in possession of notes from a Ukrainian spy showing that the conspiracy had three thousand fighters, all in possession of arms and ammunition.[232] Needless to say the conspiracy existed only in the committee members' imagination. In July 1919 the committee demanded the introduction of a state of emergency on the railway, which it saw as infected with Bolshevism and infested with alien nationals.[233] Simultaneously the railway workforce was also accused of harbouring imperial pro-German sentiments.[234] In September 1919 the committee's information section complained of "the sad relations among the railway personnel," the "sad relations" consisting of the single fact that there were "a great number of Jews" among railway employees. Karol Barwicz, the new railway director in Lviv, blamed the ministry in Warsaw for "imposing on him Jews as officials."[235] While on the one hand Jews were suspected of being both pro-Ukrainian and pro-Bolshevik, on the other hand they were seen as the embodiment of speculative capitalism.[236] The denunciations of Jews also came from below as early as 1919.[237]

The Bolsheviks, who allegedly arrived with the railway workers from the former Russian partition, were "spreading agitation in the workshops and barracks." Railway workers were accused of "trading in a speculative way with food they had brought, against which the engineers and higher officials were completely powerless."[238] During the Soviet-Polish war in 1920, Lviv's Polish patriots warned their government that Ukrainians, especially the railway workers, looked forward to the arrival of the Bolsheviks.[239] Although "alien" national groups became the prime suspects, the railway workers as a social group that provided vital services to the community were also distrusted. Social and national, political and behavioural in the frightened patriotic imagination converged on the image of a single enemy, omnipresent and many-faceted.

Exclusive, aggressive, and racialized patriotism became the mainstream. The Committee of National Defence listed Ukrainians, Jews, Germans, and Czechs as the "elements inimical to our nation," and believed that there was no place for those ethnicities in the state service.[240] The "Ten Commandments for the Poles on the Eastern Borders of the Commonwealth," created in the same milieu, imagined a racially pure Polish community. Commandment Five forbade marrying people of another nation or rite, an obvious reference to Greek Catholics, who could also pose as Poles.[241] The political and emotional climate of the new Polish state was intolerance born in fighting, where front lines were drawn along ethnic boundaries, and social tensions were often interpreted as enemy infiltration.

In 1919 Galician railways became part of the Polish state railways (*Polskie Koleje Państwowe*, PKP), whose abbreviation PKP was now painted on train cars.[242] Lviv was the seat of the PKP's Regional Directorate of State Railways. Regular passenger traffic between Lviv and Przemyśl was restored in March 1919, but the next two years saw major interruptions during multiple emergencies. The city was flooded with refugees, and passenger traffic was suspended in June 1919 during the Ukrainian offensive.[243] As late as July 1920, fearing the Bolshevik offensive, Lvivites sent children and valuables to Krakow.[244] Panicked people stormed trains.[245] By August the situation had stabilized,[246] but the city still dwelled on rumours about a coming Bolshevik offensive, and looked as if it had been deserted.[247]

Even though the fighting stopped in fall 1920, life was far from "normal." The railway schedule, a standard of pre-war normality, continued to malfunction. Trains could suddenly stop running because of coal shortages, as happened in 1921 during Christmas.[248] A wave of strikes in 1921 also took its toll.[249] Some delays were caused by bottlenecks in freight operations. Three-hour waits for a train to depart were quite common.[250] In these conditions the travel privileges of the military and railway officials were deeply resented.[251]

The city became used to living by emergency governance, and it also became accustomed to death and deprivation. Lives and property were lost at whim. Camps confining and sheltering displaced people became a normal fixture of the urban landscape. There was a makeshift camp for Soviet POWs in the Klepariv (Kleparów) neighbourhood north of the Ianivsky (Janowski) cemetery,[252] while another camp – for refugees – was created on Janowska (Shevchenko) Street.[253]

The profound effect that the First World War had on Europe is one of those historiographic clichés that is also undeniably true. The massive death toll, the unprecedented state intervention in economic and private life, the shattering of old social boundaries and gender roles – Lviv had experienced it all. By 1920 there were around thirty thousand soldiers' graves in the city. Over ten thousand Lvivites had lost their lives in combat.[254] The war between two independent states, the defeat of the Ukrainian state and the victory of the Polish one created a rift that would only widen in inter-war Poland. Social radicalization and conflict under these conditions were often presented in national terms, with the local "Bolsheviks" defined as either Jewish or Ukrainian.

War and occupation not only exposed the fragility of the liberal order, but also showed that sophisticated modern cities and societies could do without it. Moreover, in times of emergency, liberal governance seemed the least efficient option. The occupation demonstrated that modern infrastructure, such as railways, could be easily overtaken by a foreign power. Local knowledge and local input were accepted and used, but they were not crucial. The occupation of Galicia and Lviv was not accidental. The war revealed multiple connections between the region and the Russian Empire, as well as the latter's imperialist designs on the former. Local collaboration was widespread, mostly because workers realized the precariousness of their status, which derived from their absolute dependence on wages. The large-scale replacement of free workers by the military or militarized personnel, together with the suspension of peacetime freedoms and procedures, could neutralize pre-war forms of social and political struggle. The war not only unleashed destruction, but also taught of its pleasures. Under the state of emergency, buildings were stripped to their basic functions or used as a resource in new capacities. The décor, the symbolism of signifiers, the self-regulating and precisely calculated order could be sacrificed along with splendour to wartime contingencies in praise of a heroism inseparable from destruction.

Chapter Five

Virtuti Militari

Lviv's terminal building sustained heavy damage during the Ukrainian-Polish War. Its walls withstood bombing, shelling, and the great 1919 explosion, but the interior décor was largely lost.[1] Reconstruction started in 1921, once the Soviet-Polish war was over, leaving all of former Galicia to Poland. The Polish Ministry of Communications allocated the funds, the Polish Construction Society did the works, and local architect Henryk Zaremba designed the project and oversaw its execution.[2]

Mere restoration was not an option. The design had to be updated to reflect the new reality of an independent, resurrected, and heroically defended Polish state. Explicit imperial symbols were the first to be retired: the dedication to Franz Joseph I and the two-headed eagles of the entrance doors and sheds were the first to be erased. The two-headed eagle on the frontispiece stayed a little longer. It was an integral part of the "allegory of communication" and was difficult to remove. Temporarily it was merely covered over by a Polish eagle, although "some were affronted by the zinc eagle placed over the entrance to the terminal."[3] The kitschy eagle on the terminal was not the only problematic one. The eagle on the city hall's tower did not unveil properly during the opening ceremony because of a jammed curtain mechanism. The public interpreted this incident as "a bad omen for Lviv's Polish-ness."[4]

The old dedication to Franz Joseph above the terminal's main entrance was replaced with the city's motto *Semper Fidelis* (Always Loyal) inscribed in gold beneath the city's name in Latin: Leopolis.[5] The motto had been given to Lviv by Pope Alexander III in 1658 in recognition of the city's role as an eastern bulwark of Christendom against Muslim invasion, but after 1918–20 it acquired new connotations, becoming a reminder of the city's "Polish-ness" and heroic defence first against the Ukrainians and then against the Bolsheviks.[6] A metal bell hung on a tripod in front of the motto, symbolizing the dangers the city had overcome, its readiness to respond to the call to arms, and the lives it had sacrificed.

One goal of reconstruction was to turn the terminal into a memorial commemorating the "Defence of Lviv" – Polish Lviv's central myth from the inter-war period. New sculptural compositions referring to the "defence" were commissioned by Petro Viitovych (Piotr Wójtowicz), an ethnic Ruthenian who had done the original industry and trade allegories. Viitovych sculpted four groups: "Reveille," "Attack," "After the Battle," and "The Crowning" (*Uwieńczenie*).[7] In May 1922, even before the reconstruction was finished, the "Cross of the Defence of Lviv" was opened at the terminal.[8]

The style of the reconstruction had a definite anti-Secession animus. In the words of one local critic: "First of all, care had been taken to somewhat remove the traces of Secession and to replace them with native ornaments."[9] This aversion to the style Secession was common in the 1920s – liking Art Nouveau was seen as a sign of poor taste. Inter-war Lviv architects, Henryk Zaremba being no exception, favoured constructivism and functionalism. At the same time, in the conditions of post-war poverty, a large-scale redesign of the terminal was not feasible. Zaremba opted for cheaper cosmetic replacements of the interior décor. He was a prolific architect who supervised nearly all larger constructions in the railway neighbourhood.

Zaremba would be remembered not so much for his buildings as for his personal tragedy, which became the most sensational murder story of inter-war Poland. In 1931 his lover and housekeeper, the Balkan foreigner Rita Gorgonowa, was convicted of the murder of Zaremba's sixteen-year-old daughter. All the ingredients sought after by the boulevard press were in this story: mystery, murder, innocence, semi-illicit sexuality, and suspicious foreigners. The fact that the drama happened to the family of a respectable and wealthy professional made the story even juicier.[10]

The terminal's reconstruction was far more prosaic. The arrivals hall, the restaurant, and third-class waiting hall were finished first. These were executed in the "national" style by Wiesław Grzymalski, who would become chair of interior design at the Lviv polytechnic. Grzymalski's ornaments and Gaudi-like references to "nature" were a major departure from the original "vernacular" Art Nouveau décor (Figure 5.1). A major change in the reconstructed terminal was the appearance of pillars that parsed the space of its large rooms. Besides their decorative function, they provided additional ceiling support. Local experts evidently approved of the stylistic changes. The local newspaper's

Z DWORCA KOLEJI PAŃSTWOWEJ WE LWOWIE.

W. Grzymalski.

1922 V. 26

Figure 5.1. The third-class restaurant and waiting hall after the reconstruction. Source: *Architekt*, 1922, no. 5, table 26.

only complaint was that budget constraints "did not allow a remake of the vestibule, which survived intact, and its style would somewhat contrast with the rest of the terminal."[11]

The reconstruction was completed in July 1923. "The most beautiful of the terminals" was "cleansed of crowns," its façade now featuring patriotic allegories and simpler, more "classical" lines (Figure 5.2). The only complaint again was that "the fashionable earlier Secession could not be completely removed."[12] Mieczysław Orłowicz even saw Grzymalski's work as a reconstruction in the old Secession style. According to Orłowicz, the first- and second-class restaurant, with its unadorned columns and modernist bas-reliefs, was especially elegant.[13] Zaremba himself designed the restaurant, while Viitovych made bas-reliefs representing nature's four seasons, Lviv, and the world. Apparently the original division between the folksy décor for third class and more cosmopolitan bourgeois style for first and second remained intact. Zaremba designed rooms down to the smallest detail, such as chandeliers commissioned in the local railway workshops.[14] The main vestibule preserved its pre-war décor, except for the new murals Grzymalski painted in lieu of the damaged ones (Figure 5.3).[15] By 1926 the terminal, its square, and its wide boulevard received new lighting. Arc bulbs, each with a luminous intensity of 2,000 candelas and low power consumption, were installed free of charge for trial.[16]

Although the terminal was still praised as "the largest and most beautiful" in independent Poland,[17] or "the only one in present day Poland built in the Western European way,"[18] it was also seen as stylistically outdated. The aesthetes of the inter-war period abhorred Lviv's "very ugly" *fin-de-siècle* buildings.[19] For native Lvivite Władysław Czarnecki, later famous for designing inter-war modernist Poznań, the formerly praised Mikolasch Passage was a pale imitation of Milan's Galeria Vittorio Emanuele, both "equally unhealthy for the people working there."[20] Affection for Secession was seen a sign of philistinism and ignorance.[21]

In the inter-war period the beautified territory in front of the terminal acquired new significance as a favourite location for mass rallies. Many of them were connected with the visits of state dignitaries and war heroes, who, unlike the imperial ministers, were venerated by the public. Probably the most celebrated protagonist of these pageants was Józef Piłsudski, the First World War Polish Legions commander, chief of state from 1919 to 1922, and quasi-dictator from 1926 to 1935. The cult of strong men, saviours of the nation, was another by-product of the wars fought on the wreckage of nineteenth-century empires.

Piłsudski's armed struggle for Polish independence had multiple connections with trains, dating back to the famous Bezdany robbery

Figure 5.2. View of the terminal after the reconstruction; Viitovych's "Reveille" and "Attack" are seen on the left pavilion. Source: Marek Münz, [Dworzec Główny we Lwowie, ca.1925]; Biblioteka Narodowa, Warsaw, F. 7794/II.

Figure 5.3. The main vestibule, ca. 1925. Source: Marek Münz, [Wnętrze hali Dworca Głównego we Lwowie, ca.1925]; Biblioteka Narodowa, Warsaw, F. 7796/II.

of the Russian mail train he led in 1908. (Between the wars, militant Ukrainian nationalists avidly studied Piłsudski's revolutionary deeds and tactics to use them against Piłsudski's own state.)[22] During the war, Piłsudski had become used to living on trains. Just like Trotsky and many other warlords in those revolutionary times, he had a train of his own. Passing through Lviv, he often slept in his train car at the terminal.[23] In November 1919, with the ongoing war at hand, the city still managed to stage a celebratory welcome for Piłsudski.[24] A full-fledged performance had taken place one year later on 22 November 1920, the second anniversary of the city's "liberation" from the Ukrainians, when Piłsudski came to present the city with the Virtuti Militari, Poland's highest military decoration. Lviv was the only city in inter-war Poland to receive it, and only two other cities were awarded the decoration in the order's history: Verdun for the battles of the First World War and Warsaw for its defence in 1939. At the terminal, the commanders who fought for the city, the city board (a substitute for a proper city council), and the mayor waited for Piłsudski, surrounded by the representatives of various associations. Local socialists were present, as well as Archbishop Bilczewski, who served up yet another of his train terminal liturgies.[25] An important part of the reconstruction was the broadening of the boulevard leading to the terminal from Horodotska (Gródecka) Street to give it "a world city character." Known at first as an "Exit Road" and later as the "Terminal Access Road," during the siege of Lviv it was informally known as "Death Alley" because of its frequent bombardment.[26] The procession for Piłsudski took the widened boulevard and then Horodotska before it reached the Sienkiewicz school, the centre of the Polish insurrection in November 1918. There the order was handed to the city.[27]

Both Piłsudski and his antagonist, General Józef Haller, were greeted at the terminal. Some claimed that Haller received greater applause than Piłsudski, which reflected a change in political sympathies of the Lviv street and the predominance of right-wing nationalism in the city. On 2 November 1928, Haller came to a congress of the "Hallerites," his former soldiers. Even though Piłsudski was now in power, Haller received a near-regal welcome from local National Democrats opposed to Piłsudski's regime.[28] Aleksander Raczyński, as a frequent traveller, could not suppress his irony describing the epidemic of welcome and farewell ceremonies he witnessed at the Lviv terminal.[29]

The terminal also received foreign dignitaries. The most important of them was Marshal Ferdinand Foch, the Supreme Allied commander during the First World War, who visited Lviv in 1923. He came by train from Warsaw, and the terminal was turned into a "reception hall," where the governor and the mayor gave welcoming speeches. All kinds of societies and associations, with girls in Polish national costumes forming front rows, waited at the terminal square. The boulevard leading to the terminal featured two triumphal arches. Thirty thousand university and grade school students formed two enormous files covering the whole length of the marshal's route.[30] To commemorate the visit, the former "Death Alley" was renamed the Marshal Foch Alley. The square in front of the terminal was named after another leader of the Entente and became Wilson Square.

Early on in independent Poland, the terminal became a patriotic memorial and a stage for performing national rituals. Signifiers pointing to the abstractions of the national sacrifice and the nation's general will obscured the messages of the terminal's original design (Figure 5.4). Already in March 1920, with the main battles of the Soviet-Polish war still ahead, the Society for the Protection of the Graves of Polish Heroes urged railway workers to install a memorial plaque at the terminal,[31] and the building kept amassing a clutter of memorial signs throughout the 1920s and 1930s. In 1929, to mark a decade since the great train station explosion, a cross was added to the terminal's façade.[32] In 1934, after the Organization of Ukrainian Nationalists (OUN) assassinated Bronisław Pieracki, the Union of the Defenders of Lviv unveiled a memorial plaque commemorating him on one of the terminal's platforms.[33] Bilczewski's figure of St Mary was reinstalled with great pomp in 1923.[34]

Nationalist pageants staged at the terminal often coincided with burials and reburials. Many historians of nationalism have noted the importance of the dead for re-enacting a national community by the living.[35] In the wake of seven long years of mass killing, the exploitation of dead bodies reached unprecedented heights. A true cult of death emerged in inter-war Lviv.[36] The nation, whose collective life allegedly allowed the individual to transcend finitude, trauma, and suffering, presented itself as the best way of coming to terms with the massive loss of life. In those rituals, to use Michael Taussig's words, "death comes to mean more than life."[37] New death rituals shifted accents from mourning to the celebration of heroic death as the ultimate fulfilment of one's life.

Lviv's terminal played a prominent role in these death rituals. Since dead bodies were used to chart the nation's symbolic geography, they had to be not only buried, exhumed, and reburied, but also transported. The first large-scale post-war military reburial took place in Lviv in September 1920. The remains of officers killed near Zadvir'ia (Zadwórze) in the Polish-Soviet war were brought to the city for interment in the

Figure 5.4. The terminal decorated for a patriotic occasion. Source: Polish National Digital Archive, 41-774.

Polish military pantheon being created at the Lychakiv (Łyczaków) cemetery. The reburial became Lviv's largest funeral ceremony yet in a city that "had become used to massive military burials."[38] In February 1921 the train brought the remains of fifteen *uhlans* (Polish light cavalrymen) killed near Rokytne (Rokitno).[39] Bodies from the surrounding battlefields kept coming to the cemetery in a steady flow. As late as 1936 the remains of three Polish pilots from the Polish-Soviet war were brought to the terminal, and from there carried by hand through the city to the cemetery.[40]

The most important reburial took place in 1925. On the last day of October, the remains of an unknown soldier were brought to the terminal, on their way to Warsaw to become one of the nation's greatest sanctities. Following the example set by Britain and France, a national monument to the unknown soldier was created in Warsaw as a tomb with an actual soldier's remains. A draw was organized among fifteen battlegrounds deemed as most important for the achievement and defence of Polish independence. Lviv was one of these fifteen. It won the draw, and provided the bodily remains for the national Tomb of the Unknown Soldier. After much deliberation, to make sure that a worthy body was identified, an unknown soldier was exhumed from the Lychakiv cemetery. The body was moved to the nearby chapel before transportation to the cathedral, and finally on to the terminal. At the terminal, the railway orchestra performed and the public sang patriotic songs, while the honorary railway guard stood by the casket together with soldiers. After an all-night vigil, with the public paying last honours, on 1 November the remains left for Warsaw (Figure 5.5).[41]

In the 1930s some of the transported bodies were recent sacrifices. Militant Polish nationalism, state discrimination against minorities, and a prevalent culture of political violence created a perfect breeding ground for increasingly violent and unscrupulous minority nationalisms. In August 1931 the remains of Tadeusz Hołówko stopped in Lviv for four hours. Piłsudski's collaborator and supporter of the Polish-Ukrainian compromise, Hołówko had been assassinated by Ukrainian nationalists.[42]

Piłsudski himself died in 1935. Lviv, however, was not on the itinerary of his body parts. Most of Piłsudski was buried in Krakow's royal cathedral crypt alongside Poland's medieval kings; his heart was interred in his native Vilnius, while his brain was deposited in a medical institute for study. Nonetheless Lviv wanted to be present physically at the leader's funeral and in his grave. For that purpose, samples of soil were taken from nearby battlefields and put into an urn first exhibited

Figure 5.5. Remains of the unknown soldier in the Lviv terminal. Source: Katafalk ze zwłokami Nieznanego Żólnierza w Sali Recepcyjnej dworca lwowskiego (Warsaw: nakł. Pol. Tow. Opieki nad Grobami Bogaterów, [1925]); Biblioteka Narodowa, Warsaw, Pocz. 2309.

at Lviv's city theatre, afterwards taken to the reception hall of the train terminal, and from there to Krakow.[43]

The railway moved both the nation's sacred objects and those who wanted to see them. It supplied discounted tickets and free cars for such national pilgrimages. Charter trains brought tours to the battlefields of Zadvir'ia and Horpyn (Horpin).[44] Railway workers were urged to participate in patriotic rituals. When in 1927 the remains of four "most deserving female workers on the social and national field during the defence of Lviv" were to be added to the pantheon of "Lviv Defenders," railway managers wanted their employees to take part in this solemn ceremony.[45]

The glitter of the pageants distracted from the problems plaguing the terminal. In 1925 wind gusts tore several tiles from the roof and crushed thirty-five glass panes on the ceiling of the corridor leading to the third-class waiting room.[46] In 1928 a fire started in the attic above the reception hall.[47] In 1932, during a storm, water flooded one of the tunnels to a half-metre height, signalling the first sign of problems with the terminal's sewers.[48] In 1936 a city newspaper complained that, "[y]ears ago, this terminal was the pride of our city and was admired in its every aspect by the whole country. Today, however, the appearance of this building leaves much to be desired. It is high time to take a look at the devastations time has inflicted on the walls of this building. Those walls are dirty, blackened, dented, the reliefs and ornaments disappear in blemish ... Every inch of the building begs for renovation, and as rich an institution as the railway should not be giving such a bad example. The appearance of the building's interior is no better."[49] Shortly after the article was published, six square metres of the ceiling's stucco collapsed in the corridor leading to the third-class restaurant, destroying a kiosk with confectionary and fruits and wounding its leaseholder.[50] Apparently the reconstruction had not mended the structural damage to the building in wartime.

While the design of the reconstructed first-class restaurant was praised, the restaurant disappeared from the lists of the eateries recommended to travellers. As a "very fair restaurant," it is mentioned in the 1911 Baedeker guide to Austria-Hungary.[51] It is also listed in the 1912 guidebook to the city,[52] but not in those from 1922,[53] 1925,[54] or 1936.[55] The terminal restaurant reappears in guidebooks only on the eve of the Second World War.[56] Sanitation reports from 1925 noted that the third-class waiting room and restaurant did not have sufficient ventilation and were full of tobacco smoke.[57] The third-class canteen had bare wooden tables and no hot meals. Even in the first-class canteen, only paper napkins were offered. Both canteens had spittoons, but these were missing in the terminal's other premises. Washrooms needed some reconstruction and "greater care."[58]

The condition of the terminal and the restaurant was emblematic of the transformation the city went through in the 1920s and 1930s, when it lost much of its pre-1914 lustre. Lviv was no longer a capital, even if only of a province, no longer the "Piedmont" for either Ukrainians or Poles. There was a brain drain to Warsaw, as well as a significant emigration of the Ukrainian intelligentsia to Kharkiv, the capital of Soviet Ukraine. Jewish immigration also picked up, mostly to North America, but also to Palestine. The bulk of Jewish immigration to Palestine came from inter-war Poland.

Nonetheless, unlike its former imperial capital, Vienna, Lviv continued to grow during the inter-war period. Its population was 219,000 in 1921 and reached 312,000 in 1931, with an estimated 318,000 living in the city in 1939.[59] Its territory expanded, and the city absorbed many suburban villages.[60] Much of this newly acquired territory belonged to the railway. Even before the expansion, Lviv's "railway terrain" had occupied nearly 17 hectares, nearly as much as the city's various green spaces[61] – and Lviv was seen as a very green city in inter-war Poland. Equalling one-fifth of the city's built-up territory, the sheer size of Lviv's railway terrain was second only to Warsaw's and Poznań's.[62]

The terminal building still served as the first indication of Lviv's metropolitan character for people from the region's towns and villages. During his first visit to the city as a five-year-old boy, Roman Szporluk was mightily impressed by the terminal, especially its glass train sheds.[63] Stanisław Lem, while "not a very independent" local kid and with little knowledge of the streets beyond his immediate neighbourhood, nevertheless knew "Grodecka St., which we took when went to the train station, magnificent and vast, situated at the end of the Foch Boulevard."[64]

By the mid-1920s peacetime routines returned to the terminal. Trains ran on time. Passengers of express trains from Warsaw checked their watches against platform clocks that showed exactly midnight (the trains left Warsaw at 3 p.m.).[65] Passenger movement now had a different geography. The sizable stream of passengers that had travelled to and from the Russian Empire diminished to a trickle in the 1920s and disappeared in the 1930s, when the Soviet Union closed its borders. Trips to Vienna and Budapest were reduced as well. New state borders, with all the passport and customs checks, deprived passengers of night sleep and made these journeys much longer.[66] Instead, Lviv obtained direct connections to Warsaw and Vilnius. Warsaw replaced Vienna as the primary destination for politicians, public servants, and businessmen, although those used to Vienna complained about Warsaw's inconspicuous and inconvenient stations.[67]

As Lviv's international significance declined, international traffic dwindled. Despite Lviv's aspirations to become a major trade hub for East-Central Europe, exemplified by the yearly "Eastern Fair" on the grounds of the former provincial exhibition, the closed Soviet-Polish border seriously hurt the city. At the same time, the old imperial borders within Poland were still highly visible. As late as 1930, the Polish railway followed three different movement regulations inherited from imperial times. Until 1935 the railway in former Galicia used left-side traffic, the rest of Poland right-side.[68] There were also problems with access from Lviv to nearby Volhynian towns inherited from the Russian Empire.[69]

Internal Polish tourism compensated, at least partly, for the loss of international travellers. The Carpathian Mountains were an attractive destination, as were the lakes and rivers of Polissia (Polish: Polesie; Belarusian: Palesse) to which Lviv served as a key access point. The railway remained the main means of transportation during this inter-war tourist boom, and cooperated with travel bureaus that advertised destinations and trips and recruited tourists.[70] Lviv's main terminal featured displays offering possible itineraries for one-, two-, and three-day visits.[71] In 1932 the minister of communications, Aleksandr Bobkowski, organized the "first and only Railway-Skiing Ride." A train was formed in Lviv from sleeping cars for guests from all over Poland and then moved at night, stopping during the day at locations known for downhill skiing. In the middle of this trip, the train returned to Lviv for "a great dinner and reception with dances until midnight." The minister himself was among the train's guests.[72] To facilitate tourism, the railway introduced all kinds of affordable seasonal tickets and passes. The trains also accommodated skis, toboggans, bicycles, and kayaks. Various associations and societies worked out deals with the railway for their members. Kazimierz Bartel, for example, after his resignation from the government, managed to get free transferable railway tickets for his Mathematics Society.[73]

After the war, policing of the railway intensified. Before 1914 there had been only an outpost of the city police at the Lviv main station. Now a full-fledged police commissariat was organized at the station, joining Lviv's other five territorial commissariats.[74] It busied itself mostly with theft and speculation, which flourished in the early 1920s against a backdrop of inflation, dwindling incomes, and scarce food. The police organized raids on speculators at the terminal and on trains and confiscated foreign currency[75] and foodstuffs.[76]

During the war people had become accustomed to riding on trains without a ticket. Ticketless passengers became a problem in the 1920s, however, and the railway needed police help in fighting fare-evasion. In July 1927, during a single terminal raid, police apprehended 120 ticketless travellers.[77] The inter-war period also witnessed the appearance of train beggars, including itinerant musicians.[78] Both phenomena were signs not so much of inter-war poverty as of the railway's democratization and greater accessibility.

Emigrants became a less frequent feature of the train terminal, as the United States and Canada had changed their pre-war "open door" policy in favour of more selective intakes. Migrants from the villages, including young women looking for job opportunities, were still flowing into the cities. Women's organizations helped lone female travellers evade the hands of pimps and other "traders dealing in humans" allegedly hunting them in the terminals of large cities. Although similar concerns and assistance were common everywhere, Lviv's case was special. The first court trial dealing with the "white slavery" of women allegedly entrapped by cross-border human traffickers had taken place there as early as 1892.[79] Many young women came to Lviv's station not for the sake of the provincial capital and the limited opportunities it offered, but for the glitter of European metropolises and overseas destinations, which formed a distinct strand in the massive Galician emigration.[80]

The Lviv chapter of the Austrian League to Combat Traffic of Women began to monitor the Lviv terminal in 1903, its patrols screening the public for potential victims.[81] The league was multi-ethnic and multiconfessional, but a nationalist Catholic organization soon took over the monitoring of the train station, compartmentalizing aid to travelling women along national and confessional lines. Another organization, the Patronage of Young Women Society, affiliated with the Catholic Union of Poles, had established a "mission" at the Lviv terminal in 1910. In 1913 the society provided 3,789 nights of accommodation and assisted 1,374 women find jobs.[82] The society had to suspend its activities at the station for the duration of the war, however, after it was banned from the platforms by the military. It resumed its work in the 1920s and expanded its scope, and by May 1929 was assisting almost six hundred women a month.[83] The society had a duty room and shelter at the terminal and another shelter in the city.

In the early 1920s the railway economy was still recovering from the war. The passenger car fleet was insufficient and many had missing windows.[84] Accidents were common, partly because worn-out equipment was used owing to the lack of replacements.[85] As late as 1929 there was no guarantee that even passengers with first-class tickets would find seats.[86] Real modernity, a better functioning economy, and a more efficient, comfortable railway were still considered to be located west of Poland. Old Herman Diamand, used to the splendour of *fin-de-siècle* Vienna, was greatly impressed by Weimar Berlin in 1929.[87] When Raczyński changed trains in Berlin on his way to Nice, he noted that the German sleeping car, "unlike ours, was unbelievably clean and elegant, I travelled alone in a compartment and could not stop wondering how this train car looked as if brand new and was much more comfortable than ours."[88]

An alternative modernity was emerging to the east. For local "Sovietophiles," Soviet trains looked better than Polish trains. In 1927 Ukrainian professor Kyrylo Studynsky, travelling to a conference in Kharkiv, found that Poland's eastern border was much more closely guarded, on both sides, than either its western or southern borders. The border crossing took six painful hours. The Soviet station restaurant in Zhmerynka, however, had "first rate meals," and Soviet "soft" cars were "very comfortable ... Greater comfort can be found only in European sleeping cars."[89]

Social shifts that had begun during the war persisted throughout the inter-war years. The resentment of "European-looking" Jews who travelled first and second class did not cease with the end of the war. Some observers in the early 1920s claimed that "Jewish speculators" formed the majority of passengers on Lviv's regional trains.[90] The ideal Jew of Poland's conservative establishment was traditional, and deferred to state authorities in political matters. The Lviv governor Piotr Dunin Borkowski allegedly secured the votes of the Hasidim for Piłsudski's bloc in exchange for the delayed departure of a six o'clock train to Belzec. This was at the request of the Belzec rabbi, who was seeking to strengthen his authority with yet another miracle: a train that would not depart without him.[91]

Jews were not the only passengers who challenged the predominant expectations of the upper classes. The same Raczyński who was offended by "Jewish speculators" complained in 1923 about a peasant returning from America and sleeping in a first-class compartment, since "first class costs only two and half dollars he can afford it."[92] In March 1929 Raczyński paid 95 zloty for his first-class ride to Warsaw, while MPs entitled to ride for free filled the rest of the car. Raczyński's seat was next to the peasant deputy Józef Sanojca, who slept on both chairs and "stank impossibly of garlic and feet odour." Next morning Sanocja kept irritating Raczyński with "endless talk about politics, referring to Boleslaw the Brave and all the 'strong' kings."[93] That same year Raczyński found himself on the train with Wincenty Witos, the famous leader of the Peasant Party and premier of Poland. Raczyński described him as fairly intelligent, but could not hide his social resentment: Witos travelled first class while Raczyński was forced to take second for financial reasons.[94]

Jan Sudoł's memoirs allow us a glimpse into the mindset of those on the other side of the social divide. Sudoł became a frequent train traveller after his election to the Constitutional Diet in 1919. Riding in third class he realized that peasants, especially peasant women, "were denigrated, condescendingly seen as something worse only because they differed from the 'ladies' by clothing, language and manners."[95] This contrasted with his American experience, where all passengers were treated with equal respect.[96] Once, Sudoł and another peasant deputy entered the second-class compartment where three "gentlemen" sat. The deputies had no ties and wore moustaches and high bootlegs, as was the custom among peasant activists. Even though "relatively well dressed," they were immediately recognized as peasants. The gentlemen started harassing them verbally, certain that the peasants had entered second class by mistake. Sudoł played a dense peasant, apologized, and promised to leave at the next station. Since he did not leave as promised, the "gentlemen" requested the conductor check the peasants' tickets. When the conductor saw their MP cards, he saluted them instantly, while Sudoł enjoyed observing the "gentlemen's" faces.[97] Once, in 1920, Sudoł entered the first-class waiting hall in Lviv's terminal, but the porter asked him to leave. At first Sudoł ignored him, then showed his identification, but the porter "either did not understand what deputy meant, or was illiterate, or no longer cared about anything in his frenzy, but he continued shouting at me to leave the waiting room." Eventually the stationmaster came, apologized to Sudoł, and asked "to forgive that other guy, because he was a Ruthenian and illiterate."[98]

Inter-war encounters at the Lviv terminal revealed not only a shattering of the social hierarchy, but also the structural problems of Piłsudski's regime, where personal connections, not public offices, gave real power. In 1927 Raczyński witnessed "a funny scene at the train terminal, because governor Borkowski was running along the train asking where colonel Sławek was." Noting this scene down in his voluminous diaries, Raczyński expressed his longing for "those times when governors at the terminal, surrounded by the police chair, railway director and his grand retinue, majestically waited for distinguished guests (ministries, the leader of a state)."[99] Walery Sławek, the *éminence grise* in Piłsudski's coterie, officially held no governmental office. Later in the year Raczyński arrived in Lviv with a cabinet minister who complained that no one had met him, nor had he been seen off on departure.[100]

The terminal had a sufficient number of tracks to handle passenger traffic.[101] Freight was a different story. In the 1920s and 1930s the Lviv junction had five "freight stations." Lviv I was next to the former Chernivtsi terminal; Lviv II, behind the main terminal. The newer Lviv III was the wartime "Lviv-Russian" station. Lviv IV was west of the main terminal and north of the main westward line. Finally, there was Lviv-Pidzamche. Lviv IV became the junction's main marshalling yards.[102] According to projections, Lviv's population was expected to reach 404,500 by 1955, with more than four thousand freight cars handled daily.[103] The military also had growing demands for the junction's throughput capacity. Transit from western to eastern lines ideally should be able to bypass the junction's narrow neck leading to the main terminal.[104] Four proposals were prepared for the new marshalling yards as a solution to this problem. Three of them would have placed the new yards north of Lviv II, near Bilohorshcha (Białohorszcze), while the fourth would locate them closer to Lviv IV, north of Klepariv (Kleparów) passenger station.[105] The fourth proposal was eventually implemented, although not by the Polish authorities, for whom the costs of the project were prohibitive.[106]

Although Lviv still had very little large-scale industry, it was nearly as densely populated as industrial Łódź, with 96.3 and 102.9 people per hectare, Respectively, while Warsaw, the largest Polish city, had a similarly dense population of 96.9 per hectare. Krakow, with its 45.0 per hectare, and Vilnius, with its 18.7, although often compared to Lviv by historians, clearly were in a different league.

Even in the inter-war period Lviv remained, after Warsaw, Poland's most important intellectual centre judging from the number of periodicals published there.[107] Lviv's workers' neighbourhoods kept swelling, with the Krakow ward remaining the city's most populous.[108] In the 1930s the city tried to create wards more equal in population by raising their number from five to six, and later to nine – the mammoth Krakow ward was the first to split.[109] The Krakow and Zhovkva wards were still the city's poorest neighbourhoods. Apartment buildings there approached the railway tracks, and passengers leaving the station could indulge their voyeuristic side by "gazing into the blinking lights of gas lampposts on the streets ... running parallel to the tracks."[110] Public kitchens maintained by the city and philanthropic organizations, which had appeared during the First World War, continued operating in working-class neighbourhoods into the 1920s and 1930s.[111] These neighbourhoods also attracted social reformers and young socialists in search of the real working class.[112]

The roaring 1920s brought film, jazz, and radio to Lviv. A local radio comedy program helped to etch the image of Horodotska (Gródecka) Street as a neighbourhood of romantic hooligans in popular culture. The program featured two young men, Tońko and Szczepko, who stood for Lychakiv (Łyczaków) and Horodotska – thanks to local parish priests, these names were the most common in their respective neighbourhoods.[113] Both spoke the unique dialect of Lviv's streets and gently mocked their subculture.[114] The writers who tried to poetize new Lviv with its working-class neighbourhoods could not escape Horodotska either. It was in neighbourhoods like these that Ukrainian writers were most likely to find genuine urban Ukrainians, part and parcel of the city's lower classes.[115]

After the First World War, Archbishop Bilczewski continued his institutional crusade in the railway neighbourhoods. In 1921 a new parish church was founded in the workers' suburb of Levandivka (Lewandówka), designed, unsurprisingly, by Zaremba. In 1923, the year this church was finished, Bilczewski died.[116] Although, throughout the 1920s, the parish priest of St Elizabeth, Father Sigmunt, was "in a state of small-scale war with the railway workers' world,"[117] the Catholic Church was no longer the main adversary of socialist labour. Instead the main threat to the workers' movement came from the new state, born in war and claiming legitimacy because of a mystical bond with its people: the Polish nation. In its birth pangs this state faced two kinds of enemies: other nations making territorial claims, and Bolshevism, an insidious and therefore even more dangerous adversary that eroded the Polish nation from within. To be legitimate in the eyes of the state, labour had to separate itself clearly from the Bolsheviks. Those who harboured internationalist sentiments found themselves threatened with exclusion from institutionalized politics and the national public sphere.

The first years of Polish independence saw a spectacular increase in the intensity and number of railway workers' strikes. Warsaw, with its strong revolutionary tradition, took the lead, but although Warsaw's working class was experienced in street battles, Galicia's was the most unionized.[118] As early as December 1918 in Warsaw, delegates of the railway workers' unions had created the Trade Union of Railway Workers (*Związek Zawodowy Kolejarzy*, ZZK), co-founded by the former Galician socialist union.[119] The founding congress also witnessed the union's first split. The Union of Railway Officials left, since it was against joining the socialist Central Commission of Trade Unions.[120] Fractures only multiplied in the years to follow. In June 1919, in response to strikes, state authorities created the ZZK's main competitor, the Polish Union of Railwaymen (after 1929, the Union of Polish Railwaymen, (*Związek Kolejarzy Polskich*, ZKP).[121] All in all, over twenty railway unions came into existence during the inter-war period.

Lviv's railway workers went on strike in independent Poland first in November 1919 and again in 1920 and 1921.[122] These strikes were part of the revolutionary turmoil that rocked Poland in those years. These confrontations with railway workers posed an existential threat to the new state, and triggered immediate counteraction.[123] The most significant coordinated strike action of railway workers in inter-war Poland took place in 1923, and Lviv railway workers were an integral part of it.[124] Job action was accompanied by street demonstrations and physical confrontation with the authorities. Horodotska (Gródecka) Street, between the railway housing project and the union headquarters, was a major arena of this confrontation. Store and tram windows were broken, and a rifle and sabre were wrestled from the police.[125] The state learned its lessons from those conflicts with restless railway workers, responding with layoffs, arrests, and the splintering of unions. Even workers loyal to the state fell victim.[126] Using experience gained in the First World War, the army prepared contingency plans to deal with strikes – in cooperation with the railway administration, it was prepared to take over essential services, such as signalling and the operation of locomotives and switches, to secure uninterrupted movement.[127] New unions nevertheless continued to proliferate, and the ZZK's membership declined precipitously from nearly 93,000 in 1920 to fewer than 59,000 in 1924, with a slight increase to 67,000 in 1926.[128] The state of the railway unions was symptomatic of a more general trend: in 1924 socialist unions claimed only a third of Poland's total union membership, and in 1925 the ZZK, although still the largest railway union, accounted for less than half of unionized railway workers.[129]

A coup in 1926 by Piłsudski was supported by the Polish Socialist Party (*Polska Partia Socjalistyczna*, PPS) and allied unions because of Piłsudski's socialist past. In Lviv, just as in the rest of Poland, socialists who supported the coup in the streets in violent clashes with the National Democrats eventually found themselves in opposition to Piłsudski's "Sanation" (*Sanacja*, or healing) regime.[130] They protested "Sanation's" antiparliamentarism and its offensive against municipal self-government, which subordinated the latter to the executive authorities and curtailed its jurisdiction. In 1928 and 1929 socialists were dismissed from city and occupational insurance boards throughout Poland, Lviv being no exception.[131]

The position of socialists in Lviv weakened. The pre-war socialist leaders were replaced by people who lacked their intellectual or organizational abilities. Socialist intellectuals abandoned their favourite café in the Mikolasch arcade, which was taken over by the liberals.[132] Even in his personal life, the inter-war leader of Lviv's Polish socialists suffered a loss that eerily paralleled the misfortunes of his party: Jan Szczyrek's wife abandoned him, and married the commandant of the infamous Brest camp, where political enemies of the "Sanation" were held.[133]

The bleeding of socialist unions continued under the "Sanation" regime. Former Galician socialist Jędrzej Moraczewski contributed to it with his pro-Sanation Union of Trade Unions. His supporters split from the ZZK and created the Federation of Polish Railwaymen,[134] and the ZZK's membership continued to decline, from sixty thousand in 1928 to forty thousand in 1933.[135] The reform of the Polish railways contributed to the decline. In 1926 the railway became an independent state enterprise that could no longer draw freely on the state budget. This "commercialization," with an emphasis on profitability was fully implemented in 1930,[136] resulting in extensive layoffs.

The government justified its anti-union policies by the need for national solidarity in the face of existential threats to the Polish nation. Militarism was pervasive. The nation prepared for war and demonized its enemies. As early as 1921, Polish posters in train stations depicting the enemy aesthetically were replicas of militant Soviet posters, the only difference being the reversal of roles of heroes and villains.[137] Both states also shared a propensity for acronyms that multiplied with uncanny speed. In the 1930s those tendencies only strengthened. In 1934 membership in a militarized organization founded in 1927 – the Railway Military Preparation (*Kolejowe Przysposobienie Wojskowe*, KPW) – became mandatory for all railwaymen. In the best of paternalistic traditions, a parallel organization, "Railway Family," was created for workers' and officials' families.[138] Thanks to mandatory membership, the KPW became the largest railway association.

The role of railway workers declined both in the socialist movement and in society at large. The First World War had seriously compromised the image of the railway system as a well-functioning, meritocratic mechanism. By the early 1920s public resentment towards the privileged "caste" of railway men was commonplace. Some railway officials did indeed use their positions for illicit private gain. Stationmasters took bribes from merchants to despatch their freight on time; they could orchestrate not only delays but also the disappearance of freight from unguarded tracks.[139] Others, however, were unjustly slandered, as happened in the Lviv suburb of Sykhiv (Sichów), where a local priest accused the stationmaster of speculation and private use of railway labour.[140]

Just as before the war, the most scandalous instances of corruption occurred in the ranks of senior management. Karol Barwicz, Lviv's railway director since 1918, was moved over his objections to Krakow in 1925,[141] while Paweł Prachtel-Morawiański moved from Krakow to Lviv. Three years later, one of the great embezzlement scandals of the Second Republic – "a railway Panama" – erupted in Lviv. At its centre was the engineer Władysław Pawłowicz, who had come from the Russian partition and claimed to have lost his engineering diploma during the war. He rose to the head of the supplies department nonetheless and purchased extensive real estate in the prestigious "New World" neighbourhoods. The investigation triggered by his conspicuous lifestyle showed that he had taken payoffs from suppliers on every railway contract. Altogether, he had embezzled roughly 250,000 zloty.[142] In May 1928, "the whole of Lviv talked only about railway frauds ... There is a general depression, everyone despairs because it happened specifically in Lviv."[143] Corruption is notoriously hard to measure: was the new Polish railway more corrupt than the old Galician railway? In a private conversation, Kazimierz Bartel himself assured Raczyński that, "every railwayman steals, and not only in ours, but in all the states."[144] In Bartel's view the scandal had been blown out of proportion to compromise him personally. Public perception, however, was definitely not in favour of the Polish railways.

On top of the scandal, the winter of 1928–29 proved especially harsh. Temperatures dropped to −40 C in February, and cut off the city from the outside world. In February the weather accomplished something the Ukrainian forces failed to do in the winter of 1918–19: freeze both train and telegraph connections.[145] Lviv suffered from a lack of coal, and it took the railway four weeks to resume normal operations.[146] Artur Hausner blamed the government for investing too little in eastern borderland railway infrastructure. He argued that handsome profits made on the railway in 1926–27 had gone mostly to the Silesia–Gdynia railway corridor, which served Poland's heavy industry or, in Hausner's words, its "coal barons." The connection between Lviv and Warsaw remained "scandalous."[147]

The criticism was not entirely justified. Polish railways performed well in the inter-war years, especially taking into account the economic and infrastructural disaster inherited after the First World War, together with three different railway systems. Poland was making modern high-speed locomotives and building new lines, and average speeds increased steadily. A direct connection between Lviv and Warsaw was created. In the 1930s express trains on first-category routes, such as Lviv–Stanisławów (Stanislau, today Ivano-Frankivsk), Lviv–Przemyśl, and Lviv–Warsaw had a normal running speed (excluding stops and braking) of a hundred kilometres an hour. On second-category lines, such as Lviv–Sambir, passenger trains ran at eighty kilometres an hour, and on third-category, which included all other lines, at fifty.[148] Moreover, in the 1930s, so-called *luxtorpedos*, or superfast first-class single cars, appeared in Lviv. Streamlined, and equipped with diesel engines and rubberized wheels, these cars were capable of 120–130 kilometres an hour. Their commercial speed (with stops) was seventy-five kilometres an hour for the Lviv–Boryslav (Borysław) route, which served the resort town of Truskavets (Truskawiec), and ninety-three on the Lviv–Kolomyia route.[149] When it came to the development of the railway network, labour productivity, and capital returns, Polish railways were among the most efficient in Europe.

These achievements, however, could not placate the public. The railway was no longer a cutting-edge transportation technology. It faced competition from road transport in convenience and from aviation in speed. The railway became a convenient scapegoat, on which a number of inter-war Poland's anxieties converged. Frustrations with inefficient paternalistic government, where personal connections often mattered more than merit, and Poland's relative economic backwardness were projected upon the railway. Senior railway officials and regular railway workers felt the consequences. One of them complained that "the importance of the railway service and thus of the railway workers, is underestimated. Moreover, it is likely that they are maltreated ... Everyone reads about the abuses by railway workers and various railway frauds. But does it mean that every worker in the railway service should be treated as a potential criminal?"[150] The public was now easily irritated by the perceived impertinence of railway officials. Raczyński dutifully noted down his own altercations with railway officials in the summer of 1928.[151] Similar conflicts pepper sources from the inter-war period. Railway officials were often just as frustrated with groundless abuse, especially from those in power.[152]

In Lviv the problems of inter-war Poland were further complicated by the legacy of the Ukrainian-Polish war. The offices of a short-lived Ukrainian union of railway workers on Horodotska (Gródecka) Street had been destroyed by Polish troops in November 1918.[153] Mykola Hankevych, a Lvivite and leading Ukrainian Social Democrats, never came to terms with it. During the war he even joined the temporary Polish City Council, where he became the most eloquent defender of the city's Jewish population in the wake of the 1918 pogrom. Frustrated with an aggressive Polish nationalism, he stepped down from this, his last prominent public role, in February 1919. Estranged from his own

Ukrainian Social Democratic Party, with the pre-1914 internationalist cooperation in shambles, Hankevych became a marginal figure in local socialist politics.

Polish right-wing socialists earned solid patriotic credentials during the war, and became part of the political establishment in Warsaw. The defence of the Polish nation from external enemies became common ground between them and their erstwhile political opponents. Even Zofia Romaniczówna, whose attitudes were shaped in a mid-nineteenth-century patriotic middle-class milieu, now confessed her fondness for Adam Kuryłowicz, a PPS MP, one of the organizers of the anti-Brest railway strike in 1918, and a veteran of the Ukrainian-Polish war in Lviv.[154]

Since Lviv was now on the front line of the national conflict, even patriotic socialism was losing ground to aggressive nationalism. Lviv witnessed antisemitic and anti-Ukrainian pogroms, as well as assassination attempts organized by the clandestine Ukrainian Military Organization and its successor, the OUN. Anti-Jewish violence picked up after Piłsudski's death. Before the First World War, the polytechnic had been a socialist fortress, much redder than the university.[155] It sent interns to railway workshops, while some engineers saw themselves as an intellectual subspecies of the proletariat.[156] Brotherly Aid, the polytechnic's student association, had been dominated by socialists since 1906.[157] In the 1920s Brotherly Aid became National Democratic, while the polytechnic turned into an arena of violent attacks against Jews. The violence culminated in 1938–39 with the murder of six Jewish students by the nationalists.[158]

Only one party in Lviv remained truly internationalist: the Communist Party of Western Ukraine (*Komunistychna partiia Zakhidnoï Ukraïny*, KPZU). It united Poles, Jews, and Ukrainians until it was disbanded by the Stalin-controlled Comintern in 1938 together with the Communist Party of Poland (*Komunistyczna Partia Polski*, KPP), of which it formed an autonomous part. The KPZU had suffered a serious blow as early as 1928, when its majority was accused of Ukrainian "national deviation" and expelled from the Comintern. The Communist Party was not especially strong among the railway workers: former members recalled that there were only five or six communist cells in Lviv's railway workshops and depots in the 1920s,[159] with no more than five members each.[160] In the mainstream PPS, railway workers remained an important group, accounting for about 12 per cent of the activists, second only to the metal or machine workers and miners.[161] In the KPP, in contrast, transportation workers accounted for meagre 0.2 per cent of the membership.[162] Even though railway workers were a tiny minority among the communists, they were the most unionized group among them.[163]

The terminal saw its share of communist agitation and anti-communist police action. In August 1924 a "Communist agitator," a local cobbler's apprentice, was arrested there and later sentenced to ten years' hard labour.[164] The same month a distributor of illegal communist papers was caught at the terminal.[165] Although the terminal was a place of strengthened police presence and periodic document checkups, in 1931 communist activists managed to hang a banner, "Down with War!" on the terminal building itself.[166] The communists had secret flats in the neighbourhood, too. One was at Horodotska (Gródecka) 95,[167] near the former union headquarters, and another was at Janowska (Shevchenko) 1.[168]

Tiny islands of genuine internationalism also existed outside of formal party structures. The intellectual milieu of the literary monthly *Sygnały* (Signals) brought together Polish, Jewish, and Ukrainian writers.[169] Another informal hub for leftist internationalist intellectuals in Lviv was in the apartments and studio of the photographer Wanda Diamand.[170] Many regulars from all three of the city's main ethnic groups left for the Spanish Civil War to fight as volunteers on the republican side.[171]

Although fractured and bled by national conflicts, Lviv remained one of the most internationalist and leftist cities of inter-war Poland – or at least Lvivites at both ends of the political spectrum believed so. Wiktor Chajes, a banker and deputy major, observed during the 1927 congress of Sokol, the physical education movement, that, "by and large we do not see any enthusiasm in the city. During the war the Sokol went a bit to the right, and Lviv is still always red."[172] Bronisław Łotocki claimed that "the Lviv workers' movement can boast that on the territory that was back then Poland, it moved furthest in the direction of the united front."[173]

In Lviv cooperation between communist sympathisers and leftist socialists predated the Comintern's anti-fascist policy of 1934–39. Polish, Ukrainian, and Jewish socialists (both Zionists and anti-Zionists) and communists still organized joint May Day demonstrations in the 1920s.[174] Some activists of the mainstream PPS exhibited antisemitism – Artur Hausner in particular worked in Lviv towards "the elimination [of Jews] from the positions of influence within the party."[175] The left faction of PPS, however, formed in Lviv in 1927,[176] was open to Jews and Ukrainians, and cooperated with crypto-communist organizations.[177] PPS-left was organized around Jan Szczyrek, who started Lviv's new socialist newspaper, *Trybuna Robotnicza* (Workers' Tribune), in 1934.[178] The final break between Lviv's right and left PPS factions took place in 1936.

This was the year when Lviv witnessed one of the greatest social explosions and the bloodiest police massacre in its history. Just as in 1901, weakened union and socialist organizations played only secondary roles in these events. The main actors in this social drama were again the unemployed. "Commercialized" state railways had contributed to unemployment by laying off forty thousand railway workers nationwide over a twelve-month period in 1929 and 1930.[179] Lviv may have been the third-largest and a very densely built Polish city, but it was also the poorest: in 1936, 45 per cent of Lviv taxpayers belonged to the bottom bracket, compared with 43 in Vilnius, 39 in Krakow, and 37 per cent in Poznań. Only 1.34 per cent of Lviv taxpayers were in the three top income brackets, compared with 2.11 in Vilnius, 2.65 in Krakow, and 3.16 in Poznań.[180] In spring 1936 the expected seasonal reawakening of the job market did not materialize, and there were strikes and demonstrations.[181] On 14 April the police shot dead a protester, Władysław Kozak.[182] For Kozak's burial, workers insisted on the Ianivsky (Janowski) cemetery, even though the remains were in a morgue by the Lychakiv (Łyczaków) cemetery, and the authorities had ordered the funeral to take place there. The issue was not only that the Ianivsky cemetery was a proletarian cemetery, but also that the funeral procession there would turn into a march through the whole city. The authorities forbade the march, but the funeral committee decided to carry it through.[183] The itinerary of Kozak's funeral procession became a geographic reversal of the patriotic reburials when remains were usually carried from the train terminal to the pantheon at the Lychakiv cemetery. Kozak's body was taken from the prestigious Lychakiv to the working-class Ianivsky cemetery – to the neighbourhood of railway depots, workshops, and warehouses. It was the cemetery of the poor and discriminated, forming essentially a single necropolis with the adjacent new Jewish cemetery and containing the main field of the Ukrainian military burials from the 1918–19 war.

The police turned the funeral procession into a massacre. The fiercest street battles were fought on Kazimierzska, today a section of Horodotska (Gródecka), where barricades were raised and tram cars overturned.[184] Kozak's home was nearby too.[185] Although Horodotska was not on the route of the burial procession, it saw its share of heavy fighting on the stretch from St Elizabeth Church to Kazimierzska. This stretch, with its eight barricades that stopped the police, turned Horodotska into the most barricaded street in Lviv.[186] Organized workers of the Horodotska ward picked up the casket near St Anna, accompanied by railwaymen from the workshops, coalers from the freight yards, and workers from the munitions factory.[187] They carried it along Janowska

(Shevchenko) relatively peacefully, crossing through the heart of the workers' neighbourhoods.

The number of casualties on that day was unprecedented, as was the workers' determination to continue with the procession despite the mounting numbers of wounded and killed.[188] The lowest estimate gave eighteen people killed and close to a hundred wounded; sixty-nine policemen were also injured.[189] The left claimed that thirty-one marchers were shot dead during the demonstration itself, and rumours claimed there were sixty-eight corpses altogether.[190]

In the wake of the massacre, Lviv's workers' groups managed to overcome disagreements and organized a general strike on 20 April.[191] Then, the May Day demonstration turned into a massive manifestation of solidarity, with papers estimating the number of participants at thirty to forty thousand.[192] For the first time, Lviv workers came to the May Day events armed with clubs. The police did not dare touch the participants, but nationalist students attacked a column of railway workers marching from their gathering point on Horodotska (Gródecka) to Gosiewski Square (today Tershakivtsiv Street), where the main rally was held. Nationalist hooligans also attacked near the polytechnic, but were badly beaten and had to retreat.[193]

For the authorities, the events of April were proof the PPS had lost whatever influence it had among Lviv's workers and that the People's Front was rallying support.[194] In June 1936 the PPS central executive decided to cleanse its Lviv organization of leftists, and authorized Hausner to reconstitute it. Szczyrek was expelled from the party. Maria Kelles-Krauz, a widow of the prominent Marxist thinker Kazimierz, was in Szczyrek's group among the united front's supporters.[195] Archbishop Sheptytsky also sensed the danger of the broader leftist alliance, and in summer 1936 warned his Ukrainian flock that "those who help Communists ... betray the Church ... Those who help Communists with their plans of the so-called people's front with Socialists and Radicals betray their people ... betray the cause of the poor, suffering and wronged in the whole world."[196]

Even before Kozak's murder, Lviv had been chosen as the seat of Poland's Anti-Fascist Congress of Cultural Workers. Although Warsaw had an even greater number of leftist intellectuals, it had nothing comparable to Lviv's *Sygnały* magazine. Lviv was also the only city in Poland where an alliance between socialists and communists seemed to work. The congress opened in the barely finished red-brick building of the municipal workers' union. This "red fortress"[197] stood by the railway track approaching Pidzamche station from the city. The choice of building for the congress was no accident: during the inter-war period, municipal workers replaced railway workers as the backbone of the local socialist movement. The relative weight of railway labour was declining as well, with city infrastructure expanding more than that of the railway. The city, in fact, became Lviv's leading employer,[198] although the railway workshops, with their eighteen hundred employees at the end of the 1930s, remained Lviv's largest enterprise.[199] All in all, railwaymen and their families constituted little more than 5 per cent of the city's total population by the start of the Second World War.[200]

A similar change was occurring all over Poland. As one railwayman observed: "There is no doubt that the social position of railway workers is lower today."[201] He also commented on the rising prestige of municipal workers. At the end of the nineteenth century, railway workshops had served as a window into the world of modern technology and industrial labour, but in the early 1920s engineer Edmund Romer recalled his disappointment as an intern with Lviv's workshops. Even in their most sophisticated part, the engines' section, "the workshops had almost no mechanized instruments, everything hinged on the skill, strength and persistence of artisans." The workers' lifestyle appeared anachronistic too: only one worker was commuting to work by bicycle, while even village youth by then had mastered bikes.[202] City enterprises, electrical works, and new tramway and trolley depots were more modern by comparison.

After the First World War, the ZZK left its old neighbourhood and moved down the street to Horodotska (Gródecka) 69. The heart of the railway neighbourhood was now occupied by the rival Federation of Polish Railwaymen, with offices in the Sokol building at Kętrzyński (Fedkovych) Street 32; the Sokol premises were also used for the federation's social events in cooperation with St Elizabeth parish.[203] The KPW held its events, including national congresses, in its own theatre on Foch Alley, next to the railway school.[204] Since the new ZZK premises were too small to accommodate large gatherings, even socialist meetings took place in the Sokol building.[205]

The ZZK remained the most influential railway union in Lviv. When Moraczewski tried to organize his syndicalist alternative, he could not find much support in the city.[206] The best monument to the ZZK's perseverance was its own Bauhaus building, finally completed in 1938 (Figure 3.9). Eclipsing the Sokol hall on the same street, the building was designed by Romuald Miller, known for his leftist sympathies and opposition to the "Sanation." Miller also designed ZZK's central headquarters in Warsaw.[207] Zaremba oversaw the building's actual construction. The new premises immediately became a centre for the social and cultural life of the railway workers. The premises featured a large library,[208] a modern cinema called the Roxy, and even ping-pong tables – the game was Lviv's last pre-war craze.[209]

The railway and municipal workers' unions were the only unions that managed to construct buildings of their own in inter-war Lviv. Although the municipal workers' building became a focal point for organized labour in the former Zhovkva ward, the railway workers' building served the same role in the former Krakow ward, especially its upper part, the new Horodok ward.[210] In 1934 the Workers' Sports Club finished a large sports complex at Bohdanivka (Bogdanówka), near Horodotska's (Gródecka's) former tollgate.[211] Evicted from the vicinity of St Elizabeth Church, the centre of organized labour's activities in the railway neighbourhood moved along the Horodotska axis farther away from the city centre.

The railway workers, however, remained the wage earners about whom the state was concerned most. Security concerns were at the forefront, but they were not the only ones. Many believed that, to survive, the Polish state had to modernize both its economy and society. The two social groups crucial to the success of this project were workers and engineers.[212] Although global flows of capital set limits to economic modernization under the capitalist system of production, relatively cheap experiments in the modern organization of work proliferated. Railway workers were subjected to detailed medical scrutiny, with ever-expanding disabilities classifications.[213] Psychometrics was recognized as a science, psychometric institutions were created, and psychometric testing introduced in all railway occupations connected with movement (dispatchers, engine drivers, conductors, and switchmen.[214]

The crudest, but at the same time easiest method of "improving" the social body of railway labour was to purge potentially unreliable elements. For a national state that equated ethnicity with loyalty, occupational ethnic cleansing was an obvious way to create a more loyal body of workers in a strategically important occupation. Already in 1919–20, thousands of workers, overwhelmingly Ukrainians and Jews, had been suspended from work[215] and eventually lost their jobs, seven hundred of them in Lviv alone.[216] In support of those workers, in 1922 Lviv's ZZK passed a resolution demanding the free acceptance of Jews into the public service in "Eastern Little Poland," the newly invented name for the former eastern Galicia.[217] Despite ethnic purges, the Lviv directorate in the 1930s still had the highest number of "PKP employees of foreign nationality" – once again Jews and Ukrainians. There were still 992 of them in Lviv at the beginning of 1936, and 851 a year later, after yet another purge. By comparison, directorates in Vilnius, Warsaw, and Radom had fewer than two hundred each. The majority of the "foreigners" worked as switchmen, brakemen, shunters, and car inspectors.[218] In a region where such "foreigners" were the majority, they accounted for less than 5 per cent of railway workers. Polish authorities nevertheless were concerned by these ridiculously low numbers.[219] Even on the eve of war, when the railway was almost purely Polish, the ministry still perceived the few remaining non-Polish employees as a serious threat.[220] Both employees and supplying firms were checked regarding the nationality of their directors. Security forces compiled blacklists of mostly Jewish Lviv firms.[221] Eventually the nationality of shareholders was also checked, since "Jewish capital" allegedly hid behind Christian frontmen.[222]

The fear of war and OUN sabotage contributed to the heightened security concerns in the 1930s. In 1927 four youngsters, including Roman Shukhevych, future commander of the Ukrainian Insurgent Army, were caught with cameras and notes near the military airfield behind the terminal.[223] There were also alleged acts of sabotage in Lviv at switchpoints and arson of stations and warehouses.[224] The Ministry of Interior prepared anti-sabotage plans for the railways and enacted them periodically.[225] Trial bomb alarms were practised from time to time at the Lviv terminal,[226] and bomb shelters were built in the vicinity of train stations.[227] The frequency of sabotage allegedly increased spectacularly in 1935 and 1936, with 136 and 150 incidents each year, respectively, compared with only 46 in 1934.[228] Almost half of these incidents occurred in the Lviv directorate.[229] This increase had more to do with the authorities' fears and expectations in the wake of Piłsudski's death than with some coordinated action of the Ukrainian underground. Such "sabotage" was often difficult to distinguish from hooliganism: broken train windows, cartridges placed on rails, stolen spikes – although, in former Galicia, hooliganism could also be politically motivated.[230] In any case, even during peaks of alleged sabotage, the absolute majority of railway accidents occurred because of employees' mistakes and defective infrastructure.[231]

The first professional group of saboteurs was caught in Lviv at the end of July 1939, and it was German. Its tasks were to blow up switchpoints at the main terminal and railway administration offices, set the main freight yards on fire, damage the power plant, and cut off communication lines.[232] Germany also sent across the border armed and trained groups of Ukrainian diversionists.[233] By summer 1939 the railway had fully stocked its warehouses and increased the throughput capacity of its main lines. Its fleet of engines and cars was repaired, while the remaining Ukrainian and German workers were being laid off and placed under police surveillance. The military itself was mining railway infrastructure, preparing for possible retreat.[234] Just as in summer 1914, in summer 1939 Lviv expected war.

Even though Polish statehood was barely two decades old, the changes it had brought were profound. The pre-1914 generation saw them as extremely menacing. Both Diamand and former Galician Polish Social Democratic Party leader Ignacy Daszyński, who in the meantime had drifted apart, saw inter-war developments as a great tragedy for Poland and complained that there was no one to replace their passing generation.[235] Wiktor Chajes, although no socialist, had an equally gloomy view of global and local developments.[236] Żuławski, the leader of the socialist trade unions, shared this pessimism and observed "dictatorial tendencies" across all political camps.[237]

Diamand and Daszyński had their casual conversation about the passing generation in 1929. Diamand died in 1931, as did Lviv's Jewish socialist Rafał Buber and Ukrainian socialist Mykola Hankevych. Daszyński passed away in 1936, followed by Kazimierz Kaczanowski, the editor of *Kolejarz*. Ukrainian socialist Semen Vityk was executed in a Soviet prison in 1937. It was not only the socialists. Teobald Orkasiewicz, a sculptor who worked on the terminal's interior in 1904, died in 1933 and was buried in the Ianivsky (Janowski) cemetery.[238] The sculptor Petro Viitovych (Piotr Wójtowicz) died in either 1936 or 1938 in the poor artists' shelter near St Elizabeth's and most likely was also buried in the Ianivsky.[239] Alfred Zachariewicz died in 1937,[240] and Władysław Sadłowski in 1940. Some survivors, such as Jan Szczyrek and Zygmunt Żuławski, would die in the late 1940s. As its bearers passed away, the institutional culture of Austrian Galicia disintegrated. As Henryk Wereszycki remarked, for the generation of Polish politicians and intellectuals formed in the pre–First World War world, the Second World War was their last collective appearance in significant public roles.[241] Many, if not most, would perish at the hands of Nazis and Soviets. The post–Second World War political and intellectual leadership was shaped by war and, in peacetime, by the realities of inter-war Poland. Those realities, however, offered no taste of either a functioning democracy or the rule of law.

Chapter Six

The Catastrophe

The 1920s and 1930s passed in the shadow of war. Lviv had faced war for seven years (1914–21), and now a new war was a distinct possibility, and independent Poland was actively preparing for it. By 1938 the menacing international situation convinced many that war was imminent.[1] At the end of August 1939, all doubts were cast aside. At the main terminal, troops were boarding trains heading west.[2] What came as a surprise was the speed with which fighting reached the city. The Luftwaffe bombed Lviv on the first day of war, 1 September. German planes targeted the main train station, the city's most important strategic object, wreaking havoc and causing panic.[3] Just as twenty years ago, the spires of St Elizabeth served as a reliable point of orientation, helping the Germans bomb with precision even in overcast skies.[4] In less than two weeks, German artillery joined aviation, turning the pyramidal roofs of St Elizabeth into charred skeletons. By then Horodotska (Gródecka), the city's westward entryway, was crisscrossed with barricades, while columns of smoke billowed over the train terminal.[5] Only one German detachment managed to reach the terminal, but it had to withdraw when the city surrendered to the Red Army.[6] The Soviet invasion of 17 September came to most Lvivites as an unexpected blow that sealed Poland's fate.

During the campaign, passenger traffic and civilian shipments were suspended, and only goods vital to the war effort were allowed.[7] The public doubled its vigilance in hunting down spies and saboteurs. In an eerie echo of the Stalinist campaign against "wreckers," technicians and engineers, including polytechnic students, became prime suspects.[8] Lviv's small German population had been well represented in the technical professions since at least 1860, when a small colony of German railway workers settled in the city.[9] In August 1939 the public watched with suspicion as they congregated at St Elizabeth, their parish church, wearing white stockings and socks and wide trousers – their customary Sunday clothes.[10] According to the 1931 Polish census, 2,448 Lvivites acknowledged German as their native tongue.[11] Once the repatriations of ethnic Germans from Soviet Western Ukraine to Germany started, 7,563 Lvivites registered as German. The Germans claimed that as many as thirteen thousand left the city.[12]

After the Polish capitulation, Lviv went through a brief interregnum. Just as in 1914, 1915, and 1918, Lvivites helped themselves to the supplies in the railway warehouses. At the Klepariv station, freight trains stood fully loaded with food and equipment. Nothing was guarded, and people took as much as they could.[13] Their main concern was coal, necessary for cooking and heating. Even a tiny apartment required hundreds of kilograms a month in winter.[14] From the railway yards, "coal was carried in baskets, in buckets, in bags, wash tubs, skirts, in old torn carpets, drawn in carts, wheelbarrows and prams."[15] Only once the Soviet military took over the stations and warehouses did the looting stop.

Western Ukraine was incorporated into the Soviet Union as an integral part of the Soviet state. Former eastern Galicia, together with Volhynia, became part of the Ukrainian Soviet Socialist Republic. The railway was integrated into the Soviet network, administratively divided into "railroads." Galician railway lines became the Lviv Railroad. Soviet authorities decided to change the Galician tracks to the broader Soviet gauge inherited from the Russian Empire. This regauging, however, was drawn out because of a shortage of funds. The double-tracked Pidvolochysk–Lviv–Przemyśl section was regauged first, at the end of 1940, as the main line providing access through Lviv to the Soviet Union's new western border.[16]

Changing gauges was but one element in the mammoth reconstruction needed to bring Polish infrastructure up to Soviet standards. Regauging aside, 24.3 million rubles was allocated in 1939 for works on the former Polish railway system. The People's Commissariat of Communications (*Narodnyi Kommisariat Putei Soobshcheniia*, NKPS) asked the government for an additional 66 million,[17] and the government obliged, even though the rest of the ministry's budget suffered serious cuts.[18]

The NKPS proceeded slowly, according to the seven-year plan adopted for the reconstruction of the western railroads and totalling 10 billion rubles.[19] The slow pace was a serious concern for the Soviet military command – Georgii Zhukov, chief of the general staff, had noted repeatedly that the throughput capacity of the German railway at the border was several times higher than that of the Soviet Union.

In February 1941 the government heeded him and reassigned three military railway brigades from the Far East to the reconstruction of western railroads.[20] The urgency was so great that the brigades started work even before the blueprints arrived.[21] The Lviv junction itself needed reconstruction, its eastern necks had seen no heavy traffic in the 1920s and 1930s, but now were expected to let through thousands of "special trains" rolling towards the new border.[22] The NKPS was also ordered to finish regauging all newly acquired western railroads,[23] a task it completed by 19 May 1941.[24]

Soviet standards were applied both to the material part of the Lviv Railroad and equally to its human component. Just as in the First World War, employees from other railroads were mobilized to operate the newly acquired lines. This time the network was much larger, the occupation more permanent, and local workers had nowhere to go. As in the First World War, there were complaints about the quality of labour received from other railroads.[25] In Lviv most engine drivers were importees who had not worked in this capacity for their home railroads. This explained a very high number of accidents and poor locomotive performance.[26] There were also problems with discipline. For the newcomers, Western Ukraine, with its capitalist abundance of consumer goods and institutions in transition, offered many temptations. In 1940 forty senior accountants of the Lviv Railroad, all of them pre-1939 Soviet citizens, had either been arrested, sentenced, or were on the run in relation to charges of fraud and embezzlement.[27]

Misbehaving newcomers from the east, however, were not the main concern of the new railroad. In September 1939 it inherited 23,504 employees from the Lviv Regional Directorate of State Railways. By 1 January 1940, 1,572 of these had been fired. Then, after "Iron Narkom" [People's Commissar of the Routes of Communications] Lazar Kaganovich reproached the Lviv Railroad for lack of vigilance, 12,022 more people were "purged." In the course of just a year, the ratio of Poles to non-Poles in the Railroad's employ was reversed. Now there were 2,355 Russians, 20,370 Ukrainians, 1,579 Jews, and only 507 Poles among its 29,570 employees. Of these, 28,237 had been hired in 1940.[28] Although some Polish railway workers might have posed as Ukrainians, many railway employees were not only fired but deported to special settlements in the USSR's sparsely populated and inhospitable interior.

At the Lviv junction the Soviets created the Lviv-Passenger and the Lviv-Freight stations, with 401 and 923 employees, respectively. Lviv-Klepariv was the third largest, followed by Lviv-Pidzamche. In total there were now 8,770 railway employees in Lviv – a very large increase of at least three thousand since August 1939, and more proof of low Soviet labour productivity.[29] When Kaganovich's plenipotentiary visited the Lviv Railroad in June 1940, he was appalled by its state.[30] The Railroad's managers blamed the lack of resources at their disposal, but the plenipotentiary insisted that the real problem was poor planning and the abysmal organization of work.[31] These disagreements notwithstanding, both parties saw locals in the workforce as a major impediment.

Although the locals were blamed for the Railroad's shortcomings, they were absent among its senior and middle officials. Even local Poles, who complained that Ukrainians had replaced them in the Lviv Railroad headquarters, acknowledged that their replacements were "imported" Soviet Ukrainians.[32] The Soviet purge of the railway workforce had opened employment opportunities for local villagers and the urban poor, but these workers no longer had independent associations of their own and no means to articulate an independent opinion or take independent action. Their "union" was part of the institutional machinery of the Soviet state.

The well-being of the average worker did not improve. Lviv became accustomed to long Soviet-style lines in front of the few remaining grocery stores. The nationalization of all trade was accompanied by the drastic reduction of retail outlets: four-fifths of all the pre-war stores disappeared.[33] Prices became "unbearable" even for basic consumables.[34] The currency exchange robbed locals of their savings. Aleksander Wat (Aleksander Chwat), a Warsaw-born Polish writer who moved to Soviet-occupied Lviv in 1939, witnessed workers in the city "fainting from hunger," and testified to "the incredible blossoming of speculation," Lvivites traded valuables, clothing, kitchenware, and other material "riches" for food and Soviet currency.[35] Hugo Steinhaus observed that the Soviet regime also dealt a heavy psychological blow to the workers, who, "during the Polish period, could at least condemn capitalists and explain their own misery by the capitalist taking a lion share of the earnings due to them." Now there were no capitalists, "but they were still sitting in basements, ate potatoes with cabbage, and could not afford boots for their children."[36]

Aleksander Wat recalled his prison mate, a local railway worker, who kept addressing his guards as "comrades," while they would remind him every time that "a Siberian wolf's your comrade."[37] It took some time for former socialists to realize that neither a working-class background nor leftist affiliations guaranteed sympathy or safety – only unquestionable loyalty to the new state and obedience to the authorities.

Lviv's railway workers voiced their discontent in private conservations. An informer working for the NKVD (*Narodnyi Kommisariat*

Vnutrennikh Del, People's Commissariat of Internal Affairs) denounced engine driver Stanisław Mark, who refused to use "Lunin's method" – named after Nikolai Lunin, the Stakhanov of Soviet engine drivers. Lunin had started doing maintenance and light repairs on the engines himself, but Mark, who had worked as a mechanic for fifteen years, allegedly said this was a mechanic's job, not an engine driver's. A mechanic from the depot supported him: "If all the engine drivers will be repairing their engines, what would we do?"[38] Some denunciations reported "nationalist talk,"[39] but most complaints were about terrible living and working conditions. One junior conductor reportedly said, "No matter how much we work, soon we and our families will die." A depot's janitor echoed this sentiment: "We are paid little, barely enough for bread and water. We'll wear out Polish clothes and will be going around naked, while we are forced to work hard."[40]

The middle classes resented Soviet power even more. Even in Soviet rhetoric they were alien to the new society. Their complaints were not only about living standards, but also about the city's public space, both associational and material. While the state funded work on the tracks, the terminal remained in half-ruins. In her biographical novel *Buria nad L'vovom* (Storm over Lviv), Maria Strutynska describes the building:

> The whole front of the building is in ruins, amidst the heap of debris, straps of concrete stick out, and behind them, inside, twisted tin frames of the glass roof of a gigantic hangar ... Now the rails lead only east, to Kyiv, Moscow, Siberia, to the East, where Ukraine, dreamed about since childhood, is ... [she] peeks through the large gap, where a wall used to be, the ruined hall of the first class restaurant. Caryatides with the beaten off heads, stucco spatters from the walls, and in the middle of the ceiling – convulsively bent shoulders of a hanging bronze chandelier.
>
> Inside, the former second class waiting room is beyond recognition, its wall-wide window nailed with boards. In a corner, next to the doors a low masonry stove, on which a beggar in rugs squats. An old woman and a boy warm their hands near its red glowing leaf.
>
> Along the walls, on the benches, muffled women, men with their feet in straw shoes and children sleep on the bags. The floor is covered with cigarette butts, stench and smoke.[41]

Soviet poverty was striking, even in a city that by Western European standards had hardly been prosperous before 1939. Since poverty was accompanied by the apparent renunciation of beauty and propriety as understood in inter-war Poland, civilizational explanations with racial overtones resurfaced. Some blamed "Asiatic" Russia, others

Ukrainians, those "barbaric" "descendants of Khmelnytsky."[42] These explanations were consistent with the dominant nationalist discourses of the inter-war period. More important, there was no other explanation for the observable differences in behaviour, personal hygiene, and taste. Even leftists committed to internationalism and the rejection of ethnic stereotypes resorted to deeply embedded civilizational traits as the reason for this clash of strikingly different cultures in the everyday. For Aleksander Wat the Soviets in Western Ukraine were "Asia at its most Asian," even though he had previously "thought that to oppose the European and Asian was merely empty anti-Soviet propaganda."[43] Soviet officials also recognized striking contrasts in appearance and behaviour between locals and Soviet newcomers.[44]

At the same time there were those who were ready to play by the Soviet rules of the game. Ethnic Ukrainians were obviously in an advantageous position, if they were ready to join the Soviet body politic. Since the "Ukrainian-ness" of the city and the region was used as an official justification for Soviet annexation, the Soviet state was keen to show that Soviet Ukrainian culture was supported and flourishing. The condition was loyalty to Stalin's Marxism-Leninism and to the authorities. Many Jews also "felt relief. Jews could breathe more freely."[45] Unlike inter-war Poland, the new state did not discriminate against Jews, and all kinds of employment and educational opportunities were now opened for them.

By 1941 the Soviets began work on the city's infrastructure, laying down gas pipes, cleaning, and planting in city parks and gardens.[46] Repairs to the main train terminal began, too. As late as March 1941, however, Lviv's official newspaper complained about "the mega-dump of debris" in front of the main terminal and the blocked sewage inside. A journalist reported from an inspection walkthrough: "Apparently, the terminal managers know what they are doing when they keep their noses to the platforms, maintained in relative order. With covered noses we approach, for example, baggage warehouses, only a dozen of steps to the left from the main terminal. No longer do we care about the garbage heaps sitting in front of the warehouse, we close our eyes to its dirty interior when we realize what is happening behind its back wall. This large territory under the open sky is one large public toilet."[47] Freight cars on the depot tracks were filled with garbage and excrement.[48] Railway canteens were filthy and stank, the tables were stained, and employees' hands dirty.[49] Another visitor to the terminal, once "one of most beautiful and largest in contemporary Europe," found it in 1941 "in a pitiful state: wartime damages were not repaired, windows in the halls were broken, steel structure bent over, and most of all – fouled to the utmost. All the corners and empty cars were turned into cesspools, with the concomitant smell."[50]

The state of the terminal was nothing exceptional. The Hotel George café, "one of the most elegant" in Lviv, looked "like stables."[51] Soviet work on the city's space mostly consisted of covering it with innumerable posters, flags, banners, portraits, and cheap gypsum monuments to Soviet leaders. Middle-class Lvivites saw these embellishments as aesthetic profanation.[52] The Church of St Elizabeth had lost all its windows in September 1939. For two years it could not repair them, and the window openings were covered with makeshift materials, including: "innumerable ironing boards" from "railwaymen's wives."[53]

The parish priest of St Elizabeth noted increased religiosity among local people under Soviet occupation. On one occasion, at the end of May 1941, close to a thousand people took communion there.[54] The Church remained the only non-Soviet institution still openly available to people. Not only associational life, but also informal socializing took a heavy blow. In Lviv socializing was tied to privately owned bars and cafés, clubs, and association halls. All of these had disappeared, while Soviet forms of socializing had yet to take root. This led Hugo Steinhaus to conclude that "there is no social life under the Soviets."[55]

The Polish state had removed "undesirable" groups from certain occupations and barred access to higher education, while resorting only occasionally to non-judicial repression. The Soviet state, unrestrained by law or political opposition, resorted to "social surgery" on a massive scale. Arrests and executions were part of it, but the state's most important tool was deportation to special settlements in Siberia with the simultaneous stripping of mostly fictitious Soviet civic rights. From the very beginning, the Soviets arrested and deported local elites: state officials (including railway administration), officers, political activists, landowners, the bourgeoisie, and "settlers" – Polish colonists who had come to the region in the 1920 and 1930s. During the first months of Soviet occupation, the overwhelming majority of deportees were Poles. In 1940 and the first month of 1941, Jews were the second-largest ethnic group among the deportees. These were mostly refugees from Nazi-occupied Poland, as well as local "bourgeoisie." According to Soviet internal statistics, as of April 1941, among 177,043 former Polish citizens in special settlements, 54.6 per cent were ethnic Poles and 33.3 per cent were ethnic Jews.[56] By August 1941 the NKVD was in charge of over 390,000 former Polish citizens, as many as 329,000 of them deportees.[57] This unprecedented and unrestrained state terror – plucking people out of their homes and regular lives – was for educated and middle-class Lvivites the single most important feature of the new regime.

Lviv's first large-scale deportation took place on 10 February 1940, when twenty thousand people were deported from the city.[58] Trains brought the deportees, those deemed as political or social enemies, from the main terminal to the Second freight yard. They stood there for two days in the cold; the elderly and children were the first to die from hypothermia.[59] Eventually the junction's other freight yards also turned into departure points for deportations.[60] Relatives and friends spent long hours trying to locate those to be deported in Lviv's massive railway infrastructure. Trains were closely guarded by soldiers, but meetings and conversations with the deportees were permitted as a rule.[61] Because of the shortage of trains, week-long waits at the station's collecting points were not uncommon.[62]

Overcrowded cars brought together people from all social backgrounds. One prisoner recalled that his companions in one such car were a Lviv engine driver, a deputy-president of the Lviv PPS, a senator, a German schoolteacher, a driver, and a pilot.[63] The dirty freight cars used to transport the deportees were often divided by wooden boards into two decks, thus doubling congestion.[64] Trains with human "contingents" were notoriously slow.[65] On average it took trains two to four weeks to reach their destination in the Soviet interior.[66] Deportees spent days in trains even before they left former Galicia.[67] Starvation, extreme temperatures, unsanitary conditions, and resulting diseases decimated deportees on trains and in the "special settlements" – the end points of their journey.

Some claimed that escapes from trains were rare;[68] others believed they were quite common.[69] All agreed that the waiting period in Lviv offered the best opportunity for escape. Bribes and connections worked best.[70] There were no group breakouts. The deportations continued until the very end of the first Soviet occupation, and trains with convicts or deportees were seen at the Klepariv station even in June 1941.[71] The Soviet railway was the indispensable tool that made these deportations possible. Following the routine established in 1930, railroads provided train cars according to NKVD requests, together with locomotives and their crews. In railroads' reporting, these trains were referred to as "special contingents," a category that also included convicts sent to prisons and labour camps.

The Lviv Railroad also moved regular passengers. Initially, only those travelling on government business could use the railroad.[72] Entry into the newly annexed regions was granted only to those on official business, although many used official business as an excuse to access the territorial shopping paradise.[73] The Railroad's plan for passengers in 1940 was overfulfilled thanks to overcrowding. Even official occupancy per axle exceeded tight Soviet standards by 40 per cent.[74] People were riding on doorsteps and hanging from broken windows in unlit and unheated cars.[75] The timetable was completely jeopardized.[76] While strategic freight moved, Lviv's population's supply was irregular – for several weeks in the winter of 1939–40, the city lived without any bread at all.[77]

A breakdown of public order accompanied the annexation. Ticketless riding skyrocketed.[78] Street thieves worked openly in the terminal. According to one memoir, "city scum, among whom Jews were the majority, created artificial scrums in the crowd" and relieved travellers of purses, suitcases, and pocket money. The eyewitness believed that the Soviet police (*militsiia*) were complicit in this.[79] Since 1914, when the term was used to describe those who plundered abandoned warehouses and stores,[80] "city scum" (*szumowiny, shumovynnia*) became convenient culprits for the violent breakdown of public order. The Polish public had readily resorted to this label in the aftermath of the 1918 pogrom and again after the wrecking of Ukrainian institutions in the 1920s to exonerate Polish patriots.[81] Although there is little doubt that the lower classes partook in street violence and property plunder, in both cases, politically motivated and organized perpetrators were both the catalyst and the coordinators of violence. Under the Bolsheviks, the alleged "scum" suddenly became Jewish. In less than a year, the same "scum" would be blamed for torturing and murdering Lviv's Jews.

The city's first Soviet period lasted less than two years. On 22 June 1941, Germany attacked the Soviet Union, and Nazi troops quickly moved deep into Soviet territory. There was panic in Lviv, not unlike that experienced in August 1914. The haste was perhaps greater in 1941, and the direction was different: east instead of west. Terminal platforms were full of those desperate to leave. People "travelled strapped with their belts to the carriage steps."[82] Nearly all of the evacuated were pre-1939 Soviet citizens; only a few locals were taken. Bronisław Łotocki, a sincere supporter of the Soviet regime, was emotionally traumatized when ordered to stay. The justification was that locals had greater chances of survival.[83] What helped Łotocki to survive most, however, was his ethnicity: he was Polish, not Jewish.

The Railroad fell victim to the general disorganization, panic, and breakdown of communications. Only on 29 June did local Railroad officials receive a directive regarding mobilization and, in the case of retreat, evacuation.[84] By then the Lviv junction had been abandoned. Tracks were scrapped; the repair plant's main shop, depot, power plant, and turntable were blown up. The main terminal survived because of the retreat's panicky haste. The evacuation took place amid German air raids and gunfire by insurgents from OUN-B (Bandera's faction).[85] The majority of the evacuated employees – 2,135 of them – were sent to the Stalingrad Railroad.[86] All of them were pre-1939 Soviet citizens.[87] Almost twenty-five thousand local workers of the Lviv Railroad were left to the Germans.

In the early morning hours of 30 June, German troops marched into the city from the west, through Janowska (Shevchenko) and Horodotska (Gródecka) streets. As they moved, the pillaging of warehouses and stores stopped.[88] A Ukrainian unit, "Nightingale," formed from OUN members, accompanied the German troops. Although some Poles undoubtedly saw the entering Germans as liberators from Soviet "barbarism," underground Poland was still at war with Germany. The city's Jewish population could not expect any good from the Germans. Only Ukrainian nationalists rejoiced, seeing Nazi Germany as a powerful and victorious ally, at war with their two deadly enemies: Poland and the Soviet Union.

As was often the case with such organizations, the OUN usurped the right to represent the organized Ukrainian community. Not only was it the only pre-war organization that survived the Soviet occupation, both its factions shared ideological affinities with Nazi Germany. They were ultranationalist, authoritarian, and had no reservations about violence and war. Moreover, they saw violence and war as natural and necessary means. Although many Lvivites expected a rule of law from the Germans, the reality of the occupation was just the opposite. The extrajudicial killing of civilians became the norm.

When the Germans took Lviv and opened its prisons, they discovered the bodies of over three thousand prisoners, executed in a hurry by the NKVD during the Soviet evacuation.[89] The city was shocked. As the exhumation of corpses got under way, the city's population, with the blessing of the German authorities, perpetrated an infamous pogrom. This 1941 progrom had structural similarities with the progrom of 1918. Both incidents of mass violence took place during the wartime change of a political regime. In both cases Jews were charged with assisting the previous regime, while torture, sexual violence, and humiliation were used as street spectacles to be watched by the public. Armed Polish servicemen had formed the core of perpetrators in 1918; armed Ukrainians and Germans played the same role in 1941.[90]

There were also important differences between the two pogroms. In 1941 the atrocious humiliation and killing took place with the clear sanction of the German and self-appointed OUN-B Ukrainian authorities; in 1918 the Polish state had not encouraged pogroms. The number of those killed in 1941, in the range of five-to-seven hundred, was many times higher than in 1918. The most important difference was that, although the 1918 pogrom had been tolerated as a temporary excess, the 1941 pogrom marked the beginning of mass murder. According to the Nazi interpretation, Jews not only collaborated with the Soviets, the Soviet regime itself was Jewish – a view shared by many Ukrainian and Polish nationalists. Jewish civilians of both sexes and all ages, who had lived under the Soviet regime for less than two years, were assigned collective responsibility for Soviet crimes. The executions continued after the pogrom, and in subsequent months reached into the thousands.

In Lviv, on 30 June 1941, without German pre-authorization, the OUN-B declared the restoration of the Ukrainian state. In less than a week, the Germans firmly established direct rule over the city, and proved their intolerance for even nominal Ukrainian statehood in their plans for the region. Soon after the pogrom, educated Ukrainians in conversations with their Jewish colleagues blamed the pogrom on the proverbial "city scum."[91] Later, it became a standard explanation Ukrainian patriots used to try to exonerate the Ukrainian community.[92] Local Poles blamed "Ukrainian chauvinists" and Polish "city scum" that had joined them.[93] Just as before, Lviv's underclass was blamed for the crimes instigated by more "respectable" patriots.

Ivan Klymiv, a leader of the OUN-B responsible for the formation of the Ukrainian militia, estimated that there were twelve hundred OUN members in Lviv in summer 1941 among the city's more than sixty thousand Ukrainians. Five hundred of them belonged to the "workers," three hundred were university students, and another three hundred were gymnasium students. One hundred and ten women wee also listed separately.[94] Even though this social categorization is imprecise and "workers" probably encompassed all salaried employees, it shows that the OUN in Lviv was hardly composed of lower-class brutes. The better educated youth constituted its backbone, but education did not make one immune to violence and murder, especially if framed as a "struggle" and directed against those defined as the "enemy."

One Polish eyewitness observed that there was no correlation between social status and antisemitism. He also believed that probably in Lviv "Polish society had a better record than the Ukrainian."[95] This general assessment rings true. Several factors contributed to the likelihood that collaboration with the Germans would be higher among Ukrainians than among Poles in Lviv. Ukrainians in the *Generalgouvernement*, to which former eastern Galicia was attached as *Distrikt Galizien*, enjoyed a relatively privileged position, just below the Germans. Politically engaged Ukrainians had fewer reservations than did Poles about collaborating with the Germans. Moreover, in *Distrikt Galizien*, the organized national Ukrainian community, while deprived of political organization, had relative freedom of cultural expression.

As to aiding the Germans in the murder of Jews in Lviv, besides the overall greater likelihood of collaboration, the fact that the auxiliary police in *Distrikt Galizien* were Ukrainian played an important role. Another additional factor was Jewish assimilation into Polish culture, which integrated them better with Polish society but estranged them from Ukrainians. A survivor, whose family spoke Ukrainian fluently and had socialized before the war with Ukrainians, found this to be an invaluable asset during the war.[96] The persecuted Jews, who saw Ukrainians in German employ and were tortured and killed by Ukrainian police and willing civilian helpers working under Ukrainian flags, naturally tended to blame Ukrainians as a group.

When on 30 June OUN militia were dispatched to Lviv's strategic establishments, the main train station alongside the railway workshops topped their list. The militia commander acknowledged that he had learned the lesson of November 1918.[97] Ukrainian flags appeared above the terminal alongside German flags, and remained there throughout July. There was also a visible "Ukrainization" of Lviv, which had already begun during the Soviet occupation of 1939–41: city signs were in Ukrainian, and workers' conversations in Ukrainian could be heard.[98] On 1 August all the Ukrainian flags throughout the city were taken down.[99] The honeymoon of the OUN-B with Nazi Germany was over, although the collaboration did not end.

For those who welcomed the Germans, the appearance of the terminal in summer 1941 was testimony to "Bolshevik stupidity and mismanagement," Its left wing was in ruins, just as it had been when the Soviets arrived in 1939. In the train sheds not a single pane of glass was left unshattered (Figure 6.1).[100] Built in haste, the gypsum, wooden, and papier-mâché Soviet monuments were easily smashed immediately after the Soviet retreat. One of them was a monument to Stalin in front of the former ZZK building.[101] More, however, was expected from the Germans. "Liberated" from the "Bolshevik Asians," Lviv was supposed to "return to its old appearance."[102]

Collaborators with the local newspapers claimed that, under "Western" and "European" rule, Lviv would not only regain its former "clean" and "joyous" appearance; it would become even "better" than before. The newspapers had already celebrated the disappearance of Jews from the city streets in the summer of 1941. Now only "a shade of the hated Semite" could be glimpsed in the former Jewish neighbourhoods, and even there "after 8 o'clock not a single one would dare to appear, even in front of their own house." Jews were marked with the

Figure 6.1. Lviv terminal, summer 1941. Source: Ihor Kotlobulatov collection, courtesy of Ihor Kotlobulatov.

yellow star and assigned "work duty." A Ukrainian journalist reported his "joy in seeing how these 'sons of the chosen people' march in files for work on mornings."[103] Anti-Jewish legislation and discrimination were presented as a continuation of nineteenth-century urban reform and city improvements.

To a visitor from Warsaw, inter-war Lviv had appeared as "very colorful, very exotic," a slightly "eastern," or even "southern" city.[104] Under the Germans it was reimagined as the easternmost outpost of Western civilization in its Nazi edition. The sad irony was that this vision was embraced by many intellectuals who belonged to the ethnic group that had contributed to the city's "eastern" appearance. In 1941 the Ukrainians' claim to a place in "Europe" often entailed approval of the disappearance of the city's other "eastern" group.

In September passenger traffic on the railway resumed for state officials and civilians in possession of a special permit. The ride was free in *Galizien*.[105] In December regular civilian passenger movement resumed, although non-Germans required a permit and had no right to platform tickets.[106] The collaborator press, both Polish and Ukrainian, praised the Germans' work on the terminal's reconstruction, which for "the last two years stood half demolished and neglected – a tragic ruin of the old glory, the symbol of unconditional separation from western culture, the place, from where for us only one road could begin – to the east."[107] The building was covered with scaffolds and bustled with activity. This "German approach" to work was yet more proof that "the ruined building ... soon will come back to its old beauty."[108]

The end of the German "reconstruction" of the terminal, however, was not covered by the local press, and for a reason. The Germans had sealed gaps in the walls and installed windows, but they could not have cared less about the building's aesthetic appearance. The terminal had to serve its function, but its stylistic unity was ignored. Instead of becoming the symbol of Lviv's return to Europe, it signified Lviv's conquest and humiliation. The left-wing gallery had been crudely fixed, without the slightest attempt to match the surviving right gallery. It was a makeshift blotch on the fabric of the terminal, a slap to the city and its architectural ensemble. The German repair was bare, unadorned, red factory brick: the barrack-industrial architecture of Auschwitz had broken through the façade of liberal modernity (Figure 6.2).

The "repair" exposed the lie behind the rhetoric of improvement and a return to the fold of Western civilization. The myth of Western civilization and Eastern barbarity, cherished in the city since the First World War, was crumbling: "Even our less educated strata realized, with great astonishment, that despite everything, the Germans are very similar

Figure 6.2. The terminal after the German reconstruction. Source: David Lee Preston collection, "Moja przygoda fotograficzna," 21 November 2011, http://dalel.blog.onet.pl/2011/11/21, accessed 31 July 2016.

to the Bolsheviks, who used to be seen as terrible brutes. Nowadays people stress that despite the murders committed in prisons, the Bolsheviks were not as brutal as the Germans."[109] Locals perceived the Germans' treatment of the city space as a humiliation. Although Lviv had its share of brothels and dives, the Germans opened army brothels on main streets, allegedly to make finding them easier for soldiers – yet another slap in the city's face.[110] One was located at Horodotska (Gródecka) 46.[111]

Many repairs, such as the work on the heavily damaged St Elizabeth Church, were community initiated, funded and executed by the neighbourhood.[112] Just like the Soviets, the Germans invested mostly in a symbolic marking of space, especially in road signs, direction boards, and the renaming of streets.[113] The city's central boulevard became Adolf Hitler Ring, while Horodotska (Gródecka), from the terminal to St Anne Church, became Vienna Street.[114]

Lviv's constructed environment survived the German occupation largely intact – only 4.3 per cent of the city's housing stock was damaged in the Second World War.[115] Three years of German rule did, however, leave an indelible imprint on the city. The single most important consequence of the city's life under Nazi occupation was the murder of at least a third of its pre-war inhabitants whom the Germans identified as Jewish. The murder of these people also changed the cityscape. First, there was the material destruction of Jewish Lviv, its synagogues and cemeteries. Concurrent with this destruction of brick and mortar was the perceptional transformation of city space. Whole neighbourhoods were to carry the stain of atrocity committed there for posterity.

Two decades later, Stanislaw Lem confessed his astonishment at being at all able, "straining against the current of time with my memory, to restore innocence to such words as Janow, Zniesienie, Piaski, Lackiego, to which the years 1941 and 1942 gave such evil meaning, when the streets from Bernstein's and past the theatre, towards Sloneczna and beyond, one day were empty, silent, their windows open and curtains moving in the wind. The walls, courtyards, balconies – deserted, and in the distance appeared, then disappeared, the wooden fence of the ghetto."[116]

The dark geography of the Holocaust in Lviv invoked in Lem's account is intimately connected with the city's railway space. Indeed the link between the Holocaust and the railway has become commonplace in the immense literature on the Holocaust. As early as 1935, well before the Soviet and Nazi deportations started, Lviv writer Józef Wittlin prophetically had drawn attention to the First World War's ominous cattle cars, "in which emperor and king Franz Joseph moved his soldiers (40 Mann.) or his livestock (8 Pferde)."[117] Since the railway was built and perfected to handle the mass movement of people, any policy involving the large-scale removal of people logistically had to be tied to the railway. Trains carrying Jews to the death camps became a symbol of the Holocaust – as a modern technology easily turned into an instrument of mass murder.[118] Trains were also central to the experience of those sent to the camps, herded into overcrowded collection points, crammed into fully packed freight cars, and dispatched on a torturous journey to death.[119] Railway employees, from engine drivers to managers, became a symbol of the wider public's collaboration in the Holocaust.[120]

The link between the Holocaust and Lviv's railway terrain is far less explored. The railway both marked the city and served as a code for reading it. Scholars have pointed out the importance of Eastern Europe and "the Holocaust by bullets" in the mass murder of Jews.[121] The vast Eastern European landscape of the Holocaust, however, was also immensely varied. There was a "communal genocide" in smaller, close-knit communities of neighbours[122] and mass murder in the more anonymous and variegated space of the modern city, imbued with previous uses and meanings.

Mass violence during the first days of the occupation had occurred in Lviv near prison sites, but adult Jewish males were also herded into collecting points near stations.[123] Spacious premises located by the station for storing and loading goods were perfectly suited for concentrating large numbers of people. Once the Nazis made plans for the large-scale reshuffling of the city's population, the use of the railway terrain changed from tactical and situational to strategic.

In summer 1941 rumours appeared that Lviv would be divided into three districts: German, Polish-Ukrainian, and Jewish.[124] Spatial segregation started with the creation of an "Aryanized" zone, free of Jews, in August 1941. The bulk of this zone was in the prestigious "New World" area.[125] These were the neighbourhoods where arrivals from Germany settled.[126]

Simultaneously, mass executions started taking place. For their location the Germans selected the suburban forests behind the railway tracks. One of them was in the Bilohorshcha (Biłohorszcze) forest, west of Levandivka (Lewandówka) and the Fifth freight yard, in a corner created by the tracks.[127] This location, however, proved too close to city apartment blocks, so two other sites – the "Sands," north of the Ianivsky (Janowski) cemetery, and the forest near Lysynychi (Lesienice), next to the railway track – were turned into killing fields for massive concealed executions.

The German Armament Works (*Deutsche Ausrüstungswerke*) took over the milling machines factory at Janowska (Shevchenko) 134, and in the fall built barracks there and fenced them with barbed wire. On

31 October the first group of approximately two hundred inmates was ordered to stay there overnight.[128] Thus was created the Janowska (Ianivska) camp, located in an industrial neighbourhood itself created by the railway. The camp was next to the Klepariv station and the Ianivsky (Janowski) cemetery, in a dystopian space of death and machines, hidden from the city's inhabitants. During and in the aftermath of the First World War, the POW and refugee camps had been located in this area.

In November 1941, the Lviv ghetto was created, also next to the railway track. All Jews were ordered to move to the city's poorest neighbourhoods, Zamarstyniv (Zamarstynów) and Klepariv (Kleparów), north of the railway track. Non-Jews had to leave the ghetto area, to be assigned former Jewish apartments in the "Aryan" parts of the city (Figure 6.3). The creation of the Jewish ghetto was presented as a continuation of urban reforms: the "improvement," the "ordering and cleaning" of city space.[129] The ghetto's main gate, to be used by Jews, was under the railway bridge on Poltviana (Pełtewna) Street. Guarded by the Germans and Ukrainian police, this checkpoint itself became a site of continuous massacres,[130] and was known as the "Bridge of Death."[131]

The first massive transfer of Jews from the ghetto to the Belzec death camp, as the implementation of the "Final Solution," took place in spring 1942. Jews were also moved from the ghetto to the Janowska camp. These transfers, accompanied by massive manhunts and massacres in the ghetto, were euphemistically called "actions." In the camp itself, mass executions of large groups started in June 1942.[132] For a while the area of the ghetto and the size of its population shrank, while the population of the camp expanded. The largest single "action" in the ghetto took place in August, when thousands of people were brought to the Janowska camp. Healthy adult men were selected to remain; the rest were sent to their deaths in Belzec. In September the ghetto area was greatly reduced in size, but still delimited in the south by the railway tracks and in the north by the Poltva (Pełtew) River, where the city's main sewage collector was visible (Figure 6.4). In the ghetto the Germans explored to the utmost extent already existing features of the city's poorest working-class areas. Overcrowding, bad sanitation, hunger, dirt, and cold became yet another set of instruments to perpetrate mass murder.[133]

The Holocaust in Lviv was not a momentary affair. It constituted a prolonged cry of agony from Galicia's Jewry. In January 1943, in the course of yet another massive "action," the Jewish Council – the ghetto's caricature of municipal self-government – was abolished and the ghetto reduced to the *Judenlager Lemberg*, a mini-concentration camp restricted to a couple of blocks pressed against the tracks. In June 1943

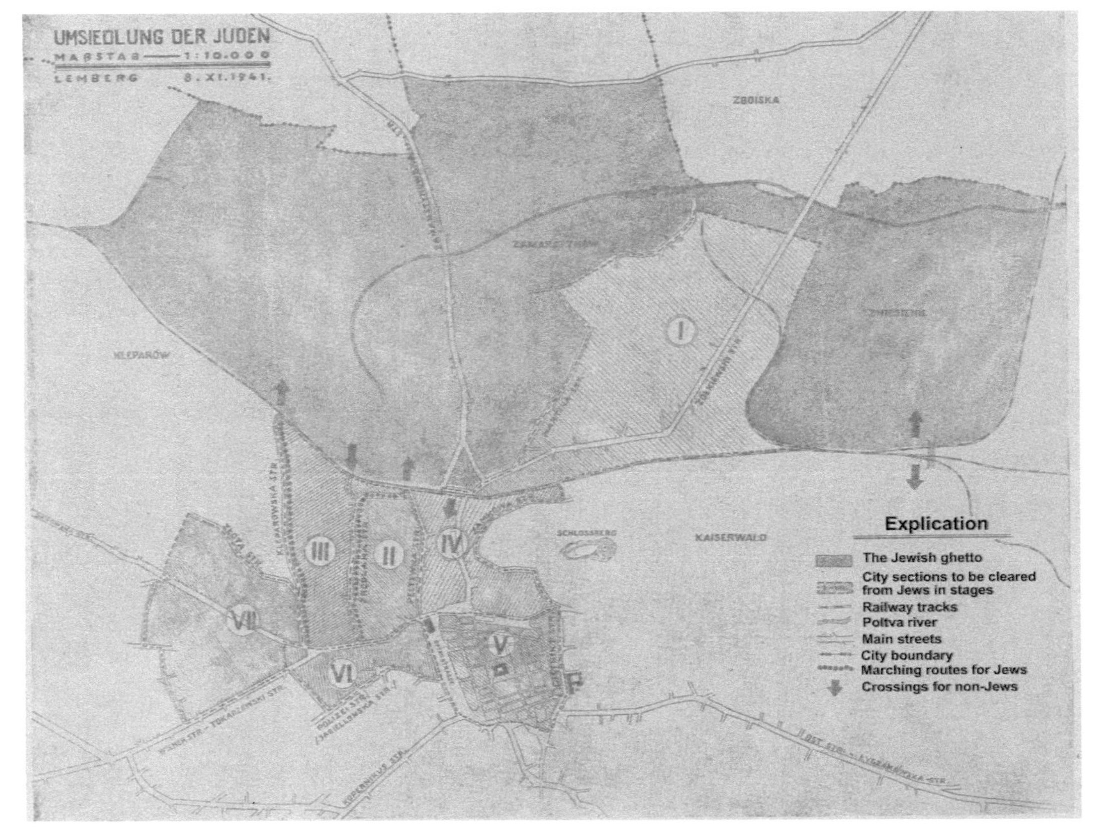

Figure 6.3. The resettlement of Lviv's Jewish population in a ghetto. Source: Based on a poster in the Steegh/Teunissen collection, Dordrecht, Netherlands.

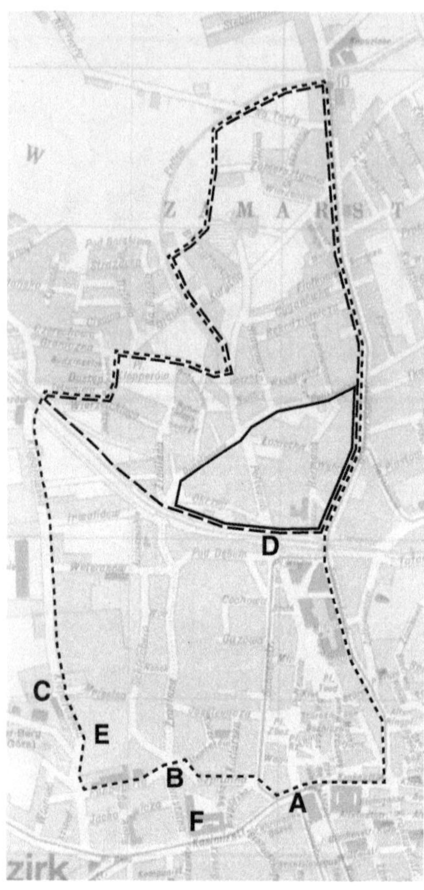

A Main Gate Pełtewna Street (today Viacheslav Chornovil Avenue)
B Gate Dzherelna (Żródlana) Street
C Gate Kleparivska (Kleparowska) Street
D Main Gate Pełtewna Bridge
E Jewish Cemetary
F Brygidki Prison

···· 1941–August 1942
– – After the "Great Action," August 1942
— Autumn 1942

Figure 6.4. The Lviv ghetto after August 1942. Source: Map courtesy of Iryna Kotlobulatova, annotations adapted from Chris Webb and Carmelo Lisciotto, "Lvov Ghetto Map," Aktion Reinhard Camps website, http://www.deathcamps.org/occupation/pic/biglvovmap.jpg.

this camp was "liquidated." The Jewish population of the Janowska camp was murdered at the end of 1943. Nearly all of Lviv's Jews – close to 150,000 – were killed, either in Lviv or at the Belzec death camp.

Jews were not the only group killed en masse in Lviv. Soviet POWs, held in the old Austrian citadel, died of starvation and disease or were executed in the Lysynychi (Lesienice) forest and at the Sands. Patients of the mental hospital were poisoned, while Roma were sent to the Janowska camp.[134] Jews, however, were by far the largest group and a core part of the city's pre-war population.

In the genocide, the Germans utilized not only the workers' neighbourhoods, but work itself. As one of the Lviv's largest employers, the railway made extensive use of slave labour. Jews had already been plucked off the streets in July 1941 and sent to work at the train stations. An eyewitness saw them there, unloading heavy howitzers with their bare hands.[135] This was no isolated incident. From the very beginning, it was not only about cheap labour, but also about labour as pure punishment, completely stripped of skill and satisfaction, and transformed into an intentionally unbearable extraction of bodily energy.

On the railway, Jews from the Janowska concentration camp were used to unload coal – a job even the unemployed had often declined before the war.[136] One day, when a group of Jews from the Janowska camp was unloading coal, the dust smeared the rails to such an extent that the engine could not pull a train. A German officer ordered Jewish inmates to move it with their bare hands.[137] Railway machines that used to empower industrial workers, making of them true proletarians, now became a dead weight used to break the workers' willpower.

Captive Jewish workers were used to demolish Jewish sacred sites, including cemeteries. Turning tombstones into masonry stone, the Nazis were dismantling culture and turning it into mere raw material. The Nazis definitely exploited the dystopian potential of the industrial neighbourhoods to its fullest, turning genocide into a macabre ritual meant to settle their accounts with Jewish culture.

Slave labour in the industrial working-class neighbourhoods that capitalism had created, together with extrajudicial killings and the genocidal mass murder of the Jews, signified Lviv's transformation into a colonial setting for the first time in its history. It was "colonial" not only because Nazi Germany was building its colonial empire in the east, but also because in the east it practised "dominance without hegemony,"[138] which was so characteristic of modern Europe's overseas colonies. Unmediated coercion and naked murderous violence became the preferred method of governing.

Jewish labour was not the only unfree labour the Germans used, although the degree of unfreedom mattered immensely. The Janowska camp had Polish, Ukrainian, and even Russian inmates – usually arrested for petty crimes – but people were also plucked from the streets and sent as labourers to Germany. Lviv also became a major transit point for "eastern workers" sent to Germany from elsewhere. A temporary camp with barracks for these workers was created by the terminal. Those to be sent to Germany were assembled there, together with those arriving on a rare leave, in special trains supervised by German officials.[139]

The local non-Jewish population also experienced segregation, albeit not one designed to kill but only to display and affirm racial hierarchies.

The Germans enjoyed spaces reserved for their exclusive use: separate tram and train cars, cafés, and cinemas. At the train terminal, instead of being divided by class, ticket windows were divided by nationality. There were now windows "for Germans and Allies," while former third-class windows were "for non-Germans."[140]

Ethnicity under the new regime became a pivotal part of an individual's experience, a matter of life and death. The ethnicization of policies, which had started in Lviv during the First World War, reached its culmination under the Nazis. The Nazis made ethnicity and origin absolute, but previous regimes had prepared the ground and accustomed people to seeing their fate as inseparable from their nationality. Still, even during the Second World War people changed their identities. A massive reversal of the ethnicity of railway workers – first in the 1920s, then in 1939–40 – most probably involved a significant number of national "conversions." The growing number of *Volksdeutsche* – local people of German descent rediscovering and declaring their German-ness under the Nazi occupation – was another such identity change.

The Nazi authorities were not the only ones to equate ethnicity with political choice. The Ukrainian and Polish undergrounds in Lviv operated on the same assumption. The Polish Home Army's reports from Lviv provide a detailed ethnic breakdown of the employees of the city's strategic enterprises, including the railway. Statistics compiled by the Polish underground show that senior and middle railway officials were German and Polish, while lower officials and workers were Poles and Ukrainians. In Lviv's railway workforce, Poles outnumbered Ukrainians.[141]

The railway infrastructure was guarded by railway security (*Bahnschutz*), normally recruited from former railway workers.[142] The headquarters of railway security for the whole of *Distrikt Galizien* and the Lviv sector was at Foch Alley 2, which the Germans renamed Bahnhofstrasse (Station Street). Railway security also had a larger reserve force of about four hundred people, also on Station Street.[143] In Polish memoirs, railway security was Ukrainian and German; Ukrainian memoirists claim it was composed mostly of culturally Polish *Volksdeutsche*.[144] In the Lviv railway security force, Ukrainians were the largest ethnic group, followed closely by Germans, and then by Poles. According to the Polish underground, Ukrainians were mostly OUN members.[145]

For the Polish underground, Poles working for the Germans were an asset, not a problem. The Ukrainian underground seconded this reasoning. The logic that applied to locals employed on the railway resembled the one applied to the police. Both undergrounds, with equal success, tried to penetrate the German service.

The Ukrainian policeman, a brutal and willing helper of Nazis, is a common figure in Polish and Jewish memories of wartime Lviv. Railway officials and workers do not evoke the same negative connotations. Even German officials are often portrayed as essentially decent human beings. Simon Wiesenthal's recollections are among the best known. At first he cleaned furnaces in the railway workshops, now known as the *Ostbahn-Ausbesserungswerke*, but eventually received a desk job thanks to Heinrich Günther, the new German director of the former railway workshops. Wiesenthal also portrays his immediate superior, Adolf Kohlrautz, as a conscientious human being.[146] Wiesenthal sees them as examples of decency and humanity in the midst of the most inhuman system, yet never raises the issue of the relationship between their jobs and the execution of mass murder.

In December 1941 Lviv's railway directorate assumed responsibility for the railway network in the whole of *Distrikt Galizien*, which became part of the *Generalgouvernment*'s *Ostbahn* (eastern railway), with headquarters in Krakow. Memoirs by former Polish *Ostbahn* employees betray a conscience not entirely at peace with their work for the Germans. The most common justification former workers provide is their usefulness to the underground in this capacity to execute occasional sabotage of the German war effort.[147] Some present their work with the *Ostbahn* as a means to avoid forced labour in Germany.[148] Reports of the Polish underground corroborate the memoirists' claims. They mention "their men" "on every station,"[149] and identify unemployment as the main reason for joining the railway workforce.

The wage labourer's total dependence on employment for survival was certainly the main motivation for the majority of Lviv's railway workers. Even though the *Generalgouvernement* was a quiet haven in comparison with the territories farther east, the German occupation of Lviv proved to be hungrier than the Soviet occupation, not only because of worse supplies but also because of widespread unemployment.[150] Life in Lviv under the Germans was much harder than in the Galician countryside, where food was more plentiful.[151] For those railway workers who lived in railway housing, abandoning the railway also meant eviction. At the same time, even under the Nazis, employment on the railway was more secure and better paid than other occupations. The *Ostbahn* even honoured service under its Polish and Austrian predecessors, which counted towards insurance and retirement pensions.[152]

A youngster who joined the Lviv junction's machine office as a courier appreciated this job. It provided him identification, which helped him avoid work in Germany amid the frequent roundups on Lviv streets. In addition to salary, he received a free tram pass, a uniform, and free meals in a canteen on Horodotska (Gródecka).[153] Despite German reluctance to open educational institutions for locals, they maintained a railway mechanical school at Station Street that provided meals twice a day, as well as some money.[154] The terminal also offered unofficial employment such as assisting travellers with baggage or working as boot polishers.[155]

During the war, the terminal bustled with people. A Ukrainian eyewitness recalled that, in summer 1941, the crowd at the terminal was even greater than in peacetime. People in uniform were as numerous as civilians.[156] Since the city was an important point in the Germans' eastern communications system, wounded German soldiers and those on leave flowed through Lviv in a constant stream (Figure 6.5). Not by accident, the soldier who is the protagonist of Heinrich Böll's *The Train Was On Time* spends much of the novel on the train, musing about the premonition that he will live long enough to see Lviv again and "is going to die between Lviv and Chernivtsi," even though there is no front between the two. Finally he does reach Lviv, "a big station, black iron frame and grimy white signboards," a city with bars and restaurants "as good as any in Europe." In the city he meets Olina, who works in a bordello and is part of the Polish underground. They leave the city together, only to be killed by partisans "somewhere between Lviv and Chernivtsi."[157] For the soldiers, Lviv was a mandatory stop for quarantine and delousing; special barracks had been built behind the terminal for this purpose.[158]

When passenger movement was again permitted, a great number of people started to move – to trade, to survive, to escape. Villagers normally would sell food, while the trade in documents was mostly a German prerogative.[159] Train tickets were hard to obtain, and "Germans" – most of them allegedly newly minted – besieged ticket counters buying out all the tickets, only to resell them later.[160]

The terminal was a place of heightened security, guarded by the railway, order, and security police.[161] Routine document checks were quite common, and members of the underground were frequently caught there.[162] Under the German occupation, IDs were a vital part of everyone's life, a crucial element in policing the populace. If the First World War ended the era of passport-free foreign travel, the Second World War made identification mandatory for everyone all the time. Under Nazi rule in Lviv, life without a German *Kennkarte* – the most important non-German identification document in the *Generalgouvernment* – was virtually impossible.[163]

The presence of the police and a heightened security regime did not save the terminal from its share of atrocities; it rather invited them. As a boy working at the terminal later recalled: "The Main Terminal back

Figure 6.5. German soldiers by a makeshift latrine on the terminal's platform. Source: David Lee Preston collection.

then was a mirror for everything that took place in the city and at the frontline. Arrests, inspections, and robbing travellers of whatever the Hitlerites and the Ukrainian police took a liking to, occurred there regularly."[164] In summer 1941 Soviet POWs lay on the bare cement floor, "weak, hungry, cold, and inhumanly treated, worse than cattle."[165] One witness remembered how a German soldier marching from the terminal struck a boy standing on the sidewalk on the head for no apparent reason. The boy died at once, while the murderer casually shoved the dead body into a gutter.[166] By fall 1942 starving Jews could be seen dying on the nearby streets.[167] Another witness remembered Ukrainian soldiers from the Waffen-SS Division "Galizien" killing his colleague from the railway workshops for speaking to them in Polish.[168] As a stage of brutal policing and killing, the terminal firmly belonged to the murderous urban railway terrain.

There was virtually no organized resistance to the Nazi occupation among Lviv's leftist milieu. Some workers saw the Soviet and Nazi occupations as a great reversal of roles, empowering them at the expense of their former masters. There are reports of building concierges extorting money from helpless Jewish tenants in 1941[169] – the same concierges who lived with inadequate salaries in tiny basement suites and had been defended by the city's socialists since the 1900s.[170] At the same time, the concierge and launderer Zofiia Tik, who lived in a tiny cellar room, sheltered Jews there at the risk of her own life.[171] Class and social background did not determine human decency. Doctor Henryk (Ryszard) Axer, brother of the renowned theatre director Maurycy Axer, helped numerous inmates from the Janowska camp to escape.[172] So did a prostitute who came to the camp to sell sex to SS personnel. Both were executed.[173] In the words of one survivor, it was impossible to guess people's intentions on the basis of their social background or appearance: "I could never sense who was a friend or who an enemy."[174] Real scum did not have to be lower class, they could be well clad and come to the ghetto only to indulge their sadistic desires.[175]

Yitzhak Sternberg, who lived in Lviv under an assumed Ukrainian identity, stayed in the home of a worker from the railway workshops who was connected with the Polish resistance.[176] At the same, Sternberg observed strong antisemitic prejudices among his fellow workers.[177] The majority of workers remained actively uninvolved in the tragedy unfolding before their eyes, although this lack of action should not be taken for indifference.

The destruction by the Soviets of the workers' associational life and political parties largely predetermined the political paralysis of the working class. Artur Hausner and Volodymyr Starosolsky, the pre-war PPS and USDP leaders in Lviv, had both been arrested by the Soviets and died in Soviet camps. Jan Szczyrek, the leader of the local united front, also met the outbreak of the Soviet-German war in a Soviet prison. Some of his comrades had avoided arrest and stayed in Lviv under the Germans. Most of them, however – Wincenty and Jadwiga Markowsky, Jan Fel, and Samuel Herschthal, among others – moved to Warsaw after less than a year under German rule in Lviv.[178] According to Jadwiga Markowsky, there was nothing for socialist activists in Lviv. Warsaw had experienced neither the demoralizing Soviet occupation nor the poisonous Ukrainian-Polish conflict. In Lviv, organized resistance was in the hands of nationalists, both Polish and Ukrainian. Even under Nazi rule, Lviv's Polish and Ukrainian underground waged a deadly war against each other, mostly with "enemy" civilians as victims.[179]

The sisters Hermina and Fryderyka Lazarus, Herman Diamand's widow and sisters-in-law, stayed in Nazi-occupied Lviv as the last prominent activists of the Austrian period's socialist movement. Hermina was the editor of Lviv's first children's magazine, while Fryderyka, a children's writer and pedagogue, dedicated her life to destitute and orphaned children. During the inter-war years she had belonged to the circle of the more famous pedagogue and writer Janusz Korczak, who in 1942 joined the children from his orphanage in Warsaw's ghetto when they were sent to a death camp. Fryderyka and Hermina had managed to avoid resettlement to the ghetto through the protection of their Christian neighbours, who knew and appreciated their work. Once, even a Ukrainian policeman, Fryderyka's neighbour, saved her from the German gendarmes. She was caught by the Germans nonetheless, during one of their systematic neighbourhood sweeps in August 1942, and most likely killed together with other Jews deemed unfit for work.[180] Hermina survived.

Besides employing permanent railway workers with full benefits and temporary wage workers, the *Ostbahn* in Lviv also made extensive use of slave labour. At first, Jewish men were rounded up randomly on the street and sent for hard physical work on the railway.[181] After the Janowska camp was established, a part of its population was assigned to the *Ostbahn*.[182] Szymon Kahane, for example, laid down tracks. The work was non-mechanized and backbreaking, the supervisors cruel.[183] According to Abraham Beer, out of roughly five thousand inmates at the Ianivska camp, a thousand were working on the railway at the end of 1941.[184] Beer worked on the main terminal's repairs, laying bricks, blending lime, and helping free civilian masons.[185]

Torture and group executions were a regular occurrence at the Janowska camp.[186] Besides being a labour camp, it was also a transit camp for Jews from *Distrikt Galizien* being sent to the Belzec death camp. Trains would depart from the Klepariv station; public spaces by the station were used as an assembly point. The Germans did not want too many witnesses. When people were marched to the station to be put on a train to Belzec, the stretch of Janowska (Shevchenko) Street near the station was closed to pedestrians and vehicles and guarded by a double row of policemen.[187] Accidental witnesses still saw people being sorted at the station, undressed to prevent escapes and jammed into overcrowded train cars.[188]

Many Ukrainian memoirs of Lviv under the Germans avoid the subject of the Holocaust completely.[189] Such silence not only focuses attention on the sufferings of their own ethnic group; it also helps to avoid discussion of Ukrainian complicity in the genocide. This silence cannot be explained by a lack of knowledge. Although mass executions normally took place out of sight of the city's non-Jewish population, they were still a well-known fact. The Germans also used murder as a pedagogical tool: summary public executions were introduced, and carried out on Strzelecki (Danylo Halytsky) and Solskis (Zernova Street) squares,[190] the former locations of socialist rallies. A Jewish eyewitness recalled his indignation at the reaction of some passersby, who idly watched Jews boarding freight cars. While no approval was present per se, he interpreted the watchers' facial expressions as curiosity akin to observing exotic animals.[191] For him this reaction was proof that the Christian public no longer saw Jews as human.

Beneath the mask of indifference and the infrequency of compassionate acts, however, some people did hide strong emotions and fear. The likelihood of encountering mass murder was greatest while on the railway's terrain, and railway workers had more intimate knowledge of Nazi killings than did average civilians. One witness saw an attempted escape from a car: naked people had jumped through a hole in the floor onto the tracks during a signals stop, but were hunted down and killed on spot. These were Hungarian Jews being transported to Belzec.[192] A railway worker accidently witnessed the execution of a group of naked people when he got off a train between stops in Lviv's northern suburbs. After that, he was feverish and sleepless for several days, feeling an irresistible urge to return to the site. When he did so, there were no people, but the horror was imprinted in the landscape: "The bottom [of the dale] was covered with the sand, which heaved as yeasty dough, on which large bubbles would grow continuously and burst with a loud splash. A terrible stench was rising up over it all."[193] The same young worker witnessed an escape of Jewish women from a train bound for Belzec and armed Ukrainian policemen hunting them down along the tracks.[194]

The paradox was that the very same railway terrain often served as the only means to survive, and railway workers provided indispensable assistance. To Lviv's Christian population, beside employment, the railway offered access to food and fuel carried by the trains – loaded, unloaded, and stored. Casual work on unloading could reward one with food in addition to money.[195] Bread crumbs and food leftovers could be picked from the garbage bins next to the military and railway canteens.[196] Most important, there were plentiful opportunities for theft. Teenagers would jump onto moving freight cars or sneak into freight yards at night. As usual, coal was the most popular prize.[197] Theft fed the illicit trade, in which railway workers were often involved.[198] The railway was at the very centre of the black market, of both official and unofficial supply chains.

The railway's role in the life of Lviv's Jewish population was even greater. Jewish inmates from the *Ostbahn* group were in a better position than camp inmates in other lines of work. According to Beer, "the Ostbahn group had the most freedom because they went to the city, where they were in contact with people."[199] Simon Wiesenthal, in the railway workshops, was able to contact the Polish underground and prepare his escape attempt.[200] A friend of Reuven Rimer's escaped from the *Ostbahn* construction group during work. Rimer recalled that "construction work was difficult but it was not humiliating" when compared to, for example, the unloading of coal.[201]

The relative freedom of working for the railway helped Abraham Beer to escape. Working in the terminal, he and two co-workers pulled out a board separating their room from the main vestibule. They tore the labels off their uniforms and blended in with the crowd.[202] Another survivor who worked for the *Ostbahn* in Lviv was Abraham Schuss. He had been assigned to the demolition of Jewish tombstones, often staying at the cemetery overnight, which facilitated his escape.[203] Jakób Birkendfeld escaped from an execution site during the ghetto's liquidation in June 1943. He ran along the railway tracks and was saved by a passing train full of German soldiers moving east. He jumped on a car unnoticed, and jumped off near Vynnyky (Winniki). He still ended up in the Ianivska camp, working as a mason, but escaped again with several others from the Jewish cemetery.[204] Non-Jewish captives also used the railway as a guiding light out. A group of Soviet POWs escaped from the Citadel camp in March 1944, disappearing into the streets next to the railway tracks.[205]

Although closely watched, the railway remained the most reliable and convenient escape route. Sabina Berger managed to board a train west without any documents with her two-year-old son. Threatened with detention by a Polish policeman near Tarnów, she bribed him with a watch and continued her trip.[206] Leon Halbersberg's mother escaped the Lviv ghetto and left for Warsaw. Eventually she returned and freed her detained son. The next day, with forged papers, they "managed to reach the station and board a train" for Warsaw.[207] Runia Rotter and her family purchased "Aryan" papers from a German, who eventually took them to the terminal, where they boarded a train.[208] Many Jewish women sought safe haven in Germany as "eastern labourers" with forged "Aryan" papers.[209] Helen Kaplan succeeded in this, although she had to surrender her suitcase to a blackmailer who identified her as Jewish.[210]

In the survivors' stories the terminal usually appears in connection with escape – as a gateway, however illusory and dangerous, out of a nightmare. These escapes never lead out of Nazi-ruled territory or end fear and suffering for good. Still, train journeys out of Lviv are plotted as memories of major relief, or even the potential thereof. One survivor recalled the longing he had while watching trains with soldiers leaving for Stalingrad. He dreamt of taking the place of those soldiers.[211]

Marek Gutwirt was a Jewish Lvivite drafted by the Red Army in the first days of the war. After three days in the Janowska camp, he escaped and hid at his Polish friend's place in the railway workers' neighbourhood. With the help of that friend, a local engine driver took him to Przemyśl disguised as a stoker. Gurtwirt recalled that eventually he obtained "a forged railway ID, and in a railway uniform moved through Poland's larger cities, without permanent residence not willing to stay for long in the same milieu." After eight months of such life, he left for Hungary and survived.[212] The Allerhands, mother and son, hid for a while in a railway worker's home.[213] The railway neighbourhood, however, was not a safe haven. As children Maurycy and Hania Allerhand waited for their mother at the small park by St Elizabeth Church, other children playing there identified them as Jewish and called the police.[214]

Escape attempts from the transports to Belzec were regular. Ana Selinger was put on a train in Lviv and "jumped" with a friend just north of the city. They walked all the way to Zhovkva (Żółkiew), where with the help of local Jews they found a whole community of "jumpers."[215] Felicja Heller, who was only twelve, was put on a train to Belzec at the Klepariv station. On the train the captives managed to burn a hole through the car's floor. Felicja was the fourth to jump off. Passing by numerous corpses of those shot during previous escape attempts and left by the track bed, she walked with another girl all the way to the Zhovkva ghetto, "directed by a railwayman."[216]

Railway workers knew that the trains with Lviv's "deportees" were taking them to the Belzec death camp. Their work helped these trains to run smoothly. There were also those who warned Jews about their destination.[217] One survivor recalled that, when his train reached Zhovkva, he asked a passing railwayman about the distance to Belzec, the latter "leaped on me, abusing me for being an absolute ass, a coward, and used abusive invective about my family, which would have made every street urchin of Lviv proud. He shouted – 'Jump you idiot! Why do you let yourself be taken to death?! TRY!'"[218] The survivor heeded this advice and avoided death.

Ostbahn workers who left recollections emphasize resisting the Germans. Usually they describe spontaneous petty sabotage.[219] The same people, however, acknowledge getting along with the German workers "well, and sometimes even amicably."[220] Sabotage and defiance led some railway workers to the organized underground or to joining partisan units in the countryside.[221] The terminal also actions by the underground:[222] during one roundup, a searched man threw a hand grenade, wounding three German policemen,[223] a woman in charge of public washrooms at the main terminal was reportedly hiding a Soviet officer and his wife,[224] and subversive graffiti was found on Horodotska (Gródecka), by the former trade union headquarters.[225] The most dramatic and massive acts of resistance, however, took place in the ghetto and in the Janowska camp. When it became clear that the Germans did not intend to leave survivors, people attacked guards, wrestled weapons from them, and used them to escape.[226]

In Lviv, as everywhere else, the Germans tried to hide the evidence of mass murder. Using the remaining Jewish inmates, they opened graves and burned bodies. Leon Weliczker was one of those inmates. He believed that his team burnt more than 310,000 bodies, 170,000 in the vicinity of the Janowska camp and another 140,000 in the Lysynychi (Lesienice) forest.[227] According to Soviet calculations, 200,000 people from the Janowska camp and 140,000 from the Citadel camp were killed. Over 130,000 inhabitants of the Lviv ghetto were killed as well, although many of them perished in Belzec, not in Lviv itself.[228] These numbers might need correcting, but they convey the mind-boggling scale of mass murder that took place. By 1944 the population of recently murdered Lvivites in the city was at least twice as large as of those still alive. Probably no other city under the Nazi occupation witnessed as many executions as Lviv, even though the total loss of human life was undoubtedly higher in Warsaw and Leningrad (Saint Petersburg). In Lviv the absolute majority of victims were Jews, killed on the outskirts of the city and in the ghetto.

In 1944 Lviv experienced yet another evacuation and retreat. The steamroller of the victorious Red Army was unstoppable. The evacuation of industry to Vienna began in January.[229] In April Soviet aircraft targeted the area of the railway terminal, damaging the tracks between the main terminal and Klepariv, and burning down the largest city bakery, on Horodotska (Gródecka).[230] The heaviest bombing took place during the first two days of May.[231] Shortly thereafter the Germans announced a voluntary evacuation.[232] As the front approached, Germans and Ukrainians left in increasing numbers. The Polish underground rejoiced: "Lwów is again Polish ... Rarely one can hear Ukrainian on the street. The Polish language again dominates everywhere: on the streets, in the offices, in the stores."[233]

This time it was the Germans' turn to destroy Lviv's railway infrastructure, and they did a much more thorough job than the Austrians had in 1914, the Russians in 1915, or the Soviets in 1941. The main terminal suffered the heaviest damage of its century-long history. This time the explosives went off even in the terminal's tunnels. The left wing, "rebuilt" by the Germans, collapsed again.[234] Freight yard warehouses and ramps, turntables, the power plant, and water stations were set on fire or demolished with explosives.[235] Aerial bombs were placed under the western depot, and only by chance failed to explode.[236] Engineer Pavel Kabanov, who entered Lviv with the Red Army, discovered that "the unique building of the terminal presented a heap of glass and bricks. Not a single line of tracks, not a single yard neck survived."[237]

During the German retreat, when the Red Army was entering Lviv, the Polish Home Army organized an insurrection, taking over key buildings and whole neighbourhoods, including the main terminal.[238] This was part of the all-national "Operation Tempest." The Home Army tried to seize control of cities and towns before the arrival of the Red Army, showing that Polish forces were in charge on Polish soil. After taking Lviv, however, the Red Army promptly disarmed the Poles and disbanded Home Army units. In the OUN report on murders of Ukrainian activists by Polish insurgents, the perpetrators are identified by the familiar trope of "scum, workers, some students."[239] This was one of the last appearances of the term "city scum" to label the perpetrators in narratives purporting to describe gruesome acts in Lviv. As was often the case, the very same "city scum" had just before been accused of collaborating with the Germans.[240] Nothing could be further from the truth. Describing the "Jewish police" (*Ordnungdienst*) used in ghetto "actions" to search, convoy, and guard, a Jewish survivor insisted they were not "scum," but, to the contrary, "the blossom of Jewish youth ... members of sports clubs, and boy scout organizations."[241] The same was probably true of the 1941 Ukrainian militia or auxiliary police. Ascribing violence to the lower class, to people of dubious moral standards and no convictions, once again created a false sense of safe distance, of one's own milieu's normality.

On 27 July 1944 the Soviet Lviv Railroad resumed its operations. The People's Commissariat of Communications restored the Railroad to its pre-war boundaries and "to the borders with Czechoslovakia and Poland" of May 1941.[242] Tracks were briskly laid to move trains with people and equipment west and south. The most heroic wartime deed of the Soviet Lviv Railroad was the reconstruction of viaducts and tunnels in the Carpathians, to support the Soviet offensive in Hungary and Czechoslovakia.[243] The Lviv junction was also crucial for supplying troops west and south of the city. Still, it took ten days before the first Soviet train was able to enter Lviv in 1944.[244] On 11 August the first cars with freight arrived, and regular loading operations resumed.[245] For its achievements, in August 1944 the Lviv Railroad received the State Defence Committee's transferrable Red Banner.[246]

Locals worked with railway troops on the station's reconstruction.[247] There were still occasional air raids, but eventually the front moved farther west. The peace, however, was relative. At first Polish and Ukrainian, and later the Ukrainian underground, continued their low-intensity guerrilla warfare. Their actions sometimes were indistinguishable from those of criminal gangs.[248] Young men were mobilized into the Red Army and many never returned. Despite all this, for Lviv the war was essentially over. Less than half of the city's pre-war population, approximately 149,000 people, remained.[249] Lviv's Jews, murdered in the Holocaust, constituted the bulk of the missing Lvivites. Only 1,689 Jews registered with the Soviet authorities in the whole of Lviv Oblast (basic administrative region of the Ukrainian SSR) by 1 October 1944.[250] We do not know the exact number of Jewish survivors from the city itself, but most likely it was not more than a thousand.

The end of the war brought no catharsis, nor was there any reckoning with the things that happened in Lviv. The new regime was oppressive, brutal, and exploitive, no better than its first edition in 1939–41. It had no interest in truth or reconciliation. Under Stalin, mass terror, including mass deportations from the region and the city, continued. Nevertheless the new regime did stop mass murder, secured a lasting peace, and treated the region as an integral part of the Soviet Union. Lviv was to become a very special, but at the same time normal, Soviet city.

"We Shall Rebuild Splendidly"[1]

Nikita Khrushchev, Soviet Ukraine's leader, had spent some time in Lviv in 1939 visiting the city's main train terminal.[2] He came again in 1944, on the heels of the victorious Red Army. In 1945–46 the terminal was reconstructed under Khrushchev's personal supervision.[3] Writing on behalf of the Central Committee of the Communist Party of Ukraine (CC CP(b)U) to the NKPS in 1946, Khrushchev put the Lviv terminal as number seven on his list of "the most important (*glavneishie*) works" to be finished on Ukraine's railways during the Fourth Five-Year Plan (1946–50).[4] The fact that the terminal is listed alongside important railway lines and major junctions reveals its singular importance for Khrushchev. The position on the list is even more striking considering that, from 1946 to 1952, a total of 1,863 other train terminals were built and rebuilt in the Soviet Union, including terminals in all of Soviet Ukraine's largest cities.[5]

Scholarship tends to speak of post-war Stalinist architecture and urban planning in Lviv in terms of a massive rebuilding aimed at the creation of a thoroughly new socialist city. The city's master development plan indeed entailed the complete disregard and destruction of Lviv's historical architectural heritage.[6] Nonetheless the grand transformative vision outlined in that master plan never materialized. Moreover, Soviet authorities handled the existing cityscape sparingly, avoiding unnecessary destruction and demolition. The general dearth of resources and labour forced the authorities to preserve surviving buildings. Not by accident did the wholesale post-war urban reconstruction take place in thoroughly war-torn cities such as Minsk, Kyiv, and Sevastopol.

Soviet frugality, however, does not explain the reconstruction of Lviv's main railway terminal. The terminal did not survive the war intact, and could have been replaced by a completely new structure. But the reconstruction was supposed to serve as proof of the Soviet state's caring attitude towards Lviv, Western Ukraine, and their historical heritage.

Official rhetoric juxtaposed Soviet care and "culturedness" and German barbarity: "Throughout the occupation the Germans had done nothing for the restoration of the station. Moreover, while retreating, they reduced it to ruins."[7] In reality the Germans did repair the terminal, however unimpressively. Nevertheless there is no denying that the terminal was in far worse condition in 1944 than in 1941.[8]

Repairs to the terminal had begun even before the architects prepared blueprints. The Railroad's priority was the tunnels to the platforms; one was cleared by the end of 1944.[9] By then the Railroad had also installed passenger and baggage ticket counters, and opened a baggage department and storage facility and two makeshift waiting halls, one for civilians and the other for the military. Passenger traffic was lively: storage facilities handled almost fifty thousand pieces of luggage in 1944,[10] although passenger movement was irregular and many travellers rode trains without baggage or tickets.[11]

Kievtransuzelproekt – Kyiv's engineering and architectural institute for transportation infrastructure – was entrusted with the reconstruction designs for the terminal. The head architect was Heorhii Domashenko, who worked on the Kyiv terminal's reconstruction in the same capacity. Among the institute's pre-war employees was Oleksandr Marchenko, a tank crew member who had hoisted the red flag over Lviv's city council in July 1944 and was killed in action the same day. In 1945 *Kievtransuzelproekt's* Party organization lobbied for Marchenko's bas-relief to be installed at Lviv's terminal.[12] Eventually, however, the bas-relief appeared on the city hall – unlike the Polish terminal, the Soviet terminal was not a proper place for solemn commemoration.

The preparation of blueprints and their approval was a prolonged process. In June 1945 the overall design proposal was vetted by the NKPS and the Architecture Committee of the USSR's Council of Ministers (CM).[13] A year later the Architecture Department of the Ukrainian CM also approved the artistic part of the project and forwarded it to the Lviv Obkom (Oblast Party Committee).[14] The Obkom approved the proposed "sculptural-artistic design" on 24 September 1946.[15] More detailed blueprints again would have to be first approved by the CC CP(b)U.[16] There was no local input into the design, and the approval began at the top, with the USSR's central government.

Heorhii Domashenko had already worked on the design for the terminal back in 1940. His proposal then involved significant changes to the symbols on the façade. The Soviet coat of arms would replace the Polish eagle, and the text, "Proletarians of all countries unite," would appear instead of "Semper Fidelis." As well, figures of a soldier and worker were to replace the original allegories of industry and trade. Two additional similar figures were to be added to the allegory of communication as shield-bearers. Likewise, sculptures representing the "Defence of Lviv" were to be replaced with new Soviet compositions.[17] By contrast his 1945–46 designs anticipated changes only to explicitly ideological symbols and inscriptions, while most of the original sculptural elements were to be preserved and restored. At first the façade of the Soviet-era terminal had no ideological embellishments at all. After the old symbols were scrapped, the shield of the coat of arms remained empty, and in the 1950s the large cartouche over the main entrance carried the modest inscription "Lviv-Passenger" in Ukrainian – the official name of the station (Figure 7.1). After the Lviv-Passenger and Lviv-Freight stations merged in 1962 and the city received the Order of Lenin in 1971, a replica of the order and the single word "Lviv" appeared there (Figure 7.2).

The fact that the terminal façade was marked with more or less permanent Soviet symbols only under Brezhnev is remarkable. Commissions representing the Party and government did not hesitate to intervene in the symbolic solutions proposed by architects. In 1950, for example, one such commission requested replacing the Soviet Union's coat of arms with Soviet Ukraine's in the design for a small train stop near a sanatorium named after Khrushchev.[18] The architectural workshop of the *Kievtransuzelproekt* had regular discussions on how "Soviet architecture has to reflect Communist ideology" and "Soviet architects should properly display the Stalinist époque's greatness."[19] Those who "succumbed" to "Western influences" were condemned regularly.[20] In such a climate, the decision not to add Soviet symbols to early twentieth-century sculptural solutions could not have been made without a sanction from above, most probably by Nikita Khrushchev himself. It reflected the emphasis placed on the preservation of Lviv's architectural heritage.

Besides the station itself, the first Soviet enterprise to work on the terminal was Lviv Railroad's USVR (*Upravleniie stroitel'no-vosstanovitel'nykh rabot*, Department of Construction-Rebuilding Works) No. 22.[21] Exorbitant amounts of work, meagre resources, and scarce labour caused major backlogs and delays in its work. In 1945 USVR 22 completed only 36 per cent of the work scheduled for the terminal that year.[22] The terminal was not the USVR's only problem: [23] out of 220 projects scheduled for completion in 1945, only thirty-five were finished.[24] The USVR's performance was far below that of other construction enterprises in the region, which experienced similar constraints in terms of resources and labour.[25] Apparently, work on railway infrastructure was far more

Figure 7.1. The façade of the Lviv terminal in the 1950s. Source: Volodymyr Rumiantsev collection, courtesy of Volodymyr Rumiantsev and Center for Urban History of East Central Europe.

complex than regular construction. Moreover, it had to be done without interrupting the railway's operations.

At the Lviv station, tracks, switches, and signals were the USVR's main priorities;[26] the only larger project USVR 22 finished in Lviv in 1945 was the junction's tracks.[27] The Railroad's management, meanwhile, accused the USVR of treating the terminal as a project of secondary importance.[28] In reality, their priorities were similar. The reconstruction of passenger infrastructure would lag behind other projects in the years to follow. In 1947, for example, USVR 22 completed 77 per cent of the capital investment planned for the projects of the movement service, but only 34 per cent of that for the passenger service.[29] Even accounting for the low priority assigned to passenger infrastructure, the pace of the terminal's reconstruction was far below the USVR's average. Only about a third of planned work was completed at the Lviv terminal, while the average completion rate for all railway terminals was about

Figure 7.2. The façade of the Lviv terminal in the 1970s. Source: Mykhailo Tsimerman collection, courtesy of the Center for Urban History of East Central Europe.

two-thirds.[30] To improve its completion statistics, the USVR focused on smaller projects – out of thirty-five completed projects, thirty-four were small scale.[31]

Even though the USVR was able to find overachievers and Stakhanovites among its workers,[32] when it came to labour, the main problem was not that people worked too little, but that there were too few of them. Labour shortages were acute at all levels. Particularly lacking were specialists and foremen – in 1945 only four USVR employees were pre-war specialists in railway construction.[33] Low-skilled labour was also hard to contract. Labour mobilization was taking place simultaneously with military mobilization in 1944, but without the expected results.[34] Instead of the planned four hundred workers, only half that many were working on terminal repairs at the end of 1944.[35]

During the initial stage of reconstruction, the solution was to use soldiers from special railway detachments and German POWs. Indeed, for a couple of years, POWs were the reconstruction's main labour source on Ukraine's railway network – in 1945 USVR 22 was using eleven hundred POWS at the Lviv junction alone. In 1947, however, the authorities told the railways to stop relying on POWs and switch to permanently employed free labour.[36] In June 1947, on orders from the Obkom, the number of POWs working at the junction was reduced to about five hundred; the rest were redirected to other city enterprises.[37] The days of POW labour were nearing an end. In October 1947, railway officials asked Soviet Ukraine's minister of the interior to use 2,250 convicts at USVR 22 as substitutes for POWs, with 1,000 to be deployed in Lviv itself.[38] Free labour at USVR 22 came primarily from local villages. Since the pay was low, demobilized soldiers were not especially eager to join this line of work.

All the typical problems of the Soviet economy plagued the terminal's reconstruction. Simple things, such as files to sharpen carpenters' saws, were missing. The technical documentation from *Kievtransuzelproekt* was flawed: it assumed the use of standard Soviet bricks, but these were not available in Lviv. Not all measurements were included, and workers had to improvise.[39] By fall 1945 foremen had enough people but not enough lumber for scaffolding to put them all to work. The solution was to produce the lumber themselves from forest plots in the Carpathians assigned to the Lviv Railroad. Felling the forest, they realized that round trunks had to be sawn into boards at the Lviv parquet factory, which was fully occupied with other jobs. The solution was to purchase their own saw bench. [40] Drawing on the experience of other construction enterprises, USVR 22 decided that the most efficient solution was to make as much auxiliary material and tools themselves as possible. Although this was a rational solution from a single enterprise's point of view, multiplying auxiliary enterprises slowed down the Soviet economy as a whole. Instead of the division of labour and horizontal ties, enterprises opted for self-sufficiency, diverting resources and labour away from their main objectives to side projects. The South-Western district as a whole followed the same strategy. Tired of endless "procuring," it started producing plumbing appliances, pipes, finished hardware, and stoves in the district's own plants and workshops.[41]

In 1944 the Lviv Railroad had spent 2.17 million rubles on the terminal's reconstruction even before the reconstruction budget was approved.[42] That budget totalled 14.8 million rubles, with 3.5 million disbursed for 1945. The main problem was not obtaining funds but spending them: purchasing labour and materials. Not by accident the term used in Soviet parlance was to "master" (*osvoit'*) funds. In 1945 USVR 22 managed to "master" only 1.9 million out of the 3.5 million it received, even though the cost of the completed works exceeded budget estimates. In 1945 the builders failed to complete a single square metre of the first floor in the terminal's left wing, which had been scheduled for completion that year. Instead of expanding, the usable space in the terminal shrank in 1945 because "existing space for serving the passengers was demolished to rebuild the restaurant,"[43] which was not finished either. Nineteen forty-five was a year of abysmal failure at the reconstruction site (Figure 7.3).

This failure occurred even though the NKPS had assigned extraordinarily prioritized (*vneocherednoi*) status to the terminal's reconstruction. Senior Party officials were more interested in the terminal building than were the railway management; for them it was a representative civic building full of symbolic significance. In winter 1945–46, a special commission from the CC CP(b)U inspected the building. Although management customarily blamed USVR 22, the commission accused the Railroad's headquarters of endlessly burdening the USVR with evermore new projects.[44] The explanation was simple: the Railroad's plan was mostly about freight, its amounts, and efficient handling; a passenger terminal would not help it at all. The Railroad reported directly to a powerful ministry in Moscow, and cared little about the wishes of the republic's authorities. Only when dealing with heavyweights like Khrushchev, who had a say in Moscow, need the railroad tread cautiously.

Because of 1945's failures the reconstruction of the terminal was transferred from USVR 22 to USVZ (*Upravleniie stroitel'stva i vosstanovleniia zavodov*) 22 – the Railroad's Department of Construction and Rebuilding of Plants.[45] Since the USVZ worked on the nearby engine

Figure 7.3. The terminal under reconstruction. Source: *Al'bom vosstanovleniia L'vovskogo vokzala*, Lviv Railway Museum.

and cars repair plant (the former railway workshops), the assumption was that it could handle the terminal's reconstruction more efficiently. This transfer, however, did not bring the expected improvements. In January 1946 USVZ 22 and the Railroad's headquarters planned to finish the terminal by the end of the year.[46] In reality the fulfilment of the adjusted 1946 plan was a disastrous 40.9 per cent, a meagre 5 per cent improvement over the previous year.[47] USVZ 22 suffered from the same problems as USVR 22, experiencing similar backlogs and delays. The terminal was not alone in this predicament. Lviv-East depot, scheduled for completion in 1946, was still under construction in 1948.[48]

In 1946 the NKPS allocated only 2 million rubles for the terminal's reconstruction. The USVZ planned to spend 8 million[49] and requested another 6 million,[50]which was granted, although only 3 million was actually disbursed. This was still a record sum for terminals in the region – Kyiv's received only 1 million rubles and Chisinau 2 million.[51] The NKPS proved correct, however, in its reluctance to commit funds. Out of 5 million rubles it received for the terminal, USVZ 22 spent less than 2 million.[52] Two waiting halls in the terminal's left wing originally scheduled for completion in 1945 were still in progress at the end of 1946.

The terminal remained a low priority for both USVZ 22 and the Lviv Railroad as a whole. Both Lviv and the management of the South-Western Railroad in Kyiv believed that the junction's bypasses and the widening of its western neck should trump all other projects in Lviv.[53] Although the funds for the Lviv terminal were significant, they were dwarfed by the investment in the Railroad's industrial sites.[54]

Labour remained a problem.[55] There were seasonal fluctuations, and work came to a virtual standstill in winter: only 0.7 per cent of the yearly plan was met in January 1946.[56] In 1946–47, famine starved workers.[57] As the reconstruction progressed, new problems with materials arose. Laying bricks and pouring concrete was relatively easy, but the installation of plumbing, electricity, and heating required unavailable skill and valuable materials. The USVZ tried to leave those jobs to the Lviv Railroad.[58] Since the latter refused them, the USVZ continued to expand its own "material-technical base," establishing various workshops.[59]

In the meantime, the management of the Lviv Railroad continued to criticize the reconstruction departments for their slow pace, fraud, and "alienating themselves from the Railroad."[60] Complaints to Moscow were of no avail: the reconstruction departments were sheltered by their own superior, the Main Department of Reconstruction Works.[61] Although officially attached to the railroads, the reconstruction organizations were in fact quite independent, established ad hoc at the end of the war.

In December 1946 the head of the Lviv Railroad listed the terminal as one of two "main impediments and bottlenecks" in its work.[62] Newspaper articles described the situation at the terminal as intolerable. Ticket counters could not be reached in the overcrowded main vestibule. Waiting halls were stuffy and dirty, and passengers were forced to sit on bare concrete since there were no benches.[63] Simultaneously with these articles, a public challenge came from South-Western Railroad to organize a socialist competition between the Kyiv and Lviv terminals. The Lviv terminal's management and the Railroad's passenger service believed they had a strong chance to win.[64] Petro Shakhrai, the Railroad's head, warned, however, that "this address of the Kievites in the press is not about people's thoughts that appeared out of nowhere, this task was given by Khrushchev to bring order to our terminal; he prompted (*podskazal*) this action."[65]

The story of the Lviv terminal was not unique. The construction of the Kyiv terminal advanced at a slightly faster pace, but had very similar problems. Between 1943 and 1947 more than 8 million rubles was spent on its reconstruction, but as of June 1947 none of the main rooms was finished. The terminal had not a single working clock. Twice glass panes had been installed on the roof, only to fall off quickly.[66] In 1948 the Donetsk terminal consisted of two temporary barracks, while Dnipropetrovsk's (Dnipro's) was located in a former school building.[67] The reconstruction of train terminals was well behind schedule all over the Soviet Union.[68]

By the end of 1947, 68 per cent of the Lviv terminal plan for that year had been completed[69] – a far cry from fulfilment, but still a major improvement over previous years. The construction departments by then were fully supplied with labour,[70] the credit for which should go the authorities in Kyiv. In February 1947 the heads of both the USVR and USVZ were summoned to Kyiv. Also at the meeting were the managers of the South-Western Railroad, the transportation secretary from the CC CP(b)U, and an inspector from the ministry in Moscow. The criticism of Lviv's departments was devastating.[71] Architect Domashenko, who was also present, explained that "all our construction organizations think only about making a foundation, raising walls and covering them with roof, and later stuccoing it. While we can work like that with technical buildings, it is unacceptable in the case of a building with some architectural face, architectural specificity."[72] He argued that transferring the terminal from the USVR to the USVZ had been a mistake. The USVZ thought it could complete the terminal with little effort simply because it had a much larger construction project nearby, but the terminal was "over their head." Instead of doing "the quality work as outlined in the blueprints," the USVZ was constantly petitioning the ministry to "simplify it." The USVZ allegedly was also diverting labour and material from the terminal to its other, industrial, sites.[73]

The Lviv Railroad also received its share of scolding. Allegedly, its head, Shakhrai, "approached the construction of the terminal indifferently, never took a look at the blueprints, did not take them even once into his hands."[74] But railway managers at the meeting defended their priorities. The head of the district's engine repair service argued that the terminal was stealing resources from the USVZ's industrial projects, not vice versa. He alleged that, in Lviv, the terminal was the only site that employed only free labour, while convicts worked on all other projects. Nonetheless, he agreed with Domashenko that the terminal should be taken from the USVZ, to let the latter focus on industrial sites.[75] The railway managers also agreed that "the Lviv terminal was in such a condition that it was a shame for the Oblast centre to have such a terminal."[76]

The USVZ and USVR managers defended themselves, blaming the Railroad for being unwilling to help.[77] Forty per cent of their workers were still POWs, who had to be kept under supervision in large groups of twenty to thirty; at work, most of them were "merely standing in the same pit not doing anything substantial." The free workers did not work during low temperatures or religious holidays.[78] Detailed plans were sent with delays,[79] and materials were missing.[80] Construction managers apparently also treated their stints in Lviv as temporary, and did not care sufficiently about their reputation there.[81] It was suggested that they be dismissed, but the Central Committee representative explained that this had been tried and had never solved the problem: "People could not be changed endlessly."[82] The construction bosses and the head of the Lviv Railroad were merely reprimanded.[83] Before the war, when defects were discovered in the newly built Vinnytsia terminal, its designers and builders had been arrested and sentenced as wreckers.[84] After the war, the deficit of cadres protected valuable specialists.

Nineteen forty-seven was also the thirtieth anniversary of the October Revolution, and public buildings acquired particular significance. Attention to the terminal, however, slowed down work on other railway projects. By September only 43 per cent of the total plan of capital investments had been fulfilled, worse than in the previous year.[85] Full staffing on some projects meant greater deficits elsewhere. In the first quarter of 1947, USVZ 22 still had only 3,423 out of the required 4,249 workers.[86] By the end of the year, the terminal reconstruction's total budget was raised to 16,775,000 rubles – 2 million above the 1945 estimate – but only 41 per cent had been spent. After more than three years, the reconstruction was not even half-finished. Only the exclusive "government rooms" had both stucco and parquet. The gallery of the left wing was allegedly 90 per cent ready. Terrazzo floors were being laid in washrooms, and walls were being prepared for marble panels. In the right wing gallery, only the cement underlay of the floors in two rooms was finished. The main vestibule was in use, but its walls still had to be tiled and the domes finished. There was no stucco on the station's façade. Telephone, telegraph, radio, and fire alarm systems were installed and then uninstalled because of numerous defects. In the sheds, metal frames were fixed but not painted. They were covered with glass panes and temporary zinc-coated iron sheets. One thousand square metres of glass panes were not glued with putty.

USVZ 22 requested that the Railroad open an account containing 350,000 rubles in Moscow to purchase marble, but the funds sat there for two months without moving. Eventually, only 83,000 rubles was disbursed; the rest was returned to the Railroad's account only to have the same request repeated later. Domashenko complained that, according to his design, the terminal's domes were to be roofed with ceramic tiles, and he had even sourced the tiles in Chernivtsi. The USVZ, however, insisted on metallic domes, which were easier to roof. The Railroad approved the modification, but even these domes of zinc were not finished in 1947.[87]

At the beginning of 1948, reconstruction came to standstill; requests and threats from the Railroad and the local Party organization were ignored.[88] The Railroad appealed to the district, and the district in turn appealed to the Central Committee in Kyiv, complaining not only about USVZ 22, but also about its supervisors in Moscow.[89] The plan for 1948 was to finish the first round of rooms.[90] A reminder came from the Ukrainian Council of Ministers in the form of a resolution about the services offered in the republic's stations and terminals. The resolution stressed that the most important task was to secure the implementation of reconstruction plans. The Council also disbursed 1 million rubles from its own funds for furniture in the Lviv terminal, which was to come from the Mukachevo factory, a top-notch furniture maker – it also made furniture for the Supreme Soviet of Soviet Ukraine. Lviv had its own furniture factory, but it was tasked with making furniture worth only 600,000 rubles for the Chisinau terminal, which was of secondary importance.[91]

In 1948 the reconstruction plan became more realistic, but still was adjusted downwards nine times in the course of the year. The construction enterprises of the Lviv Railroad ended the year with a 71.1 per cent plan-fulfilment rate, but only 50.9 of the originally approved plan.[92] At the Lviv terminal, 76 per cent of the adjusted yearly plan was completed.[93] The most important achievements of the year were the partial completion of the rooms for mothers and children and the beautification of the terminal surroundings with grass and plant beds.[94] On 1 October the reconstruction of the terminal was transferred from the disbanded USVZ 22 to Department 56 of the Main Railway Construction of the West.[95]

In April 1949 the Council of Ministers of the USSR passed a resolution ordering the completion by 1952 of the reconstruction of all damaged train terminals.[96] Railway authorities in Kyiv responded by revising the schedule for the Lviv terminal and set 1 October 1949 as the new completion date. When that deadline arrived, however, only the left wing was largely finished.[97] The construction department tried to declare the whole left wing as finished, but the commission did not accept it. There were too many defects: the baseboards were not fixed properly, there was no stucco behind the radiators, windows and doors were cracked and bent, and floors in some rooms were not finished. The staircase was still waiting for marble; parquet floors had to be scraped. There were no mouldings from non-ferrous metals, and ventilation and stoves in the restaurant were still being installed.[98] By December only the offices on the third floor of the right wing – for the local Party committee, trade union, and military commandant, and the radio and time-synchronization rooms – had been completed and handed over to the Railroad.[99]

Department 56 argued that its budget only allowed for either the full completion of the right wing or the completion of the right wing and the central part without final touches. Since parts of the terminal already had luxurious finishing touches such as marble and terrazzo floors, the authorities decided that, at this stage, simplification would "damage the general architectural ensemble of the terminal."[100] The construction bosses asked for another increase to the budget, but the railway district declined the request. Instead it assured them that, once the commission had officially accepted the terminal as completed, unfinished parts – such as passenger tunnels, platforms, and finishes (*blagoustroistvo*) – would be authorized and funded as a new, renovation project.[101] In 1949, 5.6 million rubles was allocated for the terminal's reconstruction, but only 1.75 million was actually spent.[102] Plan-fulfilment dropped to 30 per cent, even lower than in 1945 and 1946.[103] The construction managers blamed administrative reorganization – namely, the dissolution of the USVZ.

In 1950 the post-war reconstruction of the Soviet economy officially ended. According to Soviet statistics, the output of Ukraine's economy was 15 per cent higher than in 1940, while consumption reached its pre-war level. The terminal in Lviv, however, was still unfinished. Most work now was on expensive finishing: the marble and black granite, mosaic, and terrazzo floors (Figure 7.4). In the waiting halls, columns and pilasters were riveted with anhydrite.[104] Lviv's glass factory was working on the "porthole" glass for the fountain and fire booster.[105] The officers' hall and ticket counters reserved for privileged groups were to have floors of parquet and Mettlach tile.[106] Marble had to come from the Office of Special Construction Materials of the Main Railway Construction-West Trust in Moscow, and there was no bronze or aluminum wire for the terrazzo floors.[107] The right wing was still waiting for wiring to come from Electrical Installations-South. When the marble finally arrived, there was too much of it, and the excess was shipped to the Mukachevo terminal even though there was no marble in the original designs for that building.[108]

Figure 7.4. Sanding terrazzo floors in the terminal's right wing. Source: *Al'bom vosstanovleniia L'vovskogo vokzala*, Lviv Railway Museum.

In 1950, among the Lviv Railroad's projects, the Lviv terminal was once again singled out as an especially unsatisfactory case.[109] The head of Department 56 complained that, while large unused amounts sat in the accounts, they were designated for specific expenses, and there was no budget line for other things, such as armoured glass for the sheds or putty to hold the glass to the frame. As a result, there were broken glass and leaks, which in turn damaged cellars, causing a serious safety hazard.[110]

Some of the construction problems in 1950 were also connected to yet another administrative reorganization of construction enterprises. On 1 October Department 56 was liquidated and all its works were transferred to the *Dorstroi* (Department of Railway Construction) of the Lviv Railroad. Aware of the coming reorganization, Department 56 had little incentive to perform, filling only a lacklustre 68.4 per cent of the plan.[111] Old problems still plagued the construction site. Even basic materials such as concrete were in deficit.[112] Labour shortages persisted.[113] *Kievtransuzelproekt* still owed the construction site certain blueprints, in particular for ventilation and lighting.[114]

Nonetheless, at the end of March 1950, Hryhorii Holovchenko, the new head of the Lviv Railroad, sent the minister of communications a photo album celebrating the reconstruction of the terminal, and promised that the terminal would be fully rebuilt that year.[115] This was easier said than done. On 16 November the right wing of the terminal passed the government commission as completed.[116] The terminal's general technical readiness was estimated at 94.3 per cent, but this was almost certainly inflated. Financially, out of 2.4 million rubles disbursed for the reconstruction in 1950, only 1.1 million was spent.[117] Support rings from reinforced concrete still had to be installed for the central vestibule's columns, as well as thermo-insulation of the inter-floor space and the vestibule's mosaic floors. The new deadline for completion of the terminal was 1 May 1951.[118]

The 1951 deadline was not met either. That year *Dorstroi* used only 57 per cent of the funds allocated for the terminal. In October the Railroad explained that completion was postponed due to the lack of concrete, asphalt, Mettlach and glazed tiles, ceruse, wires, cables, gas pipes, and water radiators.[119] *Dorstroi*'s work, like that of its predecessors, was characterized by "numerous defects, which are being fixed for a very long time after the unit is officially completed."[120]

In 1952 it was decided that the reconstruction was essentially over. The completion went largely uncelebrated, since *de facto* work on the terminal continued apace. In July the Railroad's newspaper sang the praises of "the reconstructed Lviv terminal," which "became much better, more beautiful than it had been before the war." The same article, however, described "dirty tunnels with cracked walls and floors, chock-full of construction material."[121] The Railroad allocated more than a million rubles for further reconstruction in 1953 and 1954, but since the reconstruction officially was over, someone deleted the word "reconstruction" (*vosstanovlenie*) from the register of capital projects and replaced it with "finishing the works on tunnels."[122]

Finishing the tunnels, and hanging the still missing obligatory portraits of Party leaders, "pictures and slogans approved by the Party and Soviet organizations,"[123] were not the only things left to do. Construction work on the exterior of the left wing and platforms continued.[124] Moreover, in 1952, a number of "construction defects" transpired. Putty was still missing for the train sheds' glass panes and, "as a result gusts of wind blow through the glass of the roof destroying it." By the beginning of March, 215 square metres of the roof and 73 square metres of the sheds' vertical ends had lost their glass. Puddles formed on the platforms, and freezing damaged the terminal's cellars and tunnels.[125] The façade had to be repainted, since the paint had peeled off, and the rusting roof had to be treated with anti-corrosion paint.[126] Capital renovation was needed. It started in 1953, immediately after the official end of reconstruction.[127]

In a way the Soviet reconstruction of the terminal never ended. One cycle of repairs followed another. The problem with the glass panes of the train sheds was fixed only after the fall of the Soviet Union, when glass was replaced with plastic. All the problems notwithstanding, the main terminal was a success story if compared to Pidzamche, Lviv's second terminal. The latter still lay in ruins in 1954, while its passengers used a temporary shed.[128]

Even if we accept 1952 as the end date, the post-war reconstruction took three times longer than the original construction of the terminal. Instead of becoming a symbol of Stalin's post-war economic miracle, it became an eloquent testimony to the inefficiency of Soviet economics. One Soviet study claimed that the rebuilding of the Lviv terminal was cheaper than the construction of new terminals in Odesa and Stalingrad (Volgograd): 125 rubles per cubic metre, against 234 and 352 roubles in the Odesa and Stalingrad cases.[129] The actual price of the reconstruction seems to have been more than 166 rubles per cubic metre, but the indicator itself is quite misleading. Both the Stalingrad and Odesa terminals were more lavishly decorated than Lviv's, and therefore more expensive. Moreover, their total volume was much smaller – 45,000 and 67,600 cubic metres, respectively – which explains the higher price per cubic metre. In fact the reconstruction of the Lviv terminal was just as expensive as the construction of a new one would have been.

There is more to the story of the terminal's reconstruction than the inherent problems of the administrative economy, its priorities, institutional in-fighting, unrealistic plans, post-war scarcity, and poor organization of work. It is also about the role and functioning of the public space in the post-war Soviet Union.

There was no shortage of explicit ideological messages literally built into the terminal: sheaves of wheat, hammers and sickles, five-pointed stars, profiles of Party leaders (Figure 7.5). Those orthodox ideological symbols, however, did not form narratives. Their overabundance was chaotic. They marked the space as Soviet, but did not provide a story, instead shying away from complex messages prone to alternative interpretations. There were almost no murals – except in the mothers' and children's room, which was illustrated with characters from Russian folk tales[130] – but framed paintings hung aplenty. The most popular painting was of the Great Leader himself. Stalin could be seen with Lenin in the men's section of the "government rooms," shaking hands with a female delegate in the women's room, playing with children in the mothers' and children's room, towering over the senior officers' room, conversing with Gorky at the stationmaster's guest table, and serving night duty in the terminal head's office (Figure 7.6). Not least,

Figure 7.5. Fragment of the vestibule of the "government rooms" and the waiting hall for transit passengers in the left wing. Source: *Al'bom vosstanovleniia L'vovskogo vokzala*, Lviv Railway Museum.

a larger-than-life, full-height sculpture of Stalin stood at the end of the main vestibule, where the stained glass of St Michael used to let light in (Figure 7.7).

Post-war Soviet terminals were uniform in their aesthetics. A total remake, with only the appearance of continuity, was not unique to Lviv. A terminal originally built in the inter-war Soviet Ukraine went through the similar disfiguration. Viktor Nekrasov, a war veteran and famous writer and dissident, described the outrageous "reconstruction" of the once beautifully modernist Kyiv terminal:

> It was rebuilt. But how? Someone decided that the triumph of victory is inseparable from the pompousness of form. More columns, cornices, capitals, volutes, moulded decorations. This was called an "enrichment." Enriched it was ...
>
> No, visitor, I beg you not to enter the terminal. Everything tasteless, deprived of any architectural logic, is assembled there together. The arches are destroyed and replaced with the paired columns, parabolic windows walled wherever possible and "decorated" on the sides with absurd pilasters; the ceiling is sprinkled with some kind of starlets, idyllic production landscapes hang on the walls of waiting halls, instead of luminescent plafonds – heavy *Metrostroi*[131] chandeliers. Nothing was left from the architect's conception. Was the author of this carnage – let's not name him – looking into Verbytsky's[132] eyes, while destroying his creation? After all, apparently he was Verbytsky's pupil.[133]

The unnamed architect in this quote was, of course, Domashenko. As in Kyiv, Lviv's reconstruction both changed the interior décor and signalled a radical departure from the original Secession design. The addition of the second storey brought the terminal closer to Stalinist post-war monumentalism, sometimes called "Stalin's Baroque" or "Stalin's Empire" – essentially Neo-Classicism, with Empire and Art Deco elements.

The reconstructed Lviv terminal, just like its other post-war Soviet siblings, was meant to showcase the achievement of the country's socialist economy, the riches held in common by Soviet citizens. As Mikhail Ryklin observed in the case of the Moscow metro, its grandeur offered a symbolic "compensation" for the loss of individual property rights.[134] Large train terminals, with thousands of people passing through them every day, just like metro stations, were the most logical place for Stalinist palaces, intended for everyday visual consumption. Architectural over-aestheticization aimed at celebrating speed and technology in fact "debased" and deprived them of symbolic depth.[135]

Figure 7.6. Portraits of Stalin in the Lviv terminal. Source: *Al'bom vosstanovleniia L'vovskogo vokzala*, Lviv Railway Museum.

Figure 7.7. Sculpture of Stalin in the main vestibule. Source: S.V. Kostenko, ed., *Arkhitektura Sovetskoi Ukrainy, 1951–1952* (Moscow: Gosudarstvennoe izdatel'stvo po stroitel'stvu i arkhitekture, 1955), 112.

The new design was not only about new aesthetics. It also exposed the Soviet inability to equal the uniquely detailed artistic craftsmanship of the old terminal. Even expensive "enrichment" consisted of heavily standardized uniform items. Moreover, luxurious marble finish could not quell the stench from lousy plumbing or compensate for inadequate ventilation. The sheds of iron and glass turned into a skeleton covered with improvised boards. Such mundane problems would keep subverting the Stalinist grandeur of the terminal's interior throughout the whole Soviet period.

The original spatial arrangement of the terminal layout was also lost. Soviet terminals were supposed to reflect a society without class antagonisms. The division into classes was abolished at ticket counters and in waiting rooms, even though there were still better and worse, more and less expensive, train cars and tickets. Instead of spaces segregated by class, new spaces were to appear in Soviet terminals. They were the spaces of "public organizations, technical creativity, and common conveniences, necessary for the active everyday life of the service personnel."[136] The Lviv terminal acquired a barber shop, a "red corner" where communist ideology and its bearers could be honoured, and a library.[137] In 1951 a cinema opened on the second floor, with 144 (later 183) seats and regular show times.[138] There were also the room of mothers and children and sleeping rooms (*komnaty otdykha*) for transit passengers. Neither the former nor the latter, with their twenty-two "shining nickel beds" made with "snow-white linen,"[139] were even remotely sufficient to accommodate all those in need of them. These "conveniences" pointed to the domestication of the terminal's space, blurring the boundary between public and private, work and leisure, railway workers and passengers, and changing the nature of the terminal's public space.

This blurring of boundaries should not be confused with the disappearance of hierarchy and privilege. The military were singled out, with separate premises for soldiers, officers, and senior officers. The Party Committee for the station had its own room, as did the station's military commandant. There were also special ticket counters for soldiers, officers, and deputies of the Supreme Soviets. These high-ranking people also enjoyed access to the station's most exclusive space: the former emperor's rooms, now called the "government rooms," encompassed a larg space, with a separate vestibule, staircase, and even a winter garden (Figure 7.8). Just like the emperor's rooms, this new space would be used very infrequently in a provincial city; accordingly, in 1962, the Minister of Communications ordered that special rooms for deputies should be maintained only in the capitals of republics, although in

Figure 7.8. The "government rooms" of the Lviv terminal after the reconstruction. Source: *Al'bom vosstanovleniia L'vovskogo vokzala*, Lviv Railway Museum.

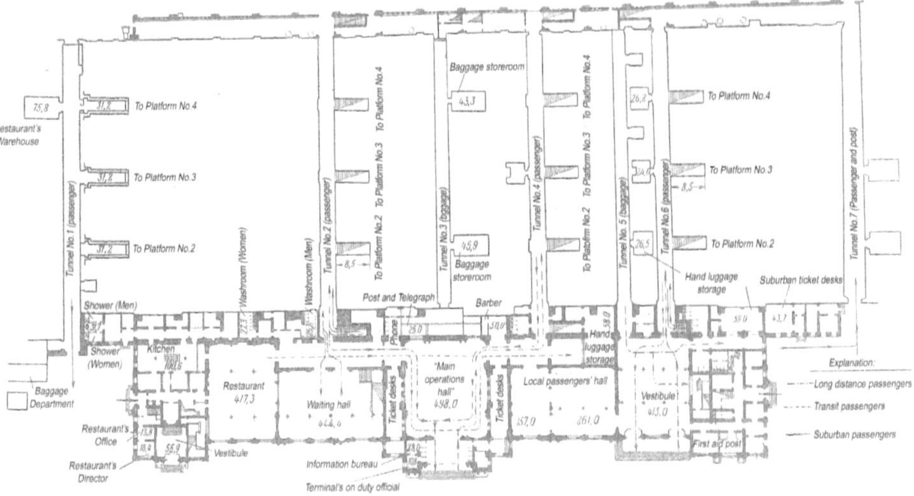

Terminal's first floor after the reconstruction

Terminal's second floor after the resconstruction

Figure 7.9. The layout of the terminal's floors after the reconstruction. Source: Based on G.P. Zaporozhtsev and S.I. Iakushin, *Novye zheleznodorozhnye vokzaly* (Moscow: Transzheldorizdat, 1957), 212–13.

Ukraine Odesa and Simferopol were added to Kyiv.[140] In Lviv, however, the resolution was tacitly ignored. Part of this exclusive space was converted into a hall for foreign passengers, still closed to the regular Soviet public, while the rest remained an exclusive space for deputies and senior officials. In 1969 the Transportation Department of the CC CP(b)U took this space under its direct supervision.[141]

Although the original terminal had been celebrated as an illustration of nearly perfect organization of early twentieth-century public space, the Soviet terminal became an equally germane illustration of a specifically Soviet organization of space (Figure 7.9). It was a physical incarnation of the contradictions of Soviet ideology itself and of the specific

Figure 7.10. The restaurant and the waiting hall for transit passengers in the left wing. Source: *Al'bom vosstanovleniia L'vovskogo vokzala*, Lviv Railway Museum.

Figure 7.11. The terminal's façade in the 1980s. Source: Ihor Kotlobulatov collection, courtesy of Ihor Kotlobulatov.

Soviet governmentality. It was a confusing maze of private and public, exclusive and open space, without single, equally applicable rules, and with as little transparency as possible. Dining and waiting spaces were intermixed, exits and corridors proliferated, and special-purpose pockets of all kinds abounded. Lavishly covered with granite and marble, the terminal's space was fragmented with numerous columns. Obstructed views, numerous mirrors, and polished surfaces gave it a labyrinthine appearance (Figure 7.10). Multiplying reflections complicated the task of understanding the space. Instead of directing eyes to ornaments and representations, as had been the case in the original terminal, mirrors drew attention to the subject itself, inviting self-examination and self-discipline.

The new Soviet arrangements and embellishments were a poor fit with the remnants of the old terminal. The façade, with its original symbols, was especially problematic. By the early 1980s, because of technical problems, the façade had lost its Soviet symbols and inscriptions (Figure 7.11). Its cartouche remained blank for the rest of the decade,[142] with only the occasional poster hung over the entrance to communicate standard ideological messages. The blank cartouche of the façade also sent a message of its own – about the problematic nature of Soviet modernity. In the post-Soviet 1990s the cartouche acquired its present-day appearance, with the word "Lviv" and the city's coat of arms on it. While also aesthetically dubious, it has thus far held up much better than the Soviet symbols.

Chapter Eight

Order without Law

In 1944 the terminal became the central part of the Lviv-Passenger station. The station received an acting stationmaster, who had already served as a deputy there in 1941.[1] in December, after the acting stationmaster was arrested for embezzlement, Pavel Selivestrov was appointed to the post.[2] In September 1945, the *militsiia* caught one of Selivestrov's acquaintances on a platform selling overpriced tickets for the Moscow train. The culprit claimed he was acting on Selivestrov's behalf.[3] This was not the first time Selivestrov had been accused of speculation,[4] and it came on top of other problems with his "moral make-up." Already paying alimony to two ex-wives in Russia, he had married for a third time in Lviv.[5] Then there were his drinking bouts, one of which ended in his detention.[6] He had also been charged with sexual harassment or, rather, attempted rape. After two young female passengers refused to join him in his office Selivestrov "applied brutal force, which was registered in a medical certificate."[7] The head of the Lviv Railroad requested Selivestrov's removal, and the ministry complied.

Selivestrov's replacement was Rostislav Obvintsev. Born in 1910, Obvintsev had worked on the railway since 1928, served in the army in between 1932 and 1934, joined the Party in 1942, and graduated from the Military-Transportation Academy in 1943.[8] Upon graduation he was despatched to the Stalingrad Railroad. There he earned the Order of the Labour Red Banner and the medals "For Battle Merit" and "For the Defence of Stalingrad." Wounded in the Battle of Stalingrad, he acquired what was called a permanent second-degree disability.[9] From 1945 to 1947 he was the only person with a higher education working at the Lviv-Passenger station.

It soon transpired that Obvintsev had problems of his own. The station's Party secretary reported his "proclivity towards alcoholic drinks," which showed up "systematically at work and outside," and accused the stationmaster of being "unscrupulous in private life." In Lviv Obvintsev divorced his second wife and began "cohabitating with a certain Olga, who had a higher education but did not work – practising speculation." Both women appeared occasionally at the terminal, "making scenes." Once, Obvintsev's ex-wife gave him a public thrashing and broke an inkstand against his head; allegedly, Obvintsev was "venting" his frustrations "on the station's workers."[10] The secretary described Obvintsev as a "great grabber," vengeful and arrogant, who "considers himself to be smarter and more knowledgeable than anyone else."[11]

Obvintsev had his defenders. Some suspected the secretary was trying to avenge the dismissal of his protégé from the ticket office.[12] Obvintsev acknowledged social drinking and complications in his private life, but denied drinking at work.[13] He also reminded the secretary that, under his watch, the station had won first place in the South-Western district's ranking.[14] Eventually his personal problems and intrigues took their toll, causing a mental breakdown. Obvintsev was hospitalized in a psychiatric clinic and diagnosed with schizophrenia.[15]

The terminal experienced similar personnel problems. Its first head, Mikhail Bezlepkin, was dismissed and sentenced to six years imprisonment soon after his appointment.[16] He had been part of the stationmaster's ring, had taken bribes and issued fake work IDs.[17] His replacement, Pavel Lebedev, managed to rein in the terminal's staff. Born in 1915 and a Russian – just like all of Lviv's other Soviet stationmasters and terminal heads – Lebedev had a secondary technical education and had worked on the railway since 1934. Similar to Obvintsev, albeit slightly younger, Lebedev belonged to the new cohort of Stalinist managers who had begun their careers as young workers in the 1930s. Characterized by the Party as a "technically literate commander, full of initiative," he wore the badges of the "Shock Worker of Stalin's Draft Call" (*Udarnik Stalinskogo prizyva*) and "Excellent Movement Specialist" (*Otlichnyi dvizhenets*).[18] Under Lebedev the terminal rapidly improved its performance and overfulfilled its targets by more than double.[19] Lebedev also replaced his deputy, who "did not cope with the work, was not on site; often showed up at work noticeably drunk, had a wide circle of acquaintances in the city."[20]

With Obvintsev's breakdown, Lebedev was promoted to stationmaster of Lviv-Passenger, providing the station with stable leadership. Obvintsev recovered, however, and returned to work as the stationmaster of Lviv-Main – the city's main freight station. After Lebedev's promotion, misrule returned to the terminal. As a public space and service enterprise, the terminal was prone to petty fraud, theft, bribery, and other typical ills of the Soviet service sector.[21] Only in 1951, with Vasilii Vishnevich (b. 1918) did the terminal acquire an efficient Soviet boss, who reined in the workers and headed the terminal till the end of the Soviet period.[22]

The Lviv Railroad headquarters during the 1944–49 period saw its fair share of squabbling, fraud, and poor discipline. Petro Shakhrai, head of the Railroad since 1939, was relieved of his position in November 1946 "for abuses in the line of duty to selfish ends."[23] Shakhrai claimed that these were the insinuations of resentful subordinates – the headquarters' Party secretary, in particular. Conflicts between "production managers" and Party secretaries were common in Soviet industries, and the railway was no exception. There were similar conflicts at the district[24] and station[25] levels.

An Obkom commission had started investigating this conflict in October 1945.[26] Shakhrai was accused of profiteering. He, in turn, charged his accusers with the very same misdeeds – in particular, his former deputy Kononov, who procured railway equipment in Germany on behalf of the NKPS.[27] Shakhrai did not deny that people helped themselves to the goods coming from Germany as reparations: "back then it was seen as completely normal, since there were so many instances of taking property from Germany to the east by trains and special groups, no one attached any significance to that."[28] But Shakhrai claimed that it was not on his order and outside of his purview. He also denied helping himself to the "trophies" found in Lviv. The only exception was a dining set, but even in this case he had followed proper procedures: the Railroad's provisioning department had appraised six dining sets, and then he and his deputies bought them.[29] Others were less scrupulous. Kononov, in particular, allegedly approached Shakhrai several times with a bribe to secure a green light for his loot from Germany.[30] The stationmaster from Lviv-Main, together with his accountant, also developed a scheme for stealing transported German goods.[31]

In the accusations against Shakhrai, the evidence included housing and luxury goods. When top Railroad's officials returned to Lviv, they found their pre-war apartments and furniture largely intact. According to Shakhrai's estimate, close to 60 per cent of his pre-war furniture was still there in 1944. Moreover, senior German railway officials, who lived in the 1913 building next to the Railroad's headquarters, had left behind some new items, such as grand pianos. Apparently Shakhrai ordered the surrender of all the new furniture from the apartments, although for compliance he could rely only on people's words. Shakhrai acknowledged commissioning a bedroom set for himself from the railway workshops, but had paid for it officially.[32] He also had a personal car, but, as he explained, it was not from Germany but purchased legally in Lviv. Both his sons had motorbikes – one was purchased in Lviv, the other was a gift from Shakhrai's friend, a senior counterintelligence officer.[33]

There was also the issue of a villa in a prestigious "New World" neighbourhood, which Shakhrai allegedly seized from a nursery. In his version, the villa at Hipsova 36, one of the most famous Bauhaus villas in the city, had been allocated to him in 1944. Since he was then still waiting for his family, he had let the railway nursery use it and taken an apartment closer to headquarters. Once the nursery outgrew the premises, it had to be moved, and the new use for the villa had not yet been decided.

Accused of expelling tenants from three apartment buildings in the same prestigious area, which had been "Aryanized" by the Germans, Shakhrai retorted that these originally had been allocated to the Railroad as housing for its managers, but later were seized with the help of armed men by the Lviv tank-repair plant for its employees. There was a prolonged litigation between the Railroad and the plant about these apartment buildings, not in court, of course, but in the offices of local Party and Soviet committees.[34]

Shakhrai denied that he had bribed ministry officials with furniture, as his enemies claimed; rather, the furniture had been legally commissioned by the ministry from the Railroad's workshops. Some ministry officials had purchased furniture for their private apartments, too, but there was nothing unusual in it: "Thousands of people were buying it in Lviv and taking it nearly all over the Soviet Union. People came not only from the [Ministry of Communications], but from all other Ministries and organizations, from Moscow and Kiev, completed purchases and shipped them by all means, including strings of east-bound trucks loaded with furniture."[35] State organizations and private citizens worked hand in hand to execute this large-scale plunder of a territory still saturated with the accessories of a "bourgeois" lifestyle. Shakhrai claimed that "the Railroad conducted itself very strictly, providing cars only in individual cases on direct requests from Sovnarkom, the Central Committee, Narkomat, or Obkom, with at least 70 per cent of freight cars provided on direct orders from the Central Planning Department in the Ministry of Communications."[36] The train car registers show dozens of them were sent east monthly, mostly loaded with furniture. The furniture was often sold by ethnic Poles, who were forced to leave for Poland but not allowed to take bulkier items with them. Besides the Ministry of Communications and its railroads, various NKGB offices in Moscow and the provinces, departments of Central Committees of the USSR and its republics, and trade ministries were among the recipients. Also receiving furniture were prominent individual citizens, such as the aircraft designer Iakovlev (one car of furniture), the stand-up comedian Raikin (two cars), and the Kievan Metropolitan of the Russian Orthodox Church (four cars).[37] Shakhrai also denounced his Party secretary for the ideological gaffe of saying "Soviet scoundrels had devastated us," instead of the intended "fascist scoundrels," at a meeting celebrating the Soviet victory on 9 May 1945.[38]

This entire defence notwithstanding, Shakhrai was removed from office and reprimanded by the Party Commission of the Central Committee of the Communist Party of the Soviet Union in May 1947. Nonetheless, in August, Shakhrai was appointed to head the North Donetsk Railroad. As a Party secretary there with whom Shakhrai also had a conflict[39] remarked: "No one is taken off the executive position forever."[40] Experienced railway managers were valuable. After Shakhrai, the Lviv Railroad went through two heads – Ivan Kraiovyi and Mikhail Osintsev – before obtaining an effective and more permanent leader in Hryhorii Holovchenko, who led it from 1950 to 1959.

What can be made of this managerial turbulence? First, these problems were not railway-specific. At the Lviv terminal alone, the restaurant and the railway security force (later to become the railway *militsiia*) of the MGB (*Ministerstvo Gosudarstvennoi Bezopasnosti*, Ministry of State Security, changed from the NKVD in 1946) experienced identical problems. The war and the traumas it inflicted were to blame. There was also Lviv's peculiarly tempting and very un-Soviet milieu, with its material riches and people inexperienced in Soviet ways. Lviv at the time was witnessing a bonanza of illegality, attracting suspect elements of all kinds while also experiencing a crime wave common to all Soviet cities at the end of the war.

Georgii Trifonov recalled that Lviv, as "the most western of all Soviet cities," with its nationalist underground movements and proximity to a still porous border, was especially attractive to Soviet criminals. Trifonov, himself a train thief (*maidanshchik*), tried to leave the country using connections in Lviv's Ukrainian nationalist underground. He also took part in a "conference" of the Soviet and Central European criminal underworld that assembled in Lviv's railway neighbourhoods to discuss new border arrangements.[41] After the war Lviv turned into a centre of the important railway corridor connecting the USSR with its Eastern European satellites. The new Soviet western border, now within the socialist bloc, was more open to freight and passenger traffic than the pre-war border had been.

Although Lviv's surfeit of material riches was eventually exhausted and the stream of goods from occupied Central Europe dried up, most problems associated with the scandals of the 1940s, such as drinking, poor discipline, and theft, persisted. After 1950, however, these became the vices of workers instead of managers. A misbehaving workforce would become one of the main concerns for the cohort of more disciplined Soviet managers that emerged from the tribulations and temptations of the 1940s.

When the Lviv Railroad resumed operations in 1944, its largest problem was managerial cadres. NKPS-appointed positions (the Railroad's top management) were staffed at 50 per cent. A total of 776 pre-1941 officials returned from evacuation, and 586 were sent from other Soviet railroads.[42] The situation with workers was easier at first. The Railroad inherited most of them from the Germans. Only 1,564 returned from evacuation, and 2,507 were received from other Soviet railroads. Some 31,197 came from the "local population." Pre-war Soviet workers concentrated in the locomotive service; 499 of them were re-evacuees and 533 came from other railroads. Even in this elite service, however, 86 per cent were locals.[43] In the passenger service, in charge of the terminal, locals constituted 94 per cent.[44]

In 1944–45 the main concern was the political reliability of local workers. The Railroad conducted a massive screening of its workforce, checking the backgrounds of 22,391 employees. The check flagged 673 people who were sent to rear railroads. Fifty-eight employees were found guilty of wartime crimes and sent to the army's punitive companies, while forty-seven were transferred to positions that did not deal with the actual movement of trains.[45] The MGB screened 13,500 railway employees in Lviv in spring 1945 as part of its larger city sweep. A total of 382 railway workers were identified as anti-Soviet elements, Gestapo agents, collaborators, members of OUN or the Ukrainian Insurgent Army (UPA, *Ukraïns'ka Povstans'ka Armiia*), deserters, or other "enemy elements."[46] Only twenty-two of them belonged to "nationalist organizations." Ninety-three others had been arrested and later released by the Gestapo, which was deemed suspicious.[47]

After 1945 political arrests at the station became rare,[48] although in post-war years the Lviv station saw it share of the state's struggle against the Ukrainian nationalist underground. In 1944–45 Soviet authorities also targeted and eliminated the city's Polish underground. Arrests and shootouts occurred at the station from time to time until the death in 1950 of Roman Shukhevych, the UPA's chief commander, during his attempted arrest in his hideout in Bilohorshcha, a part of the Lviv railway terrain.

Just as in 1940–41 the Soviet state resorted to massive deportations to pacify and secure the region. Deportations to the Soviet interior aimed at destroying the popular base of the UPA and peasant resistance to collectivization peaked in 1947 and continued until Stalin's death in 1953. The largest of all Stalin's deportations, however, was intended to change the region's ethnic composition. It took place in 1945 and 1946 as a population exchange between Poland and Soviet Ukraine, with ethnic Poles and Ukrainians being "evacuated" to the states of their nations. In a way, this resettlement was a culmination of the great forced migrations inaugurated in the region by the First World War. Although not as deadly and physically torturous as deportations to special settlements in the Soviet interior, the exchange had more profound consequences for the cultural landscape. Ethnic Poles, who had lived in the region for centuries, shaping its culture and society, became a statistically inconsequential minority in Western Ukraine. In Lviv, according to the first post-war Soviet census in 1959, the former ethnic Polish majority had been reduced to a paltry 3.9 per cent of the city's population, even less than the remaining Jewish share.[49]

Insisting in 1944 on the rebuilding of Lviv's Polish-designed grand railway terminal, Nikita Khrushchev also urged Stalin to adopt policies that would hasten the "evacuation" of Poles from the city, as well as from all other territories that Soviet Ukraine had acquired at the expense of inter-war Poland.[50] Khrushchev was preaching to the choir: Stalin's redrawing of Poland's boundaries certainly entailed "population transfers." Indeed the leaders of the Allied powers that won the Second World War agreed that the mass transfer of populations was a legitimate and perhaps the only way to disentangle Europe's "nationality problems."[51] For the populations concerned, however, "repatriation" to "national homelands" was an immense personal tragedy. Many left homes, native landscapes, and familiar streets, never to see them again. Most Poles from Western Ukraine eventually complied, fearing Soviet state terror and the Ukrainian nationalist insurgents. There were also resistance and hesitation, however – Polish patriotism and hopes that the international situation would change sustained them for a while.[52]

For the Soviet railway in Lviv, the population transfer posed a twofold problem. First, it meant the loss of qualified labour and the challenge of replacing it. Second, there were logistical difficulties, since the deportation placed additional demands on an already overburdened system. In March 1945 stationmaster Selivestrov complained that "the issue of cadres is very serious. Since all the Poles are returning to Poland, we have no one to rely on; the question is who we shall work with; it is necessary to select people from among Ukrainians and train them."[53] At the time the station employed 194 Poles and 142 Ukrainians.[54] In June the station management complained that the situation "was worsening with every day."[55] Poles were leaving, there were no replacements, and a mammoth stream of passengers was flowing eastward.[56] The Lviv station choked under the mass of people moved by force, the "repatriated" often camping in front of the terminal.[57]

For most deportees from Lviv, the terminal and railway neighbourhoods to the west of it were the last familiar sights of their native city. Those leaving on trucks would pass by the same neighbourhoods, taking Horodotska (Gródecka) Street, the city's main western exit. Formally the repatriation was voluntary; in reality many were forced to leave. The conditions of their journey were harsh. In winter and spring 1945, people camped by stations waiting for trains all over the region. Cars were packed and limitations on belongings imposed, forcing people to sell most of their property.[58] Trains were slow. Covering the short distance to Poland took days. Fleas and hunger plagued the deported as they travelled.[59]

There is little compassion for the deportees in official documents of the Soviet railway administrators, but neither is there even a trace of joy or celebration. The managers themselves were no strangers to the experience of uprooting and frequent transfer. Moreover, like managers in other industries and the local authorities, they were upset by the loss of valuable specialists. One Party official complained of a quiet sabotage by railway managers who would not provide requested trains. He also explained that Party officials often moved the "repatriants" to stations, where they would have to camp for days and weeks, on purpose, hoping to compel the Railroad to supply trains.[60]

There is also little evidence that Lviv's Ukrainian population rejoiced at the deportation of the Poles, despite decades of "nationalizing" politics and the murderous inter-ethnic violence of the war years. Polish historian Roman Aftanazy noted in his diary that, as late as spring 1946, both Poles and "local Ukrainian society" – to be distinguished from Ukrainians from the east – cherished the same vague hope that the international situation would change – that the USSR would surrender Lviv. Some local Ukrainians placed their hopes in General Władysław Anders' Polish army, which many Ukrainians had joined.[61] Polish intellectual Ryszard Gansiniec, however, had little sympathy for Ukrainians, and suspected collusion between the Soviet authorities and the UPA in terrorizing rural Poles in the region. Nevertheless, in December 1945, he was very moved by Christmas greetings from his Ukrainian students, who sang carols in Latin, Polish, and Ukrainian (local Ukrainians, like their Orthodox brethren, celebrated Christmas in January).[62] He also noticed that local Ukrainians, whose Greek Catholic Church, by the decision of the Soviet state, had been "reunited" with the Russian Orthodox Church, began to attend Polish Roman Catholic churches rather than Orthodox ones.[63] For the Lviv station's Party organization in 1945, Ukrainian and Polish "locals" were equally problematic, while its "agitational work" was directed against "Polish-Ukrainian" nationalists.[64]

The "evacuation" of Poles from Lviv was over by July 1946.[65] A symbolic remarking of the city space followed. Streets and institutions were renamed, monuments moved or removed, and new histories of the city were written. New narratives would invent for the city an identity fully compatible with its new position as the centre of Soviet Western Ukraine. The very same narratives systematically underplayed and demonized the city's Polish past. For deported Polish Lvivites returning to the city as visitors after decades of absence, this erasure of the city's Polish-ness and "sack" of the Polish contribution were more striking than the proverbial Soviet poverty and negligence.[66] The Poles who departed the city in 1945 and 1946 also conceptualized it in ethnic or "civilizational" terms. Leaving the city, Gansiniec, "with bleeding heart," sees Lviv as a "symbol of Poland and Polish-ness, which drowns slowly in the barbarity of the steppe."[67] Some larger narrative and the longer-than-life history of a larger community helped to make sense of a deeply personal tragedy: "I am sitting on the wreckage of my life and experience the longings of a dying. I have never realized how grown into this land I am, how this city impressed itself into my heart and my being."[68]

There is no doubt that the forced resettlement of the city's Polish population changed Lviv. Ethnic composition, however, was not the only change that happened in Lviv under the new Soviet regime. Work and leisure, streets and homes, the way people made a living and navigated a world controlled by the modern state, all changed in profound ways that cannot be reduced to changes in the city's ethnicity.

Lviv's main terminal after the Second World War also changed, and not only in its physical appearance. The massive intake of locals secured the growth of the workforce, notwithstanding the exodus of ethnic Poles. By 1949 the Lviv Railroad had 38,765 workers of "mass occupations."[69] This expansion of the labour force continued throughout the whole Soviet period, despite the Railroad's wholesale conversion to diesel and electricity in the 1950s through the 1980s. Both the absolute number of railway workers and their share of the region's adult population kept increasing – yet another evidence of mounting problems with Soviet productivity.[70] By the 1970s, the problems were obvious to state authorities and railway management alike. When in

1971 someone made the usual complaint about the lack of workers needed to improve performance, stationmaster Badiuk angrily replied there would be no additional hiring, only layoffs in the future.[71] He was wrong. The workforce kept expanding until the 1990s.

Lviv-Passenger's workforce reached 579 in 1951.[72] More than half, 295, worked at the terminal.[73] Only six years later the terminal's workforce was 40 per cent larger, accounting for nearly all the station's new hires.[74] After the single Lviv station (both freight and passenger) was formed in 1962, it employed fifteen hundred people,[75] with six hundred working at the terminal.[76] By the end of the 1970s the terminal had almost seven hundred employees.[77] It was an enormously high number, and does not include numerous restaurant employees, station managers, and the *militsiia*, who also worked in the terminal building. By comparison, in 2015 VIA Rail, Canada's national passenger rail service operating 121 stations, had a total of only 2,600 employees.[78]

The station's labour turnover was very high in the late 1940s – over 30 per cent in 1948.[79] It declined to slightly above 10 per cent in the 1950s.[80] Indeed the workforce stabilized to such an extent that the proverbial "clannishness" of railway labour re-emerged. Around 1950, 80 per cent of new cadres at the Lviv station were children of railway workers.[81] In the 1960 and 1970s, however, salaries on the railway lagged those in industry, and workers began deserting it in search of better pay. As late as 1980 management complained about this "old illness" of the station.[82]

Women's share of the workforce was higher than ever before. In 1946, 33 per cent of station's workforce was female;[83] by 1957 that share had increased to 39 per cent.[84] Although the same trend was seen across the post-war Soviet economy, the terminal was exceptional because its female employees on average were better paid than the males.[85] Most women worked in the traditional female (but now relatively better paid) occupation of ticket cashier, but there was also the new phenomenon of female accountants.

Soviet Lviv's most important peculiarity was the "locals": people with non-Soviet background and experiences. According to the official discourse, problems with them stemmed from their ignorance and backwardness. The Railroad's management had used inexperienced "locals" as a convenient excuse for its numerous failures during the 1944–46 period.[86] In fact, when it came to the level of education, the difference between locals and pre-1939 Soviet citizens was negligible. Nearly all the locals had an elementary education, while secondary education was equally a rarity among newcomers from the east. By the end of the 1950s, secondary education was the new norm; only 16 per cent of the station's workers did not have it.[87] The expansion of higher education also led to more demanding educational requirements for managers and officials. In 1964 the government reserved a number of managerial and engineering positions for people with a higher or specialized secondary education. The station at this point had thirty-four vacancies for educated specialists,[88] while the Lviv Railroad as whole had more than three thousand.[89] In terms of employment, the golden age for Soviet graduates had begun. Despite all the station's efforts and its willingness to wait for employees to finish their degrees,[90] open vacancies for qualified workers persisted throughout the 1970s.[91] In 1981 the station was still short seven certified engineers and twenty-one technicians.[92]

Just as post-war Lviv in the 1940s and 1950s had a greater share of ethnic Russians than did most large cities of Central and Southern Ukraine, so the management of the Lviv Railroad was more Russian than that of the South-Western or Odesa Railroads (Table 8.1). By 1953 the share of Ukrainians among them in Lviv declined even further, to 33 per cent.[93] Ethnic Ukrainians among the Railroad's management were "easterners" – newcomers from pre-1939 Soviet Ukraine.

Since the Soviet goal in Western Ukraine was integration, locals were promoted, but only to lower- and middle-rank managerial positions. The promotion was faster in less skilled and less well paid occupations. Of one hundred foremen in the mostly menial tracks service, as early as 1947 all were locals.[94] Training replacements for the deported Poles, the management favoured youth as more reliable and mouldable.[95] The majority of "locals" were now new hires, but there were exceptions. Havrylo Vanio, for example, had worked in 1939–41 as a porter; under the Germans he moved to the workshops, returning to the terminal in September 1944.[96]

Table 8.1. Ethnic composition of senior management of three main railroads of the South-Western district, 1 January 1947

Ethnic Group	Railroad		
	Lviv	South-Western	Odesa
Ukrainians	457	647	870
Russians	622	446	349
Jews	35	44	146

Source: TsDAVO, f. 4920, op. 1, spr. 510, 32, 93, 153.

The promotion of locals was often intended to showcase successful integration. Many had pre-war connections to the Soviet authorities. Vasyl Sadovy, for example, had come to Lviv as a teenager to learn metalworking. In 1921 he joined the railway workshops. In 1939, under the Soviets, he became a chair of the workshops' union committee and a delegate to the People's Assembly that voted for the unification of Western and Soviet Ukraine. In 1940 Sadovy was elected to the Supreme Soviet of the USSR. As a Soviet official he was evacuated in 1941, and returned to Lviv in 1946. As a local who had proven his loyalty, he became a chair of the executive committee of Lviv's Shevchenko district, the poorest northern part of the city.[97] Sadovy retained his seat in both the 1946 and 1950 Supreme Soviet.

There were also some veterans of the local communist movement from the inter-war period. Two of them (a Ukrainian and a Jew) worked at the station. One of them was Mykola Shevchuk, hailed in the 1940s as one of the best local workers at the terminal.[98] Born in 1885, with only an elementary education,[99] from 1926 to 1929 he was a member of PPS-Left, which served as a legal front for communist activities. Shevchuk worked at the terminal from 1939 to 1941, then spent the German occupation in his home village. After the war he returned to work on the terminal's reconstruction. In 1946 he joined the Communist Party of the Soviet Union.[100]

Another communist from the inter-war period at the station was Hersh Malets, a member of the Communist Party of Western Ukraine (KPZU) since 1924 who had spent five years in a Polish prison and served as a secretary of the KPZU's district committee. He had worked at the Lviv station since 1945, serving occasionally on the Party bureau and chairing his shop union committee.[101] When he was about to retire in the 1960s, he asked for a "personal pension," which was awarded prominent communist activists by the Ukrainian Central Committee. A fellow Russian Party member pointed out, however, that Malets had a sister in Israel and received parcels from her, arguing that a communist should reject "alms like that." Malets argued that he did not ask for the gifts, but neither was he going to offend his sister by refusing them.[102] Even though it was 1966 and an antisemitic campaign was in full swing, the station's Party organization supported Malets's application.[103]

During the first post-war years, occupational divides often coincided with ethnic boundaries. Shunters, for example, were mostly local Ukrainians. One of them, Ivan Karashkevych, even became the shunters' "Stakhanov" after he developed a special method for the rapid assembling of trains. As with similar cases, this "method" depended much on Karashkevych's individual skill and the peculiarities of the

Lviv railway marshalling yard, and was not easily transferable to other stations. Nonetheless the Railroad needed a local Stakhanovite and so did the Party. After an enquiry and internal debate, officials decided to acknowledge Karashkevych's achievement and advertise it. Ticket cashiers at the terminal, on the other hand, were mostly Russians.[104] This was an occupation that required not only literacy and arithmetic skills, but also proficiency in Russian.

Recorded ethnic tensions during the first post-war years were usually between local Ukrainians and Russian newcomers. As a rule there was a social dimension to them as well. They often occurred between superiors and subordinates, as in the case of an on-duty official who called "all the local workers 'Banderites' and 'bandits.'"[105] Tensions also arose about the newcomers' sense of superiority. Even in 1951 communists who arrived from the east believed their duty was "to educate the local population."[106] Pre-1939 Soviet citizens tended to stick together, and even had separate rest areas at the station.[107]

The position of locals was ambivalent. On the one hand, they were, to use Tarik Cyril Amar's apt characterization, "redeemable."[108] On the other hand, they were suspected of disloyalty and locked out of key positions. Newcomers reported on the locals and their nostalgic recollections of the pre-war era.[109] Locals were concentrated in low-paid departments and were also the most suspect and unruly. The station's management claimed that the greatest "infestation" (*zasorennost*) of cadres was in the terminal and in the baggage departments.[110]

By 1950 locals accounted for 65 per cent of the station's workforce.[111] Managers and Party activists complained that they were not able to monitor locals or agitate them successfully because of linguistic and cultural barriers.[112] Locals knew very little Russian, and newcomers did not know Ukrainian.[113] During the 1944–46 period, Russian-speaking communists had had the same problem with Polish.[114] As late as 1965 the station's Party activists complained: "We have many nationalists here, while many – the majority – of our Communists cannot strike a conversation in Ukrainian."[115]

The number of commuting locals peaked in the 1960s – after the station had added new workers, but before it could offer them sufficient urban housing. In 1967 more than 60 per cent of the station's workers still lived in villages, causing managers and ideological watchdogs to complain constantly about the difficulties of reaching out to them.[116] As one Party member complained, "we do not know what they are doing there; we are not sufficiently informed."[117] The 1970s saw large-scale housing construction, and by 1980 less than a third of the workers still commuted.[118]

The growing number of locals made the co-optation of at least some of them into management and the Party essential. From 1944 to 1949 Mykola Shevchuk was the only local among the station's middle-rank officials; in 1950 two more locals were promoted to similar positions.[119] Such promoted locals were expected to help the authorities with their inside knowledge. Shevchuk, for example, reported that locals were joining the workforce to escape from collective farms. In a pattern of chain migration, they brought their relatives and friends to the station. According to Shevchuk, in one shop's shift, all the workers were from the same village.[120]

Some promoted locals proved to be problematic. A connection with the OUN-UPA underground could be uncovered, even of people whose relatives had reportedly been killed by nationalists.[121] Other locals simply evaded Party work and remained ignorant of ideological nuances. A certain Vasyl Lesiv, a full Party member since 1952, was reprimanded several times for inactivity.[122] Eventually, in 1973, Lesiv was expelled from the Party during an exchange of Party membership cards. No longer a dreaded "purge," as in the 1930s, the exchange still involved ideological examination. Lesiv surprised everyone: "an old communist, and he does not know who comrade Brezhnev is."[123] Lesiv surely was aware of Brezhnev, but apparently did not know his formal position in the state and Party hierarchy.[124]

In 1953, when Stalin died, the station's party organization had forty-eight members. Only ten were Ukrainians, a mere three of them "local."[125] The "leading and guiding force" of Soviet society opened up to locals fully at the end of the 1950s with a significant expansion of the station's workforce. In 1959 Russians were still the plurality (forty-six people), but ethnic Ukrainians were catching up (thirty-six).[126] When a single station was formed, the terminal obtained a Party organization of its own, and it was even more Russian than the station's.[127] The number of Ukrainians in the terminal's Party organization nearly reached parity with the Russians only in 1971.[128] Locals, however, remained a minority.[129] Not a single Western Ukrainian served on the terminal's Party bureau at least until Brezhnev's death.

At the Lviv Railroad, Russian was not only the language of official communication, but also of Party meetings and protocols. This became a concern for the authorities for the first time in 1953, after Stalin's death, when Lavrentii Beria, one of the main contenders for the position of Stalin's successor, ordered a halt to Russification and entertained concessions to national sensibilities, especially in the western borderlands. At a closed Party meeting of the Railroad's headquarters, Holovchenko, the head of the Railroad, drew attention to the fact that, even though "on the Lviv Railroad 73.4 per cent of workers are from local population, all the lectures ... are in Russian. The Railroad's newspaper, *L'vovskii Zheleznodorozhnik* [Lviv Railwayman], is published in Russian. This is an obvious deficiency and we should correct it. Even though there are people from the local population on the Railroad with higher and secondary education, we have paid very little attention to their promotion."[130] Holovchenko also criticized the policy of intentional ethnic reshuffling – 70 per cent of local graduates from specialized railway schools were sent to work on eastern railroads. Beria's directive was to end this policy, too. Holovchenko announced the establishment of Ukrainian-language study circles in the Railroad's headquarters. The Party secretary even said that all correspondence and directives should now be in Ukrainian, but Holovchenko corrected him: only correspondence with the Ukrainian state and Party offices would be in Ukrainian. To be able to correspond in Ukrainian, headquarters ordered two typewriters with Ukrainian keys.

Holovchenko summarized the need for "Ukrainization" with an anecdote about his encounter with "Iron Narkom" Kaganovich. The latter asked him if he was a khokhol – pejorative for a Ukrainian. When the answer was affirmative, Kaganovich enquired about his ability to speak the language (*a balakat' umeete*?). Holovchenko confessed that he could not speak it. "That is bad," continued Kaganovich. "Imagine that you are coming to a depot and the engine driver addresses you in Ukrainian, while you answer in Rostovian or some other [dialect], but if you answered him in Ukrainian he would have opened his soul to you." Holovchenko conceded that Kaganovich was correct.[131] Beria's Ukrainization attempt was short lived, ending the same year he was arrested and executed. The Railroad's newspaper continued to be published in Russian for ten more years, switching to Ukrainian only in the mid-1960s during the first years of Petro Shelest's tenure as First Secretary of the CC CPU. The Railroad would maintain official correspondence with local and Kyivan authorities in Russian, however, until the end of the Soviet Union. More lasting linguistic Ukrainization occurred from below, at the workplace and at home. By 1968 local Ukrainians had become assertive enough to demand the right to speak Ukrainian at official meetings. The stationmaster interpreted this as a dangerous manifestation of nationalism awoken by the Prague Spring, because "at the station people of many nationalities work."[132]

In time locals and newcomers forged friendships, started families, worked and socialized together. At first, management frowned upon these relationships. In 1951 the Party card of Anatolii Zavialov, a shunter, was torn to pieces by his three-year-old child. The Party organization suspected foul play: "Tell us sincerely, who destroyed the candidate's card, because a three-year-old could not damage the card so much." The main reason for their suspicions was Zavialov's marriage to a local woman: "You are surrounded by the foreign element." Zavialov refused to "confess," and defended himself and his family. He was expelled from the Party and reported to state security.[133]

Generational change, together with the more liberal post-Stalinist climate, was one of the most important factors in the integration of "locals" and "easterners." In 1972 Bohdan Dudykevych died. He had been a long-time director of the city's Lenin museum, a former KPZU member, and one of the locals co-opted into the regional Soviet establishment. At a Party meeting Gurii Nesterov, a retired station manager, spoke against a state funeral for Dudykevych, since "there was more nationalism than communism in Dudykevych." Nesterov's remarks reflected the lasting antipathy of Stalinist arrivals towards the locals, even when the latter were pro-communist. In 1972, however, younger leaders of the station's Party organization dismissed Nesterov's words as the "nonsense" of an old man.[134] In 1980 a Russian-speaking station restaurant Komsomol (League of Young Communists) leader explicitly reproached his older managerial cadres for their disdainful attitude towards younger, Ukrainian-speaking workers.[135]

Antisemitism was also present, although less prominent than the tension between local Ukrainians and Russian newcomers. One of the earliest cases involved the station's cadre inspector, Tsipris, who accused stationmaster Obvintsev of "chauvinism." When Tsipris missed work because of a wounded finger, Obvintsev said, "This is not a Jewish synagogue for you. It will heal; it's not much of illness." Obvintsev, in turn, accused Tsipris of spying on him and visiting Obvintsev's family in his absence on false pretences to find evidence of Obvintsev's "moral and domestic decomposition." As in other such cases, ethnic slurs usually appeared in the context of some other non-ethnic conflict – in this case, between the cadre inspector and the stationmaster.[136]

Antisemitic incidents usually involved name calling, as in the case of Fedor Demidov, a Russian, who called one of his workers a "kike" (*zhid*).[137] In 1966 Mikhail Starovoitov called his fellow co-worker Iosif Beider a "scabby kike."[138] In 1977 there was a work-related conflict between a Ukrainian canteen sales clerk, Ivan Fundela, and the Jewish restaurant supply manager, Folkenflik. Although both were communists, there was a heated exchange of words such as "scabby kike" and "banderite" (*bandera*). Folkenflik's family had perished in the Holocaust, while Fundela's sister had been killed by the Banderite underground. Both felt deeply offended.[139]

Ethnic tensions were rare, however, and abated with time. Nonetheless the Party remained alert to the dangers of both "Ukrainian nationalism" and "Zionism" until the very end, although in the context of the Cold War the line between "bourgeois nationalisms" and broader anti-Soviet sentiment became blurred. In 1967 Party activists complained that workers listened to the Voice of America and the BBC and supported Israel.[140] Every event that heightened international tensions, such as the Hungarian crisis of 1956, was accompanied by a rise of anti-Soviet sentiment.[141] Moreover, as the Soviet Union's borders became more open to foreigners, their interactions with the local population had to be monitored.[142] As "the gateway to Western Europe," the terminal was subjected to close ideological scrutiny.

After the Second World War, the terminal was no longer described as a modern building. When Vishnevich praised it to visitors as "one of the most beautiful buildings of our city," in line with productivist Soviet rhetoric he emphasized the size of the terminal (12,794 square metres and 71,534 cubic metres), the flow of passengers (15 million in 1964), and the amount of work (165 daily trains).[143] For railway managers, it was the "flagship" of the Lviv Railroad, "a true scientific laboratory, the school of advanced experience, complex application of everything advanced that has been created and accumulated in the business of organizing passenger transportation."[144] The fact that the terminal was a Soviet enterprise in the official discourse overshadowed other possible significations.

The single most important fact in the lives of Soviet Lviv's workers was the absence of any independent associational life. During the first post-war years, Soviet managers discovered that local station workers had the wrong idea about union activism. Locals in the union committee "did not understand trade union work," therefore they "had to be re-elected, and workers who arrived from the eastern provinces should be brought in."[145] Proper Soviet trade unions were totally dependent not only on the Party, but also on the enterprise managers. The head of the Lviv terminal did not tolerate independent action from the union, and could override decisions that did not meet his prior approval.[146] The absence of an independent working-class organization, however, cannot be reduced to "total" domination by an all-powerful "state." The state proper, in the form of a public service or bureaucracy, was extremely weak. Executive committees of various levels – or state authorities proper – had little power over the managers of large enterprises, who often ignored not only them, but also Party secretaries of district and city committees. Moreover, the competence of industrial managers was much broader than the administration of the state's economic assets. This was especially true in the case of the railway. Top management of the Lviv Railroad was part of a mammoth railway empire subordinated to the ministry in Moscow, and enjoyed significant independence both from local Party bosses and from the CC CPU and the Council of Ministers of Soviet Ukraine. The Party was ubiquitous, present in every department and structural unit. But the local Party organization was integrated with the management of the enterprise. As a rule, the secretary of the Party organization was a deputy of the head of the enterprise, while the latter served on the bureau of the local Party organization. Management used railway Party organizations to communicate with territorial Party committees in matters that went beyond the scope of internal railway affairs.

Under Stalin the Party had been charged with overseeing the production process. The best workers were expected to join the Party, although in Lviv locals were often unsuitable for Party membership because of their "compromised" backgrounds.[147] Even in the 1970s, Party membership was expected of all enterprise "commanders."[148] Communists devised strategies for improving the performance of the enterprise and discussed its problems. The Party bureau screened candidates for sensitive positions such as the crews of international trains.[149] The local Party organization functioned as arbiter in conflicts between workers and management,[150] and handled the station's public relations.[151] The Party, however, was not separated from the workforce by an impenetrable wall. Rank-and-file communists were as likely to violate work discipline as their non-Party co-workers.[152]

Numerically, station and terminal Party membership never exceeded 11–12 per cent of the workforce, and in 1944–45 it had encompassed a meagre 2–4 per cent. Close to a quarter of its members were women.[153] In the 1960s and 1970s, however, the role of the Party organization in managing the terminal declined. Professionalism and the importance of properly trained specialists gained in importance at the expense of aging Party activists. War veterans began to retire in the 1960s, while remaining in the Party organizations of their former workplaces. By 1972 one-third of the Party members at the terminal were retirees.[154] Aged Party organizations, however, meant more power for management.

Much of the Party organization's work was ideological and social. Its members studied Marxism-Leninism and served as volunteer agitators. Many communists, however, treated those obligations lightly, especially after Stalin's death. Agitators played dominos with co-workers during political education sessions, and non-Party members were often better informed about current events than the communists.[155] Communists were expected to secure high participation in the elections to the Soviets,[156] and served at voting stations in the terminal and on some trains.[157] They were also in charge of newspaper subscriptions, which were seen as evidence of the workers' political consciousness. By 1952 thirty per cent of the station's employees subscribed to at least one periodical.[158] The most popular newspaper was the Railroad's own *L'vovskii zheleznodorozhnik*, which accounted for almost half of all subscriptions. A 70 per cent subscription rate was achieved by the end of the 1960s.[159] In the 1970s nearly every station employee subscribed to at least one title, and many to several.[160] Although an all-embracing subscription rate should not be equated with successful ideological indoctrination, it did make Soviet discourse all-pervasive.

Besides "locals," the Party paid special attention to women, yet another "minority" group in the workforce. The station's "Women's Council" was organized in 1948, and consisted of employees and the wives of male managers. Most of the council's work consisted of providing free labour to the station. The women's role was reduced to that of a collective wife in the workplace's patriarchal family, with the council working for free on tasks seen as "suitable" to the women's gender. The wives of managers dominated the council, organizing the cleaning, painting, and decorating of the terminal. They also oversaw an orphanage and organized a Red Cross circle.[161] Since the council's "activism" (*obshchestvennaia rabota*) was often tantamount to unpaid work for the benefit of their male colleagues, most women workers abstained from it. In 1953, of the 195 women working at the station, only 20 to 25 were involved in the council's work.[162] In 1954 the women's council was even chaired by a man.[163] Starting in the mid-1950s, the council was in charge of organized "cultured leisure" for the workers. It oversaw an amateur drama circle[164] and group visits to theatres and museums.[165] Even when the council tried to do more serious work, it was still within the same solid framework of Soviet patriarchy. In 1972 council activists started interviewing employees' families, probing for "family problems" and offering any possible help.[166] Women activists were used for this, since they were seen as natural guardians of the family hearth who could help management reach into this delicate sphere of their workers' lives.

Organized workers' leisure was connected to the workplace, and sports were part of it from the very beginning.[167] Sports circles were united through the Railroad's sports club, "Locomotive," now housed in the former Sokol building. Starting in the 1960s, there was also a choir[168]and an annual New Year's Eve celebration for terminal employees.[169] The physical centre of organized leisure for the workers was the former ZZK building, renamed the Palace of Culture of Railway Workers. It had a library, cinema, various circles for children and adults, and a planetarium, which reflected the post-war fascination with space and astronomy. Officially under the purview of the Railroad's trade union committee, the Palace of Culture had a large full-time staff paid by the Railroad.

The less the Party was involved in the actual management of the enterprise, the more it paid attention to public activism. It oversaw the local union committee, whose chair was a member of the Party bureau together with the head of the enterprise and the Party secretary – the ruling triumvirate of a Soviet enterprise. Many benefits were distributed through the union. It also administered the "comrades' courts," which dealt with disciplinary infractions.[170] The Party organization was also in charge of the system of "people's control," set up to provide an "outside" public check on enterprises.[171] Every shop received its quota of "people's controllers" from the station's Party secretary.[172]

A web of interconnected organizations enveloped all aspects of workers' lives in a paternalistic cocoon. The head of the enterprise was at the centre of it, wielding immense power over workers. Although Austrian and Polish directors had tried to create obedient workers' associations and cultural institutions, Soviet managers succeeded, surpassing even the most daring hopes of their predecessors. Hypothetically workers could appeal to the Party or state offices, but an enterprise boss with a good record and years of experience, such as the terminal's head, Vishnevich, had nothing to fear. Moreover, workers' appeals could be made only from the position of plaintiffs humbly petitioning high authorities.

In the absence of an autonomous legal arena, private property, and market mechanisms, workers depended upon management's good will in nearly all aspects of their lives. Even employees' private lives were under constant scrutiny. So-called immorality cases were routinely considered by the managers and the Party bureau, which looked into issues of abandoned wives, alimony, and unwed lovers. Workplace managers were regularly approached by outside institutions and people that ran into problems not only with their workers, but also with their workers' wives and children.[173] There was, in fact, little separation between workers' private lives and work. Under an all-encompassing Soviet paternalism, bosses were responsible for their subordinates' family lives and friendships. Good managers were supposed to serve as model parents, as in the case of Vishnevich and his chief accountant, Anna Milrud.[174] Complaints from the school of a worker's son could result in a fine levied by the terminal head.[175] "Immorality" cases were often intertwined with other problems of everyday Soviet life, most notably inadequate housing.[176] Neighbours complained about workers' hooliganism, especially among those living in communal apartments.[177]

Wives complained about husbands – their drinking, family violence, and sexual promiscuity.[178] Those charged with "moral degradation" were usually men, but sometimes women were investigated too.[179] Children could denounce parents for neglect and lack of financial support.[180] Finally, because of ubiquitous drinking, reports flowed in from the *militsiia* and sobering-up stations on all the workers picked up drunk in public places.[181] Insubordination and defiance, however, were seen as greater missteps than mere "moral degeneracy." One terminal head's deputy was reported by his wife for not coming home for days and weeks, while the janitor complained that the deputy had slept with her daughter. The deputy's greatest misstep, however, was refusing to explain himself and verbally attacking the Party bureau. The deputy was downgraded from his position, and banned from interacting with passengers.[182] The management often dealt with love triangles that involved co-workers by reassigning them to different positions and shifts.[183] Even in the second half of the 1970s, the enterprise and Party bosses went to the villages where their workers lived to check on the "climate" in their homes and families.[184]

Since the Soviet system had destroyed the self-regulating structures of liberal governmentality, the weight of governing shifted to personal interactions. The absence of strict rules allowed room for negotiation, but also greatly empowered senior management, which made key decisions about promotions, the allocation of resources, and benefits. Not by accident one of the most common transgressions of managers was the "lordly" treatment of subordinates.[185] In this new system, the "authoritativeness" of an official was the key indicator of his legitimacy. Party activists often quoted Stalin's observation that the Soviets were not only the "most democratic," but also the "most authoritative organizations of the masses."[186] A superior's authority in the eyes of his subordinates was perceived as the key that could unlock their "energy" and "creative potential." In the absence of any mediating autonomous institutions and spheres, this "unlocking" occurred via direct messages. Eric Naiman observes that Stalinist culture and ideology were primarily verbal.[187] Language, in turn, was seen as merely an instrument serving consciousness. In a de facto denial of a main tenet of Marxism-Leninism – that consciousness is determined by being – Soviet reality upended the formula by placing causative primacy with consciousness itself. At the Lviv station, the Party secretary once explained that, although feudal discipline was of the stick and that of capitalism hunger and poverty, "the communist organization of social labour rests and will rest on a conscious attitude toward work and conscious discipline ... In Soviet society labour discipline is founded on the consciousness of every worker."[188] Based on this assumption, various defects of work and major infractions could be explained as problems of individual consciousness, and had to be dealt with pedagogically.

Disciplinary problems at work were many, but most involved either theft or drinking. The station, with its constant flow of valuable goods, attracted thieves. Although professional thieves from the street "worked" there, too, railway management was more concerned with theft practised by employees. The immediate post-war years witnessed a large-scale embezzlement scheme in which senior managers and accountants were involved.[189] A massive theft of shipped goods also took place – seventy-six incidents at Lviv-Main alone in 1947.[190] There were gangs of employees with connections to state officials and enterprise managers. Whole train cars of freight were hijacked and readdressed to other stations. More than eight thousand people were arrested on the Lviv Railroad in 1947. At Lviv-Main alone, the cost of stolen property amounted to nearly 1.5 million rubles, and another 1 million at the Klepariv station.[191]

Lviv was not unique. After the war Leon Weliczker travelled extensively, arranging deals for the Lviv Railroad and greasing them with goods from Lviv – Lviv's furniture once helped him get out of the NKVD's hands. During one such a trip, his personal train car was hijacked from the Kyiv station. Only the car's bare frame was found later on some side track in the Kyiv region.[192]

Petty workplace theft was tacitly tolerated and essentially accepted as normal. When a worker complained about strained material circumstances, he was reminded that, in addition to his "good salary," he had a wife "working at the Confections Factory," who presumably could help herself to valuable chocolate and sweets.[193] Only when petty theft crossed a certain limit, or involved an official complaint, was action taken. Most theft at the terminal took place at the expense of passengers, and was not much different from that in other branches of the Soviet economy that dealt with individual customers. Ticket offices were especially vulnerable as they handled cash and sold a commodity, train tickets, in high demand. As early as 1945 ticket cashiers speculated by using, and sometimes losing, large amounts of cash "borrowed" from registers.[194] Cashiers were also involved in selling tickets for extra money or favours,[195] and would sometimes be denounced for "living materially not up to ... [official] incomes."[196] Ticket controllers could also be paid privately instead of with an official fine.[197] Terminal porters offered their services unofficially and kept unreported money.[198] The luggage storage area was a "tight spot" swarming with suspicious "elements," tempted by the presence of unclaimed luggage and tips.[199]

The baggage department was also problematic: checked baggage often went missing, while unauthorized people were from time to time caught in the storage area.[200]

The terminal also had its seedy hangouts, essential to its work but not subordinate to the terminal's management. The restaurant, with its numerous canteens and food kiosks, was the largest such hangout. Attracting petty crime and serving as the main source of alcohol at the terminal, the restaurant was a constant threat to public order and labour discipline. Another den of iniquity was the terminal barbershop. In the 1940s and 1950s, the master barber was involved in speculation and had frequent altercations with customers.[201] Brawls in the terminal went hand in hand with alcohol consumption. In 1948 the station's Party organization identified drinking as the main disciplinary problem.[202] People came drunk to work and drank at work.[203] Porters drank in a canteen between serving clients.[204] Employees drank on trains and were found unconscious in baggage cars.[205] Even an on-duty official in the marshalling yard, on whom shunters' lives depended, was once caught drinking at his post.[206] It was mostly a male problem, but not exclusively: a female ticket cashier was once found asleep drunk in her booth.[207] People drank alone and in groups – especially in the "shady" luggage and porters' departments. People drank at home, and management believed that a great deal of absenteeism was related to drinking, often covered up by neutral medical notes.[208] In 1959 one worker missed four consecutive workdays because of drinking.[209] Those caught drunk often claimed that they simply felt "unwell" or were "tired," while the distinct smell of alcohol was from a small dose taken before work.[210] People indeed were often overworked, especially in the 1940s, and alcohol helped to cope with it.

Drinking among workers was seen as undesirable but inevitable, and not a single terminal worker lost his or her job for drinking regularly. At worst a worker would be moved to a position that did not involve interaction with passengers.[211] Such decisions, however, were fiercely contested, since interaction with passengers meant the opportunity to earn some unreported cash.[212] For senior managers, however, drinking was a serious offence. A lack of self-control raised doubts about one's leadership qualifications, and a drunken manager's public appearance undermined respect for the Soviet authorities. When a deputy stationmaster was found drunk in the 1960s with a bottle of moonshine, he had to step down from his position despite twenty-two long years of service. The stationmaster indicated that "higher echelons" had caught wind of the incident, and the head of the Railroad himself insisted on exemplary punishment.[213] Among those positions that involved less responsibility, however, drinking was endemic. Weighers and loaders from the baggage shop were constantly reproached for it;[214] the freight shop was not much better.[215]

In the 1940s and 1950s, the most popular drink was vodka with beer, the mixture with the strongest effect on one's consciousness at the least cost. It was consumed socially and alone, in canteens and on streets.[216] With improved living standards in the 1960s and 1970s, the mixture's popularity receded.

To combat theft more systematically, in April 1964 a Public Council (*obshchestvennyi sovet*) was created at the Lviv junction consisting of twelve people representing all of the junction's railway services. It was most concerned with the theft of freight, for which the Railroad answered to its shipping and receiving organizations.[217] The council, however, did not bring any observable improvement. Moreover, several inspectors were charged with covering up encountered violations.[218] In the 1970s, the theft of freight acquired catastrophic proportions.[219] In 1971 a special commission sent from Moscow checked the "integrity of freight" at the station and reached "a very uncomplimentary verdict."[220] Most of the Railroad's "vanished" freight (90 per cent in 1967) had disappeared at the Lviv station.[221] In the late 1970s hundreds of reclamations were signed yearly in relation to missing, corrupted, and spoiled freight.[222] Although most claims were dismissed, in 1978 the station had to pay 11,000 rubles for freight-related claims,[223] rising to 26,000 in 1979[224] and to 42,000 in 1982.[225] "Solved cases" usually involved petty theft. In four months of 1967, the *militsiia* solved the following cases: a recorder of cars opened a container and stole five carpets; weighers opened a box and stole two sets of knives and forks;[226] some fireproof bricks were stolen from the warehouse;[227] and twenty rolls of toilet paper were taken from a box of freight.[228]

Railway workers' access to trains and high spatial mobility created a perfect environment for speculation. Foodstuffs and alcohol were the staples.[229] Seasonal fruits were delivered to areas that did not have them, compensating for the notorious clumsiness of the state retail system.[230] A speculation network reached from Lviv to all over the Soviet Union. Investigations of serious incidents revealed a well-functioning system, with agents at small and large stations ordering goods, and train personnel regularly delivering them.[231] Since Lviv was close to the border and serviced cross-border trains, there was also smuggling – especially heavy during the first Soviet years, when customs checkpoints were still establishing their routines. Even later, despite the well-guarded border and careful selection of the personnel operating cross-border trains, small-scale smuggling still occurred.[232] Imported goods were also an attractive prize in Lviv's prone-to-theft freight yards.[233]

Station management tried to control its workforce, but it was jealous of outside intervention. The Soviet railway police – first a branch of state security and then the transportation *militsiia* of the Ministry of Interior – were persistent intruders, maintaining a "line department" (*lineinoe otdelenie*) at the station. The management complained that "the line department does not help us to fight speculators and raise the culture of servicing passengers; [instead] they generate cases against the terminal workers to undermine the authority of the whole collective."[234] The station wanted the *militsiia* to help police the public, while the *militsiia* found it much easier to screen and investigate station employees. These contradictory impulses were never reconciled. The *militsiia* maintained independent access to the workers, bypassing management's nearly monopolistic control over them. The KGB had similar independent access and its own network of informers. Political transgressions warranting the KGB's attention, however, were extremely rare.

Chapter Nine

The Terminal for All

In 1945 more than four hundred thousand travellers passed through Lviv's main train terminal.[1] In 1950 the terminal handled almost four million.[2] Since the terminal was a Soviet enterprise, it had its own quotas to fulfil and targets to reach. The performance of a freight station was essentially about the efficient handling of trains and freight. The performance of a terminal, however, was about services offered to passengers. These services were measured through the revenues the terminal generated – the "local revenues" of Soviet railway reporting. Terminals were the main revenue-producing structure of the passenger service.[3] Revenues came from commissions on ticket sales, porters' services, and, most important, luggage storage (40 per cent in 1951).[4] Only in 1948 did the Lviv terminal fail the revenues plan, an outcome of currency reform and the abolition of rationing.[5]

In the economy of the Soviet terminal, performance could be increased with the help of additional services, but individual dedication to work was seen as the most important means. Even ticket sales had its own brand of "Stakhanovism": the so-called Aladin's method, in which a ticket cashier would pass through the arriving train punching the tickets of connecting passengers instead of waiting for them at the station ticket booth. In 1949 more than half of the passenger station's 589 employees were either Stakhanovites (127 people) or shock workers (222).[6] Additional services included advance reservations or the home delivery of tickets, with a surcharge from the terminal.[7]

In 1951 the Five-Year Plan approved for Lviv-Passenger expected that, by 1955, with twenty-one thousand trains and seventeen million passengers served, local revenues would reach 4.9 million rubles. The average salary was supposed to reach 830 roubles.[8] None of those figures had been attained even by 1960. The actual growth was impressive nonetheless. By 1955 local revenues had increased by 74 per cent, while the average salary had increased to 700 rubles from 605 in 1951. The number of passengers during the same period almost tripled, reaching 12.8 million in 1955.[9] By 1964 local revenues had reached 443,000 rubles (10 pre-1961 rubles were equal to 1 ruble after the 1961 currency reform) and the number of passengers had increased to 15 million.[10]

After the merger of the freight and passenger stations in 1962, tensions between the station and the terminal managements developed. Terminal managers believed that the Lviv terminal was entitled to *khozraschet* (self-supporting cost-accounting), which entailed significant financial autonomy.[11] Although the station's performance was average, the terminal's, by Soviet standards, was truly stellar. Moreover, more than a third of the station's employees worked at the terminal. In 1966 the terminal even received a special honorary diploma from the Exhibition of Achievements of the National Economy for dispatching its passengers well.[12] From 1967 until the end of the 1970s, the terminal held the honorary title of "Collective of Communist Work."[13] In 1968 the terminal moved 16 million passengers and made 548,000 rubles – 71,000 above plan.[14] Without financial autonomy, however, the terminal's revenues disappeared into the station's overall budget.

The terminal was finally given *khozraschet* and relative independence from the station in 1970.[15] Now the terminal started to prioritize additional services, "since this is where money is."[16] Local revenues saw rapid increases, reaching over 600,000 rubles in 1971[17] and 784,300 in 1972.[18] The terminal decided to double the volume of services sold to passengers during the 1971–75 Five-Year Plan.[19] This target reflected the high expectations connected with the Soviet citizen's growing consumer power and increased mobility, and the terminal workers' own expectations of material benefits from *khozraschet*. The terminal, however, did not come even close to this target. Nonetheless, after yearly plan readjustments, its performance was still excellent, especially compared to the freight side of the Railroad.[20]

Massive backlogs of unloaded freight and the resulting delays plagued not only Lviv, but the whole Soviet rail network. Despite its high potential, double tracks on all main lines, and high level of electrification, the railway was choking under industry's demands. Throughout the 1970s territorial Party committees tried to coordinate the work of the railway with local transportation and industrial enterprises to alleviate the situation, but without much success. Problems with freight also affected passenger traffic. In the first half of 1981, 144 passenger and 2,097 freight trains were delayed on the approaches to Lviv for a total of 3,439 hours.[21]

The growth of the terminal's operations after the war was linked with the emergence and growth of commuter traffic in an industrializing Lviv. The goal of the Soviet state was not only the economic, but also the sociological industrialization of Lviv – turning industrial workers into the city's largest occupational group. The expanding railway workforce and burgeoning population of commuting workers were both facets of this profound change. By 1950 suburban and local traffic accounted for 54 per cent of those passing through the terminal.[22] In the first half of the 1960s, suburban traffic peaked, accounting for 80 per cent of all terminal passengers.[23]

The 1960s was also the decade when regular suburban and regional bus routes opened and began diverting passengers from trains. A bus station opened on the terminal square in 1965, enabling a smooth transfer between trains and buses. By the 1970s a bus was leaving the square every two minutes. The head of the terminal described this as "astronomical growth," which also meant an "astronomical decline in the number of our suburban passengers."[24] The decline, in fact, was far from astronomical, and in absolute numbers suburban railway traffic through the terminal began to decline only in 1968, when it still accounted for 74.3 per cent of the total.[25] Eventually the number of suburban passengers stabilized – for those living in the proximity of train stations, the railway remained a cheaper and more convenient option than the bus. In the 1970s the flow of passengers increased, but only on account of long-distance passengers. In 1979 the terminal handled 116 suburban and 84 long-distance passenger trains and sixty thousand passengers daily, two-thirds of them suburban.[26]

Throughout its Soviet history, the terminal functioned as a shop (*tsekh*) of a larger enterprise: the station.[27] The story of its workers' exploitation exemplified that of Soviet urban labour. Under Stalin, Soviet workers regularly worked unpaid overtime. The overtime was not limited to supposedly "voluntary" Saturday and Sunday hours. Terminal workers' regular shifts were in reality four to five hours longer than their nominal duration.[28] In the 1940s, terminal workers were also supposed to "help" with the reconstruction of the building. One year every worker contributed forty hours of unpaid work monthly to the reconstruction.[29] All the "beautification" and "greening" of the territory was accomplished "by the [terminal] workers, during their free time, with minimal expenses."[30] The same was true of simple building, mechanical, and electrical repairs.[31] In 1948 terminal workers, without compensation, during their leisure time repaired boilers for potable water, central heating, switches, weight scales, and carts, and dug trenches for gas and water mains.[32] They also helped repair the station's tracks.

Workers complained that repairing the tracks prevented them from doing unpaid work at their own workplace, the terminal, which was in need of cleaning and decorating.[33] In 1949 terminal workers contributed 1,200 free "man-hours" on Sundays alone.[34] When in 1950 the terminal was preparing for the summer season, the management boasted that 30 per cent of the work had been accomplished without spending any funds.[35]

This merciless extraction of labour abated after Stalin's death. In 1954 desk workers demanded allocation of work time for the preparation of reports, accounts, and scheduling, which they had been doing after work.[36] In 1960 the management complained that workers were no longer doing petty maintenance, such as painting and caulking, and "neglected" their workplace.[37] Labour without compensation, however, did not disappear completely, especially when it came to cleaning and maintenance.[38] In 1965 conductors alone did 7,370 extra hours in the violation of the labour code.[39] Free Saturday work, "donated towards the fulfilment of the Five-Year Plan," continued in the USSR under Brezhnev, and the terminal was no exception.[40] The mobilization of railway workers for clearing the tracks of snow also continued throughout the whole Soviet period.[41] Even when funds were allocated for capital construction, as in 1973, the terminal head warned his employees that, in addition to contractors' work, "many tasks have to be done by our own forces."[42] Safety rules were still routinely violated to secure higher output, as in the case of workers crawling beneath train cars while unloading baggage.[43]

Salaries at the station and at the terminal in particular were low. In 1947 the average monthly salary at the Lviv Railroad was a mere 590 rubles; it declined to 548 rubles in 1948.[44] The head of the Railroad received 2,000 rubles monthly and senior managers 1,000 to 1,500; they also received hefty regular bonuses.[45] The highest paid workers at the terminal were ticket cashiers with a monthly salary of 450–500 rubles in 1953. An announcer – necessarily a "person of culture" who could speak literary Russian – received only 280–320 rubles. Information bureau clerks received 350–380, while manual workers – porters, weighers, and loaders – significantly less than that.[46] In 1948 the average monthly salary in the USSR was 684 rubles; in industry it was 762 and on the railway 746.[47] According to a Soviet statistical study of workers' budgets, average expenses of a family of low-skilled workers in 1953 were 1,238.25 rubles a month, while expenses for food alone were 515.5 rubles.[48]

In 1953 the terminal introduced a system wherein workers were paid piecework for above-plan output.[49] The average salary of stockmen in the luggage storage area under the new system increased to 600 rubles monthly from an earlier 475. The revenues the stockmen brought in for the terminal increased by 16.5 per cent.[50] In 1956 almost every worker at the station received a monetary premium in addition to salary, with 809 workers receiving 389,000 rubles. An additional 536 workers received small 40–60 ruble one-time bonuses.[51]

By the end of the 1950s, however, workers were voicing their dissatisfaction with the amount of the bonuses and their distribution, which did not reflect individual input.[52] In 1962, the year of the Novocherkassk crisis, with its violent suppression of workers' discontent, the station had no funds for premium payments.[53] The terminal was especially dissatisfied, since it was the only shop that overfulfilled the plan.[54] In 1965 workers complained that individual plans were set too high, and began to leave their jobs.[55]

Against this background, the Kosygin reforms, which gave enterprises greater autonomy and encouraged monetary rewards for good work, were very timely. The state promised that salaries would increase by 20 per cent between 1966 and 1970.[56] In 1968 the average terminal worker earned 94.8 (new) rubles monthly.[57] In 1972, together with bonuses, average monthly earnings reached 105 rubles.[58] Earnings thereafter increased at a yearly rate of 2.5 per cent, but these gains were not equally distributed. Especially high bonuses were found in the city ticket offices, which sold seat reservations with transfers.[59] Since the bonuses were not divided equally, the management and "best workers" benefited from them disproportionally. The most productive ticket cashier in summer 1969 received monthly bonuses equal to her salary.[60] This trend continued into the 1970s.

There were also collective bonuses. Shifts competed against one another. In 1966, among fifty brigades (shifts), twenty-seven earned the title of "Communist Labour."[61] One terminal ticket clerk was honoured as the best in the entire Soviet railway system. "Shock Workers of Communist Labour" accounted for two-thirds of the workforce.[62] The terminal's best department received a bonus of 150 rubles quarterly, while the best shift had a monthly bonus of 50 rubles.[63]

In terms of purchasing power, 100 rubles – the average monthly salary of a station worker in Lviv in 1970 – could buy 217 kilograms of wheat bread or 35.7 kilograms of beef. In contrast, in 1907, 67 crowns – the starting salary of a stoker or ticket cashier[64] – could buy 335 kilograms of wheat bread or 43.2 kilograms of beef. In addition, finding even basic goods in Soviet state stores was not easy. Workers were more likely to purchase a product such as beef at collective farmers' markets, where it fetched a much higher price.

Arguably, Soviet workers enjoyed greater access to a number of free services and additional benefits. The number and value of non-monetary benefits increased during the Brezhnev period. In 1952 the whole of Lviv-Passenger station, with six hundred employees, obtained only ten placements for sanatoria, twenty-three for vacation homes, thirteen for children's sanatoria, and twenty-four for young pioneers' camps.[65] Even if those placements were distributed equally, an average worker would receive one only once every ten years. There were no substantial improvements in this respect for many years – in 1963 the terminal received only five placements for children's camps.[66] The situation improved markedly only in the second half of the 1960s and first half of the 1970s. In 1974 a total of 140 workers or family members (20 to 25 per cent of all employees) spent time in sanatoria, camps, and vacation homes.[67]

Another important benefit was paid medical leave, widely used by workers starting in the 1960s. Receiving a medical note became much easier under Brezhnev, and the management recognized it as a formidable challenge. In November 1971, 115 workers – almost 8 per cent of the station's workforce – and another 125 in December were on sick leave of various durations.[68] Free work clothes and footwear were an important perk that railway workers in Austria and Poland enjoyed, but for a long time the Soviet railways could not provide these to all terminal workers; only in 1972 did all terminal workers finally receive free work uniforms and footwear.[69]

There were also once-in-a-lifetime benefits. In 1954 the station distributed parcels of land among interested workers for individual gardens in suburban areas.[70] Vegetables from those land plots were an important supplement to the diet of city workers. The most important of these benefits, however, was housing. By the 1960s a family apartment for urban workers had become an important part of the redefined welfare package promised by the Soviet state – a right and an expectation.[71] By 1949 all station employees had some dwelling space,[72] although very often it was a shared one, either in the form of dorms or communal apartments.[73] In 1957 the Soviet government promised a separate apartment to every Soviet family. This was the year the Railroad completed the first apartment building for its employees. The Stalinist-style structure, on the corner of Horodotska (Gródecka) and Iaroslav Mudryi (Bem) streets, featured spacious apartments. The station, however, did not receive a single apartment there. Instead it began construction of several small two-apartment houses for its employees in the railway suburb of Levandivka.[74] These were built with the station's own resources and workforce without contracting any construction enterprises.[75] The construction was slow, however, and shop foremen sabotaged it, arguing that fulfilling the enterprise's plan was far more important than improving housing conditions.[76] Still, in 1958 a building with eight apartments was started,[77] and by 1959 the station was working on four buildings simultaneously.[78] Completed buildings were full of "defects," but people moved in gladly nonetheless.[79]

In the 1960s the station started receiving apartments in *khrushchevka*s – mass-built, low-rise apartment blocks – built by the Railroad, but their number was minuscule. In 1963 there were three apartments for the station's 1,500 employees.[80] In 1965 the head of the Railroad promised twenty-five to thirty apartments for the station, but at the last moment changed his mind and would give only ten to fifteen.[81] In the 1970s the terminal received several apartments a year.[82] Although there was some progress in solving the housing crisis, the majority of workers did not receive an individual family apartment from the state. Overcrowded homes remained a problem. In 1967 one worker explained his drinking by the fact that his family of nine lived in a space of 15 square metres.[83] Since workers were far more likely to receive an apartment from their workplace than from the state administration – waiting lists were kept by territorial executive committees – this welfare element became an important part of the web of paternalistic patronage spun around workers and their families by the employer – a socialist enterprise.

The actual distribution of apartments confirmed workers' suspicions of prevalent favouritism and inequality. Managers were the first to receive apartments.[84] The Party bureau was involved in the decision making that favoured Party activists.[85] The manipulation of housing waitlists was not uncommon. Any particular position on these lists provoked endless negotiations, numerous petitions, and complaints. Some workers brought their grievances, sometime successfully, as far as the Supreme Soviet and central newspapers in Moscow.[86] In 1963 a Party commission confirmed that the head of conductors allocated apartments to people who were not even on the waitlist.[87]

By the end of the 1960s, workers could obtain housing without endlessly waiting for mercy from either management or the authorities. They could join a housing-construction cooperative by providing a 40 per cent down payment; a one-room apartment in Lviv cost around 4,000 rubles. To save for a down payment, an average station worker had to keep putting aside one-third of his or her salary for ten years.[88] In addition, while paying out the loan, the worker would be paying higher-than-usual apartment maintenance fees, eating up 20 per cent of the average salary. In the 1900s, in contrast, for a third of their salary, Lviv railway workers could rent a one-room apartment that was more spacious than the average Soviet apartment at a market price.[89] Austrian workers, however, had not had to sacrifice their salary at all, since they received a housing allowance, which for Lviv was set at 80 per cent of the Viennese allowance, and for lower-paid workers was usually larger than one-third of their salary.[90] It is safe to conclude that railway workers in Lviv were relatively wealthier in the 1900s than in the 1970s.

The operation of the station – its "technological process" – changed over time, especially when steam ceased to be the main locomotive power and coal the main source of energy. These tremendous changes, however, had little impact on the work of the terminal. Nonetheless, since mechanization and rationalization were the new mantras of the 1960s and 1970s, the terminal had to keep up with the times. Beginning in 1957, "rationalization suggestions" were encouraged and paid for. A special "technical council" was created to assess and implement them.[91] Most suggestions were trivial, often involving additional services – such as baggage wrapping[92] orthe acceptance of baggage directly on the platform.[93] Many of the changes were about the more rational organization of work,[94] but there were physical changes too. The terminal had its own celebrated "rationalizer": local worker Iaroslav Kravets, who built change and token machines from regular cash registers. In the luggage storage, his machines allegedly helped to increase labour productivity by 35 per cent.[95] The single most important "invention" at the Lviv terminal, however, was the centralized control of ticket sales at all ticket windows, introduced in 1960. In 1961 the system was approved by the ministry, and by 1969 108 large terminals across the Soviet rail network were using it.[96]

Major changes stemmed from state-wide technological progress, not from the initiatives of local "rationalizers." In 1960 the terminal started printing boarding cards instead of filling them out by hand.[97] In 1965 suburban ticket windows received ticket printers, and the first self-serve ticket machines were installed for suburban destinations.[98] Automated lockers appeared for luggage storage.[99] Electrical clocks replaced mechanical, and displays of free seats on long-distance trains were installed.[100] Between 1967 and 1970 the terminal received ten machines for counting and sorting change.[101] Soviet industry started producing automated luggage lockers, and by the end of the 1970s there were hundreds of them in the terminal.[102] In 1971 all ticket offices in the terminal were connected to ticket offices in the city centre,[103] and received a teletype connection with other stations for fast updates on tickets sold for the same trains.[104] In 1972 a machine automatically distributing seats on long-distance trains was introduced.[105]

Mechanisms and machines were not only help, but also a major annoyance and waste of funds. The baggage shop, for example, purchased a motor scooter in 1959 for the home delivery of baggage, but there was no one willing to drive it for the meagre 380 rubles assigned to this full-time job.[106] Machines for washing the terminal floors stood idle and rusted in the early 1960s because janitors did not know how to operate them.[107] Even trifling breakages disabled machines permanently, since there were no spare parts or repair shops.[108] Pneumatic mail was introduced in 1962, but after only a year it broke down; using human couriers proved to be cheaper than repairing it.[109] Ten years later, the pneumatic mail was still down.[110] Machines were stored in unsuitable rooms, too humid and unheated, greatly shortening their lifespans.[111]

Electrical baggage lifts to the platforms, one of the original building's technological wonders, failed more often than they worked. As late as 1965, in the middle of the mechanization and rationalization campaign, people were still carrying baggage to and from the platforms on their backs.[112] The tractor purchased in 1963 for moving baggage "worked or, to be more precise, just stood there, for only a year and a half," and in 1966 had to be "written off" as broken.[113] Even the system of centralized control of ticket sales suffered because of frequent equipment breakdowns.[114] Call quality was extremely poor, and for a while all communications had to be duplicated in writing, slowing down sales.[115]

The Lviv terminal was the largest on the Lviv Railroad, handling more than 10 per cent of its passenger traffic.[116] Although in the 1940s much of the passenger flow had consisted of people moved by the state against their will, by 1950 the situation had normalized. Regular civilian traffic dominated, having reoriented within the new political boundaries. The most popular destinations were now Kyiv, Moscow, Odesa, and Sochi – capitals and seaside resorts.[117] Long-distance traffic peaked in summer and slowed down in winter. The Soviet state abolished "classes" of train cars, which did not suit the egalitarian vision of the socialist order. In reality it abolished only the term itself, and the variation among train cars in terms of comfort and ticket price remained. Moreover, in practice, the number of those categories actually exceeded the three classes of pre-Soviet times.

Soviet trains preserved some Russian imperial traditions, such as the early appearance of departing trains at the platform. The terminal complained when trains were served only fifteen to twenty minutes before departure, arguing that it did not leave enough time for proper service.[118] Typical Soviet problems plagued passenger trains: worn-out cars, smelly and dirty washrooms, and damp linen. Some problems were the terminal's responsibility. Before automated ticket sales, "doublets," or the sale of seats twice over, were a regular occurrence.[119] A slight movement of trains during boarding was a common safety violation.[120]

The 1950s saw a resurgence of tourism. The terminal's management attributed the growth in tourist traffic to "higher living standards of workers."[121] After Stalin's death, the number of foreign tourists increased every year, with an absolute majority coming from socialist East-Central Europe. In 1955 the terminal opened a separate ticket counter for foreign tourists.[122] More popular destinations were served with better trains, and in the 1960s various "brand" trains were introduced.[123] By the 1970s the level of cross-border tourism on the Lviv Railroad was impressive: over 110,000 passengers from Poland and an equal number from Romania in 1971; 300,000 from Czechoslovakia in and 270,000 from Hungary in 1972. Passengers, likewise, travelled to these countries on the Lviv Railroad in similar numbers. Altogether there were almost a million and a half cross-border travellers yearly on the Lviv Railroad in the 1970s.[124] International trains normally originated in Moscow and Kyiv.

Soviet domestic tourism developed slowly, and the Soviet railways never matched either the number of services offered to tourists or the share of tourists of the Polish railways in the 1930s. Soviet-organized tourism had its own peculiarities. Since hotels were few and often inaccessible to ordinary citizens, charter trains were used not only to carry tourist groups, but also served as cheap night shelters. By the end of the 1960s, the Lviv Railroad had created "bases" for tourist charter trains in Lviv, Chernivtsi, Rakhiv, and Iaremche, the latter two being popular mountain resort destinations.[125] In Lviv, its "tourist base" used two dead-end tracks in one of the station's yards. In nine months of 1973, the Lviv Railroad sent 116 "tourist, excursion, theatre, and school" trains and 308 "vacation" trains, while, in turn, receiving 171 tourist trains from other railroads.[126] The tourist base near the station had poor makeshift sanitary facilities and problems with its water supply. The base also interfered with the operations of the station. In 1975 the tourist base was moved to suburban Briukhovychi, where new facilities were being built.[127] Briukhovychi was an appropriate destination, having functioned since the 1900s as Lviv's suburban resort, and had a number of sanatoria and children's camps.

The most important and newest group of post-war passenger traffic was suburban commuters. They were directly responsible for the dramatic increase in the number of passengers going through the terminal in the 1940s and 1950s. They were also the terminal's most problematic passengers.

The passengerhood that emerged in the wake of war was unruly, and resisted the incessant attempts to impose order. Although access to the platforms was restricted to people with tickets, Lviv's platform inspectors could not stop ticketless passengers, who ignored them and their orders.[128] Officials complained that enforcing payments for extra luggage on suburban trains was equally impossible.[129] When the Railroad blocked access to the platforms from the terminal, passengers sneaked through the freight yards.[130] In an attempt to maintain order, officials decided to keep suburban passengers outside the terminal and moved ticket offices for them to the terminal square.[131] The growing mass of suburban passengers refused containment. In 1950 terminal managers acknowledged that a separate suburban terminal was needed. In the meantime, a shed covering ticket offices had to be built on the terminal square.[132] There was not even a separate waiting hall for suburban passengers at the terminal.[133] In 1953 a suburban pavilion[134] and a three-kilometre-long fence[135] were proposed as a solution. Even the requested fence was not built by the next year, not to mention a suburban pavilion.[136] The *militsiia*, too, avoided trespassers, who walked the tracks and the station's territory unhindered.[137] Station workers themselves were among the violators, walking to work through restricted territory resisting and insulting those who tried to stop them.[138]

To alleviate the problem, the terminal encouraged the purchase of seasonal train passes, and in 1954 opened offices for selling them at the city's largest factories.[139] In 1955–56, ticketless passengers got on the radar of the Obkom. This was also the period when they became labelled "hooligans,"[140] adding yet another category to the multiple meanings "hooliganism" obtained during the Khrushchev period.[141] Ticketless passengers broke car windows, threw conductors off trains, and beat up ticket inspectors. The chair of the Lviv conductors' union committee himself was stabbed several times in 1956 during an encounter with ticketless working-class youth.[142] Controllers at the access points to the platforms were helpless. Terminal employees despaired, arguing that they could not solve this problem alone, and demanded additional *militsiia* outposts.[143] The terminal *militsiia* still refused to provide assistance.[144] The openness and chaotic state of unenclosed space were repeatedly identified as the main source of the terminal's complaints.[145]

In 1956 the Party authorities and Railroad management took coordinated action against fare dodgers. The fence around the Second freight yard was lengthened, access through the service tunnel was blocked, and new outposts of controllers were created. The terminal was sceptical of these measures – openings would appear, and the trails crossing the railway terrain were too numerous to control them all.[146] The scepticism proved justified – by the following year the situation had not improved.[147] In 1958 the terminal demanded additional fences.[148] Twenty years later, it was still voicing identical complaints about fences and trespassers.[149] Permanent enclosure seemed impossible. This was an aspect of Soviet "nomadism," which, as Mikhail Epstein explains, is the disorganized nature of Russian and Soviet space that results from a societal inability "to give it a distinct well-compartmentalized form."[150] The case of the terminal seems to show that the problems of Soviet urban space stemmed from the peculiarities of Soviet disciplinary mechanisms. These mechanisms worked directly with individual consciousness, neglecting mediating devices such as law or private property in the modern West.

The losses the terminal incurred because of fare dodgers were significant. In 1958 an enforced inspection group managed to seal access to the platforms and thoroughly check tickets for thirteen days in a row. Those two weeks yielded 300,000 rubles above usual sales.[151] Since ticketless hooligans were identified as young workers, following the logic of Soviet paternalism, the terminal approached their factory managers, but received no response. [152] The terminal expected factory managers to cooperate and provide their workers with passes.[153]

In the second half of the 1950s, a shift from criminal persecution to greater social self-policing took place, justified by the alleged new heights the civic consciousness of Soviet people had reached. The railway police braced for reductions, while volunteers from the Voluntary People's Druzhina (squads), created in 1959, were to assume the maintenance of public order. The terminal used the station's *druzhina* to combat fare dodgers. The head of the terminal became the *druzhina*'s first commander.[154] With the high level of petty crime, however, the *druzhina* did not have time for fare dodgers. In the first nine months of 1966, the *druzhina* detained 500 people at the terminal; of these, 183 were caught for petty theft, another 183 for petty hooliganism and violation of public order, and only 140 for riding without a ticket.[155] There was also little enthusiasm for joining the *druzhina*. People were too tired after their work shifts to dedicate free time to yet another unpaid service for the terminal.[156] Women in particular protested, arguing that their free time was filled with other chores.[157] Station *druzhina* membership declined from 250 in 1966 to 117 in 1972.[158] Twenty per cent of all *druzhina* shifts that year came to naught because no one showed up for duty.[159]

Violent hooliganism and damage to the Railroad's property decreased significantly in 1958–59.[160] The single most important cause was the lowered suburban tariff on the Lviv Railroad introduced in 1957.[161] There were also infrastructural improvements. In the early 1950s ticket desks at the terminal physically could not sell tickets to all the passengers;[162] after 1965 ticket machines eased the pressure.[163] The sales of seasonal passes in city factories also improved.[164] All these measures helped to overcome the crisis.

The terminal never eliminated fare dodgers, although it kept inventing new techniques of combatting fare evasion. Since guarding the platform did not work, the terminal switched to controlling car doors.[165] Fare dodgers responded by jumping onto cars upon departure.[166] Structural problems also remained. Even in the 1970s, there were long lines, and many passengers were physically unable to purchase suburban tickets.[167] Lower tariffs and improved living standards made fare dodging less pervasive, but the terminal had learned to live with it. This forced tolerance resulted from the failure of direct face-to-face policing and the profound inability of the railway and state authorities to create a self-regulating public space.

Within the terminal, public space and workplace were not separated. There was a certain indeterminacy of space as well as an excessive openness about it that invited neglect and dilapidation. The terminal's work algorithms were not synchronized with the needs and interests of other agencies or passengers. In November 1945 the *militsiia* complained about dark waiting halls, ticket, and baggage desks, and tunnels without electrical light after dark. No one checked people's IDs, and the terminal was open to everyone.[168] Several years later, the problems remained the same.[169] Terminal employees suffered too. Even in the early 1950s, ticket booths had no heat, and windows were without glass.[170]

The 1950s was a decade of beautification. Flower beds and trees were planted on the terminal square.[171] In 1954 all terminal rooms obtained furniture and "artistic paintings," curtains, and carpets. A little park on the square with alleys and benches was set up by the terminal,[172] The 1957 the Moscow International Youth Festival also helped to improve the appearance of the terminal. Walls were painted, additional lights were installed on the platforms,[173] and a fountain was placed in front of the main entrance. The fountain waited several years for water[174] before it was finally connected to the mains.[175]

Some things, however, changed little. Even after proper lights were installed, they were normally switched off at night – to reduce expenses.[176] There was never enough light – not only in the terminal and on the platforms, but also in the freight yards and on the square.[177] The problem with the glass sheds was perennial, as were the plans to repair them.[178] Vishnevich, in a slip of tongue typical of Soviet managers, called the train sheds a "breach of impediment" instead of a "stumbling block" (*bresh'* instead of *kamen' pretknoveniia*) that "nothing could tackle."[179] The electrical grid could not cope with the increased power consumption.[180] The fountain operated briefly in 1957, but then the water disappeared from it again. This was a major problem because the fountain was also supposed to function as a main fire reservoir.[181]

Terminal employees were regularly reproached for poor sanitation. They, in turn, blamed the infrastructure.[182] Roofs were leaky and ticket booths cold.[183] Even after the reconstruction, at the end of the 1950s, the terminal was still using a Polish boiler from the 1930s.[184] In 1964 an inspection found that most of the premises were unsuitable for workers. There were problems with dampness, ventilation, and heating.[185] In the 1970s, the "fat" decade of relative Soviet prosperity, ticket desks waited for two years for the replacement of damp, rotten floors and the installation of a toilet stall.[186] Workers also felt vulnerable in their offices. Drunken passengers and hooligans sometimes walked in, even into the office of an on-duty official.[187]

For the terminal as a whole, a separate zone for suburban passengers was the top priority. The terminal had asked for one in 1953 in connection with fare dodgers. In 1955 the passenger service pointed out that the simultaneous arrival and departure of suburban trains with daily commuters produced a crowd of five thousand people, which the existing terminal could not handle physically. The only solution was a separate suburban terminal for two or three thousand people on the territory of the First freight yard.[188] In 1958 the terminal requested a suburban terminal be built in 1959.[189] The Railroad's head replied that, according to the Railroad's Seven-Year Plan, the suburban terminal would open in 1962, together with the electrification of the Lviv–Stryi section of the line.[190] By 1962 it became clear that, although electrification was the ministry's priority, the suburban terminal was not. Instead of a separate terminal, a suburban pavilion was promised.[191] Even for this pavilion, neither space nor funds were found. The design of the suburban terminal was ready, but approval of construction was delayed year after year.[192]

The sheds, tunnels,[193] and washrooms[194] were a permanent problem. Capital repair of the sewers had already been long overdue in the 1950s;[195] no funds were secured for it over the whole Soviet period. Capital renovations during the 1968–71 period conformed to the well-established pattern: small repairs by the terminal itself were completed on time and decently; everything contracted to the construction enterprise suffered from delays and poor workmanship – the sheds and ventilation, in particular.[196]

The Soviet terminal remained darker, both inside and outside, than its Polish predecessor. The contrast with the abundance of light in the cities of the developed West was even more striking. Incandescent lamps in the terminal were replaced by fluorescent lamps in 1973 as part of a republic-wide campaign to save energy;[197] the first neon clocks were installed only in 1974.[198] Both technological lag and attitudes towards space were manifested in the terminal's state of permanent disrepair. Locomotives flushed engines on platforms, flooding tunnels and damaging the foundations.[199] Although one of the best terminals on the Soviet network, it remained dirty, both inside and out.[200] At the end of the 1970s, terminal porters swept platforms with wooden brooms, mostly just scattering dust around, often right in front of international trains.[201]

Visual ideological agitation was easy to produce and cheap. Uninviting and neglected premises were generously sprinkled with an outcropping of ideological signs. Posters with the agendas and materials of Party Congresses and highlights of Five-Year Plans were plastered on the terminal walls, together with Khrushchev's "Moral Code of the Builder of Communism."[202] Posters hung on the entrance to the terminal, concealing a simple, poorly made gate, a mockery of the original Art Nouveau masterpiece.

Since there was no private property and virtually no property law, the use of space could rarely be adjudicated in court. The clumsy administrative machinery functioned through permanent negotiations. Users of the premises were never in full control of their space and never fully responsible for it. The restaurant and the *militsiia* had rooms and mandates of their own, and were not subordinated to the Railroad. Conflicts and mutual accusations between the employees of all three organizations were the rule, not the exception.[203] Territorial Party committees served as arbiters in such conflicts but offered no permanent solutions. In 1954 the terminal complained that the station's *militsiia*, instead of helping, "only intrude into business which is not theirs."[204] In 1963 the terminal head complained about the restaurant and retail stores: "All the platforms are covered with kiosks, portable canteens, and there is no space for machines, and all the branches of retail trade are represented; there are several tables from the restaurant, jewellery, industrial goods, and no space for a passenger. In fact the terminal has turned into a shopping mall. Beer and wine are being sold by the glass."[205] The station wanted the Party to prohibit the sale of beer in the terminal, which the government was unwilling to do since that would undermine revenues.[206] The *militsiia* argued that its main task was to protect passengers from abuses by unscrupulous employees of both organizations, instead of solving those organizations' problems.[207]

Outside, on the terminal square, things were even worse. Retail and public dining outlets mushroomed and occupied the square with a variety of pavilions, turning it, in Vishnevich's words, into the "Sorochyntsi Fair" (immortalized by Nikolai Gogol).[208] There was also the city's central bus station, invited to the terminal square by Vishnevich. Having realized that the growth of road and air transportation was an inevitable long-term trend, he had decided to turn the terminal into a hub of intermodal passenger transportation. The terminal's information bureau started providing information about all public transportation options available in Lviv, while the city bus connected the terminal with the airport. In 1965 the terminal started selling tickets for both trains and buses. Combined train and bus tickets were sold for local resort destinations. The downside of this arrangement was more work for the terminal employees, since the bus station consisted only of ticket booths and bus stops and did not have many employees. Terminal ticket cashiers complained that their bus ticket sales did not count towards their salary, and the workload for terminal janitors tripled.[209]

In the 1970s the terminal repeatedly complained to the district Party committee about the presence of beer kiosks on every platform. Workers drank there before heading home and often had accidents afterwards.[210] The complaints were to no avail. The authorities were in the process of expanding small retail outlets, and those at the terminal would keep multiplying. In 1975 several new canteens, cafés, and a delicatessen with tables appeared on the terminal square, augmenting its seating capacity to eight hundred, not counting counters and kiosks.[211]

The station could not even seal the railway terrain proper. In the late 1960s despairing managers complained that "the station is open from all the sides. The fence is of the kind that thieves jump over."[212] Efforts to enclose the space continued with remarkable futility. Instead of organizing the space, officials locked entrance doors and posted checkpoints at the entrances to the platforms. In those face-to-face encounters, the public as a rule triumphed.[213]

The defiant behaviour of the Soviet public in the early 1960s was noticed by John N. Westwood, a renowned expert on Soviet and Russian railroading: "After visiting most of the Moscow terminal, I came away impressed with the Russians' contempt for regulations; they not only refused to buy platform tickets but scorned the assistance of the subways to cross the tracks. Despite notices warning of the heavy fines levied on track-walkers, passengers in a hurry would gaily clamber over the platform edge to take a short cut."[214] This "unruliness" was the consequence of the particular Soviet unmediated and educational approach to discipline and of the specificity of Soviet space. Private boundaries were rare, while commons were plentiful. Public space was a resource to use to supplement private incomes and to compensate for the lack of private space. The absence of property laws and city by-laws invited informal use. The nature of the railway terrain, adjacent to never-ending tracks, made breaking rules easier. Simple fencing, however inefficient even for industrial factories, was impossible here.

Since the very beginning of Soviet rule, all those who could not afford or obtain accommodation in the city used the terminal as a shelter. *Militsiia* reports from 1944 speak of the "vagabond element" found in waiting halls.[215] Even *militsiia* convoying prisoners occasionally requisitioned the terminal in this capacity.[216] The terminal had tried to "liquidate overnight stays of strangers" since at least 1945, but without success.[217] Instead various people on move also started camping in front of the terminal.[218] In this respect Lviv was not unique. Railway stations attracted suspicious people all over the Soviet Union. In Leningrad (Saint Petersburg), after the war, hundreds of "criminals" essentially lived in the sanitary railway yard.[219] In Lviv security forces complained that terminal workers "themselves bring to the terminal various vagabonds, who are not passengers, and drink with them."[220] "Speculators" were selling foodstuffs at the terminal square, and in the 1960s illegal private services offered at the terminal expanded to include unofficial taxis.[221]

In the 1960s, people from the city came to the terminal, attracted by the restaurant and alcohol sold after hours. The terminal's management complained that they "engage in hooliganism, violate passengers' peace, and stroll along the tracks."[222] Tracks leading from the terminal to station's freight and equipping yards were a liminal space, where fights between local youth gangs took place and women abandoned their unwanted children.[223] Terminal waiting halls were full at night. There were not only various "idly loafing people,"[224] but also legitimate transit passengers, especially those who had failed to validate their tickets in time and had to wait overnight, and those on business trips who had failed to check in to city hotels.[225] In 1965 an inspector from the district Party committee complained about "gypsies" "pestering passengers."[226] Various "strangers" with easy access to the terminal were an indefatigable concern for the *militsiia*.Statistics of those detained at the terminal show that the most common offence was public drunkenness. Street urchins were the second-largest group and petty hooligans the third (Table 9.1). The terminal served as a magnet attracting a "criminal element,"[227] despite substantial police presence. There were forty-one *militsiia* men at the terminal's station in 1979. For special occasions this presence was increased: for the duration of the 1980 Olympics it was doubled.[228]

A constant stream of indoctrination campaigns centred on the notion of "culturedness" attempted to compensate for the inability to secure

Table 9.1. Detainees at the Lviv terminal, by offence, 1971 and 1972

Offence	1971	1972
Hooliganism	63	57
Petty hooliganism	905	1,058
Drunkenness, sent to detoxification	1,338	1,208
Accidents	183	161
Glass breaking	41	40
Emergency stops by passengers	112	51
Homeless children	1,293	1,479

Source: DALO, f. 2037, op. 4, spr. 25, 44.

public order. In a pioneering article, Vadim Volkov showed how in the 1930s this versatile term had been used as an instrument to deal with public disorder and help rural newcomers assimilate new norms and ideological messages.[229] Categories of "cultured" and "uncultured" behaviour remained strong during the post-war period, especially in the Soviet economy's service sector. The alleged "lack of culture" explained everything from dirty floors and absent janitors, to the absurd ticket desk queues and overcrowded premises with five thousand people instead of the expected two thousand.[230] Culture was an all-encompassing master signifier used to signify desired outcomes. Basic politeness towards customers was "culture"[231] – so was the lack of theft,[232] painted walls, and potable water.[233] Drinking and cheating, on the other hand, were "unculture" (*nekul'turnost'*).[234] When the terminal head encouraged workers to be more diligent, he claimed that "there is not yet real culture among terminal workers."[235]

"Culture" and "culturedness" helped to place the burden of responsibility on human agency and to divert attention from infrastructural defects and financial shortages. With the emphasis on "culture," the state tried to compensate for its inability to create mediating mechanisms that would reshape the Soviet self without crudely direct forms of intervention. In 1951, in preparation for the busy summer season, every terminal worker spent 70 to 120 hours at lectures on the culture of service, without any discernible effect.[236] Ceaseless propaedeutic sessions and appeals to individual consciousness and conscience remained the main Soviet alternative to a self-regulating material environment of liberal governmentality.

The distinctiveness of Soviet social space is easy to overlook, since the geography of an industrializing Soviet Lviv in the 1950s and 1960s was similar to that of its capitalist predecessor. Only beginning with the 1960s, but mostly in the 1970s and 1980s, did new districts of pre-fabricated multi-storey apartment buildings appear, moving the bulk of the city's population into newly developed territory. Soviet industrial Lviv was built first by the railway, in the industrial zones that had emerged around the first stations back in Austrian times (Figure 9.1). Although historiography treats Soviet industrialization as a major break with the past, "new" Soviet factories and plants in many cases were merely greatly expanded versions of pre-existing enterprises, draining labour from other economic sectors and inflating labour productivity.

Proximity to the railway track was the main locational determinant for Lviv's first Soviet factories, which took over not only industrial but also other public buildings near the railway. A telegraph factory, essentially arriving by train from Saratov in 1946, started in the former Bilinski hospice, next to the ZZK building. Nearby a factory of electrical bulbs (later, of television tubes) took over the school that had served as the headquarters of the Polish insurrection in November 1918. Later those inherited core premises became overgrown with standard Soviet industrial buildings.

The railway, in fact, played a far more important role in the Soviet Union than in any Western country – in 1940 it was responsible for carrying 85.1 per cent of all freight and 92.2 per cent of all passengers. Even in 1970, with competition from road transport and aviation, the railway's share remained an impressive 65.1 per cent of freight and 48.4 per cent of passengers (respective US figures were 7.5 and 7.8 per cent).[237] The Soviet railway was not merely a means of transportation; it was a supra-industry with factories and plants of its own and served as a precondition for other industries. The railway was the only industry after which administrative districts in large Soviet cities were routinely named. Soviet authorities acknowledged the role of railway infrastructure to the development of cities. In Soviet Lviv, the former Krakow ward became the Railway district, one of four (later, five) city administrative districts. By the end of the 1970s, all administrative districts included vast neighbourhoods of industrially built standard Soviet apartment blocks. Ethnic communities were not ghettoized, but the traditionally working-class Railway and Shevchenko districts had a slightly higher share of Ukrainians than did the Soviet and Lenin districts, which included more prestigious neighbourhoods, such as the former "New World."[238]

Stalin famously relied on the railway for inter-city travel, but post-war Soviet leaders switched to planes. In 1975 Lviv saw the last

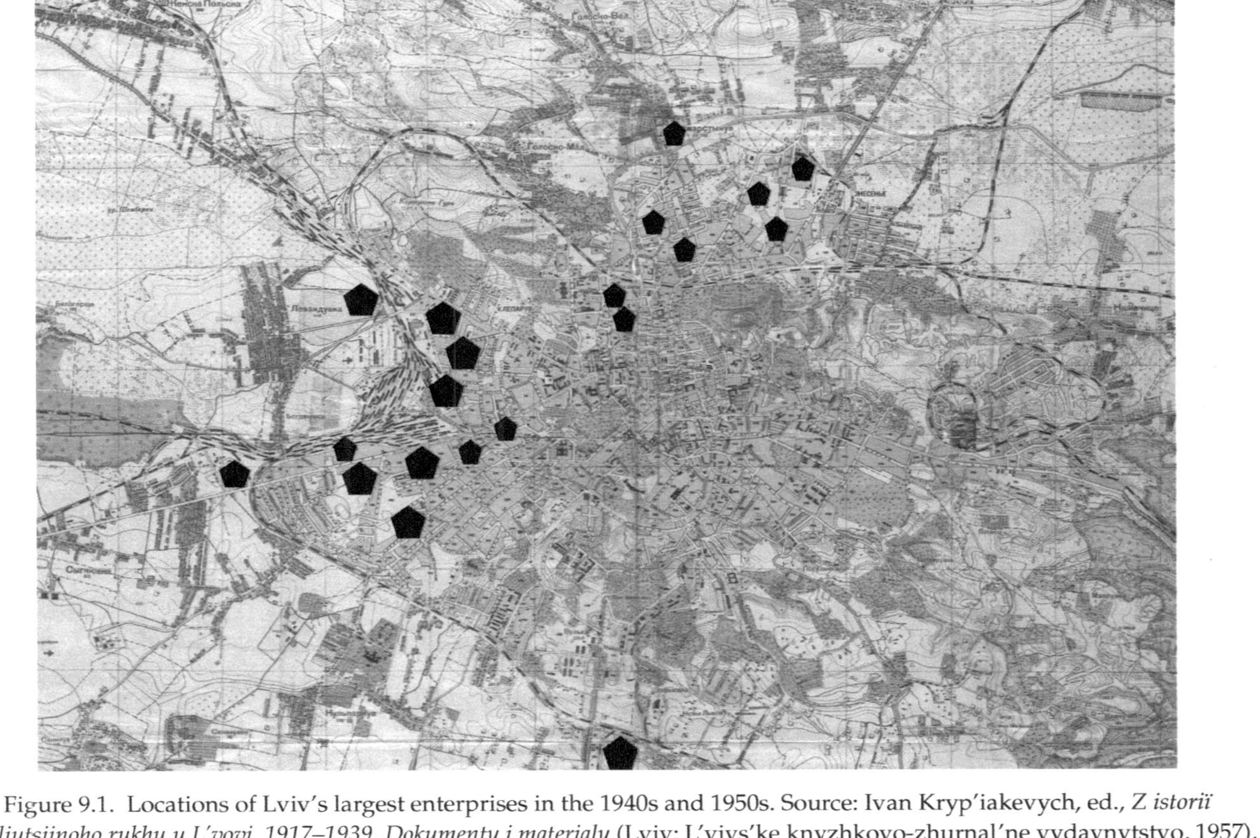

Figure 9.1. Locations of Lviv's largest enterprises in the 1940s and 1950s. Source: Ivan Kryp'iakevych, ed., *Z istoriï revoliutsiinoho rukhu u L'vovi, 1917–1939, Dokumenty i materialy* (Lviv: L'vivs'ke knyzhkovo-zhurnal'ne vydavnytstvo, 1957), 243–52; U. Ia. Iedlins'ka and Iaroslav Isaievych, eds., *Istoriia L'vova v dokumentakh i materialakh: zbirnyk dokumentiv i materialiv* (Kyiv: Naukova dumka, 1986), 270. The map is based on the 1944 city plan by Sukhorukov and Burshtein.

official visit of the head of the state by train. On 21 March Leonid Brezhnev stopped at the Lviv terminal on his way back from Hungary. The bureau of the Oblast Committee as well as "representatives of the workers of the Oblast" greeted him.[239] When Mikhail Gorbachev visited Lviv in 1989, he landed at Lviv airport.

In the public space of the railway neighbourhoods, pre-Soviet divisions became irrelevant. St Elizabeth Church lost the crosses on its spires and became a warehouse – a fitting illustration of Mikhail Epshtein's thesis that, in Soviet spatial order, the warehouse replaced the church.[240] This temple to scarce and desired goods was not maintained properly, however, and fell into dreadful disrepair. The old ZZK building – colloquially called the "Rox," from the name of its original pre-war cinema – the Sokol building, the engine drivers' club, and the former Catholic Home were now run by various "culture" departments of Soviet officialdom.

Workers' resistance lost its civic and organized dimensions, and became reduced to what Michel de Certeau calls the "tactics of everyday life."[241] As Certeau points out, those tactics are fundamentally about uses of space, structured by the strategies of power but not wholly controlled by them. The Soviet people's propensity for breaking rules was part of the repertoire of such resistance, which did not have to be intentional. Many "discipline violations" at the station were also about the appropriation of work space. Workers were most vocal when voicing concerns about the safety and comfort of their workplace.[242] They appropriated the semi-sacred ideological space of the terminal's "Red Corner" for their leisure, furnishing it with a TV set and musical instruments,[243] chessboards, and billiard tables.[244] They also demanded amenities such as drinking water and showers.[245]

Outside the workplace, people claimed public space. Railway terrain was trespassed upon, while railway neighbourhoods saw their fair share of rowdy socializing and frequent altercations with the *militsiia*.[246] Workers' neighbourhoods repurposed state-maintained premises of "socialist leisure" for old purposes. Unmarried neighbourhood youth went to evening dances there, older workers gathered for a game of chess or dominos and beer with friends. Election days and Soviet holidays were popular because the authorities enticed workers with treats, while the *militsiia* were more lenient than usual. These everyday practices were poor substitutes, however, for the loss of an autonomous public sphere, of which a contestable public space is an important dimension.

Although personal living spaces could be claimed for individual and family ownership, public space, in theory, could not be used to demonstrate or appeal by anyone other than the proletarian state itself. Only through informal and illicit practices could it be contested. Youth gangs did just that, having divided it informally into their own neighbourhood "districts." They watched over them, punished trespassers, and fought over boundaries. Neither mandatory secondary schooling nor the growing numbers of university students could eradicate them.[247]

Soviet Lviv's public space remained grim. There was an asceticism of unadorned walls, bleak display windows, and stencilled, unlit shop signs beneath the kitschy "visual propaganda" (*nagliadnaia agitatsiia*). The latter, while called illustrated or visual, relied on words rather than images. Slogans covered roofs and stretched across streets in blatant indifference to the surrounding architectural design. Visual propaganda did not use space as medium, but rather disregarded its potential and autonomy. Space was a location and a utility, oftentimes a problem, but not a means to mould people.

Using broad brush strokes to characterize a complex and variegated Soviet social space runs the risk of overgeneralization and banality. Nonetheless some aspects of the terminal space can be extrapolated to the larger Soviet social space. The USSR did have its own urban planners, architects, and designers, who tried to organize urban space conveniently for people and for the economy, and in accord with socialist ideals.[248] The public space of a socialist city was meant to inculcate collectivism and help mould good Soviet citizens. The terminal likewise was supposed to work as a "zone of estrangement" (*polosa otchuzhdeniia*), where "the citizen no longer is his own master" and becomes a passenger.[249] In Soviet reality, however, the citizen all too often became "a trouble-maker without a ticket, who makes life difficult for the teams of conductors and platform ticket-inspectors."[250] The absence of the liberal "auto-regulation of matter,"[251] coupled with the Soviet "cult of the word" and "the primacy of the word before deed,"[252] turned urban public space into a passive indeterminate substance. Soviet social space, like the train terminal in Viktor Nekrasov's novel *Zapiski zevaki* (Notes of a bystander), was something in between – somewhere "between heaven and earth."[253]

Coda

Lviv's main train terminal is still on its original site. Just as more than a hundred years ago, trains, trams, and people flow to and from the terminal, augmented by the ubiquitous traffic of minibuses scurrying about the city's routes. The neighbourhoods around the station remain the city's poorer and less desirable areas. Some things seemingly change very little. As the good soldier Švejk wisely remarked more than a century ago, "at stations there always have been thefts and always will be. It can't be otherwise."[1]

The city's post-Soviet period started similarly to its Soviet predecessor: with economic ruin, industrial profiteering, loose labour discipline, heavy drinking, and a spike in crime. During one of their drinking sessions in the terminal head's office, the deputy head killed the terminal head by hitting him with a chair. In court the deputy claimed he had overreacted to being addressed as a "Muscovite" (*moskal'*).[2] This conformed deftly with the image of the city as a hotbed of radical Ukrainian nationalism, but the rumour was that deputy's explanation was just a clever defence strategy, while his real motives were far less political.

Ironically the economic collapse of the early 1990s helped to solve some of the terminal's long-term problems. The implosion of Soviet industry and the reconfiguration of trade resulting from the socialist bloc's total collapse reduced the gulfstream of goods flowing through the Lviv railway junction to a mere trickle. The First freight yard, located on the site of the old Chernivtsi terminal, became redundant and soon closed down. Since the contraction of passenger traffic was negligible, the Railroad turned the former yard into a pavilion for suburban trains. The long-standing request of the terminal's Soviet managers was satisfied after nearly a half-century's wait.

As a child I was oblivious to the rhythms and problems of the station's economy. Neither did I pay much attention to the details of the terminal's façade and or décor of its halls. The buzz of the crowd and the spin of train axles were far more exciting. I also liked the unmistakable railway smell: a potent mixture of wet iron, machine oil, burnt coal, and rotten sleepers. It filled the train sheds and followed the tracks as they left the terminal. As I grew up, the scenery around the terminal changed, but the smell was still there, year after year, amid falling snow or on a sultry August day. The smell was my link to the past. It helped me imagine small, puffing, nineteenth-century engines and rugged crews of navvies with picks. It took years to realize that the railway had stopped using steam engines in Lviv even before I was born. The only coal around was for heating in winter on electrified routes. The smell, just as many other seemingly unchangeable fixtures, proved to be deceptive. The nineteenth century must have smelled different.

The terminal of my childhood is long gone, together with the fascinating machine of shining metal for changing coins to tokens in the terminal's luggage room. Working on this book, I discovered that this piece of Soviet steampunk was invented by a local mechanic, part of the Khrushchev's campaign to encourage the invention and rationalization of production. This was not the only finding that prompted the return of certain childhood memories.

I became aware of the terminal at about the same time that I discovered the city lying outside our apartment building. We lived on Horodotska (Gródecka) Street, on the same block that had housed the railway union's headquarters before the First World War. The building was a typical Lviv three-storey, with a courtyard ringed with long, shared balconies running the whole of its length. Another yard at the back ended with the wall of the sewing factory. In 1944 stables were there, from which my grandfather took horses every morning, carting material for the terminal's reconstruction. He spent the next half-century working at the terminal.

Somewhere in the building's cellars the remains of a resident lay, buried by the gang that murdered him in the heat of the post-war crime wave. The neighbours were too terrified to report him as missing, so his body was never retrieved. When I grew up, those fears belonged to the past. The neighbourhood was peaceful – as kids we could roam the streets after school unaccompanied, looking for adventure in the dark, locked away in St Elizabeth Church, with its boarded windows. My first library was the one at the "Rox," the Railway Workers' Palace of Culture in the former ZZK building. On my way to the library or art studio, I would take wide passageways cutting through the magnificent blocks of pre–First World War railway apartment blocks.

As to the "national problem," with which so much writing on Lviv has been preoccupied, in my life it mattered far less than Bulgakov's famous "housing problem" or even noisy and nosy neighbours – problems familiar to nearly everyone in any city. In at least half of around thirty apartments in our building, the older generation spoke Russian and never became fluent enough in Ukrainian to speak it. Their children, born after the war, spoke the same Ukrainian I did. Neighbourhood conflicts did not run along ethnic lines. Our worst long-standing neighbourly feud was with a Ukrainian woman who had come to Lviv from a Galician village, just as my grandparents had.

Language, history, and identity played a role, but not in any simplistic "us versus them" way. We knew that Russian was the language of power, that books in Ukrainian were fewer and Ukrainian newspaper thinner in their content and style compared with Moscow-based Russian publications. Since the Russian language was omnipresent and indispensable, I learned to read in Russian almost simultaneously with learning to read in Ukrainian. The first book I borrowed after registering at the "Rox" library at the age of six was in Russian. Ukrainian language and identity gave one a feeling of belonging to the non-conforming minority, and helped to develop sympathy for the oppressed, exploited, and discriminated against around the globe and across history.

Ukrainian identity also provided a connection to the hidden continents of the local past, submerged in the sea of Soviet narratives and representations. This was the past that lingered in the city's physical remains. On 1 November – All Saints' Day in the Latin tradition and the Day of the "November Deed" for Galician Ukrainians – my grandparents used to take me for a walk to the Ianivsky (Janowski) cemetery, following either the tracks from the main terminal or taking Railway (Na Błonie) Street. At the cemetery we would visit the few remaining crosses on the graves of Ukrainian Galician Army soldiers – most of them had been vandalized by the Soviets and used to pave the roads. There were also the graves of "our Premier" and "our General": Kost Levytsky and Myron Tarnavsky of the Western Ukrainian People's Republic. The phantom republic and its army was a source of major frustration for me. There were no references to them in the history books I had access to, and my grandparents avoided more detailed explanations.

The Ianivsky (Janowski) cemetery was no longer formally divided into Jewish and Christian. I roamed its Jewish section hoping to find at least one surviving pre-war Jewish tombstone there, but to no avail. There were no monuments commemorating the Holocaust in Lviv, no plaques to mark sites where it had occurred. On the territory of the former Janowska concentration camp, a Soviet labour camp was still operating, puncturing the landscape with watchtowers and barbed wire.

These memories undoubtedly shaped the way I think about Lviv and read my sources. On the other hand, memories, just as much as bricks and mortar, are the stuff that cities are made of, even when they are as unreliable as that railway smell. Walter Benjamin reminds us that "truth is not – as Marxism would have it – a merely contingent function of knowing, but is bound to a nucleus of time lying hidden within the knower and the known alike."[3]

The city, with its physicality and possibility to be experienced directly, is more difficult to "know" than the far more abstract "nation" and "culture" first constructed and later explained by intellectuals. Detached speculative explanations and interpretations cannot do justice to the imbroglio of routines and dreams, to the city's simultaneously multilayered existence on multiple temporal and material planes. Some things are best conveyed with the help of imprecise and deeply personal reminiscences.

Intimate personal connection to a place does not make one's interpretation better, observations more discerning, or narrative more convincing. They do, however, thwart a safe, ironic distancing from the subject and help to avoid a condescending exoticization – that original sin of anthropology, which is still alive and well in some Western scholarship about Eastern Europe.

The train terminal provides an excellent vantage point for re-examining the conventional stereotypes of Lviv's twentieth-century history. Not only is the terminal a microcosm or metaphor for the modern city as a place of urban vertigo – an amalgam of hopes and fears; as a clutter of diverse cityscapes, it has also become a key to the spatial history of modern Lviv. As a material embodiment of the city's global interconnectedness and a relay in the shifting political geography of the wider world, the terminal helps us to explore the physical connections between the city and the wider world of national and international politics.

The city's wider world started with the state and its juridical, ideological, and administrative frameworks. These frameworks shaped the city through state agencies, discourses, and regulations. The twentieth-century state controlled the railway directly, endowing its space with a certain extraterritoriality in the municipal context. The state wielded its powers by interpreting, marking, and setting the terms of the train terminal's use. Its symbolic appearance and economy reflected the nature of relationships among the state, intermediate territorial structures, and the city, serving as reliable indicators of local self-government's real power.

The terminal, however, is not just about strategies of political power and its mapping and regulating techniques. The terminal is the city's most public building, and unlike other public buildings, embodies and sustains an everyday public space that is much wider and far more open than allowed by partisan visions of the ideal urban *civitas*. The terminal's crowds, movement, and noise are all reflections of a fluctuating and transitory modernity that hardly aligns with the firmly normative vision of bound communities and proper governance.

In the twentieth century, the terminal was a site in which the normative modernity of state projects was constantly challenged and probed from below. As a workplace it mirrored the railway itself, with its combination of white- and blue-collar jobs spread across a variety of occupations. It presented challenges and opportunities to the workers' movement and to the railway managers. "Below" at the terminal consisted not only of railway workers. Pre-figuring the post-industrial economy of present-day cities, the terminal produced and sold services. It served passengers and was as central as the trains themselves to the culture of modern passengerhood. As a place of consumption, with its restaurant and canteens, kiosks, and bookstands, a shelter for homeless, and a police station, a site attracting city *flâneurs* and loners, petty thieves and pimps, the terminal was the quintessence of the modern city, an urban heterotopia condensed into a single structure.

Although guidebooks usually assign to the terminal building a definite style, the current building is a palimpsest. Not only twentieth-century architectural styles and their local interpretations, but also political regimes, with their distinct ideologies, economies, and techniques of governance, have left their imprint on the terminal. The building documents the profound and ubiquitous changes the city underwent in the twentieth century, when not only preferred styles and desired solutions, but even the basic structures of Lviv's social space were transformed.

Political regimes dictated regimens and set the rhythm and tone for both grand projects and daily routines, determining not only the composition and appearance of places and buildings, but also their uses and connotations. With thousands of threads, space was tied not only to the state's economic capacity, but also to the political regime's fundamental assumptions about society and the purpose of human existence. The differences between the ideology of political regimes and applied sociology were not limited to what they did to space; the most important difference was in how they saw and conceptualized social space.

Regimes' visions of the social space determined to a significant extent how the city and its population would be governed.

Some of the techniques these twentieth-century regimes used were identical. They all shared the same modern toolbox. They were familiar with the railway and its infrastructure, aware of the railway's strategic importance and functions, and read the city through its railway infrastructure. Those similarities became especially apparent in the two World Wars, with the Second drawing upon the experiences of the First.

The differences between political regimes, however, were just as important. The dividing lines were many. There were national and supranational regimes, liberal and illiberal, regimes that tried to incorporate and assimilate, and regimes that treated the city as a foreign conquered territory. There were states of law that endowed communities with autonomy and those that tried to govern their human subjects directly.

Since the arrival of the first train in Lviv, the terminal and the railway terrain that developed in the city became a liminal space, an unstable borderland embodying the finite nature of the community, municipal authority, and propriety. That liminal space of social "others," intimately linked to "real" industry, was shared with machines and the dead, and was used to demarcate city space and territorialize its hierarchies. It was no accident that the terminal and its environs found themselves at the centre of a Nazi colonial project that transformed the urban heterotopia of early twentieth-century Lviv into an urban dystopia.

Dystopian mid-century violence undermined Lviv's optimistic love affair with modernity. The deadly mid-century political projects not only claimed to be modern, but also used the familiar pathways that liberal modernity threaded through the city's space. Thus they also sabotaged and displaced turn-of-the-century hopes and expectations. In the aftermath of genocide and deportations, the restitched city took the Soviets' optimistic promise of egalitarian and sophisticated paradise with a large grain of salt.

The Soviet vision entailed not only smoke-stacked landscapes of large-scale industry, but also an all-encompassing paternalistic care that enveloped the workforce – a culture of permanent negotiation and exceptions and the receding importance of formal procedures, regulations, and laws. The paternalistic cocoon around the worker was not without its pleasures, especially after the mass violence of mid-century. It also entailed an obsession with individual consciousness and a utilitarian approach to urban space. The seemingly all-powerful Party state was slow and unwieldy when it came to capital investments in urban infrastructure or the myriad tiny maintenance tasks the modern city requires.

The inertia of rusty Soviet industrial parks smothered all attempts to encourage technological innovation and acceleration. The absence of private property and a market helped the state inject labour and capital into large-scale projects, while at the same time conserving and neglecting real estate, thus arresting the dynamism of the city's built environment. "Capital" and "real estate" in this case are actually misnomers. To paraphrase Marx, a building is just a structure with walls and roof; "only under certain circumstances does it become capital."[4] This Soviet spatial framework, together with Soviet paternalism, endowed people with greater freedom to navigate the relatively inert space of Soviet cities. They generated multiple vigorous tactics of appropriation. The blurry boundary between private and public facilitated a distinctive form of dwelling in public, characteristic of Soviet workplaces and neighbourhoods.

Although scholarship has focused on the national projects and ethnic tensions of Soviet Lviv, its post-Stalinist period was characterized by a remarkable silence on the nationalist front that remained multi-ethnic even after the Holocaust and post-war "repatriations." The internationalist ideology of the new regime and the lack of legal and political venues for national mobilization contributed to this silence, but grassroots workers' solidarity vis-à-vis the Party state and its managerial elite was just as important. On the other hand, the lack of autonomous arenas for self-organization and open discussion, as well as the conflation of nationality with allegedly biologically transmitted ethnicity, prevented any critical examination of national myths. Neither did social hierarchy and privilege fully lose their ethnic colouring. These were the mines left for post–Soviet Ukraine to disarm.

Regarding theoretical battles as to whether the organization of space is merely a reflection of social relations or can be seen as a relatively autonomous structure within the mode of production,[5] this book points to the importance of political regimes, the technologies of governing they deployed, and the social imagination that informed them in structuring urban space. In twentieth-century Lviv, the change of political regimes entailed tectonic social shifts, including a change in the very relations of production. At the same time, the nature of those political regimes cannot be fully understood without examining the transformations they enacted in urban space, and the latter cannot be merely reduced to the relations of production.

Twentieth-century Lviv and its people often faced the consequences of decisions made in faraway capitals by governments over which they had no control. The city, however, was not merely a toy in the hands of powerful states. It could be languid and proactive, accepting and resisting; but most important, the city was never homogeneous, and therefore could be all these things simultaneously. The layers of Lviv's material palimpsest demonstrate not only the ease with which space could be redrawn and reordered, but also point to alternatives and possibilities, feeding the imagination and sustaining hopes for a more fulfilling life.

Describing Kyiv, yet another great Eastern European provincial city passing through the cataclysmic decades of the twentieth century, the poet Osip Mandelshtam remarked on the "still extraordinary love of life" of "small" people, which accompanied "their deep helplessness."[6] Those little purposes of ordinary lives in this part of the world outlasted grand political projects. Lviv's streets and buildings also proved to be more resilient than ambitious social designs. Spectacular bloodbaths and frequent and dramatic political changes failed to change the texture of modern Lviv in equally spectacular fashion. The changes were subtle, but subtle is not the same as superfluous. Testimonies of exiles visiting Lviv after decades of absence show that hardly any other change is as profoundly disconcerting as the defamiliarization of things once known intimately. We tend to explain changing landscapes through people, attributing change to human agency, but people just as often are merely responding to changing space, even when change is subtle and nearly impossible to pinpoint.

Notes

Introduction

1 Although the term has several meanings, in this book "terminal" refers to the building designed primarily to serve passengers. Such a terminal is an integral part of the railway "station," a larger structure that processes trains by assembling and disassembling, receiving and sending, and handling loads.
2 Stanley Washburn, *Field Notes from the Russian Front* (London: Andrew Melrose, [1915?]), 211.
3 Iosif Il'in, *Skitaniia russkogo ofitsera: dnevnik Iosifa Il'ina, 1914–1920*, ed. Veronika Zhober (Moscow: Knizhnitsa, Russkii put', 2016), 92.
4 Walter Benjamin, *The Arcades Project* (Cambridge, MA: Belknap Press, 1999).
5 Timothy Snyder, *Bloodlands: Europe between Hitler and Stalin* (New York: Basic Books, 2010).
6 Christoph Mick, *Kriegserfahrungen in einer multiethnischen Stadt: Lemberg 1914–1947* (Wiesbaden: Harrasowitz, 2010).
7 The classic work in this respect is Wolfgang Schivelbusch, *The Railway Journey: The Industrialization of Time and Space in the Nineteenth Century* (Berkeley; Los Angeles: University of California Press, 1987). For more recent work on the railway and cultural imagination, see Michael Freeman, *Railways and the Victorian Imagination* (New Haven, CT: Yale University Press, 1999). The Russian imperial context is explored in Frithjof Benjamin Schenk, *Russlands Fahrt in die Moderne: Mobilität und sozialer Raum im Eisenbahnzeitalter* (Stuttgart: Franz Steiner Verlag, 2014).
8 Stephen Kotkin, *Magnetic Mountain: Stalinism as a Civilization* (Berkeley: University of California Press, 1997); David L. Hoffmann, *Stalinist Values: The Cultural Norms of Soviet Modernity, 1917–1941* (Ithaca, NY: Cornell University Press, 2003); idem, *Cultivating the Masses: Modern State Practices*

and Soviet Socialism, 1914–1939 (Ithaca, NY: Cornell University Press, 2011).

9 Stephen Kotkin, "1991 and the Russian Revolution: Sources, Conceptual Categories, Analytical Frameworks," *Journal of Modern History* 70, no. 2 (1994): 387.

10 Peter Holquist, *Making War, Forging Revolution: Russia's Continuum of Crisis, 1914–1921* (Cambridge, MA: Harvard University Press, 2002).

11 Michael David-Fox, *Crossing Borders: Modernity, Ideology, and Culture in Russia and the Soviet Union* (Pittsburgh: University of Pittsburgh Press, 2005), 50.

12 The first pioneering work in this direction likely was Patrick Joyce, *The Rule of Freedom: Liberalism and the City in Britain* (London: Verso, 2003).

13 One of the most powerful critiques of abstraction in the social sciences remains Derek Sayer's reading of Karl Marx's method: Derek Sayer, *The Violence of Abstraction: The Analytical Foundation of Historical Materialism* (Oxford: Basil Blackwell, 1986).

14 Geoff Eley and Keith Nield, *The Future of Class in History: What's Left of the Social?* (Ann Arbor: University of Michigan Press, 2007), 199.

15 William J. Sewell Jr., *Logics of History: Social Theory and Social Transformation* (Chicago: University of Chicago Press, 2005), 318–72.

16 Lewis H. Siegelbaum identifies both material culture and space as especially promising in the new subfield of Soviet historiography; see Lewis H. Siegelbaum, "Whither Soviet History? Some Reflections on Recent Anglophone Historiography," *Region: Regional Studies of Russia, Eastern Europe, and Central Asia* 1, no. 2 (2012): 213–30.

17 Nick Baron, "New Spatial Histories of Twentieth Century Russia and the Soviet Union: Surveying the Landscape," *Jahrbücher für Geschichte Osteuropas* Neue Folge 55, no. 3 (2007): 374–400.

18 Henri Lefebvre, *The Production of Space* (Oxford: Basil Blackwell, 1991).

19 Roman Szporluk, "West Ukraine and West Belorussia: Historical Tradition, Social Communication and Linguistic Assimilation," *Soviet Studies* 31, no. 1 (1979): 76–98; idem, "The Strange Politics of Lviv: An Essay in Search of an Explanation," in *The Politics of Nationality and the Erosion of the USSR*, ed. Zvi Gitelman (Basingstoke, UK: Palgrave Macmillan, 1992), 215–31.

20 Ia Kryp'iakevych, ed., *Z istoriï revoliutsiinoho rukhu u L'vovi, 1917–1939: dokumenty i materialy* (Lviv: Lvivske knyzhkovo-zhurnalne vydavnytstvo, 1957); Fedir Koval, Ivan Kryp'iakevych, and Volodymyr Chuhaiov, eds., *Stanovyshche trudiashchykh L'vova, 1917–1939: dokumenty ta materialy* (Lviv: Lvivske knyzhkovo-zhurnalne vydavnytstvo, 1961); M.V. Bryk and Uliana Iaroslavivna Iedlins'ka, eds., *Istoriia L'vova v dokumentakh i materialakh: zbirnyk dokumentiv i materialiv* (Kyiv: Naukova dumka, 1986).

21 Jacek Purchla, *Patterns of Influence: Lviv and Vienna in the Mirror of Architecture* (Cambridge, MA: Harvard Ukrainian Research Institute, 2000); Iurii Biriuliov, ed., *Arkhitektura L'vova: chas i styli XIII–XXI st.* (Lviv: Tsentr Ievropy, 2008); Ihor Zhuk, *L'viv Levyns'koho: misto i budivnychyi* (Lviv: Hrani, 2010).

22 Markian Prokopovych, *Habsburg Lemberg: Architecture, Public Space, and Politics in the Galician Capital, 1772–1914* (West Lafayette, IN: Purdue University Press, 2009). For a thorough critique of this work, see Ihor Zhuk, "'Teoriia arkhitekturnykh tsyvilizatsii': krytychni uvahy shchodo monohrafiï Markiiana Prokopovycha," *Ukraïna Moderna* 23 (2016): 216–71.

23 A good example of such an approach to Lviv's past is John Czaplicka, ed., *Lviv: A City in the Crosscurrents of Culture* (Cambridge, MA: Harvard Ukrainian Research Institute, 2005).

24 Roman Lozynskyi, *Etnichnyi sklad naselennia L'vova u konteksti suspil'noho rozvytku Halychyny* (Lviv: Vydavnychyi tsentr LNU im. Ivana Franka, 2005).

25 Andrzej Bonusiak, *Lwów w latach 1918–1939: ludność, przestrzeń, samorząd* (Galica i jej dziedzictwo, vol. 13) (Rzeszów: Wydawnictwo WSP, 2000); Grzegorz Hryciuk, *Polacy we Lwowie, 1939–1944: życie codzienne* (Warsaw: Książka i Wiedza, 2000); Grzegorz Mazur, *Życie polityczne polskiego Lwowa 1918–1939* (Societas 7) (Krakow: Księgarnia Akademicka, 2007).

26 I would like to single out two studies that, while being "merely" detailed, nearly daily chronicles of city life, reconstructed mostly on the basis of the city press and memoirs, are indispensable to historians working on the city: Grzegorz Mazur, Jerzy Skwara, and Jerzy Węgierski, eds., *Kronika 2350 dni wojny i okupacji Lwowa 1 IX 1939 – 5 II 1946* (Katowice: Unia, 2007); and Agnieszka Biedrzycka, ed., *Kalendarium Lwowa 1918–1939* (Warsaw: Universitas, 2012).

27 Iryna Kotlobulatova, *Lwów na dawnej* pocztówce (Krakow: Międzynarodowe Centrum Kultury, 2006); Iryna Kotlobulatova, *L'viv na fotohrafiï: 1860–2006* (Lviv: Tsentr Ievropy, 2006); idem, *L'viv na fotohrafiï-2: 1860–2011* (Lviv: Tsentr Ievropy, 2011); idem, *L'viv na fotohrafiï-3: 1844–2014* (Lviv: Tsentr Ievropy, 2014); Iurii Biriuliov and Andrii Rudnytskyi, *L'viv, turystychnyi putivnyk* (Lviv: Tsentr Ievropy, 1999); Józef Wittlin, *Mój Lwów* (London: Poslka fundacja kulturalna, 1975); Stanisław Lem, *Wysoki Zamek* (Warsaw: Wydawnictwo MON, 1966); and Volodymyr Mykhalyk and Il'ko Lemko, *L'viv povsiakdennyi (1939–2009)* (Lviv: Apriori, 2009).

28 Aleksandra Matyukhina, *W Sowieckim Lwowie: życie codzienne miasta w latach 1944–1990* (Krakow: Wydawnictwo Uniwersytetu Jagiellońskiego, 2000).

29 Halyna Bodnar, *L'viv: shchodenne zhyttia mista ochyma pereselentsiv iz sil (50-80-ti roky XX st.)* (Lviv: Vydavnychyi tsentr KNU imeni Ivana Franka, 2010); Roman Genega, *L'viv: novi mishchany, studenty ta rezhym 1944–1953 rr.* (Lviv: L'vivs'kyi natsional'nyi universytet imeni Ivana Franka, 2015).
30 Iaroslav Isaievych et al., eds., *Istoriia L'vova. U triokh tomakh*, vol. 1–3 (Lviv: Tsentr Ievropy, 2006–7).
31 Tarik Cyril Amar, *The Paradox of Ukrainian Lviv: A Borderland City between Stalinists, Nazis, and Nationalists* (Ithaca, NY: Cornell University Press, 2015).
32 William Jay Risch, *The Ukrainian West: Culture and the Fate of Empire in Soviet Lviv* (Cambridge, MA: Harvard University Press, 2011).
33 The earliest classical work was Filip Friedman, *Zagłada Żydów lwowskich* (Łódź: Wydawnictwo Centralnej Żydowskiej Komisji Historycznej przy Centralnym Komitecie Żydów Polskich, 1945). The most detailed account. which needs updating, still remains Eliyahu Yones, *Smoke in the Sand: The Jews of Lvov in the War Years 1939–1944* (Jerusalem; New York: Gefen, 2004).
34 Mick, *Kriegserfahrungen in einer multiethnischen Stadt*.
35 Kai Struve, *Deutsche Herrschaft, ukrainischer Nationalismus, antijüdische Gewalt: Der Sommer 1941 in der Westukraine* (Berlin: De Gruyter, 2015).
36 Ola Hnatiuk, *Odwaga i strach* (Wrocław: KEW, 2015).
37 This is in striking contrast to other great city histories, where the cities' space and uniqueness are at the centre of the narration; see, for example, David Harvey, *Paris, Capital of Modernity* (New York: Routledge, 2003); and Mark Mazower, *Salonica, City of Ghosts: Christians, Muslims, and Jews, 1430–1950* (New York: Alfred A. Knopf, 2005).
38 Edward W. Soja, "Writing the City Spatially," *City* 7, no. 3 (2003): 273.
39 Rogers Brubaker coined the term "nationalizing state" to describe a nation-state that attempts to consolidate and homogenize its population by strengthening and favouring the "core" nation at the expense of national minorities; see Rogers Brubaker, "National Minorities, Nationalizing States and External National Homelands in the New Europe," *Daedalus* 124, no. 2 (1995): 107–32.

Chapter 1

1 Derek Sayer uses Norman Davies' metaphor of "vanished kingdoms" in "Review of *The Idea of Galicia: History and Fantasy in Habsburg Imperial Culture*, by Larry Wolff," *Common Knowledge* 19, no. 3 (2013): 568–9.
2 Élisée Reclus, *The Earth and Its Inhabitants*, vol. 3, *Europe* (New York: D. Appleton and Company, 1882), 122.
3 Larry Wolff, *The Idea of Galicia: History and Fantasy in Habsburg Imperial Culture* (Stanford, CA: Stanford University Press, 2010), 19–32.

4 Ludwig Wierzbicki, "Rozwój sieci kolei żelaznych w Galicyi od roku 1847 włącznie do roku 1880," pt. 1, *Czasopismo Techniczne* 21 (1907): 307.
5 Ihor Zhaloba, *Infrastrukturna polityka avstriis'koho uriadu na pivnichnomu skhodi monarkhiï v ostannii chverti XVIII – 60-kh rokakh XIX st. (na prykladi shliakhiv spoluchennia)* (Chernivtsi: Knyhy-XXI, 2004), 123–4.
6 W. Bruce Lincoln, *Nicholas I: Emperor and Autocrat of All the Russias* (DeKalb: Northern Illinois University Press, 1989), 348.
7 J. Osiecki, *Koleje żelazne w Galicji i stosunek tychże do kolei w Polsce i Rosji: z Mappą topograficzną kolei europejskich* (Vienna: Zamarski, Dittmarz i spółka, 1858), 3–4.
8 Józef Skwarzyński, "Rozwój sieci kolejowej pod zaborem austrijackim," *Inżynier Kolejowy* 3, no. 24-25 (1926): 216.
9 *Sprawozdanie komissii wyznaczonej przez Sejm to wypracowania projektu kolei żelaznej w Galicii, złożone Prześwietnym Sejmującym Stanom w miesiącu wrześniu roku 1842* (Lviv, 1842), 2.
10 Fedosii Steblii, "Sotsial'no-demohrafichnyi portret," in *Istoriia Lvova y triokh tomakh*, vol. 2, ed. Iaroslav Isaievych et al. (Lviv: Tsentr Ievropy, 2007), 28.
11 Paul M. Hohenberg and Lynn Hollen Lees, *The Making of Urban Europe, 1000–1994* (Cambridge, MA: Harvard University Press, 1996), 228.
12 Prokopovych, *Habsburg Lemberg*, passim.
13 Biruliov, *Arkhitektura L'vova*, 175.
14 Wierzbicki, "Rozwój sieci kolei żelaznych w Galicyi," pt. 1, 311.
15 *Sprawozdanie komissii wyznaczonej przez Sejm do wypracowania projektu kolei żelaznej w Galicii*, 24.
16 Wierzbicki, "Rozwój sieci kolei żelaznych w Galicyi," pt. 1, 312.
17 Marta Rymar, *Architektura dworców Kolei Karola Ludwika w Galicji w latach 1855–1910* (Warsaw: Neriton, 2009), 86–7.
18 Wierzbicki, "Rozwój sieci kolei żelaznych w Galicyi," pt. 1, 310.
19 Skwarzyński, "Rozwój sieci kolejowej pod zaborem austrijackim," 217.
20 "Ruch pociągów kolejowych...," *Gazeta Lwowska*, no. 211, 16 September 1903, 6; "Spravochnyi listok," *Kievlianin*, no. 2, 2 January 1903, 5.

Chapter 2

1 David Harvey, "The Urban Process under Capitalism: A Framework for Analysis," in *The Blackwell City Reader*, ed. Gary Bridge and Sophie Watson (Oxford: Wiley-Blackwell, 2010), 32–9.
2 Klemens Kaps, *Ungleiche Entwicklung in Zentraleuropa: Galizien zwischen überregionaler Verflechtung und imperialer Politik (1772–1914)* (Vienna: Böhlau Verlag, 2015), passim.
3 "Nowy dworzec lwowski," *Kurjer Lwowski*, 10 October 1901, 1.
4 Zbigniew Adrjański, *Złota księga pieśni polskich: pieśni, gawędy, opowieści* (Warsaw: Bellona, 1994), 76–7.

5 As analysed in Brian Porter-Szücs, *Faith and Fatherland: Catholicism, Modernity, and Poland* (Oxford: Oxford University Press, 2011), 330–1.
6 "Uroczyste poświęcenie i otwarcie nowego dworca kolejowego we Lwowie," *Dziennik Lwowski,* no. 71, 27 March 1904, 5.
7 Ibid.
8 "Poświęcenie nowego dworca kolejowego we Lwowie," *Wiek Nowy,* no. 824, 27 March 1904, 6.
9 Daniel L. Unowski, *The Pomp and Politics of Patriotism: Imperial Celebrations in Habsburg Austria, 1848–1916* (West Lafayette, IN: Purdue University Press, 2006), 58–72.
10 *Kurjer Lwowski,* no. 87, 27 March 1904, 1.
11 "Poświęcenie nowego dworca kolejowego we Lwowie," 6.
12 "Uroczyste poświęcenie i otwarcie nowego dworca kolejowego we Lwowie," *Gazeta Lwowska,* no. 45, 27 February 1904, 4.
13 "Poświęcenie nowego dworca kolejowego we Lwowie," 6.
14 "Kronika," *Kolejarz,* no. 7, 1 April 1904, 9.
15 *Wiek Nowy,* no. 820, 22 March 1904, 7.
16 "Poświęcenie nowego dworca kolejowego we Lwowie," 6.
17 Ibid.
18 Stephen Parisien, *Station to Station* (London: Phaidon Press, 1997), 6–7.
19 Unowsky, *Pomp and Politics of Patriotism,* 67.
20 It is defined as such by an eminent author of numerous guidebooks published in the 1910s, 1920s, and 1930s: Mieczysław Orłowicz, *Ilustrowany przewodnik po Lwowie ze 102 ilustracjami i planem miasta,* Polska biblioteka turystyczna 13 (Lviv; Warsaw: Atlas, 1925), 59.
21 Grigorii Ostrovskii, *L'vov* (Leningrad: Iskusstvo, 1982), 177.
22 Rymar, *Architektura dworców Kolei,* 100.
23 Carl E. Schorske, *Fin-de-siècle Vienna* (New York: Random House, 1981), 24–115.
24 "Dworzec kolei państwowej we Lwowie," *Architekt,* no. 7, 1904, 102.
25 [w.], "Nowy dworzec kolejowy we Lwowie," *Gazeta Lwowska,* no. 44, 24 February 1904, 1; "Nowy dworzec kolejowy we Lwowie," *Nowa Reforma,* no. 71, 27 March 1904: 2.
26 [T.C.], "Nowy dworzec lwowski," *Tygodnik ilustrowany,* no. 13, 1904, 247.
27 *Geschichte der Eisenbahnen der Österreichisch-Ungarischen Monarchie, Band VI: Das Eisenbahnwesen Österreichs in seiner allgemeinen und technischen Entwicklung, 1898–1908,* B.II (Vienna: Karl Prochaska, 1908), 184–5; Local experts were in agreement here, too: "Nowy dworzec kolejowy we Lwowie," *Nowa Reforma,* no. 71, 27 March 1904, 2; see also Alexander Dąbrowski, *Illustriert Führer durch Lwów* (Lviv, 1939), Rkps BJ 9107 IV, 1.
28 Józef Wiczkowski, *Lwów, jego rozwój i stan kulturalny oraz przewodnik po mieście* (Lviv: Wydział gospodarczy X zjazdu lekarzy i przyrodników polskich, oraz reprezentacyi m. Lwowa, 1907), 547.

29 "Nowy dworzec lwowski," *Tygodnik ilustrowany*, no. 13, 1904, 246.
30 "Uroczyste poświęcenie i otwarcie nowego dworca kolejowego we Lwowie," *Dziennik Lwowski*, no. 71, 27 March 1904, 5.
31 Michał Banach, *Wspomnienia z lat 1897–1969*, Rkps. Ossolin. 15587/II, 28.
32 Wittlin, *Moj Lwów*, 12.
33 Nathan Wood, *Becoming Metropolitan: Urban Selfhood and the Making of Modern Cracow* (DeKalb: Northern Illinois University Press, 2010).
34 [T.C.], "Nowy dworzec lwowski," *Tygodnik ilustrowany*, no. 13, 1904, 245.
35 "Poświęcenie nowego dworca kolejowego we Lwowie," *Dziennik Lwowski*, no. 71, 27 March 1904, 6.
36 Ihor Mel'nyk and Roman Masyk, *Pam'iatnyky ta memorial'ni tablytsi mista L'vova* (Lviv: Apriori, 2012), 289.
37 Lviv literally means the lion city, and was named after the Ruthenian prince Leo (*Lev*), son of the city's founder Danylo.
38 St. Wom [Stanisław Womela], "Rzeźby na nowym dworcu," *Kurjer Lwowski*, no. 282, 11 November 1902, 1–2.
39 Matsei Ianovs'kyi, "Lemberg 1916–L'viv 2002: rozdumy nad starym putivnykom," *Krytyka* 7-8, no. 57-58 (2002): 23–7.
40 "Nowy dworzec kolejowy we Lwowie," *Nowa Reforma*, no. 71, 27 March 1904, 2.
41 [T.C.], "Nowy dworzec lwowski," *Tygodnik ilustrowany*, no. 13, 1904, 245.
42 Pieter M. Judson, *The Habsburg Empire: A New History* (Cambridge, MA: Belknap Press, 2016), 346.
43 [T.C.], "Nowy dworzec lwowski," *Tygodnik ilustrowany*, no. 13, 1904, 246.
44 [w.], "Nowy dworzec kolejowy we Lwowie," *Gazeta Lwowska*, no. 44, 24 February 1904, 1.
45 "Uroczyste poświęcenie i otwarcie nowego dworca kolejowego we Lwowie," *Gazeta Lwowska*, no. 45, 27 February 1904, 4.
46 "Dworzec kolei państwowej we Lwowie," *Architekt*, no. 7, 1904, 101. The same claim is in [T.C.], "Nowy dworzec lwowski," *Tygodnik ilustrowany*, no. 13, 1904, 246.
47 Iurii Biriuliov, "Gorgolevs'kyi Zygmunt," in *Entsyklopediia L'vova*, vol. 1, ed. Andrii Kozyts'kyi and Ihor Pidkova (Lviv: Litopys, 2007), 635.
48 Rkps. Ossolin. 18352 II, 81.
49 [w.], "Nowy dworzec kolejowy we Lwowie," *Gazeta Lwowska*, no. 45, 25 February 1904, 1.
50 "Nowy dworzec osobowy we Lwowie," *Dziennik Polski*, no. 406, 6 October 1901, 1.
51 Adam Kuryłło, *Wspomnienia z lat 1907–1946*, Rkps. Ossolin. 15513/II, 31–2.
52 [w.], "Nowy dworzec kolejowy we Lwowie," *Gazeta Lwowska*, no. 45, 25 February 1904, 1.
53 [w.], "Nowy dworzec kolejowy we Lwowie," *Gazeta Lwowska*, no. 46, 26 February 1904, 1.

54 Ibid.
55 [w.], "Nowy dworzec kolejowy we Lwowie," *Gazeta Lwowska*, no. 44, 24 February 1904, 1.
56 "Nowy dworzec kolejowy we Lwowie," *Nowa Reforma*, no. 71, 27 March 1904, 2.
57 Wojciech Dzieduszycki, *Listy ze wsi*, Serja 1 (Lviv: Gazeta Narodowa, 1889), 432.
58 Oleksander Barvins'kyi, *Spomyny z moho zhyttia*, vol. 2 (New York; Kyiv: Stylos, 2009), 682.
59 Stepan Shakh, *L'viv – misto moieï molodosty*, pt. 3, *Spomyn prysviachenyi Tiniam zabutykh L'vov'ian* (Munich: Khrystyians'kyi Holos, 1955), 232–3.
60 Ludwik Wierzbicki, "Wstęp," "Ikonostas," "Paramenta kościelne, ornaty i hafty," "Plaszczenica," "Oprawy książek i Ewangelii," "Krzyże," "Kielichy," in *Wystawa Archeologiczna Polsko-Ruska urządzona we Lwowie w roku 1885* (Lviv, 1885), 1–13.
61 Ludwik Wierzbicki, *Wzory przemysłu domowego*, various subtitles; titles and text in Polish, Ukrainian, French, and German, 10 vols. (Lviv, 1880–89).
62 Iurii Biriuliov, *Zakharevychi: tvortsi stolychnoho L'vova* (Lviv: Tsentr Ievropy, 2010), 16.
63 Archduke Rudolf, Crown Prince of Austria, ed., *Die Österreichisch-ungarische Monarchie in Wort und Bild*, vol. 12, *Galizien* (Vienna: k.k. Hof- und Staatsdruckerei, 1898), 669.
64 [w.], "Nowy dworzec kolejowy we Lwowie," *Gazeta Lwowska*, no. 45, 25 February 1904, 1.
65 Oskar Kofler, *Żydowskie dwory*: *Wspomnienia z Galicji Wschodniej od początku XIX wieku do wybuchu I wojny światowej* (Warsaw: Żydowski Instytut Historyczny, 1999), 74.
66 AGAD, zesp. C.K. Ministerstwo Kolei Żelaznych, sygn.42 a, 693.
67 Sergey R. Kravtsov, "Wooden Synagogues of the Polish-Lithuanian Commonwealth: Between Polish and Jewish Narratives" (lecture presented at the symposium, *Stella, Abstract Art and Synagogues*, Warsaw, 12 May 2016), 1–3.
68 Ludwik Wierzbicki, "Bożnica w miasteczku Jabłonowie nad Prutem," in *Sprawozdanie komisyi do badania historyi sztuki w Polsce*, vol. 4, no. 2 (Krakow: Akademia Umiejętności, 1889), 45–51.
69 Peter Vergo, *Art in Vienna, 1898–1918: Klimt, Kokoschka, Schiele and Their Contemporaries* (New York: Phaidon, 1975), 34.
70 Kazimierz Mokłowski, *Sztuka ludowa w Polsce* (Lviv: Altenberg, 1903), passim.
71 Carol Herselle Krinsky, *Synagogues of Europe: Architecture, History, Meaning* (Cambridge, MA: MIT Press, 1985), 265; Anthony Alofsin, *When Buildings Speak: Architecture as Language in the Habsburg Empire and Its Aftermath, 1867–1933* (Chicago: University of Chicago Press, 2006), 45–52.

72 Dzieduszycki, *Listy ze wsi*, 440.
73 Slightly over 1 million crowns: Michał Lityński, *Pamiątkowy opis teatru miejskiego we Lwowie* (Lviv: Michał Lityński, 1900), 3.
74 Kaps, *Ungleiche Entwicklung in Zentraleuropa*, 426–31.
75 Leon Biliński, *Wspomnienia i dokumenty*, vol. 1, *1846–1914* (Warsaw: księgarnia F. Hoesicka, 1924), 42, 66–7.
76 "Dworzec kolei państwowej we Lwowie," *Architekt*, no. 7, 1904, 101–2.
77 Archbishop Józef Bilczewski, *Listy pasterskie, odezwy, kazania i mowy okolicznościowe*, vol. 1 (Lviv; Krakow: Wydawnictwo bł. Jakuba Strzemię Archidiecezji Lwowskiej ob. Łac. Oddział w Krakowie, 2005), 369.
78 AGAD, C.K. Ministerstwo Kolei Żelaznych, sygn.241 A, 627.
79 Krzysztof Broński and Jan Szpak, "Polityka budżetowa galicyjskich władz autonomicznych (zarys problematyki)," *Zeszyty Naukowe Uniwersytetu Ekonomicznego w Krakowie*, no. 835 (2010): 62.
80 Officially, the largest industry was actually "clothing." It included not only textile works and tailors, but also laundry workers and cleaners. See Tadeusz Dyskiewicz, ed., *Wiadomości statystyczne o mieście Lwowie: 1910 i 1911*, vol. 14 (Lviv: Gmina królewskiego stołecznego miasta Lwowa, 1914), 241.
81 Edmund Kolbuszowski, *Sprawozdanie z czynności Miejskiego Biura pośrednictwa pracy*: *Wiadomości statystyczne o mieście Lwowie 9* (Lviv: Gmina królewskiego stołecznego miasta Lwowa, 1905), 31.
82 "Rozruchy głodowe we Lwowie," *Kurjer Lwowski*, 30 April 1901, 10.
83 Ibid.
84 Wolfgang Maderthaner and Lutz Musner, *Unruly Masses: The Other Side of Fin-de-Siècle Vienna*, International Studies in Social History 13 (Oxford; New York: Berghahn Books, 2008), passim.
85 "Rozruchy głodowe we Lwowie," *Kurjer Lwowski*, 30 April 1901, 10–12.
86 "Brak zarobku," *Kurjer Lwowski*, 2 May 1901, 1.
87 "Uwagi po rozruchach," *Monitor*, no. 19, 5 May 1901, 1.
88 "Kronika," *Kurjer Lwowski*, 9 October 1901, 4.
89 "Robotnicze święto," *Kurjer Lwowski*, 2 May 1901, 2.
90 "Położenie kamienia węgielnego pod nowy dworzec kolei we Lwowie," *Dziennik Polski*, no. 410 , 9 October 1901, 3.
91 "Kronika," *Dziennik Polski*, no. 413, 10 October 1901, 2.
92 AGAD, zesp. C.K. Ministerstwo Kolei Żelaznych, sygn.205, 275–7.
93 Walentyna Najdus, *Polska Partia Socjalno-Demokratyczna Galicji i Śląska, 1890–1919* (Warsaw: Państwowe Wydawnictwo Naukowe, 1983), 305.
94 Ibid., 366.
95 Ibid., 369.
96 Rymar, *Architektura dworców*, 184.
97 Kazimierz Mokłowski, "Nowy dworzec we Lwowie," *Kurjer Lwowski*, no. 80, 20 March 1904, 2.

98 Ibid., 3.
99 [w.], "Nowy dworzec kolejowy we Lwowie," *Gazeta Lwowska*, no. 45, 25 February 1904, 1.
100 [T.C.], "Nowy dworzec lwowski," *Tygodnik ilustrowany*, no. 13, 1904, 246.
101 Józef Wiczkowski, "Dział informacyjny," in *Lwów, jego rozwój i stan kulturalny oraz przewodnik po mieście*, 3.
102 P. Hrankin et al., *L'vivs'ka zaliznytsia: istoriia i suchasnist'* (Lviv: Tsentr Ievropy, 1996), 23.
103 Micheline Nilsen, "'The Other Side of the Tracks': The Implantation of the Railways in Western European Capitals," vol. 1 (PhD diss., University of Delaware, 2003), 162–3.
104 Jack Simons, *St Pancras Station*, rev. ed. (Zaragoza: Historical Publications, 2003), 75–7.
105 "Dworzec kolei państwowej we Lwowie," *Architekt*, no. 7, 1904, 104–6.
106 AAN, zesp.98, sygn.71/III-1, 21, 31.
107 Peter Stansky, *Redesigning the World: William Morris, the 1880s, and the Arts and Crafts* (Princeton, NJ: Princeton University Press, 1985), 31, 63, 122, 135.
108 Mokłowski, "Nowy dworzec we Lwowie," 2.
109 Ibid., 3.
110 Mikolaj Hankiewicz, "Jak stałem się socyalistą?" *Promień: Pismo poświęcone sprawom młodzieży szkolnej*, no. 6-7, 1903, 250–2; Bolesław Limanowski, *Historja ruchu społecznego w XIX stuleciu* (Lviv: Księgarnia Polska, 1890), 490.
111 Fyodor Dostoevsky, *Notes from Underground* (Bristol: Bristol Classical Press, 1993), 21–3.
112 Benjamin, *Arcades Project*, 5.
113 Alfred Wysocki, *Sprzed pół wieku* (Krakow: Wydawnictwo Literackie, 1974), 242. *Kolejarz*, no. 24, 15 December 1903, 7; *Kolejarz*, no. 14, 15 July 1904, 8; "Konferencya robotników warsztatów kolej w Galicyi," *Kolejarz*, no. 5, 1 March 1906, 1–2.
114 Biliński, *Wspomnienia i dokumenty*, 82–5.
115 Wiktor Chajes, *Semper Fidelis: Pamiętnik Polaka wyznania mojżeszowego z lat 1926–1939* (Krakow: Księgarnia Akademicka, 1997), 52.
116 Isaievych et al., *Istoriia Lvova*, vol. 2, 182–3.
117 George Bataille, "Museum," in *Rethinking Architecture: A Reader in Cultural Theory*, ed. Neil Leach (London; New York: Routledge, 1997), 21.
118 "Nowy dworzec i informacje dla podróżnych," *Kurjer Lwowski*, no. 85, 25 March 1904, 6.
119 [T.C.], "Nowy dworzec lwowski," *Tygodnik ilustrowany*, no. 13, 1904, 246.
120 Ibid.
121 Mokłowski, "Nowy dworzec we Lwowie," 3.
122 "Cesarz Franciszek Józef I we Lwowie," *Kurjer Lwowski*, no. 255, 14 September 1903, 1.

123 Ibid., 2.
124 [w.], "Nowy dworzec kolejowy we Lwowie," *Gazeta Lwowska*, no. 46, 26 February 1904, 1.
125 Washburn, *Field Notes from the Russian Front*, 63.
126 [w.], "Nowy dworzec kolejowy we Lwowie," *Gazeta Lwowska*, no. 46, 26 February 1904, 1.
127 See, for example, F.P. Kochnev, *Passazhirskie stantsii i vokzaly* (Moscow: Gosudarstvennoe transportnoe zheleznodorozhnoe izdatel'stvo, 1950), 82; Brian Edwards, *The Modern Station: New Approaches to Railway Architecture* (London; New York: E & FN Spon, 1997), 147.
128 [T.C.], "Nowy dworzec lwowski," *Tygodnik ilustrowany*, no. 13, 1904, 246.
129 This is the concept developed by Patrick Joyce (*Rule of Freedom*) to describe the functioning of the modern urban space.
130 Michel de Certeau, *The Practice of Everyday Life* (Berkeley: University of California Press, 1984), 111.
131 "Nowy dworzec i informacje dla podróżnych," *Kurjer Lwowski*, no. 85, 25 March 1904, 6.
132 Ibid.
133 [w.], "Nowy dworzec kolejowy we Lwowie," *Gazeta Lwowska*, no. 46, 26 February 1904, 1.
134 Tom F. Peters, *Building the Nineteenth Century* (Cambridge, MA: MIT Press, 1996), 209.
135 In 1909 G.K. Chesterton noticed that the great terminus "has many of the characteristics of a great ecclesiastical building ... vast arches, void spaces, coloured lights"; quoted in Parisien, *Station to Station*, 7.
136 "Nowy dworzec lwowski," *Tygodnik ilustrowany*, no. 13, 1904, 247.
137 Carroll L.V. Meeks, *The Railroad Station: An Architectural History* (New Haven, CT: Yale University Press, 1956), 109.
138 Steven Brindle, *Paddington Station: Its History and Architecture* (Swindon: English Heritage, 2004), 30.
139 Meeks, *Railroad Station*, 4.
140 Edmund Burke, *A Philosophical Enquiry into the Origins of Our Ideas of the Sublime and Beautiful* (London: Routledge and Paul, 1958); originally published in 1757.

Chapter 3

1 "Galicya w budżecie państwa," *Słowo Polskie*, no. 580, 10 December 1905,4.
2 Jürgen Osterhammel, *The Transformation of the World: A Global History of the Nineteenth Century* (Princeton, NJ: Princeton University Press, 2014), 300–1.
3 Volodymyr Levyns'kyi, *Narys rozvytku ukrains'koho robitnychoho rukhu v Halychyni* (Kyiv, 1914), 4.

4 "Z ogrzewalń i warsztatów," *Kolejarz*, no. 15, 1 August 1906, 7.
5 Zygmunt Żuławski, *Wspomnienia* ([Warsaw]: Niezależna Oficyna Wydawnicza, [1980]), 13.
6 Emil Haecker, *Historija socjalizmu w Galicji i na Śląsku Cieszyńskim* t.1 1846–1882 (Krakow: Nakładem Towarzystwa uniwersytetu robotniczego, 1933), 101.
7 Ibid., 131.
8 Stary towarysz, "Praca organizacyjna w Galicyi,"*Kolejarz*, no. 9, 1 May 1912, 6–7; "Organizacja nasza w r. 1899." *Kolejarz* gives a number of 386 in 1900, but two years later provides a slightly different number of 413; *Kolejarz*, no. 4, 15 May 1900, 2; "Nasza organizacya w r. 1902," *Kolejarz*, no. 10, 15 May 1903, 7.
9 "Organizacya kolejarzy a socyalna demokracya," *Kolejarz*, no. 7, 1 April 1903, 1.
10 Oleh Zhernoklieiev, *Natsional'ni sektsii avstriis'koi sotsial-demokratii v Halychyni j na Bukovyni (1890–1918 rr.)* (Ivano-Frankivs'k, Ukraine: Vydavnycho-dyzainers'kyi viddil Tsentru informatsiinykh tekhnolohii, 2006), 142.
11 "Nasza organizacya w r. 1902," *Kolejarz*, no. 10, 15 May 1903, 7.
12 Najdus, *Polska Partia Socjalno-Demokratyczna Galicji i Śląska*, 472.
13 Zhernoklieiev, *Natsional'ni sektsii avstriis'koi sotsial-demokratii*, 85.
14 Herman Lieberman, *Pamiętniki* (Warsaw: Wydawnictwo Sejmowe, 1996), 65.
15 Najdus, *Polska Partia Socjalno-Demokratyczna Galicji i Śląska*, 352.
16 Ibid., 382.
17 Geoff Eley, *Forging Democracy: The History of the Left in Europe, 1850–2000* (New York: Oxford University Press, 2002), 70.
18 "Galicyjskie związki zawodowe w roku 1911,"*Kolejarz*, no. 6, 15 March 1912, 8–9.
19 Zhernoklieiev, *Natsional'ni sektsii avstriis'koi sotsial-demokratii*, 85.
20 Wysocki, *Sprzed pół wieku*, 221.
21 Józef Buszko, *Polacy w parlamencie wiedeńskim, 1848–1918* (Warsaw: Wydawnictwo Sejmowe, 1996), 419.
22 Najdus, *Polska Partia Socjalno-Demokratyczna Galicji i Śląska*, 108–9.
23 "Z przestrzeni i warsztatów," *Kolejarz*, no. 14, 15 October 1900, 3.
24 Gary P. Steenson, *After Marx, Before Lenin: Marxism and Socialist Working Class Parties in Europe, 1884–1914* (Pittsburgh: University of Pittsburgh Press, 1991), 179.
25 Calculated on the basis of election results published in *Gazeta Lwowska*, no. 115, 22 May 1907; *Gazeta Lwowska*, no. 117, 24 May 1907; and "Vybory u Lvovi," *Dilo*, 18 May 1907, 2.
26 LNB, f. 44, spr. 24, ark. 51.

27 "Kolejarze galicyjscy wobec wyborów," *Kolejarz*, no. 13, 1 July 1907, 4.
28 Rkps. Ossolin. 12915/I, 26–30.
29 *Wiek Nowy*, no. 787, 12 February 1904.
30 Present-day Horodotska Street at the beginning of the twentieth century was composed of two streets: Kazymirivska (Kaźmierzowska) and Horodotska proper. The outgoing part, beyond the old city checkpoint, was also known as Bohdanivka (Bogdanówka).
31 Union activists complained that nearly every building on Horodotska had either a tavern or an inn, and sometimes both, which induced alcoholism among the railway workers; see "Uwagi nad wiecem kolejarzy we Lwowie 8-go listopada," *Kolejarz*, no. 22, 15 November 1908, 8.
32 "Z przestrzeni i warsztatów," *Kolejarz*, no. 1, 15 January 1901, 5.
33 Bronisław Łotocki, *Jeszcze raz się uśmiechnę*, Rkps. Ossolin. sygn.15128, 21.
34 "Lwowscy kolejarze (blog)," 19 February 2010, http://lwow.blog.onet.pl/2010/02/19/lwowscy-kolejarze
35 Rkps. BN 10 562 III, 92.
36 "Asanacya dzielnicy III," *Głos*, no. 177, 5 August 1909, 3.
37 "Rozboi v L'vovi," *Galichanin*, no. 38, 11 March 1908, 3
38 "Nasza organizacya w r. 1902," *Kolejarz*, no. 10, 15 May 1903, 7.
39 "Konferencya maszynistów kolejowych Galicyi i Bukowiny," *Kolejarz*, no. 22, 15 November 1905, 8.
40 *Kolejarz*, no. 3, 1 February 1904, 3.
41 *Kolejarz*, no. 3, 1 February 1908.
42 *Kolejarz*, no. 21, 1 November 1905, 7.
43 "Baczność kolejarze!" *Kolejarz*, no. 3, 1 April 1910, 1.
44 "Kronika," *Kolejarz*, no. 8, 15 May 1910, 12.
45 "Kronika," *Kolejarz*, no. 15, 1 August 1912, 11.
46 *Kolejarz*, no. 6, 15 March 1903, 8.
47 Fr. Reichman, ed., *Księga adresowa królewskiego stołecznego miasta Lwowa 1900*, r.4 (Lviv: A. Stryjkowskiego, 1900), 32, 64.
48 *Głos*, no. 12, 15 January 1907, 7.
49 "Publiczne zgromadzenie kolejarzy," *Kolejarz* , no. 3, 1 February 1909, 2. A meeting that followed a demonstration by the railway workers took place there on 24 March 1912: "Demonstracya kolejarzy we Lwowie," *Kolejarz*, no. 6, 1 April 1912, 2–3. And the "great demonstrating railway rally" took place at the Jad Charuzim building on 6 April, 1913: *Kolejarz*, no. 7, 1 April 1913, 1.
50 "Manifestacya kolejarzy lwowskiej dyrekcyi kolejowej," *Kolejarz*, no. 16, 15 August 1907, 2.
51 Najdus, *Polska Partia Socjalno-Demokratyczna Galicji i Śląska*, 99.
52 Stanisław Głąbiński, *Wspomnienia Polityczne* Cz. 1 Pod zaborem austriackim (Pelplin: SP. Z O. ODP, 1939), 149.

53 Rkps. Ossolin. 15397/II, 30–1.
54 Rkps. Ossolin. 14746.
55 *Kolejarz*, no. 23, 1907, 6–10.
56 "Praca kobiet na austryjackich koljach państwowych," *Kolejarz*, no. 12, 15 June 1905, 1.
57 Najdus, *Polska Partia Socjalno-Demokratyczna Galicji i Śląska*, 248.
58 Ivan Kompaniiets', *Stanovyshche i borot'ba trudiashchykh mas Halychyny, Bukovyny ta Zakarpattia na pochatku XX st.* (Kyiv: Vydavnytstvo Akademii Nauk Ukrains'koi RSR, 1960), 119–20.
59 Najdus, *Polska Partia Socjalno-Demokratyczna Galicji i Śląska*, 424.
60 Małgorzata Nitka, *Railway Defamiliarisation: The Rise of Passengerhood in the Nineteenth Century* (Katowice: Wydawnictwo Uniwersytetu Śląskiego, 2006), 9–10.
61 *Kolejarz*, no. 8, 15 April 1902, 8.
62 "Nieoświecone wagony," *Kolejarz*, no. 18, 15 December 1900, 4.
63 *Kolejarz*, no. 6, 15 March 1903, 8.
64 "Nasza organizacya w r. 1902," *Kolejarz*, no. 10, 15 May 1903, 7.
65 Edward Palmer Thompson, *Whigs and Hunters: The Origins of the Black Act* (New York: Pantheon Books, 1975), 266.
66 Najdus, *Polska Partia Socjalno-Demokratyczna Galicji i Śląska*, 328.
67 "Z przestrzeni," *Kolejarz*, no. 4, 15 March 1905, 6.
68 "Warsztaty we Lwowie," *Kolejarz*, no. 1, 1 January 1903.
69 "Koszary dla personału pociągowego w Galicyi," *Kolejarz*, no. 17, 1 September 1910, 8.
70 "Z przestrzeni i warsztatów," *Kolejarz*, no. 1, 1 January 1902, 3; "Z przestrzeni i warsztatów," *Kolejarz*, no. 14, 15 October 1900, 3.
71 "Nowy posterunok," *Kolejarz*, no. 1, 8 April 1900, 1.
72 *Kolejarz*, no. 2, 15 January 1904, 8.
73 "Praca kobiet na austryjackich koljach państwowych," *Kolejarz*, no. 12, 15 June 1905, 1.
74 "P. Wechsler urzęduje ... ," *Kolejarz*, no. 11, 1 June 1906, 5, 11.
75 Artur Gruszecki, *Kolejarze: powieść współczesna* (Krakow: G. Gebethner; Warsaw: L. Biernacki, 1909).
76 "Oszustwo z biletami kolejowymi," *Głos*, no. 62, 15 March 1907, 6–7; "Z sali sądowej," *Głos*, no. 220, 25 September 1907, 3.
77 "Z bagna kolejowego. Stosunki na stacyi Podzamcze," *Głos*, no. 32, 15 March 1909; "Z lwowskiej dyrekcyi kolejowej," *Głos*, no. 200, 1 September 1908.
78 "Korupcya w dyrekcyi kolejowej," *Głos*, no. 28, 11 March 1909.
79 "Uprzemysłowiony dygnitarz kolejowy," *Głos*, no. 258, 11 October 1908, 7.
80 "Korupcya w dyrekcyi kolejowej," *Głos*, no. 79, 6 April 1909, 3–5.
81 "Pasożyty," *Kolejarz*, no. 14, 15 October 1900, 2.

82 Stanisław Hoszowski, *Ceny we Lwowie w latach 1701–1914* (Badania z Dziejów Społecznych i Gospodarczych, v.130 (Lviv: Kasa im. Rektora J. Mianowskiego, 1934), 175.
83 "Z ogrzewalń i warsztatów," *Kolejarz* , no. 15, 1 August 1906, 7.
84 "W sprawie mieszkań dla kolejarzy," "Z przestrzeni," *Kolejarz*, no. 11, 1 June 1905, 3; "Demonstracya kolejarzy lwowskich," *Kolejarz*, no. 15, 1 August 1905, 6.
85 The excited Lviv public expected skyscrapers in the wake of the statute's abolition; see "Drapacze do nieba – we Lwowie," *Goniec Polski*, no. 88, 1 May 1907, 3.
86 Andrii Kozyts'kyi and Ihor Pidkova, eds., *Entsyklopediia L'vova*, vol. 1 (Lviv: Litopys, 2007), 523–4.
87 "Gospodarka krajowa przed forum parlamentu,"*Kolejarz*, no. 13, 1 July 1910, 1–2.
88 "Kronika,"*Kolejarz*, no. 14, 15 July 1910, 15; "Skandał mieszkaniowy w dyrekcyi lwowskiej,"*Kolejarz*, no. 18, 1 October 1911, 7.
89 "Kronika," *Kolejarz*, no. 20, 15 October 1913, 8.
90 "Stowarzyszenie galicyjskich kolejarzy," *Kolejarz*, no. 1, 8 April 1900, 2.
91 "Kronika," *Kolejarz*, no. 4, 15 February 1908, 7.
92 "Stosunki w ogrzewalni lwowskiej," *Kolejarz*, no. 15, 1 August 1907, 3.
93 "Kronika," *Kolejarz*, no. 17, 1 September 1910, 10.
94 "Kronika," *Kolejarz*, no. 8, 15 April 1903, 6.
95 "Sromotna klęska macherów dyrekcyjnych," *Kolejarz* , no. 20, 15 January 1907, 1.
96 "Sprzedali nas ... ," *Kolejarz*, no. 14, 15 August 1910, 1.
97 "Kronika," *Kolejarz*, no. 18, 15 September 1910, 7–8.
98 "Nowy minister kolejowy," *Kolejarz*, no. 2, 15 January 1911, 1.
99 "Kronika," *Kolejarz*, no. 2, 15 February 1911, 11.
100 Bilczewski, *Listy pasterskie, odezwy, kazania i mowy okolicznościowe*, vol. 1, 24–5.
101 Ibid., 366.
102 Ibid., 94.
103 Ibid., 100.
104 Ibid., 105.
105 Ibid., 134.
106 "Konkurs na kościół św. Elżbiety we Lwowie," *Architekt*, no. 4, 1903, 49.
107 Bilczewski. *Listy pasterskie, odezwy, kazania i mowy okolicznościowe*, vol. 1, 377.
108 Józef Wołczański, "Listy Anny z Działyńskich Potockiej do Arcybiskupa Józefa Bilczewskiego z lat 1901- ok. 1919," *Nasza Przeszłość* 90 (1998): 429.
109 Jurij Smirnow, "Świątynia-pomnik: kośćiół św. Elżbiety," *Kurier Galicyjski* 71, no. 19 (2008): 19.

110 "Kronika," *Kolejarz*, no. 5, 1 March 1910, 11.
111 Ibid., 18.
112 Smirnow, "Świątynia-pomnik," 19.
113 "Konkurs na kościół św. Elżbiety we Lwowie," *Architekt*, no. 4, 1903, 49.
114 The correspondence regarding planned reconstruction is in TsDIAuL, f. 146, op. 68, spr. 2111, 1–38, 119–21, 169.
115 Smirnow, "Świątynia-pomnik," 18.
116 James Shedel, *Art and Society: The New Art Movement in Vienna, 1897–1914* (New York: Sposs, 1981), 92.
117 Bilczewski, *Listy pasterskie, odezwy, kazania i mowy okolicznościowe*, vol. 1, 375.
118 Ibid., 216.
119 "Kronika," *Kolejarz*, no. 12, 15 June 1912, 12.
120 Biedrzycka, *Kalendarium Lwowa 1918–1939*, 250.
121 Małgorzata Dziedzic and Stanisław Dziedzic, *Arcybiskup Józef Bilczewski* (Krakow: Wydawnictwo WAM, 2012), 136.
122 Rkps. Ossolin. 15587/II, 79.
123 AAN, zesp. 1208, sygn. 305/V/13, 42–3.
124 "Fundusz budowy domu kolejarzy," *Kolejarz*, no. 16, 15 August 1907, 7.
125 Henry F. Reichman, *Railwaymen and Revolution: Russia, 1905* (Berkeley: University of California Press, 1987), 163.
126 Henryk Wereszycki, *Niewygasła przeszłość* (Krakow: Znak, 1987), 184.
127 "Publiczne zgromadzenie kolejarzy," *Głos*, no. 20, 2 February 1909, 3.
128 Kerstin S. Jobst, *Zwischen Nationalismus und Internationalismus: die polnische und ukrainische Sozialdemokratie in Galizien von 1890 bis 1914: ein Beitrag zur Nationalitätenfrage in Habsburgreich* (Hamburg: Dolling und Gallitz, 1996), passim; Zhernokleiev, *Natsional'ni sektsii avstriisk'koi sotsial-demokratii v Halychyni i Bukovyni*, passim.
129 AAN, zesp. 98, sygn. 71/I-118. Cz.1 t.2.
130 "Nowy posterunok," *Kolejarz*, no. 1, 8 April 1900, 1.
131 "Robitnyche s'viato," *Dilo*, no. 86, 2 May 1904, 3.
132 Jakub Beneš, "Socialist Popular Literature and the Czech-German Split in Austrian Social Democracy, 1890–1914," *Slavic Review* 72, no. 2 (2013): 327–51.
133 *Kolejarz*, no. 8, 15 April 1903, 7.
134 Najdus, *Polska Partia Socjalno-Demokratyczna Galicji i Śląska*, 211.
135 Ibid., 213–14.
136 "W sprawie ruskiego 'Kolejarza,'" *Kolejarz*, no. 8, 15 April 1910, 8.
137 Levyns'kyi, *Narys rozvytku ukraïns'koho robitnychoho rukhu v Halychyni*, 86, 89.
138 "Kiedyś a dzisiaj!" *Kolejarz*, no. 9, 1 May 1912, 5–6.
139 Michael P. Smith, *The City and Social Theory* (New York: St Martin's Press, 1979), 272.

140 Stanisław Koźmian, *Podróże i polityka* (Krakow: Czas, 1905), 188.
141 Wysocki, *Sprzed pół wieku*, 39.
142 Rkps. BN 10562 III, t. 2, 63.
143 Wysocki, *Sprzed pół wieku*, 39.
144 Rkps. Ossolin. 15430 II, 2.
145 Rkps. Ossolin. 15351 II, 103.
146 Alexander Granach, *There Goes an Actor* (Garden City, NY: Doubleday, Doran, 1945), 119.
147 Dmytro Doroshenko, *Moï spomyny pro nedavnie-mynule* (Munich: Ukrains'ke vydavnytstvo, 1969), 11–12.
148 Serhii Iefremov, "Zi spohadiv pro Ivana Franka," in *Spohady pro Ivana Franka*, ed. Mykhailo Hnatiuk (Lviv: Kameniar, 1997), 224–5.
149 Sholem Aleichem, *The Letters of Menakhem-Mendl and Sheyne-Sheyndl and Motl, the Cantor's Son*, trans. Hillel Halkin (New Haven, CT: Yale University Press, 2002), 193.
150 Rkps. Ossolin. 15327, 203–4.
151 Doroshenko, *Moï spomyny pro nedavnie-mynule*, 11–12; Barański, *Opowieść o jednym miasteczku i jednej rodzinie*, 251.
152 LNB, f. 44, spr. 34, a. 222.
153 Ibid., a. 916.
154 Ibid., a. 631.
155 Ibid., a. 946.
156 Kofler, *Żydowskie dwory*, 74.
157 LNB, f. 44, spr. 34, a. 65.
158 Adolf Inlender, *Przewodnik ilustrowany po c. k. austr. kolejach państwowych na szlakach: Lwów-Krasne-Podwołoczyska, Krasne-Brody, Lwów-Stanisławów-Kołomyja-Śniatyn-Czerniowce, Kołomyja-Słoboda rungurska, Kołomyja-Kniażdwór, Stanisławów-Buczacz-Husiatyn, Stanisławów-Woronienka, Koleje Podolskie. Wedle wskazówek c.k. Generalnej Dyrekcji austr. koleji państwowych zredagował i napisał Adolf Inlender* (Vienna: Steyrermühl, [1892]); Rkps. BJ 9106/III, t. 1, 63.
159 Ibid., 72.
160 Perkun, "Mafia Lwowska," *Kolejarz*, no. 15, 1 August 1901, 2–3.
161 Janina Mazurek-Stocka, *Wspomnienia*, Rkps. Ossolin. 15619/II, 19–20.
162 Rkps. Ossolin. 14093/II, 106.
163 Władysław Ryszkowski, *Wspomnienia lwowskie z lat 1895–1900*, vol. 2, BN, IV 10189, 362–3.
164 Zofia Romaniczówna, *Dziennik lwowski 1842–1930* (Warsaw: Ancher, 2005), 1:634, 2:232.
165 Żuławski, *Wspomnienia*, 7.
166 LNB, f. 44, spr. 34, a. 108.
167 BN, akc. 7947, 5.

168 Kofler, *Żydowskie dwory*, 136.
169 Franciszek Barański, *Przewodnik po Lwowie* (Lviv: Słowo Polskie, 1902), 11; *Kurzer Führer durch Lemberg und Umgebung mit 15 Illustrationen und 1 Karte* (Krakow: Landesverband für Fremden- und Reiseverkehr in Galizien, [1910]), 8; See also the Polish version of the same guide: *Krótki przewodnik po Lwowie i okolicy* (Krakow: Krajowy Związek Turystyczny, 1910), 3.
170 LNB, f. 44, spr. 34, a. 236.
171 Rkps. Ossolin. 13167/II, 24.
172 LNB, f. 44, spr. 34, a. 3.
173 Ibid., a. 150.
174 Ibid., a. 65.
175 Ibid. a. 839.
176 Ibid., a. 740.
177 Zenon Tarnavs'kyi, *Doroha na Vysokyi Zamok. Noveli, opovidannia, narysy* (Toronto: Homin Ukrainy, 1964), 25.
178 *Głos*, no. 231, 1 November 1908, 9.
179 "Z poczekalni kolejowej III kl.," *Głos*, no. 142, 23 June 1907, 2–3.
180 Simons, *St. Pancras Station*, 97–8.
181 *Hauptergebnisse der Österreichischen Eisenbahn-Statistik im Jahre 1897* (Vienna: Kaiserlich-Königlich Hof- und Staatsdruckerei, 1898), 132.
182 Wittlin, *Moj Lwów*, 12–13.
183 Lieberman, *Pamiętniki*, 22.
184 Jan Sudoł, *Moje wspomnienia z lat 1890–1945* (Kolbuszowa: Biblioteka Publiczna Miasta i Gminy, 1994), 47.
185 Tara Zahra, "Travel Agents on Trial: Policing Mobility in Late Imperial Austria," *Past & Present*, 223 (May 2014): 161–93.
186 Jan Stapiński, *Pamiętnik* (Warsaw: Ludowa spółdzielnia wydawnicza, 1959), 253.
187 Sudoł, *Moje wspomnienia z lat 1890–1945*, 44.
188 Ibid., 46–7.
189 Rkps. Ossolin. 15327, 251.
190 Ibid., 253.
191 Wittlin, *Moj Lwów*, 12.
192 Rkps. Ossolin. 15619/II, 19–20.
193 Georg Kohlmaier and Barna von Sartory, eds., *Houses of Glass: A Nineteenth-Century Building Type* (Cambridge, MA: MIT Press, 1981).
194 Józef Kozielecki, *Banach: geniusz ze Lwowa* (Warsaw: Żak, 1999), 25.
195 Wittlin, *Moj Lwów*, 12.
196 Ibid., 12–13.
197 Rkps. Ossolin. 15586/II, 55.
198 Stefan Grabiński, *Demon Ruchu* (Warsaw: Lampa i Iskra Boża, 1999), 50.
199 Ibid., 50–4.

200 Ivan Franko, *Zibrannia tvoriv u p'iatdesiaty tomakh* (Kyïv: Naukova dumka, 1976), 1:200–1.
201 Ibid., 2:265–6.
202 Ivan Franko, "Zakym rushyt' poïzd," *Literaturno-naukovyi* vistnyk 3, no. 1(1898): 135–39.
203 Artur Hutnikiewicz, *Twórczość literacka Stefana Grabińskiego (1870–1936)* (Toruń: Państwowe wydawnictwo naukowe, 1959), 80.
204 Grabiński, *Demon Ruchu*, 6.
205 Stefan Grabinski, *The Motion Demon* (Ashcroft, BC: Ash-Tree Press, 2005), 38.
206 "Obłąkany maszynista," *Głos*, no. 279, 4 December 1908, 2.
207 Bernard Połoniecki, *Dzienniki, pamiętniki i listy z lat 1880–1943*, Opracowała i wstępem opatrzyła Maria Konopka (Warsaw: Biblioteka Narodowa, 2006), 153.
208 Hutnikiewicz, *Twórczość literacka Stefana Grabińskiego (1870–1936)*, 59.

Chapter 4

1 Ihor Chornovol, *Pol's'ko-ukraïns'ka uhoda 1890-1894 rr.* (Lviv: L'vivs'ka akademiia mystetstv, 2000), 100–10; Klaus Bachmann, *Ein Herd der Feindschaft gegen Rußland: Galizien als Krisenherd in den Beziehungen der Donaumonarchie mit Rußland (1907-1914)*, Schriftenreihe des österreichischen Ost- und Südosteuropa-Instituts, Band 25 (Vienna: Verlag für Geschichte und Politik; Munich: Oldenbourg, 2001).
2 LNB, f. 44, spr. 34, 354.
3 Kost' Levyts'kyi, *Istoriia politychnoi dumky halyts'kykh ukraïntsiv 1848–1914: Na pidstavi spomyniv* (Lviv: OO. Vasyliiany u Zhovkvi, 1926), 630–9; Mykhailo Lozyns'kyi, *Halychyna v rr. 1918–1920* (Vienna: Ukraïns'kyi Sotsioliogichnyi Instytut, 1922), 13; Najdus, *Polska partia socjalno-demokratyczna*, 550–4.
4 Rkps. Ossolin. 15586/II, 66.
5 Rkps. Ossolin. 16180 /II, 33.
6 Rkps. Ossolin. akc. 120/7, cz. 3, 12.
7 Rkps. Ossolin. 15351/II, cz. 1, 87.
8 Karel Čapek, *R.U.R. (Rossum's Universal Robots)*, trans. David Wyllie (Adelaide: University of Adelaide, 2014), EPUB e-book, https://ebooks.adelaide.edu.au/c/capek/karel/rur/complete.html
9 Rkps. Ossolin. 16180 /II, 33; Rkps. Ossolin. 13177/II, 31.
10 Mick, *Kriegserfahrungen in einer multiethnischen Stadt*, 78; Alfred Olszewski, *Wypisy lwowskie*, Rkps. Ossolin. 17257/I, 368.
11 Rkps. Ossolin. akc. 121/99, 130.
12 Ibid.

13 Bronisław Braiter, *Z mego podwórka* (Lviv: Leopolia, 1938), 123.
14 Ibid., 124.
15 Ibid.
16 Ibid., 123–6.
17 AGAD, C.K. Ministerstwo Kolei Żelaznej, sygn. 2252, 189.
18 Rkps. Ossolin. 15385/II, t. 1, 81.
19 Rkps. Ossolin. 15351/II, cz. 1, 90.
20 Rkps. Ossolin. 12915/I, 65.
21 Ibid., 66.
22 Rkps. Osolin. akc. 120/79, cz. 3, 16.
23 Rkps. Ossolin. 12915/I, 67.
24 Ibid., 68.
25 Ibid., 71.
26 AGAD, C.K. Ministerstwo Kolei Żelaznej, sygn. 2252, 198–203.
27 Ibid., 206–7.
28 Rkps. Ossolin. 15619/II, 30.
29 RGIA, f. 273, op. 6, d. 940, 4.
30 Rkps. Ossolin. akc. 120/79, cz. 3, 19.
31 Judson, *Habsburg Empire*, 391–3.
32 Mick, *Kriegserfahrungen in einer multiethnischen Stadt*, 75–7.
33 Keely Stauter-Halsted, "Jews as Middleman Minorities in Rural Poland: Understanding the Galician Pogroms of 1898," in *Antisemitism and Its Responses*, ed. Robert Blobaum (Ithaca, NY: Cornell University Press, 2005), 39–59. Anti-Jewish pogroms did occur in Galicia in the 1890s, but were confined to Western Galicia's towns and villages. The scale and intensity of anti-Jewish violence, however, did not at all approach that of the Russian pogroms.
34 Rkps. Ossolin. akc. 120/79, cz. 3, 31.
35 Rkps. Ossolin. 13168/II, 108–9.
36 RGIA, f. 273, op. 6, d. 940, 8.
37 Ibid.
38 AGAD, C.K. Ministerstwo Kolei Żelaznej, sygn. 2252, 208.
39 RGIA, f. 273, op. 10, d. 1399.
40 RGIA, f. 273, op. 4, d. 863, 2.
41 V.I. Fedorchenko, *Imperatorskii Dom. Vydaiushchiesia sanovniki: Entsiklopediia biografii*, t.2 (Krasnoiarsk: Bonus; Moscow: Olma-Press, 2003), 115–16.
42 RGVIA, f. 2070, op. 1, d. 381, 146.
43 Ibid.
44 Ibid.
45 RGVIA, f. 2004, op. 1, d. 24, 110.
46 RGIA, f. 273, op. 6, d. 940, 8.
47 Ibid., 5.

48 RGIA, f. 273, op. 12, d. 1682, 6.
49 *Al'bom vidov postroiki i evakuatsii voennykh zheleznykh dorog Vladimir-Volynskii-Sokal' i Sokal'-Kamenka-L'vov. 1914–1915 gg.* (Kyiv: S.V. Kul'zhenko, 1916).
50 RGVIA, f. 2067, op. 1, d. 546, 143.
51 Ibid.
52 Ibid.
53 Ibid., 144.
54 RGIA, f. 273, op. 6, d. 940, 10–12.
55 RGVIA, f. 2067, op. 1, d. 546, 148.
56 RGIA, f. 273, op. 6, d. 940, 27.
57 RGVIA, f. 2070, op. 1, d. 381, 922.
58 RGVIA, f. 2067, op. 1, d. 546, 270.
59 Ibid., 29.
60 RGIA, f. 273, op. 17, d. 109, 6.
61 RGIA, f. 350, op. 35, d. 411.
62 RGIA, f. 350, op. 35, d. 396, 1.
63 RGIA, f. 350, op. 35, d. 397, 3–12.
64 RGVIA, f. 2067, op. 1, d. 546, 30.
65 Ibid., 36, 90.
66 RGIA, f. 273, op. 6, d. 940, 131.
67 RGVIA, f. 2067, op. 1, d. 546, 9.
68 Ibid., 11.
69 Ibid., 7.
70 RGVIA, f. 2004, op. 1, d. 24, 123.
71 RGVIA, f. 2067, op. 1, d. 546, 5.
72 [Nikolai Romanov], *Dnevniki imperatora Nikolaia II* (Moscow: Orbita, 1991), 523.
73 Ibid.
74 RGIA, f. 273, op. 6, d. 940, 154.
75 RGIA, f. 237, op. 1, d. 733, 13.
76 RGIA, f. 237, op. 1, d. 735, 282.
77 RGIA, f. 237, op. 1, d. 734, 24.
78 RGIA, f. 237, op. 1, d. 733, 45–6.
79 Ibid., 68, 71.
80 Alison Fleig Frank, *Oil Empire: Visions of Prosperity in Austrian Galicia* (Cambridge, MA: Harvard University Press, 2007), 167–9.
81 Leszek Zakrewski, "Stacja ropałowa w Nowym Sączu," *Zeszyty Naukowo-Techniczne Stowarzyszenia Inżynierów i Techników Komunikacji Rzeczypospolitej Polskiej. Oddział w Krakowie* 1, no. 108 (2016): 135–6.
82 RGVIA, f. 2004, op. 1, d. 26, 71–2.
83 RGIA, f. 273, op. 11, d. 838, 4.

84 RGVIA, f. 2067, op. 1, d. 546, 96.
85 RGVIA, f. 2004, op. 1, d. 26, 530.
86 Rkps. BN akc. 7947, 94–9.
87 RGVIA, f. 2004, op. 1, d. 14, l.29, 30, 38, 43, 101, 111, 141, 178.
88 Eric Lohr, *Nationalizing the Russian Empire: The Campaign against Enemy Aliens during World War I* (Cambridge, MA: Harvard University Press, 2003), passim.
89 RGVIA, f. 2070, op. 1, d. 379, 2.
90 Ibid.
91 Ibid., 24.
92 RGIA, f. 273, op. 6, d. 108, 3.
93 Ibid., 438.
94 Ibid., 9, 20, 44.
95 Ibid., 126, 144, 203–4, 237.
96 RGVIA, f. 2004, op. 1, d. 24, 35–36.
97 RGVIA, f. 2004, op. 1, d. 26, 2–7, 83–92.
98 Ibid., 2–7, 36–60, 334, 536.
99 Ibid., 320.
100 RGVIA, f. 2004, op. 1, d. 24, 43.
101 Ibid., 41.
102 Ibid., 10.
103 Ibid., 112.
104 RGVIA, f. 2070, op. 1, d. 381, 128.
105 Ibid., 120.
106 RGIA, f. 273, op. 6, d. 940, 30.
107 Rkps. Ossolin. 13539/II, 130.
108 RGVIA, f. 2070, op. 1, d. 379, 2.
109 Ibid., 56–7.
110 RGVIA, f. 2004, op. 1, d. 115, 16.
111 RGVIA, f. 2070, op. 1, d. 342, 133.
112 RGVIA, f. 2070, op. 1, d. 381, 576.
113 RGIA, f. 273, op. 12, d. 1682, 1–2.
114 RGIA, f. 273, op. 15, d. 188, 7, 38.
115 RGVIA, f. 2004, op. 1, d. 115, 15.
116 Rkps. Ossolin. 15385/II, 101.
117 RGIA, f. 273, op. 10, d. 2632, 154.
118 RGIA, f. 273, op. 12, d. 1490, 2, 74; RGVIA, f. 2070, op. 1, d. 381, 716, 727.
119 RGVIA, f. 2070, op. 1, d. 381, 424.
120 Wasburn, *Field Notes*, 61.
121 Il'in, *Skitaniia russkogo ofitsera*, 93.
122 S. Ansky [Shloyme Zanvl Rappoport], *The Enemy at His Pleasure: A Journey through the Jewish Pale of Settlement during World War I* (New York: Metropolitan Books, 2002), 74.

123 Washburn, *Field Notes*, 62.
124 Ibid., 213.
125 Ansky, *Enemy at His Pleasure*, 113.
126 Il'in, *Skitaniia russkogo ofitsera*, 100.
127 RGVIA, f. 2004, op. 1, d. 24, 23.
128 RGVIA, f. 2070, op. 1, d. 67, 98.
129 Ibid., 100.
130 RGVIA, f. 2004, op. 1, d. 24, 110.
131 RGVIA, f. 2070, op. 1, d. 74, 51, 130.
132 RGVIA, f. 2004, op. 1, d. 26, 261.
133 RGVIA, f. 2070, op. 1, d. 67, 75b.
134 RGVIA, f. 2067, op. 1, d. 546, 170.
135 Ibid., 136.
136 RGVIA, f. 2070, op. 1, d. 381, 70.
137 RGVIA, f. 2070, op. 1, d. 74, 149.
138 Ibid., 1.
139 RGVIA, f. 2070, op. 1, d. 381, 732, 735.
140 RGVIA, f. 2004, op. 1, d. 26, 530, 670.
141 RGVIA, f. 2067, op. 1, d. 546, 35
142 *Al'bom vidov postroiki*.
143 RGVIA, f. 2067, op. 1, d. 547, 272.
144 RGIA, f. 273, op. 10, d. 3054, 10.
145 RGVIA, f. 2067, op. 1, d. 547, 116.
146 Ibid., 46.
147 Ansky, *Enemy at His Pleasure*, 74.
148 RGVIA, f. 2067, op. 1, d. 547, 11.
149 Ibid., 32.
150 RGVIA, f. 2004, op. 2, d.2 09, 12–14.
151 RGIA, f. 273, op. 4, d. 863, 4, 17; RGVIA, f. 2004, op. 3, d. 2008, 63.
152 RGVIA, f. 2070, op. 1, d. 379, 60–1, 74.
153 Ibid., 389.
154 Ibid., 80.
155 Ibid., 88.
156 Ibid., 91.
157 RGVIA, f. 2004, op. 2, d. 209, 32.
158 Ibid., 33–6, 217.
159 Ibid., 268.
160 RGVIA, f. 2004, op. 3, d. 252, 1–8.
161 RGVIA, f. 2004, op. 3, d. 1598, 3–4.
162 AGAD, C.K. Ministerstwo Kolei Żelaznej, sygn. 204, 529; Henryka Kramarz, *Samorząd Lwowa w czasie pierwszej wojny światowej i jego rola w życiu miasta* (Krakow: Wydawnictwo Naukowe WSP, 1994), 64.
163 Biruliov, *Zakharevychi*.

164 Rkps. Ossolin. 13174/II,154–6.
165 Ansky, *Enemy at His Pleasure*, 134.
166 Rkps. Ossolin. 15351/II, cz. 1, 102.
167 AGAD, C.K. Ministerstwo Kolei Żelaznej, sygn. 40, 360.
168 AGAD, C.K. Ministerstwo Kolei Żelaznej, sygn. 21, 131.
169 AGAD, C.K. Ministerstwo Kolei Żelaznej, sygn. 2252, 147.
170 Ibid., 167.
171 AGAD, C.K. Ministerstwo Kolei Żelaznej, sygn. 204, s. 454; AGAD, C.K. Ministerstwo Kolei Żelaznej sygn. 2252, 148.
172 AGAD, C.K. Ministerstwo Kolei Żelaznej, sygn. 2252, 170.
173 AGAD, C.K. Ministerstwo Kolei Żelaznej, sygn. 35, 578.
174 AGAD, C.K. Ministerstwo Kolei Żelaznej, sygn. 2252, 185.
175 Ibid., 217.
176 Ibid., 218–19.
177 Ibid., 241–72.
178 "Jeszcze echa wojny światowej," *Kolejarz*, no. 9 (143), 1 May 1928, 3.
179 John Reed, *The War in Eastern Europe* (New York: Charles Scribner's Sons, 1916), 160.
180 Zieliński, *Lwów po inwazyi rosyjskiej, wrzesień-grudzień 1914: Opowiadanie naocznego świadka* (Vienna: Z. Machnowski, 1915), 20.
181 Vejas Gabriel Liulevicius, *War Land on the Eastern Front: Culture, National Identity, and German Occupation in World War I* (Cambridge: Cambridge University Press, 2000), 154.
182 AGAD, C.K. Ministerstwo Kolei Żelaznej, sygn. 204, s.493; AGAD, C.K. Ministerstwo Kolei Żelaznej, sygn. 2252, s. 148.
183 Rkps. Ossolin. 14038/III, 1.
184 Rkps. Ossolin. 16191/I, t. 3, 170.
185 Rkps. Ossolin. 15327, 354–5.
186 Rkps. Ossolin. 16191/I, t. 3, 164.
187 LNB, f. 44, spr. 36, a. 540.
188 LNB, f. 44, spr. 36, a. 631.
189 Rkps. Ossolin. 16191/I, t. 3, 169.
190 LNB, f. 44, spr. 36, a. 503.
191 LNB, f. 44, spr. 36, a. 639.
192 LNB, f. 44, spr. 36, a. 588.
193 Rkps. Ossolin. 16191/I, t. 1, 14.
194 LNB, f. 44, spr. 36, a. 614.
195 Rkps. Ossolin. 16191/I, t. 3, 164.
196 Rkps. Ossolin. 16191/I, t. 5, 100.
197 Rkps. Ossolin. 16191/I, t. 3, 170.
198 Rkps. Ossolin. 15128, 8.
199 BN 10 562/III, t. 2, 108.

200 LNB, f. 44, spr. 36, a. 577.
201 Najdus, *Polska Partia Socjalno-Demokratyczna Galicji i Śląska*, 594.
202 Rkps. Ossolin. 15128, 10.
203 The Ukrainian People's Republic created on the Ukrainian territories of the former Russian Empire, declared its independence on 22 January 1918.
204 Najdus, *Polska Partia Socjalno-Demokratyczna Galicji i Śląska*, 596.
205 Rkps. Ossolin. 15397/II, 31–2.
206 Najdus, *Polska Partia Socjalno-Demokratyczna Galicji i Śląska*, 588.
207 Iosyf Slipyi, *Spomyny* (Lviv; Rome: Vydavnytstvo Ukrains'koho Katolyts'koho Universytetu, 2014), 112.
208 Rkps. Ossolin. 14093/II, 320–1.
209 Oleksa Kuz'ma, *Lystopadovi dni u L'vovi: Zi shkitsamy* (Lviv: Chervona Kalyna, 1931), 100–1
210 Włodzimierz Michał Bułat, "Pamiętnik-Dziennik," in *Lwów i lwowianie. Pamiętniki-Wspomnienia-Relacje*, ed. Jerzy Kowalczuk (Krakow, 2011), 3:19.
211 Rkps. Ossolin. 14093/II, 320–1.
212 Rkps. Ossolin. 12 925 II, 38.
213 Kuz'ma, *Lystopadovi dni u L'vovi*, 144.
214 Rkps. Ossolin. akc. 120/79, cz. 3,123–4.
215 Ibid., 125.
216 Ignacy Daszyński, *Pamiętniki*, 2 v. (Krakow: Z.R.S.S. "Proletarjat," 1925), 2:302.
217 Lieberman, *Pamiętniki*, 145.
218 Mick, *Kriegserfahrungen in einer multiethnischen Stadt*, 234.
219 Józef Wołczański, ed., *Nieznana korespondencja metropolitów lwowskich Józefa Bilczewskiego z Andrzejem Szeptyckim w czasie wojny polsko-ukraińskiej 1918–1919* (Lviv; Krakow: Wydawnictwo bł. Jakuba Strzemię Archidiecezji Lwowskiej ob. Łac. Oddział w Krakowie, 1997), 85 ft.6, 86.
220 Rkps. Ossolin. 16191/I, t. 8, 77.
221 Dyoniza Wieczffińska, "Wspomnienia," in *Lwów i lwowianie. Pamiętniki-Wspomnienia-Relacje*, ed. Jerzy Kowalczuk (Krakow, 2011), 3:109–10.
222 Ibid., 109–11.
223 Hieronim Wirzyński, "W bohaterskim Lwowie," *Tygodnik Ilustrowany*, no. 5, 1 Feburary 1919, 82.
224 Wieczffińska, "Wspomnienia," 113.
225 *Jednodniówka Walki z Pożarem: W 10-lecie wybuchu amunicji w Magaz. Kolej. we Lwowie: 1919–1929* (Lviv: Zakł. Graficzne "Druk. Mieszczańskiej," 1929), 2.
226 Wieczffińska, "Wspomnienia," 113.
227 Rkps. Ossolin. 16191/I, t. 8, 505.
228 Biedrzycka, *Kalendarium Lwowa 1918–1939*, 18.

229 Rkps. Ossolin. 16191/I, t. 8, 440.
230 Rkps. Ossolin. sygn. 15128, 12.
231 Rkps. Ossolin. 13498/II, 253.
232 Rkps. Ossolin. 13499/II, 209.
233 Rkps. Ossolin. 13498/II, 84.
234 Rkps. Ossolin. 13499/II, 34.
235 Rkps. Ossolin. 13498/II, 199.
236 Rkps. Ossolin. 16191/I, t. 11, 671.
237 Rkps. Ossolin. 13499/II., 35.
238 Ibid., 201.
239 Rkps. Ossolin. 13500/III, 451.
240 Ibid., 5.
241 Ibid., 30.
242 Rkps. Ossolin. 16191/I, t. 9, 548.
243 Ibid., 566.
244 Rkps. Ossolin. 16191/I, t. 26, 722.
245 Biedrzycka, *Kalendarium Lwowa 1918–1939*, 29.
246 Ibid., 84.
247 Rkps. Ossolin. 16191/I, t. 26, 740.
248 Biedrzycka, *Kalendarium Lwowa 1918–1939*, 157.
249 Rkps. Ossolin. 16191/I, 133.
250 LNB, f. 44, 38/3, 78, 93, 106.
251 Rkps. Ossolin. 16191/I, t. 10, 591.
252 Biedrzycka, *Kalendarium Lwowa 1918–1939*, 91.
253 Ibid., 59, 149.
254 Olszewski, *Wypisy lwowskie*, 367.

Chapter 5

1 Orłowicz, *Ilustrowany przewodnik po Lwowie*, 155.
2 AAN, zesp. 98, sygn. 18, 267.
3 Biedrzycka, *Kalendarium Lwowa 1918–1939*, 126.
4 Rkps. Ossolin. 16191/I, t. 15, 954.
5 Rkps. BJ 9107 IV, 1.
6 Rkps. Ossolin. akc. 133/73, 3.
7 Biedrzycka, *Kalendarium Lwowa 1918–1939*, 207.
8 Ibid., 158.
9 Ibid., 126.
10 Małgorzata I. Niemczyńska, "Ta, która chciała być panią," *Gazeta Wyborcza*, no. 117, 22 May 2014, 11–13.
11 Biedrzycka, *Kalendarium Lwowa 1918–1939*, 126.
12 Ibid., 207.

13 Orłowicz, *Ilustrowany przewodnik po Lwowie*, 156.
14 Biedrzycka, *Kalendarium Lwowa 1918–1939*, 207.
15 Orłowicz, *Ilustrowany przewodnik po Lwowie*, 156.
16 Biedrzycka, *Kalendarium Lwowa 1918–1939*, 342.
17 Orłowicz, *Ilustrowany przewodnik po Lwowie*, 155.
18 Michał Lityński, "Oblicze dzisiejszego Lwowa," in *Lwów dawny i dzisiejszy*, ed. B. Janusz (Lviv: Mar, 1928), 85.
19 BN 10 562 III t. 1, 33.
20 Władysław Czarnecki, *Wspomnienia architekta*, vol. 1, ed. Hanna Grzeszczuk-Brendel (Poznań: Wydawnictwo Mijeskie, 2005), 40.
21 Rkps. Ossolin. 16189, 46.
22 Handziuk, "Fenomenolohiia ta propahandysts'ka diial'nist' hazety UVO 'Surma' u 1927–1929 rr.," 39.
23 Biedrzycka, *Kalendarium Lwowa 1918–1939*, 110.
24 Rkps. Ossolin. 13498/II, 227.
25 Biedrzycka, *Kalendarium Lwowa 1918–1939*, 97.
26 Rkps. Ossolin. 15351 II, 63.
27 Biedrzycka, *Kalendarium Lwowa 1918–1939*, 97.
28 Rkps. Ossolin. akc. 41/68, 2.
29 Rkps. Ossolin. 16191/I, t. 25, 1614.
30 "Marszałek Foch we Lwowie," *Republika*, no. 122, 11 May 1923, s.1.
31 Biedrzycka, *Kalendarium Lwowa 1918–1939*, 63.
32 Ibid., 470.
33 Ibid., 729.
34 Ibid., 250.
35 Derek Sayer, *The Coasts of Bohemia: A Czech History* (Princeton, NJ: Princeton University Press, 1998); Katherine Verdery, *The Political Lives of Dead Bodies: Reburial and Postsocialist Change* (New York: Columbia University Press, 1999).
36 Mick, *Kriegserfahrungen in einer multiethnischen Stadt*, 360–401.
37 Michael Taussig, *Walter Benjamin's Grave* (Chicago: University of Chicago Press, 2006), 6.
38 Rkps. Ossolin. 16191/I, t. 26, 753.
39 Biedrzycka, *Kalendarium Lwowa 1918–1939*, 188.
40 Ibid., 767.
41 Ibid., 302.
42 Ibid., 58.
43 Ibid., 752.
44 Rkps. Ossolin. akc. 41/68, 1.
45 Ibid.
46 Biedrzycka, *Kalendarium Lwowa 1918–1939*, 309.
47 Ibid., 449.

48 Ibid., 625.
49 Ibid., 776.
50 Ibid., 822.
51 Karl Baedeker, *Austria-Hungary with Excursions to Cetinje, Belgrade, and Bucharest: Handbook for Travellers* (Leipzig: Karl Baedeker, 1911), 378.
52 *Kurzer Führer durch Lemberg und Umgebung* (Lviv: Landesverbande für Fremden, 1912), 8.
53 Bohdan Janusz, *Przewodnik po Lwowie (z planem miasta)* (Lviv: Wszechświat, 1922), 4–5.
54 Orłowicz, *Ilustrowany przewodnik po Lwowie*, 2–3.
55 *Ilustrowany przewodnik po Lwowie z planem orjentacyjnym ze wskaźnikiem* (Lviv: Reklama Lwowska, 1936), 11.
56 Aleksander Medyński, *Lwów: Ilustrowany przewodnik dla zwiedzających z planem miasta* (Lviv: Księgarnia Gubrzynowicz i syn, 1938), 27.
57 DALO, f. 1, op. 9, spr. 489, 58.
58 Ibid., 61–2.
59 *Mały rocznik statystyczny: 1939* (Warsaw: Główny Urząd Statystyczny, 1939), 36.
60 *Wielki Lwów: Przewodnik i informator* (Lviv: Komitet Wydawniczy, 1933), 33.
61 Roman Shporliuk, "Try (?) nenapysani statti pro L'viv," in *Leopolis multiplex*, ed. Ihor Balyns'kyi and Bohdana Matiiash (Kyiv: Hrani-T, 2008), 295.
62 Rkps. Ossolin. 16154 III, 9.
63 Shporliuk, "Try (?) nenapysani statti pro L'viv," 295.
64 Stanislaw Lem, *Highcastle: A Remembrance* (New York: Harcourt, Brace, 1995), 45.
65 Rkps. Ossolin. 15620/II, 247.
66 LNB, f. 44, 38/3, 66.
67 Ibid., 2.
68 RGAE, f. 1884, op. 88, d. 917, 19.
69 Rkps. Ossolin. 15589/II, 1.
70 Teofil Bissaga, *Geografia Kolejowa Polskiz uwzględnieniem stosunków gospodarczo-komunikacyjnych*, Wydawnictwa Techniczne Ministerstwa Komunikacji 9 (Warsaw: Ministerstwo Komunikacji, 1939), 188–92.
71 Tadeusz Krzyżewski, *Propaganda turystyczna Lwowa* (Lviv: Związek Dyplom. Abs. Akademii Handlu Zagranicznego, 1937), 10.
72 Rkps. Ossolin. 15327, 490.
73 Rkps. Ossolin. 16189, 37.
74 Biedrzycka, *Kalendarium Lwowa 1918–1939*, 142.
75 Ibid., 109.
76 Ibid., 157.
77 Ibid., 422.
78 Rkps. Ossolin. 16709, t. 1, 3.

79 Kelly Stauter-Halsted, *The Devil's Chain: Prostitution and Social Control in Partitioned Poland* (Ithaca, NY: Cornell University Press, 2015), 124–8.
80 Nancy M. Wingfield, "Destination: Alexandria, Buenos Aires, Constantinople; 'White Slavers' in Late Imperial Austria," *Journal of the History of Sexuality* 20, no. 2 (2011): 291–311.
81 Stauter-Halsted, *Devil's Chain*, 208–9.
82 AAN, zesp. 15, sygn. 218, 88–191.
83 AAN, zesp. 15, sygn. 219, 144.
84 Rkps. Ossolin. 15336, 141–3.
85 Rkps. Ossolin. 16191/I, t. 16, 1019.
86 LNB, f. 44, 38/3, 48.
87 Ibid., 25.
88 Rkps. Ossolin. 16191/I, t. 32, 1971.
89 Kyrylo Studyns'kyi, *Z pobutu na Radians'kii Ukraïni: Na marginesi pravopysnoï konferentsiï* (Lviv: nakladom Knyharni NTSh, 1927), 4–6.
90 Rkps. Ossolin. 15336, 146.
91 Rkps. Ossolin. 17499 II, 33.
92 Rkps. Ossolin. 16191/I, t. 16, 1041.
93 Rkps. Ossolin. 16191/I, t. 28, 1722.
94 Rkps. Ossolin. 16191/I, t. 29, 134.
95 Sudoł, *Moje wspomnienia z lat 1890–1945*, 119.
96 Ibid.
97 Ibid.
98 Ibid., 120.
99 Rkps. Ossolin. 16191/I, t. 24, 1532.
100 Ibid., 1535–6.
101 TsDIAUL, f. 354, op. 1, spr. 61, 60.
102 Ibid., 61–2.
103 Ibid., 67–8.
104 Ibid., 69–70.
105 Ibid., 71–2.
106 RGAE, f. 1884, op. 12, d. 1498, 9.
107 Rkps. Ossolin. 16154 III, 18.
108 Bonusiak, *Lwów w latach 1918–1939*, 35.
109 Ibid., 49–50.
110 Rkps. Ossolin. 15589/II, 1.
111 Rkps. Ossolin. sygn. 15128, 67.
112 Rkps. Ossolin. 17258 II, 34–43.
113 Czarnecki, *Wspomnienia architekta*, 18.
114 Paweł Kozłowski, "'Wesoła lwowska fala,' czyli co bawiło publiczność w II Rzeczypospolitej," *Prace Naukowe Państwowej Wyższej Szkoły Wschodnioeuropejskiej: Nauki Humanistyczne* 1 (2014): 195–205.
115 Tarnavs'kyi, *Doroha na Vysokyi Zamok*, 43.

116 Jurij Smirnow, "Historia świątyń rzymskokatolickich," *Kurjer Galicyjski*, no. 3, 14 February 2008, 15.
117 Rkps. Ossolin. 15587/II, 113.
118 Władysław Ratyński, *Lewica Związkowa w II Rzeczypospolitej* (Warsaw: PWN, 1976), 22.
119 Hanna Krauze-Jaworska, *Zarys Historii związku zawodowego pracownikow kolejowych Rzeczy Pospolitej 1918–39* (Warsaw: Wydawnictwo Związkowe CRZZ, 1968), 10–13.
120 Ibid., 14.
121 Ibid., 17.
122 Janusz Żarnowski, "Strajk kolejarzy i strajk powszechny w lutym-marcu 1921 r.," *Kwartalnik historyczny* 63, no. 1 (1956): 61.
123 Lucjan Kieszczyński, *Komunistyczna Partia Polski a ruch zawodowy 1918–1939* (Warsaw: Akademia Nauk Społecznych, Instytut Historii Ruchu Robotniczego, 1990), 205.
124 Bolesław Drobner, *Rzecz o klasowym ruchu zawodowym w Polsce w swietle prasy socjalistycznej* (Warsaw: Wydawnictwo związkowe CRZZ, 1965), 2:24.
125 Kryp'iakevych, *Z istorii revoliutsiinoho rukhu u L'vovi, 1917–1939*, 192–205.
126 AAN, zesp. 98, sygn. 18, 487, 520–3.
127 TsDIAUL, f. 248, op. 3, spr. 6.
128 Krauze-Jaworska, *Zarys Historii związku zawodowego pracownikow kolejowych Rzeczy Pospolitej 1918–39*, 20.
129 Drobner, *Rzecz o klasowym ruchu zawodowym w Polsce w swietle prasy socjalistycznej*, 2:7.
130 Mazur, *Życie polityczne polskiego Lwowa, 1918–1939*, 355.
131 Ratyński, *Lewica Związkowa w II Rzeczypospolitej*, 151.
132 Rkps. Ossolin. 15586/II, 148.
133 Rkps. Ossolin. 15352/II, 610.
134 Krauze-Jaworska, *Zarys Historii związku zawodowego pracownikow kolejowych Rzeczy Pospolitej 1918–39*, 148.
135 Drobner, *Rzecz o klasowym ruchu zawodowym w Polsce w swietle prasy socjalistycznej*, 4:64–5.
136 Bissaga, *Geografia Kolejowa Polskiz uwzględnieniem stosunków gospodarczo-komunikacyjnych*, 102.
137 Rkps. Ossolin. 51.
138 Krauze-Jaworska, *Zarys Historii związku zawodowego pracownikow kolejowych Rzeczy Pospolitej 1918–39*, 154.
139 Rkps. Ossolin. 15336, t. 2, 215.
140 Rkps. Ossolin. 15397/II, 51.
141 AAN, zesp. 98, sygn. 71/I-41, 9–9a.
142 "Wielka panama w Dyrekcji kolejowej we Lwowei: Aresztowanie naczelnika Wydziału zasobów i dwóch urzhędników oraz dostawcy," *Dziennik Ludowy*, no. 104, 7 May 1928, 10.

143 Rkps. Ossolin. 16191/I, t. 26, 1635.
144 Ibid., 1637.
145 Ibid., 456.
146 Artur Hausner, *Gospodarka kolejowa w świetle dyskusji sejmowej* (Lviv: Nakładem księgarni ludowej, 1930), 11.
147 Ibid., 7–8.
148 RGAE, f. 1884, op. 31, d. 2764, 17, 33.
149 Ibid., 37; RGAE, f. 1884, op. 88, d. 917, 47.
150 Rkps. Ossolin. 13072/II, 237.
151 Rkps. Ossolin. 16191/I, t. 27, 1666.
152 AAN, zesp. 98, sygn. 71/I-108, 44–9.
153 Antin Chernets'kyi, *Spomyny z moho zhyttia* (Kyiv: Osnovni tsinnosti, 2001), 54–5.
154 Romaniczówna, *Dziennik lwowski 1842–1930*, 2:308–10.
155 BN, IV 10189, t. 2, 578.
156 AAN, zesp. 98, sygn. 71/III-1, 3.
157 Rkps. Ossolin. 13341/II, 110.
158 Dieter Pohl, *Nationalsozialistische Judenverfolgung in Ostgalizien 1941–1944*, Studien zur Zeitgeschichte 50 (Munich: R. Oldenbourg, 1997), 27.
159 V.I. Bilous, "Pershi komunistychni orhanizatsiï l'vivs'kykh zaliznychnykiv," *KPZU – orhanizator revoliutsiinoï borot'by: Spohady kolyshnikh chleniv Komunistychnoï partiï Zakhidnoï Ukraïny* (Lviv: Knyzhkovo-zhurnal'ne vydavnytstvo, 1958), 55–8.
160 D.D. Verbovyi, "V robitnychomu seredovyshchi," *KPZU – orhanizator revoliutsiinoï borot'by: Spohady kolyshnikh chleniv Komunistychnoï partiï Zakhidnoï Ukraïny* (Lviv: Knyzhkovo-zhurnal'ne vydavnytstvo, 1958), 159.
161 Zbigniew Szczygielski, *Członkowie KPP 1918–1939 w świetle badań ankietowych* (Warsaw: Książka i Wiedza, 1988), 53.
162 Ibid., 50, 52.
163 Ibid., 137.
164 Biedrzycka, *Kalendarium Lwowa 1918–1939*, 249.
165 Ibid., 251.
166 Ibid., 585.
167 Verbovyi, "V robitnychomu seredovyshchi," 159.
168 "'Sztab' komunistów 'Zachidnej Ukrainy' aresztowany we Lwowie," *Dziennik Ludowy*, no. 230, 1928, 5.
169 Rkps. Ossolin. 15352/II, 610.
170 Rkps Ossolin. 17258 II, 289.
171 Rkps. Ossolin. 15590/II, 6–8.
172 Chajes, *Semper Fidelis*, 55.
173 Rkps. Ossolin. 15590/II, 1.
174 Mazur, *Życie polityczne polskiego Lwowa, 1918–1939*, 363.
175 Ibid., 356.

176 Rkps. Ossolin. sygn. 15128, 44.
177 Ibid., 47.
178 Rkps. Ossolin. 15590/II, 21–2.
179 Hausner, *Gospodarka kolejowa w świetle dyskusji sejmowej*, 4.
180 Rkps. Ossolin. 16154 III, 65.
181 Rkps. Ossolin. sygn. 15128, 199–200.
182 Ibid., 200, 206.
183 Ibid.
184 Ibid., 213.
185 "W izbie piwnicznej Władysława Kozaka," *Trybuna Robotnicza*, no. 18, 1936, 3.
186 Ibid., a.2.
187 Rkps. Ossolin. sygn. 15128, 214.
188 Rkps Ossolin. 17258 II, 98–9.
189 "... Bo na nim robotnicza krew...," *Trybuna Robotnicza*, no. 18, 1936, 4–5.
190 Rkps. Ossolin. sygn. 15128, 217.
191 Ibid., 215.
192 Rkps Ossolin. 17258 II, 98–9.
193 Rkps. Ossolin. sygn. 15128, 119–67.
194 DALO, f. 350, op. 1, spr. 67a, a. 213.
195 Mazur, *Życie polityczne polskiego Lwowa, 1918–1939*, 368–70.
196 Andrei Sheptyts'kyi, *Ostoroha Ioho Eksts: Vpreosviashchenoho Mytropolyta Kyr Andreia Sheptys'koho pered zahrozoiu komunizmu* (Biblioteka "Prominchyka sontsia liubovy," ch.1) (Univ: Lavra Studyts'koho Ustavu v Unevi, 1936), 1.
197 "Wykończyć czerwoną twierdzę!" *Trybuna robotnicza*, no. 12, 1936, 3.
198 Bonusiak, *Lwów w latach 1918–1939*, 209.
199 Ibid.
200 *Powszechny spis ludności z dnia 9.XII.1931*, tab. XV 12.
201 Rkps. Ossolin. 13072/II, 237.
202 Rkps. Ossolin. 15620/II, 78–9.
203 "Z okręgu Lwowskiego F.K.P.," *Front Kolejowy*, no. 11, 1935, 7.
204 *Kolejowe Przysposobienie Wojskowe*, no. 5, 1934, 6; *Kolejowe Przysposobienie Wojskowe*, no. 5, 1935, 12.
205 "Uroczystość Związku kolejarzy lwow," *Dziennik Ludowy*, no. 93, 1923, 5; "Ogólny wiec kolejarzy za P.P.S. Protest przeciwko komercjalizacji kolei," *Dziennik Ludowy*, no. 40, 1928, 4.
206 AAN, zesp. 98, sygn. 71/I-116, s. 36, 57.
207 Romuald Miller, "Dom związku zawowodego pracowników kolejowych Rzeczypospolitej Polskiej," *Architektura i budownictwo*, no. 6 (1928): 175–207.
208 "Jak pracuje biblioteka Z.Z.K. we Lwowie," *Kolejarz Związkowiec*, 1938, 104.
209 Konrad Sura, "Moja ulica Gródecka," *Cracovia-Leopolis* 17, no. 1 (1991): 19–20.

210 Rkps. Ossolin. 15590/II, 25.
211 Sura, "Moja ulica Gródecka," 21; *Piłka Nożna na Ziemi Lwowskiej 1894–1939* (Warsaw: SPAR, 1996), 105.
212 Rkps. Ossolin. 16218, 50.
213 AAN, zesp. 16, sygn. 532.
214 Ibid., 1.
215 Mick, *Kriegserfahrungen in einer multiethnischen Stadt*, 271–2.
216 Ibid., 271–2.
217 LNB, f. 44, spr. 4, 82.
218 AAN, zesp.16, sygn.520.
219 AAN, zesp. 98, sygn. 18, 481.
220 AAN, zesp. 16, sygn. 550, 2994.
221 AAN, zesp. 16, sygn. 561, 2, 8.
222 AAN, zesp. 16, sygn. 556, 160.
223 Biedrzycka, *Kalendarium Lwowa 1918–1939*, 376.
224 Ibid., 538, 540–2.
225 AAN, zesp. 16, sygn. 539, 1.
226 Ibid., 691.
227 Ibid., 814.
228 AAN, zesp. 16, sygn. 554, 86.
229 Ibid., 85.
230 Ibid., 81.
231 Ibid., 84.
232 Biedrzycka, *Kalendarium Lwowa 1918–1939*, 937.
233 Tomasz Chinciński, "Niemiecka dywersja w Polsce w 1939 r. w świetle dokumentów policyjnych i wojskowych II Rzeczypospolitej oraz służb specjalnych III Rzeszy. Cz.1, (Marzec-sierpień 1939 r.), *Pamięć i Sprawiedliwość* 4/2, no. 8 (2005): 159–95.
234 AAN, zesp. 16, sygn. 3001.
235 LNB, f. 44, spr. 38/3, 80.
236 Chajes, *Semper Fidelis*, 115.
237 Żuławski, *Wspomnienia*, 117, 120.
238 Biedrzycka, *Kalendarium Lwowa 1918–1939*, 667.
239 Ibid., 914.
240 Ibid., 863.
241 Wereszycki, *Niewygasła przeszłość*, 360.

Chapter 6

1 Rkps. Ossolin. 15620/II, 291.
2 Rkps. Ossolin. 16709, t.1, 4, 6.
3 Rkps. Ossolin. 15587/II, 160.
4 DALO, f.1, op. 1, spr. 190, a. 34–4a.

5 Rkps. Ossolin. 16709, t. 1, 28, 30.
6 Rkps. Ossolin. 16180 /II, 197.
7 Rkps. Ossolin. 15620/II, 291.
8 Rkps. Ossolin. 16709, t. 1, 30.
9 Karolina Grodziska, *Listy, listy, liście, wspomnienia ... Z dziejów lwowskich rodzin Reichertów, Peterów i Negruszów* (Krakow: Karolina Grodziska, 2012), 7.
10 Stanisław Trusz, "Wspomnienia wojenne," in *Lwów i lwowianie. Pamiętniki-Wspomnienia-Relacje*, ed. Jerzy Kowalczuk (Krakow, 2011), 3:193.
11 *Powszechny spis ludności z dnia 9.XII.1931*, tab. XV 12.
12 Amar, *Paradox of Ukrainian Lviv*, 59.
13 Mieczysław Piwowar, *Wspomnienia lwowskiego chłopaka* (Opole; Warsaw: Warsgraf, 2004), 9–10.
14 Rkps. Ossolin. 16709, t. 1, 14.
15 V. Mars'ka [Mariia Strutyns'ka], *Buria nad L'vovom: Povist' u dvokh chastynakh* (Philadelphia: Kyiv, 1952), 106.
16 RGAE, f. 1884, op. 12, d. 1498, 1.
17 RGAE, f. 1884, op. 31, d. 2650, 192.
18 Ibid., 194, 139.
19 Ivan Kovalev, *Transport v Velikoi Otechestvennoi voine (1941–1945 gg.)* (Moscow: Nauka, 1981), 63–5.
20 Pavel Kabanov, *Stal'nye peregony* (Moscow: Voenizdat, 1973), 69–70.
21 Ibid., 71–2.
22 RGAE, f. 1884, op. 31, d. 2889, 3.
23 RGASPI, f. 81, op. 3, d. 350, 1.
24 Ibid., 200.
25 RGAE, f. 1884, op. 46, d.444, 98.
26 RGASPI, f. 111, op. 12, d. 3, 285.
27 RGAE, f. 1884, op. 46, d. 444, 99.
28 RGASPI, f. 111, op. 12, d. 3, 118–19.
29 Ibid., 281–305.
30 RGAE, f. 1884, op. 31, d. 2889, 1.
31 Ibid., 4.
32 Rkps. Ossolin. 16180 /II, t. 2, 9.
33 Volodymyr Baran, "Ekonomicheskie preobrazovaniia v Zapadnoi Ukraine v 1939–1941 godakh," in *Zapadnaia Belorussiia i Zapadnaia Ukraina v 1939–1941 gg.: liudi, sobytiia, dokumenty*, ed. Oksana Petrovskaia and Elena Borisenok (Saint Petersburg: Aleteiia, 2011), 173.
34 Zbigniew Domosławski, *Mój Lwów: Pamiętnik czasu wojny. Lwów po latach* (Jelenia Góra: Kolegium Krakonoskie, 2009), 49, 52, 65, 70.
35 Wat [Aleksander Chwat], *My Century: The Odyssey of a Polish Intellectual* (Berkeley: University of California Press, 1988), 102.

36 Rkps. Osssolin. 16189, 144.
37 Wat, *My Century*, 149.
38 RGASPI, f. 111, op. 12, d. 4, 22.
39 Ibid., 23.
40 Ibid., 34.
41 Mars'ka, *Buria nad L'vovom*, 131.
42 Mick, *Kriegserfahrungen in einer multiethnischen Stadt*, 445–6; Hryciuk, *Polacy we Lwowie, 1939–1944*, 150–1.
43 Wat, *My Century*, 98–9.
44 Ivan Serov, *Zapiski iz chemodana: Tainye dnevniki pervogo predsedatelia KGB, naidennye cherez 25 let posle ego smerti* (Moscow: Prosveshchenie, 2017), 55.
45 Yitzhak Sternberg, *Under Assumed Identity* (Israel: Hakibbutz Hameuchad and Ghetto Fighters' House, 1986), 21.
46 Rkps. Ossolin. 16709, t. 2, 135.
47 Rkps. Ossolin. 17259 II, 19.
48 Ibid.
49 Ibid., 20.
50 Rkps. Ossolin. 17259 II, 35–6.
51 Ibid., 7.
52 Hryciuk, *Polacy we Lwowie, 1939–1944*, 32–3.
53 Rkps. Ossolin. 15587/II, 165.
54 Rkps. Ossolin. 16709, t. 2, 305.
55 Rkps. Osssolin. 16189, 161.
56 Iosyp Nadol's'kyi, *Deportatsiina polityka stalins'koho totalitarnoho rezhymu v zakhidnykh oblastiakh Ukraïny (1939–1953): Monohrafiia* (Luts'k: Vezha, 2008), 129.
57 Ibid., 139–40.
58 Ibid., 106.
59 Rkps. Osssolin. 16189, 152.
60 Rkps. Ossolin. 16709, t. 2, 126. Wat, *My Century*, 165, 177.
61 Maurycy Allerhand and Leszek Allerhand, *Zapiski z tamtego swiata* (Krakow: Wydawnictwo Educkacyjne, 2003), 27.
62 Rkps. Osolin. 17839 II, 80.
63 Rkps. Ossolin. 16771 II.
64 Rkps. Ossolin. 16770 II, 8–10; Rkps. Ossolin. 16778 II, 2–3.
65 Rkps. Ossolin. 16787 II, 15.
66 Nadol's'kyi, *Deportatsiina polityka stalins'koho totalitarnoho rezhymu*, 108.
67 Rkps. Ossolin. 16770 II, 8–10.
68 Rkps. Osolin. 17839 II, 80.
69 Rkps. Osssolin. 16189, 152.
70 Rkps. Ossolin. 16709, t. 2, 126–7.
71 Ibid., 247, 249, 251.

72 Ostap Tarnavs'kyi, *Literaturnyi L'viv, 1939–1944: Spomyny* (Lviv: Prosvita, 1995), 22.
73 Serov, *Zapiski iz chemodana*, 58.
74 RGAE, f. 1884, op. 48, d. 2280, 8.
75 Hryciuk, *Polacy we Lwowie, 1939–1944*, 87.
76 RGAE, f. 1884, op. 46, d. 727, 28.
77 Baran, "Ekonomicheskie preobrazovaniia v Zapadnoi Ukraine v 1939–1941 godakh," 170–1.
78 RGAE, f. 1884, op. 46, d. 727, 19.
79 Rkps. Ossolin. 15336, t. 3, 43–4.
80 Bohdan Janusz, *293 dni rządów rosyjskich we Lwowie (3.IX.1914–22.VI.1915)* (Lviv: Księgarnia Polska, 1915), 60–1.
81 Zynovii Knysh [Bohdan Mykhailiuk], *Dalekyi prytsil: Ukrains'ka viis'kova orhanizatsiia v 1927–1929 rokakh* (Toronto: Sribna surma, 1967), 247–8.
82 Anna Czekanowska, *Świat rzeczywisty – świat zapamiętany: Losy Polaków we Lwowie (1939–1941)* (Lublin: Norbertinum, 2010), 159
83 Rkps. Ossolin. 15128, 273.
84 Kabanov, *Stal'nye peregony*, 82.
85 RGASPI, f. 111, op. 16, d. 16, 5, 47.
86 Ibid., 1, 10.
87 Ibid., 129.
88 Struve, *Deutsche Herrschaft, ukrainishcer Nationalismus, antijüdische Gewalt*, 255. Iatsek Vil'chur [Jacek Wilczur], *Na nebo srazu ne popast': L'vov, 1941–1943* (Moscow: Regnum, 2012), 15.
89 Ibid., 252.
90 The most detailed reconstruction of the events can be found in ibid., 247–380; see also John-Paul Himka, "The Lviv Pogrom of 1941: The Germans, Ukrainian Nationalists, and the Carnival Crowd," *Canadian Slavonic Papers* 53, nos. 2-4 (2011): 209–42.
91 Allerhand and Allerhand, *Zapiski z tamtego świata*, 38.
92 Tarnavs'kyi, *Literaturnyi L'viv, 1939–1944*, 67.
93 BN, akc. 7123, 2.
94 Taras Hryvul, "Chysel'nist' pidpil'noï merezhi OUN na terytoriï URSR v 1940–1941 rokakh," *Ukraïna: kul'turna spadshchyna, natsional'na svidomist', derzhavnist'*, no. 52 (2012): 266.
95 BN, akc. 7123, 409.
96 Sternberg, *Under Assumed Identity*, 26. Piotr Rawicz also survived Auschwitz posing as a Ukrainian; see Lawrence Langer, "Introduction," in *Blood from the Sky*, by Piotr Rawicz (New Haven, CT: Yale University Press, 2003), vi.
97 Bohdan Kazanivs'kyi, *Shliakhom Liegendy* (London: Ukraïns'ka vydavnycha spilka, 1975), 212.

98 "L'viv distaie nove oblychchia," *L'vivs'ki visti*, no. 6, 15 August 1941, 2.
99 Rkps. Ossolin. sygn. 15587, 175.
100 "L'viv distaie nove oblychchia," *L'vivs'ki visti*, no. 6, 15 August 1941, 2.
101 Hryciuk, *Polacy we Lwowie, 1939–1944*, 191.
102 "L'viv vertaiet'sia do davnioho vyhliadu," *L'vivs'ki visti*, no. 1, 9 August 1941, 4.
103 S.D., "Mandrivka po L'vovi," *L'vivs'ki visti*, no. 9, 19 August 1941, 2.
104 Wat, *My Century*, 104.
105 "Khto mozhe korystaty z pereïzdu," *L'vivs'ki visti*, no. 23, 4 September 1941, 3.
106 "Vidnovelnnia osobovoho zaliznychnoho rukhu," *L'vivs'ki visti*, no. 102, 5 December 1941, 3.
107 "Wśród huku maszyn, stukotu młotów postaje z ruin lwowski węzeł kolejowy," *Gazeta Lwowska*, no. 41, 25 September 1941, 3.
108 "Remont l'vivs'koï zaliznychnoi stantsiï," *L'vivs'ki visti*, no. 79, 8 November 1941, 3.
109 Rkps. Ossolin. 16604, 23.
110 Rkps. Ossolin. 15587/II, 176.
111 P.P. Mykhailenko and Ia. Iu. Kondrat'ev, *Istoriia militsii Ukrainy u dokumentakh i materialakh: U 3-kh t.* (Kyiv: Heneza, 1999), 2:382.
112 Rkps. Ossolin. 14093/II, 255.
113 M.S. Chartoryis'kyi [Mykola Sydor-Chartoryis'kyi], *Mizh molotom i kovadlom: Prychynky do istoriï U.P.A. (Spomyny 1942–1945 rr.)* (New York: Ukraïns'ke vydavnytstvo "Hoverlia," 1970), 16.
114 Ibid., 19.
115 Hryciuk, *Polacy we Lwowie, 1939–1944*, 197.
116 Lem, *Highcastle*, 105.
117 Józef Wittlin, *Sól ziemi: Powieść o cierpliwym piechurze* (Warsaw: Państwowy Instytut Wydawniczy, 1988), 144. In a "post-scriptum" to his novel added in 1970, a terrified Wittlin acknowledges that the train car from his novel can be seen as a seed "from which grew and multiplied in the years of World War II those nightmarish sealed cars, where innocent people choked while carried to annihilation" (250).
118 Raul Hilberg, *The Destruction of the European Jews* (New York: Holmes and Meier, 1985), 2:407–54. Todd Samuel Presner, *Mobile Modernity: Germans, Jews, Trains* (New York: Columbia University Press, 2007).
119 Simone Gigliotti, *The Train Journey: Transit, Captivity, and Witnessing in the Holocaust*, (New York: Berghahn Books, 2009).
120 Raul Hilberg repeatedly emphasizes the railway's role as a collective perpetrator and mechanism that enabled destruction; see Raul Hilberg, "German Railroads/Jewish Souls," in *The Nazi Holocaust: Historical Articles on the Destruction of the European Jews*, ed. Michael Marrus (Westport,

CT: Meckler, 1989), 3:520–56. See also Alfred C. Mierzejewski, "A Public Enterprise in the Service of Mass Murder: The Deutsche Reichsbahn and the Holocaust," *Holocaust and Genocide Studies* 15, no. 1 (2001): 33–46.

121 Snyder, *Bloodlands*, passim.

122 Omer Bartov, "Communal Genocide: Personal Accounts of the Destruction of Buczacz, Eastern Galicia, 1941–1944," in *Shatterzone of Empires: Coexistence and Violence in the German, Habsburg, Russian and Ottoman Borderlands*, ed. Omer Bartov and Eric D. Weitz (Bloomington: Indiana University Press, 2013), 399–420.

123 BN, akc. 7123, 20; Samuel Drix, *Witness to Annihilation: Surviving the Holocaust, a Memoir* (Washington, DC; London: Brassey's, 1994), 54.

124 Jacob Gerstenfeld-Maltiel, *My Private War: One Man's Struggle to Survive the Soviets and the Nazis* (London: Vallentine Mitchell, 1993), 66.

125 Mazur, Skwara, and Węgierski, *Kronika 2350 dni wojny i okupacji Lwowa*, 225; Hryciuk, *Polacy we Lwowie, 1939–1944*, 289.

126 Friedman, *Zagłada żydów lwowskich.*

127 Ibid.

128 Leon Richman, *Why? Extermination Camp Lwów (Lemberg) 134 Janowska Street, Poland: A Documentary by an Inmate* (New York: Vantage Press, 1975), 3.

129 E., L'viv roste. "Odyn rik pratsi L'vivs'koi Mis'koi Upravy," *L'vivs'ki visti*, 1 August 1942, 4.

130 Friedman, *Zagłada żydów lwowskich.*

131 Ibid.

132 Richman, *Why?*, 101.

133 Tom Segev, *Simon Wiesenthal: The Life and Legends* (New York: Doubleday, 2010), 47.

134 Rkps. Ossolin. 15587/II, 176.

135 BN, akc. 7123, 38.

136 Rkps. Ossolin. sygn. 15128, 69.

137 Yad Vashem, O. 39, file 120, 94–5.

138 Ranajit Guha, *Dominance without Hegemony: History and Power in Colonial India* (Cambridge, MA: Harvard University Press, 1998).

139 "Robitnyky ïdut' na vidpustku," *L'vivs'ki visty*, no. 85, 14 April 1943, 6.

140 RGAE, f. 1884, op. 31, d. 5940, 14–15.

141 Rkps. Ossolin. sygn. 16598, 69, 72, 116, 169, 174–6.

142 Czesław Bakunowicz, "Koleje Generalnego Gubernatorstwa w wojennej organizacji kolejnictwa III Rzeszy Niemieckiej 1939–1945," *Dzieje Najnowsze*, no. 1 (2005): 41–2.

143 Rkps. Ossolin. 16598/II, 22.

144 Chartoryis'kyi, *Mizh molotom i kovadlom*, 59.

145 Rkps. Ossolin. 16598/II, 22.

146 Segev, *Simon Wiesenthal*, 46, 51.
147 BN, akc. 7947, 247–8; Jadwiga Chodakowska, *Pociąg berliński stoi przy peronie 2a* (Krakow: Krajowa agencja wydawnicza, 1988).
148 Witold Szczepaniec, *Wspomnienia z Ostbahnu: Żurawcia Nord Zugabfertigung Mitte 1942–1944* (Szczecin: Arsoba, 2003), 10.
149 Rkps. Ossolin. 16598/II, 103.
150 Rkps. Osolin. 17839 II, 83, 90.
151 Rkps. Ossolin. 16772, 53, 62.
152 "Pro suspil'nu zabezpeku zaliznychnykiv," *Zaliznychnyk*, no. 1, 1944, 2.
153 "Moja przygoda fotograficzna," 21 November 2011, http://dalel.blog.onet.pl/2011/11/21, accessed 31 July 2016.
154 Piwowar, *Wspomnienia lwowskiego chłopaka*, 19.
155 Ibid., 19; Vil'chur, *Na nebo srazu ne popast'*, 32.
156 Chartoryis'kyi, *Mizh molotom i kovadlom*, 17.
157 Heinrich Böll, *Der Zug war pünktlich: Erzählung* (Munich: Deutscher Taschenbuch, 1972), 11–12, 81–2.
158 "Moja przygoda fotograficzna."
159 Rkps. Osssolin. 16189, 154.
160 Chartoryis'kyi, *Mizh molotom i kovadlom*, 49.
161 "Moja przygoda fotograficzna."
162 Rkps. Ossolin. 16598/II, 131.
163 Rkps. Ossolin. 16772, 53.
164 Piwowar, *Wspomnienia lwowskiego chłopaka*, 23.
165 Chartoryis'kyi, *Mizh molotom i kovadlom*, 17.
166 Rkps. Osssolin. 16189, 188.
167 Vil'chur, *Na nebo srazu ne popast'*, 66.
168 Piwowar, *Wspomnienia lwowskiego chłopaka*, 23.
169 Yad Vashem, O. 39, file 120, 4.
170 Semen Wityk, *Jak żyje 10.500 mieszkańców Lwowa* (Lviv: Semenr Wityk, 1903).
171 Yones, *Smoke in the Sand*, 241.
172 Stanisława Gogołowska, "Przyczynek do historii obozu janowskiego: Ryszard Axer," *Przegląd Lekarski* 36, no. 2 (1979): 154–6.
173 Helene C. Kaplan, *I Never Left Janowska* (New York: Holocaust Library, 1989), 48.
174 Ibid., 81.
175 Drix, *Witness to Annihilation*, 37.
176 Sternberg, *Under Assumed Identity*, 49, 62.
177 Ibid., 65.
178 Rkps. Ossolin. 13516/II, 149.
179 Artur Węgierski, *W lwowskiej Armii Krajowej* (Warsaw: PAX, 1989). By the end of 1941, the OUN-B concluded that the Polish underground was

fighting not only against the Germans but also against Ukrainians, and defined it as an enemy; see Volodymyr V'iatrovych, ed., *Pol's'ko-Ukrains'ki stosunky v 1942–1947 rokakh u dokumentakh OUN ta UPA*, vol. 1 (Lviv: Tsentr doslidzhen' vyzvol'noho rukhu, 2011).

180 Rkps. Ossolin. 13518/II, 145.

181 Yad Vashem, O. 39, f. 120, 75.

182 Ibid., 82.

183 Yad Vashem, O. 62, f. 438.

184 Yad Vashem, M. 49, f. 857.

185 Ibid.

186 Michał Borwicz, *Uniwersytet zbirów: rzecz o Obozie Janowskim we Lwowie 1941–1944* (Krakow: Wysoki Zamek, 2014).

187 Drix, *Witness to Annihilation*, 146.

188 BN, akc. 7123, 270–1.

189 For one of the most striking examples, see Tarnavs'kyi, *Literaturnyi L'viv, 1939–1944*.

190 Hryciuk, *Polacy we Lwowie, 1939–1944*, 236–7.

191 Yad Vashem, O. 39, f. 120, 51.

192 Rkps. Ossolin. akc. 42/81, 8–9.

193 Piwowar, *Wspomnienia lwowskiego chłopaka*, 21.

194 Ibid., 23.

195 Vil'chur, *Na nebo srazu ne popast'*, 28.

196 Ibid., 32.

197 Ibid., 31.

198 Ibid., 44–5.

199 Yad Vashem, M. 49, f. 857.

200 Segev, *Simon Wiesenthal*, 50–2.

201 Yad Vashem, O. 39, f. 120, 34–7.

202 Yad Vashem, M. 49, f. 857.

203 Yad Vashem, M. 49, f. 3736.

204 Yad Vashem, M. 49, f. 3735

205 Mykhailenko and Kondrat'ev, *Istoriia militsii Ukrainy u dokumentakh i materialakh*, 2:385.

206 Yad Vashem, M. 49E, f. 2159.

207 Yad Vashem, M. 49, f. 2279.

208 Yad Vashem, M. 49, f. 3785.

209 Joachim Shoenfeld, *Holocaust Memoirs: Jews in the Lwów Ghetto, the Janowski Concentration Camp, and as Deportees in Siberia* (Hoboken, NJ: Kitav, 1985), 108–9.

210 Kaplan, *I Never Left Janowska*, 85.

211 Drix, *Witness to Annihilation*, 114.

212 Yad Vashem, M. 49, f. 1931.
213 Ibid., 110.
214 Ibid.
215 Yad Vashem, M. 49, f. 3442.
216 Yad Vashem, M. 49, f. 3510, 6.
217 Gerstenfeld-Maltiel, *My Private War*, 139.
218 Ibid., 154.
219 Szczepaniec, *Wspomnienia z Ostbahnu*, 15–20.
220 Ibid., 11–12.
221 Vil'chur, *Na nebo srazu ne popast'*, 47–8; Piwowar, *Wspomnienia lwowskiego chłopaka*, 24–6.
222 Alfons Tąkiel, "Pamiętnik," in *Lwów i lwowianie. Pamiętniki-Wspomnienia-Relacje*, ed. Jerzy Kowalczuk (Krakow, 2011), 3:159.
223 Mykhailenko and Kondrat'ev, *Istoriia militsii Ukrainy u dokumentakh i materialakh*, 2:386.
224 Vil'chur, *Na nebo srazu ne popast'*, 42.
225 Mykhailenko and Kondrat'ev, *Istoriia militsii Ukrainy u dokumentakh i materialakh*, 2:384.
226 Leon Weliczker Wells, *The Death Brigade (The Janowska Road)* (New York: Holocaust Library, 1963), 224.
227 *Soviet Statements on Nazi Atrocities* (London: Hutchinson, [1946]), 254–5.
228 *Pro zlochynstva nimtsiv na terytoriï L'vivs'koï oblasti: povidomlennia Nadzvychainoï Derzhavnoï Komisiï po vstanovlenniu i rozsliduvanniu zlochynstv nimets'ko-fashysts'kykh zaharbnykiv* (Kyiv: Ukraïns'ke derzhavne vydavnytstvo, 1945), 18.
229 Rkps. Ossolin. 16599 II, 52.
230 Rkps. Ossolin. 16598/II, 188.
231 Rkps. Ossolin. 16600, 1–2.
232 Ibid., 42.
233 Ibid., 16600, 46.
234 RGAE, f. 1884, op. 31, d. 5940, 3.
235 Ibid., 6–9.
236 Ibid., 11.
237 Kabanov, *Stal'nye peregony*, 257–60.
238 Węgierski, *W lwowskiej Armii Krajowej*, 189–241.
239 V'iatrovych, *Pol's'ko-Ukrains'ki stosunky v 1942–1947 rokakh u dokumentakh OUN ta UPA*, 575.
240 Hryciuk, *Polacy we Lwowie, 1939–1944*, 206–7.
241 Mazur, Skwara, and Węgierski, *Kronika 2350 dni wojny i okupacji Lwowa*, 247.
242 RGAE, f. 1884, op. 46, d. 1398, 28.

243 V.E. Pavlova and M.M. Uzdina, eds., *Istoriia zheleznodorozhnogo transporta Rossii i Sovetskogo Soiuza*, vol. 2, *1917–1945* (Saint Petersburg; Moscow, 1997), 368.
244 U.Ia. Iedlins'ka and Iaroslav Isaievych, eds., *Istoriia L'vova v dokumentakh i materialakh: Zbirnyk dokumentiv i materialiv* (Kyiv: Naukova dumka, 1986), 233.
245 RGAE, f. 1884, op. 31, d. 5885, 7.
246 "Slava truzhenikam prifrontovoi magistrali zavoevavshim perekhodiashchee Krasnoe znamia Gosudarstvennogo Komiteta Oborony," *L'vovskii zhelznodorozhnik*, no. 2, 19 August 1944.
247 Kabanov, *Stal'nye peregony*, 261.
248 Rkps. Ossolin. 16772, 74.
249 Hryciuk, *Polacy we Lwowie, 1939–1944*, 50.
250 Pohl, *Nationalsozialistische Judenverfolgung in Ostgalizien 1941–1944*, 385.

Chapter 7

1 Olga Burova and Viktor Ivanov, "Otstroim na slavu," 1945; Soviet post-war reconstruction poster.
2 Nikita Khrushchev, *Vospominaniia* kn.1 (Moscow: Moskovskie novosti, 1999), 568.
3 DALO, f. 239, op. 1, spr. 6, 31.
4 TsDAHO, f. 1, op. 23, spr. 3413, 30.
5 Vadim Batyrev, *Vokzaly* (Moscow: Stroiizdat, 1988), 94.
6 Bohdan Tscherkes, "Stalinist Visions for the Urban Transformation of Lviv, 1939–1955," *Harvard Ukrainian Studies* 24 (2000): 205–22.
7 N. Shabalin, "V strok vosstanovim L'vovskii vokzal," *L'vovskii zheleznodorohnik*, no. 68, 2 June 1945.
8 TsDAHO, f. 1, op. 23, spr. 1278, 13.
9 RGAE, f. 1884, op. 31, d. 5885, 27.
10 Ibid., 30–1.
11 Ibid., 233.
12 DAKO, f. 3527, op. 1, spr. 3, 46.
13 TsDAHO, f. 1, op. 77, spr. 432, 40.
14 TsDAHO, f. 1, op. 23, spr. 3435, 65.
15 Ibid., 59.
16 Ibid., 66.
17 TsDIAuL, f. 248, op. 2, spr. 2687, 8.
18 TsDAVO, f. 4920, op. 1, spr. 2849, 17.
19 DAKO, f. 3527, op. 1, spr. 4, 28.
20 Ibid., 29.
21 TsDAHO, f. 1, op. 77, spr. 103, 5–6.

22 TsDAHO, f. 1, op. 23, spr. 2171, 4.
23 TsDAHO, f. 1, op. 77, spr. 225, 65.
24 TsDAHO, f. 1, op. 77, spr. 287, 15.
25 Ibid., 16.
26 TsDAHO, f. 1, op. 23, spr. 3858, 11.
27 TsDAHO, f. 1, op. 77, spr. 287, 15.
28 TsDAHO, f. 1, op. 23, spr. 2171, 4.
29 TsDAVO, f. 4920, op. 1, spr. 381, 32.
30 TsDAHO, f. 1, op. 23, spr. 3461, 17.
31 TsDAHO, f. 1, op. 77, spr. 287, 15.
32 Shabalin, "V strok vosstanovim L'vovskii vokzal."
33 TsDAHO, f. 1, op. 77, spr. 103, 5–6.
34 TsDAHO, f. 1, op. 23, spr. 3858, 11.
35 Ibid., 12.
36 TsDAVO, f. 4920, op. 1, spr. 377, a.109.
37 TsDAVO, f. 4920, op. 1, spr. 367a, a.41.
38 Ibid., a.101.
39 Shabalin, "V strok vosstanovim L'vovskii vokzal."
40 N. Alekseev, "Chto tormozit rabotu," *L'vovskii zheleznodorozhnik*, no. 139, 13 November 1945.
41 TsDAVO, f. 4920, op. 1, spr. 377, 69.
42 RGAE, f. 1884, op. 31, d. 5885, 27.
43 DALO, f. 2037, op. 4, spr. 2, 12.
44 TsDAHO, f. 1, op. 77, spr. 225, 172.
45 TsDAVO, f. 4920, op. 1, spr. 377, 234.
46 DALO, f. 2037, op. 1, spr. 2, 59.
47 TsDAHO, f. 1, op. 77, spr. 432, 38.
48 A. Matveev, "Cherepash'imi tempami," *L'vovskii zhelznodorozhnik*, no. 100, 17 August 1948.
49 DALO, f. 2037, op. 1, spr. 2, 59.
50 DALO, f. 2037, op. 4, spr. 2, 22–3.
51 TsDAVO, f. 4920, op. 1, spr. 199, 16, 19, 26.
52 DALO, f. 2037, op. 4, spr. 2, 14.
53 TsDAVO, f. 4920, op. 1, spr. 5, 64–5.
54 TsDAVO, f. 4920, op. 1, spr. 199, 16, 19, 26.
55 DALO, f. 2037, op. 4, spr. 2, 14; TSDAVO, f. 4920, op. 1, spr. 6, 162.
56 TsDAVO, f. 4920, op. 1, spr. 377, 61.
57 Ibid., 108.
58 Ibid., 98.
59 Ibid., 106.
60 DALO, f. 2037, op. 1, spr. 6, 19–20.
61 Ibid., 8.

62 TsDAHO, f. 1, op. 23, spr. 3435, 104.
63 "Chto volnuet passazhirov vo L'vove," *L'vovskii zheleznodorozhnik*, no. 82, 1946.
64 DALO, f. 2037, op. 1, spr. 5, 54
65 Ibid., 57
66 TsDAVO, f. 4920, op. 1, spr. 379, 7–19.
67 TsDAVO, f. 4920, op. 1, spr. 973, 32.
68 V.D. Kuz'mich and B.A. Levin, eds., *Istoriia zheleznodorozhnogo transporta Sovetskogo Soiuza*, vol. 3, *1945–1991 gg*. (Moscow: Moskovskii gosudarstvennyi universitet putei soobshcheniia, 2004), 29.
69 TsDAVO, f. 4920, op. 1, spr. 534, 23.
70 TsDAVO, f. 4920, op. 1, spr. 378, 85.
71 Ibid., 126.
72 Ibid., 149.
73 Ibid.
74 TsDAVO, f. 4920, op. 1, spr. 377, 153.
75 Ibid., 203.
76 TsDAVO, f. 4920, op. 1, spr. 378, 139.
77 Ibid., 114.
78 Ibid., 103.
79 Ibid., 107.
80 Ibid., 127.
81 Ibid., 140.
82 Ibid., 143.
83 Ibid., 92.
84 RGAE, f. 1884, op. 31, d. 2657, 141–2.
85 TsDAVO, f. 4920, op. 1, spr. 381, 2.
86 TsDAVO, f. 4920, op. 1, spr. 534, 20.
87 Ibid., 27.
88 Ibid.
89 TsDAVO, f. 4920, op. 1, spr. 979, 182.
90 TsDAVO, f. 4920, op. 1, spr. 973, 45.
91 TsDAVO, f. 4920, op. 1, spr. 979, 77.
92 TsDAVO, f. 4920, op. 1, spr. 1188, 1–7.
93 Ibid., 27–8.
94 *L'vovskii zheleznodorozhnik*, no. 44, 7 April 1949.
95 TsDAHO, f. 1, op. 77, spr. 432, 38.
96 Kuz'mich and Levin, *Istoriia zheleznodorozhnogo transporta Sovetskogo Soiuza*, 3:29.
97 TsDAHO, f. 1, op. 77, spr. 432, 38.
98 DALO, f. 2037, op. 4, spr. 5, 9.
99 TsDAVO, f. 4920, op. 1, spr. 1620, 117.
100 TsDAHO, f. 1, op. 77, spr. 432, 46.

101 Ibid.
102 TsDAVO, f. 4920, op. 1, spr. 1623, 188.
103 TsDAHO, f. 1, op. 77, spr. 432, 38.
104 Ibid., 34.
105 Ibid., 36.
106 Ibid., 34.
107 Ibid., 53.
108 Ibid., 21.
109 TsDAVO, f. 4920, op. 1, spr. 2303, 71.
110 TsDAHO, f. 1, op. 77, spr. 432, 38.
111 TsDAVO, f. 4920, op. 1, spr. 2555, 4–8.
112 Ibid., 106.
113 Ibid.
114 TsDAHO, f. 1, op. 77, spr. 432, 45.
115 RGAE, f. 1884, op. 31, d. 9939.
116 TsDAVO, f.4920, op. 1, spr. 2555, 34.
117 DALO, f. 2037, op. 4, spr. 6, 24.
118 Ibid.; TsDAVO, f. 4920, op. 1, spr. 2555, 169.
119 TsDAHO, f. 1, op. 77, spr. 462, 174.
120 TsDAVO, f. 4920, op. 1, spr. 2555, 138.
121 A. Skoryi, I. Alekseev, and N. L'vov, "Na vokzale stantsii L'vov-passazhirskii," *L'vovskii zhelznodorozhnik*, no. 79, 5 July 1952, 2.
122 TsDAHO, f. 1, op. 77, spr. 567, 12.
123 DALO, f. 2037, op. 4, spr. 9, 46.
124 DALO, f. 239, op. 1, spr. 49, 83.
125 TsDAHO, f. 1, op. 77, spr. 480, 88.
126 DALO, f. 2037, op. 4, spr. 10, 38.
127 DALO, f. 239, op. 1, spr. 49, 84.
128 TsDAVO, f. 4920, op. 1, spr. 2592, 163.
129 G.P. Zaporozhtsev and S.I. Iakushin, *Novye zheleznodorozhnye vokzaly* (Moscow: Gosudarstvennoe transportnoe zheleznodorzhnoe izdatelstvo, 1957), 218.
130 "Luchshii na seti dorog," *L'vovskii zheleznodorozhnik*, no. 112, 20 September 1954, 4.
131 Soviet enterprise for the construction of subway systems.
132 Oleksandr Verbytsky, the architect who designed the Kyiv terminal built between 1928 and 1932.
133 Viktor Nekrasov, *Zapiski zevaki* (Moscow: Vagrius, 2003), 96.
134 Mikhail Ryklin, "'The Best in the World': The Discourse of the Moscow Metro in the 1930s," in *The Landscape of Stalinism: The Art and Ideology of Soviet Space*, ed. Evgenii Dobrenko and Eric Naiman (Seattle: University of Washington Press, 2003), 269.
135 Ibid., 262.

136 Batyrev, *Vokzaly*, 115.
137 DALO, f. 2037, op. 4, spr. 6, 24.
138 Nataliia Boichenko, "Kino u L'vovi: Top-10 starykh kinoteatriv," 6 June 2015, Fotohrafiï staroho L'vova, http://photo-lviv.in.ua/kino-u-lvovi-top-10-staryh-kinoteatriv
139 DALO, f. 2037, op. 4, spr. 6, 24.
140 TsDAHO, f. 1, op. 31, spr. 3716, 12–13.
141 Ibid., 10, 14.
142 Photographs in V. Vuitsyk and R. Lypka, *Zustrich zi L'vovom: Putivnyk* (Lviv: Kameniar, 1987), 118; *L'vivshchyna turysts'ka: Putivnyk* (Lviv: Kameniar, 1986).

Chapter 8

1 RGASPI, f. 111, op. 16, d. 6, 171.
2 DALO, f. 239, op. 1, spr. 6, 2.
3 DALO, f. 239, op. 1, spr. 8, 11.
4 TsDAHO, f. 1, op. 23, spr. 3436, 40.
5 TsDAHO, f. 1, op. 77, spr. 287, 94.
6 TsDAHO, f. 1, op. 23, spr. 3436, 40.
7 Ibid.
8 DALO, f. 239, op. 1, spr. 15, 3.
9 DALO, f. 239, op. 1, spr. 20, 5.
10 DALO, f. 239, op. 1, spr. 20, 5.
11 Ibid.
12 DALO, f.239, op. 1, spr. 18, 53–7.
13 Ibid., 4.
14 Ibid., 55–6.
15 TsDAHO, f. 1, op. 77, spr. 287, 94.
16 DALO, f. 239, op. 1, spr. 1, 9.
17 DALO, f. 239, op. 1, spr. 2, 10.
18 DALO, f. 239, op. 1, spr. 15, 6.
19 DALO, f. 239, op. 1, spr. 6, 1.
20 DALO, f. 239, op. 1, spr. 12, 19.
21 DALO, f. 239, op. 1, spr. 28, 12.
22 DALO, f. 239, op. 1, spr. 49, 37.
23 TsDAHO, f. 1, op. 23, spr. 3436, 1–3.
24 TsDAHO, f. 1, op. 23, spr. 6188, 70.
25 DALO, f. 239, op. 1, spr. 17, 18.
26 TsDAHO, f. 1, op. 23, spr. 3436, 4.
27 Ibid., 8.
28 Ibid., 11–12.

29 Ibid., 14–15.
30 Ibid., 19.
31 Ibid., 15.
32 Ibid., 23.
33 Ibid.
34 Ibid., 46.
35 Ibid., 20.
36 Ibid., 22.
37 Ibid., 78–96.
38 Ibid., 55.
39 TsDAHO, f. 1, op. 23, spr. 5447, 11.
40 TsDAHO, f. 1, op. 23, spr. 3436, 8.
41 Mikhail Demin, *Blatnoi* (New York: Russica Publishers, 1986).
42 RGAE, f. 1884, op. 31, d. 5885, 234.
43 Ibid., 237.
44 Ibid.
45 Ibid., 242.
46 DALO, f. 3, op. 1, spr. 213, 6.
47 Ibid.
48 DALO, f. 239, op. 1, spr. 2, 7.
49 Lozyns'kyi, *Etnichnyi sklad naselennia L'vova*, 211.
50 Iurii Slyvka, ed., *Deportatsiï: Zakhidni zemli Ukraïny kintsia 30-kh - pochatku 50-kh rr.: Dokumenty, materialy, spohady*, vol. 1 (Lviv: Instytut uraïnoznavstva NANU, 1996), 309.
51 Matthew Frank, *Making Minorities History: Population Transfer in Twentieth-Century Europe* (Oxford: Oxford University Press, 2017), 227–64.
52 Grzegorz Hryciuk, *Przemiany narodowściowe i ludnościowe w Galicji Wschodniej i na Wołyniu w latach 1931–1948* (Toruń: Adam Marszałek, 2005), 315–22.
53 DALO, f. 239, op. 1, spr. 2, 14.
54 Ibid.
55 Ibid, 25.
56 Ibid., 35.
57 DALO, f. 239, op. 1, spr. 8, a.6.
58 Hryciuk, *Przemiany narodowściowe i ludnościowe*, 325–7.
59 Mirosław Maciorowski, *Sami swoi i obcy: Reportaże z kresów na kresy* (Warsaw: Agora, 2011), 25–7.
60 Slyvka, *Deportatsiï*, 427.
61 Rkps. Ossolin. akc. 61/04, note under 22 March 1946.
62 Ryszard Gansiniec, *Notatki lwowskie (1944–1946)* (Wroclaw: Sudety), 1995, 11, 69.
63 Ibid., 157.

64 DALO, f. 239, op. 1, spr. 2, 11.
65 Hryciuk, *Przemiany narodowściowe i ludnościowe,* 330.
66 Rkps. Ossolin. 17259 II.
67 Gansiniec, *Notatki lwowskie (1944–1946),* 185.
68 Ibid., 188.
69 TsDAVO, f. 4920, op. 1, spr. 1169, 31.
70 That share more than doubled between 1931 and 1964 – see Stanisław Wiktor, "Stanisławska Dyrekscja Kolejowa w cyfrach," *Inżynier Kolejowy,* no. 3, 1 March 1931, 95; TsDAHO, f. 1, op. 32, spr. 722, 88.
71 DALO, f. 239, op. 1, spr. 116, 25.
72 DALO, f. 239, op. 1, spr. 33, a.103; DALO, f. 239, op. 1, spr. 38, 95.
73 DALO, f. 239, op. 1, spr. 39, 54.
74 DALO, f. 239, op. 1, spr. 65, 124; DALO, f. 239, op. 1, spr. 68, 15.
75 DALO, f. 239, op. 1, spr. 97, 54.
76 DALO, f. 239, op. 1, spr. 108, 98.
77 DALO, f. 239, op. 1, spr. 145, 101.
78 Via Rail Canada, *Annual report 2015,* 2, https://www.viarail.ca/sites/all/files/media/pdfs/About_VIA/our-company/annual-reports/2015/ViaRail_AnnualReport_2015_EN.pdf
79 DALO, f. 239, op. 1, spr. 29, 11.
80 DALO, f. 239, op. 1, spr. 65, 124.
81 DALO, f. 239, op. 1, spr. 38, 13.
82 DALO, f. 239, op. 1, spr. 152, 39.
83 DALO, f.239, op. 1, spr. 14, 31.
84 DALO, f. 239, op. 1, spr. 68, 15.
85 DALO, f. 2037, op. 4, spr. 25a, 63.
86 RGAE, f. 1884, op. 31, d.5885, 14.
87 DALO, f. 239, op. 1, spr. 77, a.11; DALO, f. 239, op. 1, spr. 77, 11.
88 DALO, f. 239, op. 1, spr. 86, 4.
89 TsDAHO, f. 1, op. 77, spr. 740, 57.
90 DALO, f. 239, op. 1, spr. 127, 147.
91 DALO, f. 239, op. 1, spr. 116, 110.
92 DALO, f. 239, op. 1, spr. 153, 94.
93 TsDAHO, f. 1, op. 77, spr. 502, 14.
94 TsDAVO, f. 4920, op. 1, spr. 510, 162.
95 DALO, f. 239, op. 1, spr. 12, 1–2.
96 DALO, f. 239, op. 1, spr. 15, 12.
97 "Kandidaty v deputaty Verkhovnogo Soveta SSSR," *L'vovskii zheleznodorozhnik,* no. 28, 4 March 1950, 1.
98 [Mykola Shevchuk], "Kak my obsluzhivaem passazhirov (Iz doklada dezhurnogo po vokzalu stantsii L'vov-passazhirskaia tov. N.K. Shevchuka)," *L'vovskii zheleznodorozhnik,* no. 139, 15 November, 1949, 1.

99 DALO, f. 239, op. 1, spr. 18, 59.
100 DALO, f. 239, op. 1, spr. 13, 1–3.
101 DALO, f. 239, op. 1, spr. 92, 78.
102 Ibid., 79.
103 Ibid.
104 Ibid., 10.
105 DALO, f. 239, op. 1, spr. 17, 2.
106 DALO, f. 239, op. 1, spr. 2391, 4.
107 Ibid., 8.
108 Amar, *Paradox of Ukrainian Lviv*, 14–15.
109 DALO, f. 239, op. 1, spr. 2391, 46.
110 DALO, f. 239, op. 1, spr. 18, 73.
111 DALO, f. 239, op. 1, spr. 33, 2.
112 DALO, f. 239, op. 1, spr. 29, 47.
113 DALO, f. 239, op. 1, spr. 2391, 46.
114 DALO, f. 239, op. 1, spr. 2, 28.
115 DALO, f. 239, op. 1, spr. 90, 18.
116 DALO, f. 239, op. 1, spr. 18, 1.
117 DALO, f. 239, op. 1, spr. 96, 22.
118 DALO, f. 239, op. 1, spr. 152, 65.
119 DALO, f. 239, op. 1, spr. 33, 25–6.
120 DALO, f. 239, op. 1, spr. 33, 2.
121 DALO, f. 239, op. 1, spr. 38, 113–14.
122 DALO, f. 239, op. 1, spr. 85, 35.
123 DALO, f. 239, op. 1, spr. 129, 16.
124 Ibid., 25.
125 DALO, f. 239, op. 1, spr. 49, 116.
126 DALO, f. 239, op. 1, spr. 76, 125.
127 DALO, f. 239, op. 1, spr. 91, 129.
128 DALO, f. 239, op. 1, spr. 118, 145.
129 DALO, f. 239, op. 1, spr. 101, 4–5.
130 TsDAHO, f. 1, op. 24, spr. 3325, 21.
131 Ibid.
132 DALO, f. 239, op. 1, spr. 101, 30.
133 DALO, f. 239, op. 1, spr. 23, a.32; DALO, f. 239, op. 1, spr. 39, 33–4.
134 DALO, f. 239, op. 1, spr. 122, 10.
135 DALO, f. 572, op. 1, spr. 101, 17.
136 DALO, f. 239, op. 1, spr. 18, 18.
137 DALO, f. 239, op. 1, spr. 88, 76–7.
138 DALO, f. 239, op. 1, spr. 94, 11–12.
139 DALO, f. 572, op. 1, spr. 96, 18–20.
140 DALO, f. 239, op. 1, spr. 97, 24.

141 DALO, f. 239, op. 1, spr. 68, 2.
142 DALO, f. 239, op. 1, spr. 72, 123–3.
143 DALO, f. R-2037, op. 4, spr. 22, 30
144 DALO, f. R-2037, op. 4, spr. 20, 12.
145 DALO, f. 239, op. 1, spr. 1, 2.
146 DALO, f. 239, op. 1, spr. 55, 79.
147 DALO, f. 239, op. 1, spr. 18, 25.
148 DALO, f. 239, op. 1, spr. 119, 71.
149 DALO, f. 239, op. 1, spr. 78, 24.
150 DALO, f. 239, op. 1, spr. 89, 65–75.
151 DALO, f. 239, op. 1, spr. 12, 13.
152 DALO, f. 239, op. 1, spr. 91, 131.
153 Ibid.
154 Ibid.
155 DALO, f. 239, op. 1, spr. 91, 66.
156 DALO, f. 239, op. 1, spr. 2, 40.
157 DALO, f. 239, op. 1, spr. 104, 3.
158 DALO, f. 239, op. 1, spr. 43, 84.
159 DALO, f. 239, op. 1, spr. 86, 70.
160 DALO, f. 239, op. 1, spr. 110, 88; DALO, f. 239, op. 1, spr. 118, 154.
161 DALO, f. 239, op. 1, spr. 23, 52–3.
162 DALO, f. 239, op. 1, spr. 49, 54.
163 DALO, f. 239, op. 1, spr. 55, 126.
164 DALO, f. 239, op. 1, spr. 60, 10.
165 DALO, f. 239, op. 1, spr. 105, 68.
166 DALO, f. 239, op. 1, spr. 126, 136.
167 DALO, f. 239, op. 1, spr. 91, 138.
168 DALO, f. 239, op. 1, spr. 108, 27.
169 DALO, f. 239, op. 1, spr. 89, 119.
170 Oleg Kharkhordin, ed., *Mishel' Fuko i Rossiia: sbornik stattei* (Saint Petersburg: Evropeiskii universitet v Sankt-Peterburge, 2001), 284–5.
171 DALO, f. 239, op. 1, spr. 134, 81.
172 DALO, f. 239, op. 1, spr. 123, 56.
173 DALO, f. 239, op. 1, spr. 60, 2.
174 Ibid.
175 DALO, f. 239, op. 1, spr. 123, 37.
176 DALO, f. 239, op. 1, spr. 88, 24–5.
177 DALO, f. 239, op. 1, spr. 94, 19–27.
178 DALO, f. 239, op. 1, spr. 23, 2; DALO, f. 239, op. 1, spr. 117, 50.
179 DALO, f. 239, op. 1, spr. 72, 23.
180 DALO, f. 239, op. 1, spr. 34, 26.
181 DALO, f. 239, op. 1, spr. 98, 2.

182 DALO, f. 239, op. 1, spr. 56, 16, 19.
183 DALO, f. 239, op. 1, spr. 83, 5.
184 DALO, f. 239, op. 1, spr. 147, 115.
185 DALO, f. 239, op. 1, spr. 83, 24.
186 DALO, f. 239, op. 1, spr. 49, 2.
187 Eric Naiman, "Introduction," in Dobrenko and Naiman, *Landscapes of Stalinism*, xii.
188 DALO, f. 239, op. 1, spr. 33, 67.
189 TsDAVO, f. 4920, op. 1, spr. 510, 158.
190 RGAE, f. 1884, op. 46, d. 2203, 228.
191 Ibid., 234–5.
192 Weliczker, *Death Brigade*, 263, 269.
193 DALO, f. 239, op. 1, spr. 49, 21.
194 DALO, f. 239, op. 1, spr. 6, 3.
195 DALO, f. 239, op. 1, spr. 18, 29.
196 DALO, f. 239, op. 1, spr. 8, 2–3.
197 DALO, f. 239, op. 1, spr. 72, 51.
198 DALO, f. 239, op. 1, spr. 49, 10.
199 Ibid., 11.
200 DALO, f. 239, op. 1, spr. 65, 58.
201 DALO, f. 239, op. 1, spr. 49, 24.
202 DALO, f. 239, op. 1, spr. 23, 55.
203 DALO, f. 239, op. 1, spr. 2391, 33.
204 DALO, f. 239, op. 1, spr. 29, 48.
205 DALO, f. 239, op. 1, spr. 77, 41, 43.
206 DALO, f. 239, op. 1, spr. 96, 4.
207 DALO, f. 239, op. 1, spr. 17, 7.
208 DALO, f. 239, op. 1, spr. 33, 68–73.
209 DALO, f. 239, op. 1, spr. 77, 41, 43.
210 DALO, f. 239, op. 1, spr. 18, 1–2.
211 DALO, f. 239, op. 1, spr. 39, 10–11.
212 DALO, f. 239, op. 1, spr. 65, 27–30.
213 DALO, f. 239, op. 1, spr. 92, 57–9.
214 DALO, f. 239, op. 1, spr. 94, 29–32.
215 Ibid., 56.
216 DALO, f. 239, op. 1, spr. 50, 49; DALO, f. 239, op. 1, spr. 77, 43.
217 DALO, f. 239, op. 1, spr. 89, 7.
218 Ibid., 17.
219 DALO, f. 239, op. 1, spr. 89, 80.
220 DALO, f. 239, op. 1, spr. 120, 68.
221 Ibid., 52.
222 DALO, f. 1699, op. 1, spr. 98, 24.

223 DALO, f. 239, op. 1, spr. 150, 6.
224 DALO, f. 239, op. 1, spr. 152, 96.
225 DALO, f. 239, op. 1, spr. 153, 24.
226 DALO, f. 239, op. 1, spr. 120, 69.
227 Ibid., 70.
228 Ibid.
229 DALO, f. 239, op. 1, spr. 77, 28.
230 DALO, f. 239, op. 1, spr. 76, 68.
231 Ibid., 30.
232 DALO, f. 239, op. 1, spr. 72, 63.
233 Ibid., 79.
234 DALO, f. 239, op. 1, spr. 56, 48.

Chapter 9

1 DALO, f. 239, op. 1, spr. 1, 6.
2 DALO, f. 239, op. 1, spr. 33, 106.
3 DALO, f. 239, op. 1, spr. 23, 3.
4 DALO, f. 239, op. 1, spr. 2391, 61.
5 Ibid., 63.
6 Ibid.
7 DALO, f. 239, op. 1, spr. 49, 29.
8 Ibid., 55.
9 DALO, f. 239, op. 1, spr. 65, 21.
10 DALO, f. 239, op. 1, spr. 87, 42.
11 DALO, f. 239, op. 1, spr. 91, 156.
12 DALO, f. 239, op. 1, spr. 93, 20–1.
13 DALO, f. 239, op. 1, spr. 122, 21.
14 DALO, f. 239, op. 1, spr. 108, 13.
15 DALO, f. 239, op. 1, spr. 118, 11.
16 Ibid., 138.
17 Ibid., 172.
18 DALO, f. 239, op. 1, spr. 127, 14.
19 DALO, f. 239, op. 1, spr. 116, 34.
20 DALO, f. 239, op. 1, spr. 137, 92.
21 DALO, f. 239, op. 1, spr. 153, 58.
22 DALO, f. 239, op. 1, spr. 33, 106.
23 "Vorota L'vova," *L'vovskii zheleznodorozhnik,* no. 55, 10 May 1962, 2.
24 DALO, f. 2037, op. 4, spr. 25a, 67.
25 Ibid.
26 DALO, f. 1699, op. 1, spr. 98, 24.
27 DALO, f. 239, op. 1, spr. 43, 89.

28 DALO, f. 239, op. 1, spr. 2, 35.
29 DALO, f. 239, op. 1, spr. 13, 5.
30 DALO, f. 239, op. 1, spr. 14, 14.
31 DALO, f. 239, op. 1, spr. 18, 17.
32 Ibid., 77.
33 DALO, f. 239, op. 1, spr. 29, 25.
34 Ibid., 64.
35 DALO, f. 239, op. 1, spr. 39, 55–6.
36 DALO, f. 239, op. 1, spr. 55, 54.
37 DALO, f. 239, op. 1, spr. 65, 33.
38 DALO, f. 239, op. 1, spr. 55, 118.
39 DALO, f. 239, op. 1, spr. 90, 60.
40 DALO, f. 239, op. 1, spr. 104, 13, 20.
41 TsDAHO, f. 1, op. 32, spr. 1086, 115.
42 DALO, f. 239, op. 1, spr. 129, 60.
43 Ibid., 72.
44 RGAE, f. 1884, op. 46, d. 2484, 259.
45 RGAE, f. 1884, op. 48, d. 2386, 25.
46 RGAE, f. 1884, op. 31, d. 12916, 83.
47 Elena Zubkova, ed., *Sovetskaia zhizn': 1945–1953 gg*. (Moscow: ROSSPEN, 2003), 501.
48 Ibid.
49 DALO, f. 239, op. 1, spr. 55, 14.
50 Ibid.
51 DALO, f. 239, op. 1, spr. 65, 129.
52 DALO, f. 239, op. 1, spr. 76, 22.
53 DALO, f. 239, op. 1, spr. 83, 49.
54 Ibid., 27–8.
55 DALO, f. 239, op. 1, spr. 90, 18.
56 DALO, f. 239, op. 1, spr. 93, 3.
57 DALO, f. 239, op. 1, spr. 108, 4.
58 DALO, f. 239, op. 1, spr. 126, 205.
59 DALO, f. 239, op. 1, spr. 108, 89.
60 DALO, f. 2037, op. 4, spr. 25a, 64.
61 DALO, f. 239, op. 1, spr. 92, 62.
62 DALO, f. 239, op. 1, spr. 108, 18.
63 DALO, f. 239, op. 1, spr. 127, 96.
64 DALO, f. 239, op. 1, spr. 129, a9; *Kolejarz*, no. 23, 1907, 6–10. Prices for 1907 are reconstructed on the basis of Hoszowski, *Ceny we Lwowie w latach 1701–1914*, 114.
65 DALO, f. 239, op. 1, spr. 49, 19.
66 DALO, f. 239, op. 1, spr. 84, 53.

67 DALO, f. 239, op. 1, spr. 133, 81.
68 DALO, f. 239, op. 1, spr. 116, 23.
69 DALO, f. 239, op. 1, spr. 129, 12.
70 DALO, f. 239, op. 1, spr. 55, 125.
71 Christine Varga-Harris, *Stories of House and Home: Soviet Apartment Life during the Khrushchev Years* (Ithaca, NY: Cornell University Press, 2015), passim.
72 DALO, f. 239, op. 1, spr. 29, 11.
73 DALO, f. 239, op. 1, spr. 23, 24–5.
74 DALO, f. 239, op. 1, spr. 68, 68.
75 Ibid., 2.
76 Ibid., 68.
77 DALO, f. 239, op. 1, spr. 72, 54.
78 DALO, f. 239, op. 1, spr. 76, 16.
79 Ibid., 3.
80 DALO, f. 239, op. 1, spr. 85, 51.
81 DALO, f. 239, op. 1, spr. 90, 24.
82 DALO, f. 239, op. 1, spr. 129, 12.
83 DALO, f. 239, op. 1, spr. 97, 55.
84 DALO, f. 239, op. 1, spr. 23, 24–5; DALO, f. 239, op. 1, spr. 152, 20.
85 DALO, f. 239, op. 1, spr. 84, 53.
86 DALO, f. 239, op. 1, spr. 126, 90–6.
87 DALO, f. 239, op. 1, spr. 84, 66.
88 Bodnar, *L'viv*, 82–90.
89 Hoszowski, *Ceny we Lwowie w latach 1701–1914*, 175.
90 Bureau of Railway Economics, *A Comparative Study of Railway Wages and the Cost of Living in the United States, the United Kingdom and the Principal Countries of Continental Europe* (Washington, DC, 1912), 44–5.
91 DALO, f. 239, op. 1, spr. 72, 3.
92 DALO, f. 239, op. 1, spr. 111, 34.
93 DALO, f. 239, op. 1, spr. 117, 35.
94 DALO, f. 239, op. 1, spr. 78, 30, 37; DALO, f. 239, op. 1, spr. 65, 117.
95 DALO, f. 2037, op. 4, spr. 23, 14.
96 DALO, f. 239, op. 1, spr. 105, 28.
97 DALO, f. 239, op. 1, spr. 78, 37.
98 DALO, f. 239, op. 1, spr. 95, 74.
99 DALO, f. 239, op. 1, spr. 91, 136.
100 DALO, f. 239, op. 1, spr. 105, 28.
101 DALO, f. 239, op. 1, spr. 116, 29.
102 DALO, f. 239, op. 1, spr. 127, 19.
103 DALO, f. 239, op. 1, spr. 118, 23.
104 Ibid., 24.

105 DALO, f. 239, op. 1, spr. 127, 19.
106 DALO, f. 239, op. 1, spr. 76, 22.
107 DALO, f. 239, op. 1, spr. 83, 26.
108 Ibid., 27.
109 DALO, f. 239, op. 1, spr. 85, 29.
110 DALO, f. 239, op. 1, spr. 127, 20.
111 DALO, f. 239, op. 1, spr. 87, 59.
112 DALO, f. 239, op. 1, spr. 90, 79.
113 DALO, f. 239, op. 1, spr. 91, 158.
114 DALO, f. 239, op. 1, spr. 105, 48.
115 DALO, f. 239, op. 1, spr. 110, 3.
116 TsDAHO, f. 1, op. 24, spr. 667, 11.
117 DALO, f. 239, op. 1, spr. 55, 14.
118 DALO, f. 239, op. 1, spr. 68, 2.
119 DALO, f. 239, op. 1, spr. 55, 84.
120 DALO, f. 239, op. 1, spr. 118, 4.
121 DALO, f. 239, op. 1, spr. 76, 99.
122 DALO, f. 239, op. 1, spr. 65, 2.
123 DALO, f. 239, op. 1, spr. 91, 111.
124 DALO, f. 2037, op. 4, spr. 25, 19.
125 Ibid., 20.
126 DALO, f. 2037, op. 4, spr. 26, 14.
127 DALO, f. 2037, op. 4, spr. 28, 9.
128 DALO, f. 239, op. 1, spr. 29, 47.
129 DALO, f. 239, op. 1, spr. 18, 18.
130 Ibid., 15.
131 Ibid., 25.
132 DALO, f. 239, op. 1, spr. 49, 144
133 DALO, f. 239, op. 1, spr. 29, 38.
134 DALO, f. 239, op. 1, spr. 55, 19.
135 Ibid., 22.
136 DALO, f. 239, op. 1, spr. 56, 71–2.
137 Ibid.
138 DALO, f. 239, op. 1, spr. 65, 60.
139 DALO, f. 239, op. 1, spr. 55, 53.
140 DALO, f. 239, op. 1, spr. 65, 82.
141 Brian LaPierre, *Hooligans in Khrushchev's Russia: Defining, Policing, and Producing Deviance* (Madison: University of Wisconsin Press, 2012), passim.
142 DALO, f. 2037, op. 4, spr. 12, 3.
143 DALO, f. 239, op. 1, spr. 65, 112.
144 Ibid., 117.
145 Ibid., 113.

146 DALO, f. 239, op. 1, spr. 68, 2.
147 Ibid., 5.
148 DALO, f. 239, op. 1, spr. 72, 28.
149 DALO, f. 239, op. 1, spr. 144, 150.
150 Ibid., 304.
151 DALO, f. 239, op. 1, spr. 72, 80.
152 DALO, f. 239, op. 1, spr. 65, 118.
153 Ibid., 119.
154 DALO, f. 239, op. 1, spr. 77, 15.
155 DALO, f. 239, op. 1, spr. 93, 50.
156 DALO, f. 239, op. 1, spr. 84, 24.
157 DALO, f. 239, op. 1, spr. 89, 119–20.
158 DALO, f. 239, op. 1, spr. 92, 57; DALO, f. 239, op. 1, spr. 109, 15.
159 DALO, f. 239, op. 1, spr. 121, 95.
160 DALO, f. 2037, op. 4, spr. 15, 3
161 DALO, f. 2037, op. 4, spr. 13, 2.
162 DALO, f. 239, op. 1, spr. 55, 121.
163 DALO, f. 239, op. 1, spr. 108, 32.
164 Ibid.
165 DALO, f. 239, op. 1, spr. 126, 27.
166 DALO, f. 239, op. 1, spr. 109, 37.
167 DALO, f. 239, op. 1, spr. 129, 75.
168 DALO, f. 239, op. 1, spr. 8, 1.
169 DALO, f. 239, op. 1, spr. 23, 8.
170 DALO, f. 239, op. 1, spr. 34, 51.
171 DALO, f. 239, op. 1, spr. 39, 5–6.
172 DALO, f. 239, op. 1, spr. 55, 12.
173 DALO, f. 239, op. 1, spr. 68, 61.
174 DALO, f. 239, op. 1, spr. 65, 71.
175 DALO, f. 239, op. 1, spr. 68, 63.
176 DALO, f. 239, op. 1, spr. 49, 18.
177 DALO, f. 239, op. 1, spr. 65, 71.
178 DALO, f. 239, op. 1, spr. 83, 66.
179 Ibid., 108.
180 DALO, f. 239, op. 1, spr. 95, 83.
181 DALO, f. 239, op. 1, spr. 89, 34.
182 DALO, f. 239, op. 1, spr. 95, 91.
183 DALO, f. 239, op. 1, spr. 72, 65.
184 Ibid.
185 DALO, f. 239, op. 1, spr. 86, 13.
186 DALO, f. 239, op. 1, spr. 129, 179.
187 DALO, f. 239, op. 1, spr. 126, 81.
188 DALO, f. P-2037, op. 4, spr. 11, 26.

189 DALO, f. 239, op. 1, spr. 72, 128–9.
190 Ibid., 133.
191 DALO, f. 239, op. 1, spr. 83, 66.
192 DALO, f. 239, op. 1, spr. 97, 11.
193 DALO, f. 239, op. 1, spr. 55, 90–1.
194 DALO, f. 239, op. 1, spr. 50, 39.
195 DALO, f. 239, op. 1, spr. 86, 71.
196 DALO, f. 239, op. 1, spr. 108, 15.
197 DALO, f. 239, op. 1, spr. 129, 75.
198 DALO, f. 2037, op. 4, spr. 28, 6.
199 DALO, f. 239, op. 1, spr. 78, 54.
200 DALO, f. 239, op. 1, spr. 91, 111.
201 DALO, f. 239, op. 1, spr. 118, 3.
202 DALO, f. 239, op. 1, spr. 89, 117.
203 DALO, f. 239, op. 1, spr. 95, 93.
204 DALO, f. 239, op. 1, spr. 43, 64.
205 DALO, f. 239, op. 1, spr. 85, 29.
206 Ibid., 39.
207 DALO, f. 239, op. 1, spr. 95, 81.
208 Ibid., 80.
209 DALO, f. 239, op. 1, spr. 89, 30.
210 DALO, f. 239, op. 1, spr. 127, 104.
211 DALO, f. 2037, op. 4, spr. 29, 18.
212 DALO, f. 239, op. 1, spr. 101, 9.
213 DALO, f. 239, op. 1, spr. 105, 50.
214 John N. Westwood, *Soviet Railway Today* (London: Ian Allan, 1963), 8–9.
215 DALO, f. 239, op. 1, spr. 8, 1.
216 Rkps. Ossolin. 16180 /II, 77.
217 DALO, f. 239, op. 1, spr. 2, 15.
218 DALO, f. 239, op. 1, spr. 8, 6.
219 Serov, *Zapiski iz chemodana*, 411.
220 DALO, f. 239, op. 1, spr. 29, 49.
221 DALO, f. 239, op. 1, spr. 76, 128–9.
222 DALO, f. 239, op. 1, spr. 83, 27–8.
223 DALO, f. 239, op. 1, spr. 84, 25.
224 Ibid., 60.
225 Ibid., 61.
226 DALO, f. 239, op. 1, spr. 90, 12.
227 DALO, f. 239, op. 1, spr. 103, 28.
228 DALO, f. 1699, op. 1, spr. 98, 25.
229 Vadim Volkov, "The Concept of *Kul'turnost'*: Notes on the Stalinist Civilizing Process," in *Stalinism: New Directions*, ed. Sheila Fizpatrick (New York: Routledge, 2000), 210–30.

230 DALO, f. 239, op. 1, spr. 18, 6–7.
231 Ibid., 21.
232 DALO, f. 239, op. 1, spr. 8, 16.
233 DALO, f. 239, op. 1, spr. 2, 31.
234 DALO, f. 239, op. 1, spr. 13, 33.
235 DALO, f. 239, op. 1, spr. 28, 12.
236 DALO, f. 239, op. 1, spr. 39, 55–6.
237 Rosalyn A. Wilson, *Transportation in America: Statistical Analysis of Transportation in the United States*, 18th ed. (Washington, DC: Eno Transportation Foundation, 2001), 12–13.
238 Lozyns'kyi, *Etnichnyi sklad naselennia L'vova*, 254.
239 Mankurt [Aleksandr Khokhulin], "1975-yi: mis'ki khroniky vid Mankurta," 23 May 2008, http://zaxid.net/news/showNews.do?1975y_miski_hroniki_vid_mankurta&objectId=1054261, accessed 25 September 2016.
240 Mikhail Epstein, "Russo-Soviet Topoi," in Dobrenko and Eric Naiman, *Landscape of Stalinism*, 301.
241 Certeau, *Practice of Everyday Life*.
242 DALO, f. 239, op. 1, spr. 33, 59.
243 DALO, f. 239, op. 1, spr. 96, 21.
244 DALO, f. 239, op. 1, spr. 50, 30.
245 DALO, f. 239, op. 1, spr. 137, 91.
246 DALO, f. 239, op. 1, spr. 77, a.18, 25; DALO, f. 239, op. 1, spr. 84, 13.
247 Mykhalyk and Lemko, *L'viv povsiakdennyi (1939–2009)*, 166–7.
248 Varga-Harris, *Stories of House and Home*, 81–135.
249 Il'ia Il'f and Evgenii Petrov, *The Twelve Chairs*, trans. John H.C. Richardson (New York: Random House, 1961). I use "the zone of estrangement" instead of the translator's "right of way." The original is in Il'ia Il'f and Evgenii Petrov, *Sobranie sochinenii v piati tomakh*, vol. 1 (Moscow: Gosudarstvennoie izdatel'stvo khudozhestvenoi literatury, 1961), 51.
250 Ibid.
251 Joyce, *Rule of Freedom*, 71.
252 Aleksandr Genis and Petr Vail', *60-e: Mir sovetskogo cheloveka* (Moscow: Novoe literaturnoe obozrenie, 1998), 327.
253 Viktor Nekrasov, *V rodnom gorode*, http://nekrassov-viktor.com/Books/Nekrasov-V%20rodnom%20gorode.aspx, originally published in 1954.

Coda

1 Jaroslav Hašek, *The Good Soldier Švejk and His Fortunes in the World War* (New York: Crowell, 1974), 219.
2 Zoriana Ilenko, "Obrazyvsia i ... ubyv," *Postup* 41, 15–21 March, 2001, http://postup.brama.com/010315/41_9_3.html

3 Benjamin, *Arcades Project*, 463.
4 Karl Marx, "Wage Labour and Capital," in Karl Marx and Frederick Engels, *Collected Works*, vol. 9 (Moscow: Progress, 1977), 211.
5 Edward W. Soja, *Postmodern Geographies: The Reassertion of Space in Critical Social Theory* (London, New York: Verso, 1989), 76–93.
6 Osip Mandel'shtam, *Shum vremeni: Memuarnaia proza. Pis'ma. Zapisnye knizhki* (Moscow: Olma-Press, 2003), 120.

Bibliography

Archival Sources

AAN, Warsaw: Archive of Modern Records (Archiwum Akt Nowych)

Zespół 15: Ministerstwo opieki społeczneh
Zespół 16: Ministerstwo Komunikacji w Warszawie
Zespół 98: Akta Jędrzeja i Zofii Moraczewskich
Zespół 1208, Polska Partia Socjalno-Demokratyczna Galicji i Śląska Cieszyńskiego

ANK, Krakow: National Archive in Krakow (Archiwum Narodowe w Krakowie)

Zespół: PPSD (Polska Partia Socjalno-Demokratyczna Galicji i Śląska Cieszyńskiego)

AGAD, Warsaw: Main Archive of Ancient Records (Archiwum Główne Akt Dawnych)

Zespół: C.K. Ministerstwo Kolei Żelaznej

BJ, Krakow: Manuscript Section of the Jagiellonian Library (Sekcja Rękopisów Biblioteki Jagiellońskiej)

BN, Warsaw: Manuscript Collection of the Polish National Library (Zakład Rękopisów Biblioteki Narodowej)

DAKO, Kyiv: State Archive of the Kyiv Oblast (Derzhavnyi arkhiv Kyïvs'koï oblasti)

Fond 3527: Primary Party Organization of *Kievtransuzelproekt*

DALO, Lviv: State Archive of the Lviv Oblast (Derzhavnyi arkhiv Lvivskoï oblasti)

Fond 1: Lviv Oblast Committee of the Communist Party of Ukraine
Fond 305: Lviv Police Directorate
Fond 239: Primary Organization of the CPU. Lviv-Passenger Station
Fond 1699: Primary Organization of the Lviv Office of the Transportation Department of the Ministry of Internal Affairs of the USSR
Fond 2037: Headquarters of the Lviv Railroad

LNB, Lviv: Manuscript Collection of the Lviv National Vasyl Stefanyk Scientific Library of Ukraine (Viddil rukopysiv L'vivs'koï natsional'noï naukovoï biblioteky Ukraïny imeni V. Stefanyka)

Fond 44: Herman Diamand

Rkps. Ossolin., Wroclaw: Manuscript Division of the Ossolineum Library (Dział Rękopisów Zakładu Narodowego im. Ossolińskich)

RGAE, Moscow: Rossiiskii gosudarstvennyi arkhiv ekonomiki (Russian State Archive of the Economy)

Fond 1884: Ministry of Communications

RGIA, Saint Petersburg: Rossiiskii gosudarstvennyi istoricheskii arkhiv (Russian State Historical Archive)

Fond 237: Inspection of Emperor's Trains
Fond 273: Department of Railways
Fond 350, Plans and Drawings on the Construction of Railways and Railway Structures

RGASPI, Moscow: Rossiiskii gosudarstvennyi arkhiv sotsial'no-politicheskoi istorii (Russian State Archive of Socio-Political History)

Fond 81: Lazar Kaganovich
Fond 111: Political Department of the People's Commissariat (Ministry) of Communications of the USSR

RGVIA, Moscow: Rossiiskii gosudarstvennyi voenno-istoricheskii arkhiv (Russian State Military-Historical Archvie)

Fond 2004: Department of the Chief of Military Communications in the Theatre of Opeations

Fond 2067: Headquarters of the Commander-in-Chief of the Armies of the South-Western Front
Fond 2070: Department of the Chief of Military Communications of the Armies of the South-Western Front

TsDAHO, Kyiv: Central State Archives of Public Organizations of Ukraine (Tsentral'nyi dezhavnyi arkhiv hromads'kykh orhanizatsii Ukraïny)

Fond 1: Central Committee of the Communist Party of Ukraine

TsDAVO, Kyiv: Central State Archives of Supreme Bodies of Power and Government of Ukraine (Tsentral'nyi derzhavnyi arkhiv vyshchykh orhaniv vlady ta upravlinnia Ukraïny)

Fond 4920: South-Western District of the Ministry of Communications of the USSR

TsDIAuL, Lviv: Tsentralnyi derzhanyi istorychnyi arkhiv u Lvovi (Central State Historical Archive of Ukraine in Lviv)

Fond 146: Galician Vice-Roy's Office
Fond 248: Lviv Railway Directorate
Fond 354: Design and Research Bureau of the Polish Railways

Yad Vashem, Jerusalem: Yad Vashem Archives

M.49: Jewish Historical Institute, Warsaw
M.49E: Jewish Historical Institute, Warsaw Testimonies Collection
O.39: Collection of memoirs for the 1957 Yad Vashem competition
O.62: Borwicz Collection

Periodicals

Architekt, 1903, 1904
Dilo, 1904, 1907, 1929
Dziennik Ludowy, 1923, 1928
Dziennik Lwowski, 1904
Dziennik Polski, 1901, 1903
Front Kolejowy, 1935
Galichanin, 1908
Gazeta Lwowska, 1904, 1907, 1941, 1943, 1944
Głos, 1907–09
Goniec Polski, 1907

Inżynier Kolejowy, 1931
Kolejarz Związkowiec, 1938
Kolejarz, 1901–13
Kolejowe Przysposobienie Wojskowe, 1934–36
Krajowy Kolejarz, 1908–11
Kurjer Lwowski, 1901–04
L'vivs'ki visti, 1941–43
L'vovskii zhelznodorozhnik, 1944–46, 1948–50, 1952, 1954, 1962
Lwów w cyfrach. Kwartalnik statystyczny, 1936
Monitor, 1901
Naprzód, 1926
Nowa Reforma, 1904
Republika, 1923
Słowo Polskie, 1904
Trybuna Robotnicza, 1936
Tygodnik ilustrowany, 1904, 1919
Wiek Nowy, 1904
Zaliznychnyk, 1944

Blogs/Online Sources

Aeou. "Budynky No. 165-167 na vulytsi Horodots'kii u L'vovi." 10 January 2012. https://commons.wikimedia.org/wiki/File:165-167_Horodotska_Street_(01).jpg

Artemko. 2013. http://wikimapia.org/6231301/uk/%D0%9F%D0%B0%D0%BB%D0%B0%D1%86-%D0%BA%D1%83%D0%BB%D1%8C%D1%82%D1%83%D1%80%D0%B8-%D0%B7%D0%B0%D0%BB%D1%96%D0%B7%D0%BD%D0%B8%D1%87%D0%BD%D0%B8%D0%BA%D1%96%D0%B2-%D0%A0%D0%BE%D0%BA%D1%81#/photo/3100671

Boichenko, Nataliia. "Kino u L'vovi. Top-10 starykh kinoteatriv." 6 June 2015. Fotohrafiï staroho L'vova. http://photo-lviv.in.ua/kino-u-lvovi-top-10-staryh-kinoteatriv

Ilenko, Zoriana. "Obrazyvsia i ... ubyv." *Postup* 41, 15–21 March 2001. http://postup.brama.com/010315/41_9_3.html

KVV. "Nash Lviv." 10 June 2013. http://nash.lviv.ua/viewtopic.php?f=108&t=254&p=347&hilit=%D0%B2%D0%BE%D0%BA%D0%B7%D0%B0%D0%BB#p347

"Lwowscy kolejarze (blog)." 19 February 2010. http://lwow.blog.onet.pl/2010/02/19/lwowscy-kolejarze

Mankurt [Khokhulin, Aleksandr]. "1975-yi. Mis'ki khroniky vid Mankurta." 23 May 2008. http://zaxid.net/news/showNews.do?1975y_miski_hroniki_vid_mankurta&objectId=1054261. Accessed 25 September 2016.

"Moja przygoda fotograficzna." 21 November 2011. http://dalel.blog.onet.pl/2011/11/21. Accessed 31 July 2016.

Posterr. "Zhytlovyi budynok. Lviv. Hlyboka 14." 15 February 2015. https://commons.wikimedia.org/wiki/File:%D0%93%D0%BB%D0%B8%D0%B1%D0%BE%D0%BA%D0%B0,_14_P1110105.JPG

Sashalvovskiy. "Live Journal." 25 November 2012. http://sashalvovskiy.livejournal.com/202468.html

Books and Articles

Adrjański, Zbigniew. *Złota księga pieśni polskich: pieśni, gawędy, opowieści.* Warsaw: Bellona, 1994.

Al'bom vidov postroiki i evakuatsii voennykh zheleznykh dorog Vladimir-Volynskii-Sokal' i Sokal'-Kamenka-L'vov. 1914–1915 gg. Kiev: S.V. Kul'zhenko, 1916.

Aleichem, Sholem [Solomon Rabinovich]. *The Letters of Menakhem-Mendl and Sheyne-Sheyndl and Motl, the Cantor's Son.* Translated by Hillel Halkin. New Haven, CT: Yale University Press, 2002.

Alekseev, N. "Chto tormozit rabotu." *L'vovskii zheleznodorozhnik,* no. 139, 13 November 1945.

Allerhand, Maurycy, and Allerhand, Leszek. *Zapiski z tamtego swiata.* Krakow: Wydawnictwo Educkacyjne, 2003.

Alofsin, Anthony. *When Buildings Speak: Architecture as Language in the Habsburg Empire and Its Aftermath, 1867–1933.* Chicago: University of Chicago Press, 2006.

Amar, Tarik Cyril. *The Paradox of Ukrainian Lviv: A Borderland City between Stalinists, Nazis and Nationalists.* Ithaca, NY: Cornell University Press, 2015.

Ansky, S. [Shloyme Zanvl Rappoport]. *The Enemy at His Pleasure: A Journey through the Jewish Pale of Settlement during World War I.* New York: Metropolitan Books, 2002.

Bachmann, Klaus. *Ein Herd der Feindschaft gegen Rußland: Galizien als Krisenherd in den Beziehungen der Donaumonarchie mit Rußland (1907–1914).* Schriftenreihe des österreichischen Ost- und Südosteuropa-Instituts, Band 25. Vienna: Verlag für Geschichte und Politik; Munich: Oldenbourg, 2001.

Baedeker, Karl. *Austria-Hungary with Excursions to Cetinje, Belgrade, and Bucharest: Handbook for Travellers.* Leipzig: Karl Baedeker, 1911.

Bakunowicz, Czesław. "Koleje Generalnego Gubernatorstwa w wojennej organizacji kolejnictwa III Rzeszy Niemieckiej 1939–1945." *Dzieje Najnowsze,* no.1 (2005): 41–2.

Baran, Volodymyr. "Ekonomicheskie preobrazovaniia v Zapadnoi Ukraine v 1939–1941 godakh." In *Zapadnaia Belorussiia i Zapadnaia Ukraina v 1939–1941 gg.: liudi, sobytiia, dokumenty,* edited by Oksana Petrovskaia and Elena Borisenok, 156–77. Saint Petersburg: Aleteiia, 2011.

Barański, Franciszek. *Przewodnik po Lwowie*. Lviv: Słowo Polskie, 1902.

Baron, Nick. "New Spatial Histories of Twentieth Century Russia and the Soviet Union: Surveying the Landscape." *Jahrbücher für Geschichte Osteuropas*, Neue Folge 55, no. 3 (2007): 374–400.

Bartov, Omer. "Communal Genocide: Personal Accounts of the Destruction of Buczacz, Eastern Galicia, 1941–1944." In *Shatterzone of Empires: Coexistence and Violence in the German, Habsburg, Russian and Ottoman Borderlands*, edited by Omer Bartov and Eric D. Weitz, 399–420. Bloomington: Indiana University Press, 2013.

Barvins'kyi, Oleksander. *Spomyny z moho zhyttia*. Vol. 2. New York; Kyiv: Stylos, 2009.

Bataille, George. "Museum." In *Rethinking Architecture: A Reader in Cultural Theory*, edited by Neil Leach, 22–4. London and New York: Routledge, 1997.

Batyrev, Vadim. *Vokzaly*. Moscow: Stroiizdat, 1988.

Benjamin, Walter. *The Arcades Project*. Cambridge, MA: Belknap Press, 1999.

Beneš, Jakub. "Socialist Popular Literature and the Czech-German Split in Austrian Social Democracy, 1890–1914." *Slavic Review* 72, no. 2 (2013): 327–51.

Biedrzycka, Agnieszka, ed. *Kalendarium Lwowa 1918–1939*. Warsaw: Universitas, 2012.

Bilczewski, Józef. *Listy pasterskie, odezwy, kazania i mowy okolicznościowe*. Vol. 1. Lviv; Krakow: Wydawnictwo bł. Jakuba Strzemię Archidiecezji Lwowskiej ob. Łac. Oddział w Krakowie, 2005.

Biliński, Leon. *Wspomnienia i dokumenty*. Vol. 1, *1846–1914*. Warsaw: księgarnia F. Hoesicka, 1924.

Bilous, V.I. "Pershi komunistychni orhanizatsiï l'vivs'kykh zaliznychnykiv." *KPZU-orhanizator revoliutsiinoï borot'by: spohady kolyshnikh chleniv Komunistychnoï partiï Zakhidnoï Ukraïny*. Lviv: Knyzhkovo-zhurnal'ne vydavnytstvo, 1958.

Biruliov, Iurii, ed. *Arkhitektura L'vova: chas i styli, XIII–XXI st.* Lviv: Tsentr Ievropy, 2008.

Biruliov, Iurii. "Gorgolevs'kyi Zygmunt." In *Entsyklopediia L'vova*. Vol. 1, edited by Andrii Kozyts'kyi and Ihor Pidkova, 634–5. Lviv: Litopys, 2007.

Biruliov, Iurii. *Zakharevychi: tvortsi stolychnoho L'vova*. L'viv: Tsentr Ievropy, 2010.

Biriuliov, Iurii, and Andrii Rudnytskyi. *L'viv, turystychnyi putivnyk*. Lviv: Tsentr Ievropy, 1999.

Bissaga, Teofil. *Geografia Kolejowa Polskiz uwzględnieniem stosunków gospodarczo-komunikacyjnych*. Wydawnictwa Techniczne Ministerstwa Komunikacji 9. Warsaw: Ministerstwo Komunikacji, 1939.

Bodnar, Halyna. *L'viv: shchodenne zhyttia mista ochyma pereselentsiv iz sil (50-80-ti roky XX st.)*. Lviv: Vydavnychyi tsentr KNU imeni Ivana Franka, 2010.

Böll, Heinrich. *Der Zug war pünktlich: Erzählung*. Munich: Deutscher Taschenbuch, 1972.

Bonusiak, Andrzej. *Lwów w latach 1918–1939: ludność, przestrzeń, samorząd*. Galica i jej dziedzictwo 13. Rzeszów: Wydawnictwo WSP, 2000.

Borwicz, Michał. *Uniwersytet zbirów: rzecz o Obozie Janowskim we Lwowie 1941–1944*. Krakow: Wysoki Zamek, 2014.

Braiter, Bronisław. *Z mego podwórka*. Lviv: Leopolia, 1938.

Brindle, Steven. *Paddington Station: Its History and Architecture*. Swindon: English Heritage, 2004.

Broński, Krzysztof, and Jan Szpak. "Polityka budżetowa galicyjskich władz autonomicznych (zarys problematyki)." *Zeszyty Naukowe Uniwersytetu Ekonomicznego w Krakowie*, no. 835 (2010): 47–65.

Brubaker, Rogers. "National Minorities, Nationalizing States and External National Homelands in the New Europe." *Daedalus* 124, no. 2 (1995): 107–32.

Bryk, M.V., and Uliana Iaroslavivna Iedlins'ka, eds. *Istoriia Lvova v dokumentakh i materialakh: Zbirnyk dokumentiv i materialiv*. Kyiv: Naukova dumka, 1986.

Bułat, Włodzimierz Michał. "Pamiętnik-Dziennik." In *Lwów i lwowianie: Pamiętniki-Wspomnienia-Relacje*. Vol. 3, edited by Jerzy Kowalczuk, 11–26. Krakow, 2011.

Bureau of Railway Economics. *A Comparative Study of Railway Wages and the Cost of Living in The United States, the United Kingdom and the Principal Countries of Continental Europe*. Washington, DC, 1912.

Burke, Edmund. *A Philosophical Enquiry into the Origins of Our Ideas of the Sublime and Beautiful*. London: Routledge and Paul, 1958.

Buszko, Józef. *Polacy w parlamencie wiedeńskim, 1848–1918*. Warsaw: Wydawnictwo Sejmowe, 1996.

Čapek, Karel. *R.U.R. (Rossum's Universal Robots)*. Translated by David Wyllie. Adelaide: University of Adelaide, 2014. EPUB e-book. https://ebooks.adelaide.edu.au/c/capek/karel/rur/complete.html

Certeau, Michel de. *The Practice of Everyday Life*. Berkeley: University of California Press, 1984.

Chajes, Wiktor. *Semper Fidelis: Pamiętnik Polaka wyznania mojżeszowego z lat 1926–1939*. Krakow: Księgarnia Akademicka, 1997.

Chartoryis'kyi, M.S. [Mykola Sydor-Chartoryis'kyi]. *Mizh molotom i kovadlom: prychynky do istorii U.P.A. (Spomyny 1942–1945 rr.)*. New York: Ukraïns'ke vydavnytstvo "Hoverlia," 1970.

Chernets'kyi, Antin. *Spomyny z moho zhyttia*. Kyiv: Osnovni tsinnosti, 2001.

Chinciński, Tomasz. "Niemiecka dywersja w Polsce w 1939 r. w świetle dokumentów policyjnych i wojskowych II Rzeczypospolitej oraz służb specjalnych III Rzeszy. Cz.1, (Marzec-sierpień 1939 r.)." *Pamięć i Sprawiedliwość* 4/2 (8) (2005): 159–95.

Chodakowska, Jadwiga. *Pociąg berliński stoi przy peronie 2a*. Krakow: Krajowa agencja wydawnicza, 1988.

Chornovol, Ihor. *Pol's'ko-ukraïns'ka uhoda 1890–1894 rr.* Lviv: L'vivs'ka akademiia mystetstv, 2000.

Chowaniec, Józef. *Najnowszy dokładny plan królewskiego stołecznego miasta Lwowa*. Lviv: księgarnia Hermana Altenberga, 1892.

Czaplicka, John, ed. *Lviv: A City in the Crosscurrents of Culture*. Cambridge, MA: Harvard Ukrainian Research Institute, 2005.

Czarnecki, Władysław. *Wspomnienia architekta*. Vol. 1, edited by Hanna Grzeszczuk-Brendel. Poznań: Wydawnictwo Mijeskie, 2005.

Czekanowska, Anna. *Świat rzeczywisty – świat zapamiętany: losy Polaków we Lwowie (1939–1941)*. Lublin: Norbertinum, 2010.

Dąbrowski, Alexander. *Illustriert Führer durch Lwów*. Lviv, 1939.

Daszyński, Ignacy. *Pamiętniki*. Vol. 2. Krakow: Z.R.S.S. "Proletarjat," 1925.

David-Fox, Michael. *Crossing Borders: Modernity, Ideology, and Culture in Russia and the Soviet Union*. Pittsburgh: University of Pittsburgh Press, 2005.

Demin, Mikhail. *Blatnoi*. New York: Russica Publishers, 1986.

Döblin, Alfred. *Podróż po Polsce*. Krakow: Wydawnictwo Literackie 2000.

Domosławski, Zbigniew. *Mój Lwów: pamiętnik czasu wojny. Lwów po latach*. Jelenia Góra: Kolegium Krakonoskie, 2009.

Doroshenko, Dmytro. *Moï spomyny pro nedavnie-mynule*. Miunkhen: Ukrains'ke vydavnytstvo, 1969.

Dostoevsky, Fyodor. *Notes from Underground*. Bristol: Bristol Classical Press, 1993.

Drix, Samuel. *Witness to Annihilation: Surviving the Holocaust: A Memoir*. Washington; London: Brassey's, 1994.

Drobner, Bolesław. *Rzecz o klasowym ruchu zawodowym w Polsce w swietle prasy socjalistycznej*. Vol. 2 (lata 1918–23); Vol. 4 (lata 1929–33); Vol. 5 (lata 1934–39). Warsaw: Wydawnictwo związkowe CRZZ, 1965.

Dyskiewicz, Tadeusz, ed. *Wiadomości statystyczne o mieście Lwowie: 1910 i 1911*. Vol. 14. Lviv: Gmina królewskiego stołecznego miasta Lwowa, 1914.

Dzieduszycki, Wojciech. *Listy ze wsi*. Part 1. Lviv: Gazeta Narodowa, 1889.

Dziedzic, Małgorzata, and Stanisław Dziedzic. *Arcybiskup Józef Bilczewski*. Krakow: Wydawnictwo WAM, 2012.

Edwards, Brian. *The Modern Station: New Approaches to Railway Architecture*. London; NewYork: E & FN Spon, 1997.

Eley, Geoff. *Forging Democracy: The History of the Left in Europe, 1850–2000*. New York: Oxford University Press, 2002.

Eley, Geoff, and Keith Nield, *The Future of Class in History: What's Left of the Social?* Ann Arbor: University of Michigan Press, 2007.

Epstein, Mikhail. "Russo-Soviet Topoi." In *The Landscape of Stalinism: The Art and Ideology of Soviet Space*, edited by Evgenii Dobrenko and Eric Naiman, 277–306. Seattle: University of Washington Press, 2003.

Fedorchenko, V.I. *Imperatorskii Dom: vydaiushchiesia sanovniki – entsiklopediia biografii*. Vol. 2. Krasnoiarsk: Bonus; Moscow: Olma-Press, 2003.
Frank, Alison Fleig. *Oil Empire: Visions of Prosperity in Austrian Galicia*. Cambridge, MA: Harvard University Press, 2007.
Frank, Matthew. *Making Minorities History: Population Transfer in Twentieth-Century Europe*. Oxford: Oxford University Press, 2017.
Franko, Ivan. "Zakym rushyt' poïzd." *Literaturno-naukovyi* vistnyk 3, no. 1 (1898): 135–9.
Franko, Ivan. *Zibrannia tvoriv u p'iatdesiaty tomakh*. 2 vols. Kyiv: Naukova dumka, 1976.
Freeman, Michael. *Railways and the Victorian Imagination*. New Haven, CT: Yale University Press, 1999.
Friedman, Filip. *Zagłada Żydów lwowskich*. Łódź: Wydawnictwo Centralnej Żydowskiej Komisji Historycznej przy Centralnym Komitecie Żydoów Polskich, 1945.
Gansiniec, Ryszard. *Notatki lwowskie (1944–1946)*. Wroclaw: Sudety, 1995.
Genega, Roman. *L'viv: novi mishchany, studenty ta rezhym 1944–1953 rr.* Lviv: Lvivskyi natsionalnyi universytet imeni Ivana Franka, 2015.
Genis, Aleksandr, and Petr Vail'. *60-e: mir sovetskogo cheloveka*. Moscow: Novoe literaturnoe obozrenie, 1998.
Gerstenfeld-Maltiel, Jacob. *My Private War: One Man's Struggle to Survive the Soviets and the Nazis*. London: Vallentine Mitchell, 1993.
Gigliotti, Simone. *The Train Journey: Transit, Captivity, and Witnessing in the Holocaust*. New York: Berghahn Books, 2009.
Głąbiński, Stanisław. *Wspomnienia Polityczne*. Vol. 1, *Pod zaborem austriackim*. Pelplin: SP. Z O. ODP, 1939.
Gogołowska, Stanisława. "Przyczynek do historii obozu janowskiego: Ryszard Axer." *Przegląd Lekarski* 36, no. 1 (1979): 154–6.
Grabiński, Stefan. *Demon Ruchu*. Warsaw: Lampa i Iskra Boża, 1999.
Grabiński, Stefan. *The Motion Demon*. Ashcroft, BC: Ash-Tree Press, 2005.
Granach, Alexander. *There Goes an Actor*. Garden City, NY: Doubleday, Doran and Company, 1945.
Grodziska, Karolina. *Listy, listy, liście, wspomnienia ... Z dziejów lwowskich rodzin Reichertów, Peterów i Negruszów*. Krakow: Karolina Grodziska, 2012.
Gruszecki, Artur. *Kolejarze: powieść współczesna*. Krakow: G. Gebethner; Warsaw: L. Biernacki, 1909.
Guha, Ranajit. *Dominance without Hegemony: History and Power in Colonial India*. Cambridge, MA: Harvard University Press, 1998.
Haecker, Emil. *Historija socjalizmu w Galicji i na Śląsku Cieszyńskim*. Vol. 1, *1846–1882*. Krakow: Nakładem Towarzystwa uniwersytetu robotniczego, 1933.
Handziuk, Vitalii. "Fenomenolohiia ta propahandysts'ka diial'nist' hazety UVO 'Surma' u 1927–1929 rr." *Naukovi zapysky Vinnyts'koho derzhavnoho*

pedahohichnoho universytetu imeni Mykhaila Kotsiubyns'koho. Seriia: Istoriia 21 (2013): 37–42.

Hankiewicz, Mikolaj. "Jak stałem się socyalistą?" *Promień. Pismo poświęcone sprawom młodzieży szkolnej*, no. 6–7 (1903): 250–2.

Harvey, David. *Paris, Capital of Modernity*. New York: Routledge, 2003.

Harvey, David. "The Urban Process under Capitalism: A Framework for Analysis." In *The Blackwell City Reader*, edited by Gary Bridge and Sophie Watson, 32–9. Oxford: Wiley-Blackwell, 2010.

Hašek, Jaroslav. *The Good Soldier Švejk and His Fortunes in the World War*. New York: Crowell, 1974.

Hauptergebnisse der Österreichischen Eisenbahn-Statistik im Jahre 1897. Vienna: Kaiserlich-Königlich Hof- und Staatsdruckerei, 1898.

Hausner, Artur. *Gospodarka kolejowa w świetle dyskusji sejmowej*. Lviv: Nakładem księgarni ludowej, 1930.

Herselle Krinsky, Carol. *Synagogues of Europe: Architecture, History, Meaning*. Cambridge, MA: MIT Press, 1985.

Hilberg, Raul. *The Destruction of the European Jews*. Vol. 2. New York: Holmes and Meier, 1985.

Hilberg, Raul. "German Railroads/Jewish Souls." In *The Nazi Holocaust: Historical Articles on the Destruction of the European Jews*. Vol. 3, edited by Michael Marrus, 520–56. Westport, CT: Meckler, 1989.

Himka, John-Paul. "The Lviv Pogrom of 1941: The Germans, Ukrainian Nationalists, and the Carnival Crowd." *Canadian Slavonic Papers* 53, nos. 2–4 (2011): 209–42.

Hnatiuk, Ola. *Odwaga i strach*. Wrocław: KEW, 2015.

Hoffmann, David L. *Cultivating the Masses: Modern State Practices and Soviet Socialism, 1914–1939*. Ithaca, NY: Cornell University Press, 2011.

Hoffmann, David L. *Stalinist Values: the Cultural Norms of Soviet Modernity, 1917–1941*. Ithaca. NY: Cornell University Press, 2003.

Hohenberg, Paul M., and Lynn Hollen Lees. *The Making of Urban Europe, 1000–1994*. Cambridge, MA: Harvard University Press, 1996.

Holquist, Peter. *Making War, Forging Revolution: Russia's Continuum of Crisis, 1914–1921*. Cambridge, MA: Harvard University Press, 2002.

Hoszowski, Stanisław. *Ceny we Lwowie w latach 1701–1914* (Badania z Dziejów Społecznych i Gospodarczych, v. 130). Lviv: Kasa im. Rektora J. Mianowskiego, 1934.

Hrankin, P., P. Lazechko, I. Siomochkin, and H. Shramko. *L'vivs'ka zaliznytsia: istoriia i suchasnist'*. Lviv: Tsentr Ievropy, 1996.

Hryciuk, Grzegorz. *Polacy we Lwowie, 1939–1944: życie codzienne*. Warsaw: Książka i Wiedza, 2000.

Hryciuk, Grzegorz. *Przemiany narodowściowe i ludnościowe w Galicji Wschodniej i na Wołyniu w latach 1931–1948*. Toruń: Adam Marszałek, 2005.

Hryvul, Taras. "Chysel'nist' pidpil'noï merezhi OUN na terytoriï URSR v 1940–1941 rokakh." *Ukraïna: kul'turna spadshchyna, natsional'na svidomist', derzhavnist'*, 52 (2012): 260–8.

Hutnikiewicz, Artur. *Twórczość literacka Stefana Grabińskiego (1870–1936).* Toruń: Państwowe wydawnictwo naukowe, 1959.

Ianovs'kyi, Matsei. "Lemberg 1916–L'viv 2002: rozdumy nad starym putivnykom." *Krytyka* 7–8, no. 57–58 (2002): 21–4.

Iedlins'ka, U.Ia., and Iaroslav Isaievych, eds. *Istoriia L'vova v dokumentakh i materialakh: zbirnyk dokumentiv i materialiv.* Kyiv: Naukova dumka, 1986.

Iefremov, Serhii. "Zi spohadiv pro Ivana Franka." In *Spohady pro Ivana Franka,* edited by Mykhailo Hnatiuk, 223–9. Lviv: Kameniar, 1997.

Il'f, Il'ia, and Evgenii Petrov. *The Twelve Chairs.* Translated by John H.C. Richardson. New York: Random House, 1961.

Il'in, Iosif. *Skitaniia russkogo ofitsera: dnevnik Iosifa Il'ina, 1914–1920.* Edited by Veronika Zhober. Moscow: Knizhnitsa, Russkii put', 2016.

Ilustrowany przewodnik po Lwowie z planem orjentacyjnym ze wskaźnikiem. Lviv: Reklama Lwowska, 1936.

Inlender, Adolf. *Przewodnik ilustrowany po c. k. austr. kolejach państwowych na szlakach: Lwów-Krasne-Podwołoczyska, Krasne-Brody, Lwów-Stanisławów-Kołomyja-Śniatyn-Czerniowce, Kołomyja-Słoboda rungurska, Kołomyja-Kniażdwór, Stanisławów-Buczacz-Husiatyn, Stanisławów-Woronienka, Koleje Podolskie. Wedle wskazówek c.k. Generalnej Dyrekcji austr. koleji państwowych zredagował i napisał Adolf Inlender.* Vienna: Steyrermühl, [1892].

Isaievych, Iaroslav, Mykola Lytvtyn, Feodosii Steblii, and Liudmyla Batrak, eds. *Istoriia Lvova.* 3 vols. Lviv: Tsentr Ievropy, 2006–7.

Janusz, Bohdan. *Przewodnik po Lwowie (z planem miasta).* Lviv: Wszechświat, 1922.

Janusz, Bohdan. *293 dni rządów rosyjskich we Lwowie (3.IX.1914–22.VI.1915).* Lviv: Księgarnia Polska, 1915.

Jednodniówka Walki z Po¿arem: w 10-lecie wybuchu amunicji w Magaz. Kolej. we Lwowie: 1919–1929. Lviv: Zakł. Graficzne "Druk. Mieszczańskiej," 1929.

Jobst, Kerstin S. *Zwischen Nationalismus und Internationalismus: Die polnische und ukrainische Sozialdemokratie in Galizien von 1890 bis 1914: Ein Beitrag zur Nationalitätenfrage in Habsburgreich.* Hamburg: Dolling und Gallitz, 1996.

Joyce, Patrick. *The Rule of Freedom: Liberalism and the Modern City.* London: Verso, 2003.

Judson, Pieter M. *The Habsburg Empire: A New History.* Cambirdge, MA: Belknap Press, 2016.

Kabanov, Pavel. *Stal'nye peregony.* Moscow: Voenizdat, 1973.

Kaplan, Helene C. *I Never Left Janowska.* New York: Holocaust Library, 1989.

Kaps, Klemens. *Ungleiche Entwicklung in Zentraleuropa: Galizien zwischen überregionaler Verflechtung und imperialer Politik (1772–1914).* Vienna: Böhlau Verlag, 2015.

Kazanivs'kyi, Bohdan. *Shliakhom Liegendy*. London: Ukraïns'ka vydavnycha spilka, 1975.

Kharkhordin, Oleg. ed. *Mishel' Fuko i Rossiia: sbornik stattei*. Saint Petersburg: Evropeiskii universitet v Sankt-Peterburge, 2001.

Khrushchev, Nikita. *Vospominaniia*. Vol. 1. Moscow: Moskovskie novosti, 1999.

Kieszczyński, Lucjan. *Komunistyczna Partia Polski a ruch zawodowy 1918–1939*. Warsaw: Akademia Nauk Społecznych, Instytut Historii Ruchu Robotniczego, 1990.

Knysh, Zynovii [Bohdan Mykhailiuk]. *Dalekyi prytsil: Ukrains'ka viis'kova orhanizatsiia v 1927–1929 rokakh*. Toronto: Sribna surma, 1967.

Kochnev, F.P. *Passazhirskie stantsii i vokzaly*. Moscow: Gosudarstvennoe transportnoe zheleznodorozhnoe izdatel'stvo, 1950.

Kofler, Oskar. *Żydowskie dwory: Wspomnienia z Galicji Wschodniej od początku XIX wieku do wybuchu I wojny światowej*. Warsaw: Żydowski Instytut Historyczny, 1999.

Kohlmaier, Georg, and Barna von Sartory, eds. *Houses of Glass: A Nineteenth-Century Building Type*. Cambridge, MA: MIT Press, 1981.

Kolbuszowski, Edmund. *Sprawozdanie z czynności Miejskiego Biura pośrednictwa pracy*. Wiadomości statystyczne o mieście Lwowie 9. Lviv: Gmina królewskiego stołecznego miasta Lwowa, 1905.

Kompaniiets', Ivan. *Stanovyshche i borot'ba trudiashchykh mas Halychyny, Bukovyny ta Zakarpattia na pochatku XX st*. Kyiv: Vydavnytstvo Akademii Nauk Ukrains'koi RSR, 1960.

Kornman, S. *Map of Galicia and Bukovina's Highways, Railways and Waterways*. Lviv: H. Altenberg, 1898.

Kostenko, S.V., ed. *Arkhitektura Sovetskoi Ukrainy, 1951–1952*. Moscow: Gosudarstvennoe izdatel'stvo po stroitel'stvu i arkhitekture, 1955.

Kotkin, Stephen. *Magnetic Mountain: Stalinism as a Civilization*. Berkeley: University of California Press, 1997.

Kotkin, Stephen. "1991 and the Russian Revolution: Sources, Conceptual Categories, Analytical Frameworks." *Journal of Modern History* 70, no. 2 (1994): 384–425.

Kotlobulatova, Iryna. *Lwów na dawnej* pocztówce. Krakow: Międzynarodowe Centrum Kultury, 2006.

Kotlobulatova, Iryna. *Lviv na fotohrafiï: 1860–2006*. Lviv: Tsentr Ievropy, 2006.

Kotlobulatova, Iryna. *Lviv na fotohrafiï-2: 1860–2011*. Lviv: Tsentr Ievropy, 2011.

Kotlobulatova, Iryna. *Lviv na fotohrafiï-3: 1844–2014*. Lviv: Tsentr Ievropy, 2014.

Koval, Fedir, Ivan Kryp'iakevych, and Volodymyr Chuhaiov, eds. *Stanovyshche trudiashchykh L'vova, 1917–1939: dokumenty ta materialy*. Lviv: Lvivske knyzhkovo-zhurnalne vydavnytstvo, 1961.

Kovalev, Ivan. *Transport v Velikoi Otechestvennoi voine (1941–1945 gg.)*. Moscow: Nauka, 1981.

Kozielecki, Józef. *Banach: geniusz ze Lwowa*. Warsaw: Żak, 1999.

Kozłowski, Paweł. "'Wesoła lwowska fala,' czyli co bawiło publiczność w II Rzeczypospolitej." *Prace Naukowe Państwowej Wyższej Szkoły Wschodnioeuropejskiej: Nauki Humanistyczne* 1 (2014): 195–205.

Koźmian, Stanisław. *Podróże i polityka*. Krakow: Czas, 1905.

Kozyts'kyi, Andrii, and Ihor Pidkova, eds. *Entsyklopediia L'vova*. Vol. 1. Lviv: Litopys, 2007.

Kramarz, Henryka. *Samorząd Lwowa w czasie pierwszej wojny światowej i jego rola w życiu miasta*. Krakow: Wydawnictwo Naukowe WSP, 1994.

Krauze-Jaworska, Hanna. *Zarys Historii związku zawodowego pracownikow kolejowych Rzeczy Pospolitej 1918–39*. Warsaw: Wydawnictwo Związkowe CRZZ, 1968.

Kravtsov, Sergey R. "Wooden Synagogues of the Polish-Lithuanian Commonwealth: Between Polish and Jewish Narratives." Lecture presented at the symposium *Stella, Abstract Art and Synagogues*, Warsaw. 12 May 2016. https://www.academia.edu/25342727/Wooden_Synagogues_of_Polish-Lithuanian_Commonwealth_between_Polish_and_Jewish_Narratives._Lecture_at_the_symposium_Stella_Abstract_Art_and_Synagogues_Museum_of_the_History_of_Polish_Jews_Warsaw_May_12_2016

Krótki przewodnik po Lwowie i okolicy. Krakow: Krajowy Związek Turystyczny, 1910.

Kryp'iakevych, Ivan, ed., *Z istorii revoliutsiinoho rukhu u L'vovi, 1917–1939, Dokumenty i materialy*. Lviv: Lvivske knyzhkovo-zhurnalne vydavnytstvo, 1957.

Krzyżewski, Tadeusz. *Propaganda turystyczna Lwowa*. Lviv: Związek Dyplom. Abs. Akademii Handlu Zagranicznego, 1937.

Kurzer Führer durch Lemberg und Umgebung mit 15 Illustrationen und 1 Karte. Krakow: Landesverband für Fremden- und Reiseverkehr in Galizien, [1910].

Kurzer Führer durch Lemberg und Umgebung. Lemberg: Landesverbande für Fremden, 1912.

Kuz'ma, Oleksa. *Lystopadovi dni u L'vovi: zi shkitsamy*. Lviv: Chervona Kalyna, 1931.

Kuz'mich, V.D., and B.A. Levin, eds. *Istoriia zheleznodorozhnogo transporta Sovetskogo Soiuza*. Vol. 3, *1945–1991 gg*. Moscow: Moskovskii gosudarstvennyi universitet putei soobshcheniia, 2004.

LaPierre, Brian. *Hooligans in Khrushchev's Russia: Defining, Policing, and Producing Deviance*. Madison: University of Wisconsin Press, 2012.

Langer, Lawrence. "Introduction." In *Blood from the Sky*, by Piotr Rawicz, i–xvii. New Haven, CT: Yale University Press, 2003.

Lefebvre, Henri. *The Production of Space*. Oxford: Basil Blackwell, 1991.

Lem, Stanisław. *Highcastle: A Remembrance*. New York: Harcourt, Brace, 1995.

Lem, Stanisław. *Wysoki Zamek*. Warsaw: Wydawnictwo MON, 1966.

Levyns'kyi, Volodymyr. *Narys rozvytku ukrains'koho robitnychoho rukhu v Halychyni* (Kyïv, 1914).
Levyts'kyi, Kost'. *Istoriia politychnoi dumky halyts'kykh ukraïntsiv 1848–1914: na pidstavi spomyniv.* Lviv: OO. Vasyliiany u Zhovkvi, 1926.
Lieberman, Herman. *Pamiętniki.* Warsaw: Wydawnictwo Sejmowe, 1996.
Limanowski, Bolesław. *Historja ruchu społecznego w XIX stuleciu.* Lviv: Księgarnia Polska, 1890.
Lincoln, W. Bruce. *Nicholas I: Emperor and Autocrat of All the Russias.* DeKalb: Northern Illinois University Press, 1989.
Lityński, Michał. "Oblicze dzisiejszego Lwowa." In *Lwów dawny i dzisiejszy,* edited by B. Janusz. Lviv: Mar, 1928.
Lityński, Michał. *Pamiątkowy opis teatru miejskiego we Lwowie.* Lviv: Michał Lityński, 1900.
Liulevicius, Vejas Gabriel. *War Land on the Eastern Front: Culture, National Identity, and German Occupation in World War I.* Cambridge: Cambridge University Press, 2000.
Lohr, Eric. *Nationalizing the Russian Empire: The Campaign against Enemy Aliens during World War I.* Cambridge, MA: Harvard University Press, 2003.
Lozyns'kyi, Mykhailo. *Halychyna v rr. 1918–1920.* Vienna: Ukraïns'kyi Sotsioliogichnyi Instytut, 1922.
Lozyns'kyi, Roman. *Etnichnyi sklad naselennia Lvova u konteksti suspilnoho rozvytku Halychyny.* Lviv: Vydavnychyi tsentr LNU im. Ivana Franka, 2005.
L'vivshchyna turysts'ka: Putivnyk. Lviv: Kameniar, 1986.
Maciorowski, Mirosław. *Sami swoi i obcy: reportaże z kresów na kresy.* Warsaw: Agora, 2011.
Maderthaner, Wolfgang, and Lutz Musner. *Unruly Masses: The Other Side of Fin-de-Siècle Vienna.* International Studies in Social History 13. Oxford; New York: Berghahn Books, 2008.
Mały rocznik statystyczny: 1939. Warsaw: Główny Urzęd Statystyczny, 1939.
Mandel'shtam, Osip. *Shum vremeni: Memuarnaia proza: pis'ma: zapisnye knizhki.* Moscow: Olma-Press, 2003.
Mars'ka, V. [Mariia Strutyns'ka]. *Buria nad L'vovom: povist' u dvokh chastynakh.* Philadelphia; Kyiv, 1952.
Marx, Karl. "Wage Labour and Capital." In Karl Marx and Frederick Engels, *Collected Works.* Vol. 9. Moscow: Progress, 1977.
Matveev, A. "Cherepash'imi tempami." *L'vovskii zhelznodorozhnik,* no. 100, 17 August 1948.
Matyukhina, Aleksandra. *W Sowieckim Lwowie: życie codzienne miasta w latach 1944–1990.* Krakow: Wydawnictwo Uniwersytetu Jagielonńskiego, 2000.
Mazower, Mark. *Salonica, City of Ghosts: Christians, Muslims, and Jews, 1430–1950.* New York: Alfred A. Knopf, 2005.

Mazur, Grzegorz. *Życie polityczne polskiego Lwowa 1918–1939*. Societas 7. Krakow: Księgarnia Akademicka, 2007.

Mazur, Grzegorz, Jerzy Skwara, and Jerzy Węgierski, eds. *Kronika 2350 dni wojny i okupacji Lwowa 1 IX 1939–5 II 1946*. Katowice: Unia, 2007.

Medyński, Aleksander. *Lwów: Ilustrowany przewodnik dla zwiedzających z planem miasta*. Lviv: Księgarnia Gubrzynowicz i syn, 1938.

Meeks, Carroll L.V. *The Railroad Station: An Architectural History*. New Haven, CT: Yale University Press, 1956.

Mel'nyk, Ihor, and Roman Masyk. *Pam'iatnyky ta memorial'ni tablytsi mista L'vova*. Lviv: Apriori, 2012.

Mick, Christoph. *Kriegserfahrungen in einer multiethnischen Stadt: Lemberg 1914–1947*. Wiesbaden: Harrasowitz, 2010.

Mierzejewski, Alfred C. "A Public Enterprise in the Service of Mass Murder: the Deutsche Reichsbahn and the Holocaust." *Holocaust and Genocide Studies* 15, no. 1 (2001): 33–46.

Miller, Romuald. "Dom związku zawowodego pracowników kolejowych Rzeczypospolitej Polskiej." *Architektura i budownictwo*, no. 6 (1928): 175–207.

Mokłowski, Kazimierz. *Sztuka ludowa w Polsce*. Lviv: Altenberg, 1903.

Mykhailenko, P.P., and Ia.Iu. Kondrat'ev, eds. *Istoriia militsiï Ukraïny u dokumentakh i materialakh: U 3-kh t*. Vol. 2. Kyiv: Heneza, 1999.

Mykhalyk, Volodymyr, and Il'ko Lemko. *L'viv povsiakdennyi (1939–2009)*. Lviv: Apriori, 2009.

Nadol's'kyi, Iosyp. *Deportatsiina polityka stalins'koho totalitarnoho rezhymu v zakhidnykh oblastiakh Ukraïny (1939–1953): Monohrafiia*. Luts'k: Vezha, 2008.

Naiman, Eric. "Introduction." In *Landscapes of Stalinism: The Art and Ideology of Soviet Space*, edited by Evgenii Dobrenko and Eric Naiman, xi–xvii. Seattle: University of Washington Press, 2003.

Najdus. Walentyuna. *Polska Partia Socjalno-Demokratyczna Galicji i Śląska, 1890–1919*. Warsaw: Państwowe Wydawnictwo Naukowe, 1983.

Nekrasov, Viktor. *Zapiski zevaki*. Moscow: Vagrius, 2003.

Niemczyńska, Małgorzata I. "Ta, która chciała być panią." *Gazeta Wyborcza*, no. 117, 22 May 2014, 11–13.

Nilsen, Micheline. '"The Other Side of the Tracks': The Implantation of the Railways in Western European Capitals." Vol. 1. PhD diss., University of Delaware, 2003.

Nitka, Małgorzata. *Railway Defamiliarisation: The Rise of Passengerhood in the Nineteenth Century*. Katowice: Wydawnictwo Uniwersytetu Śląskiego, 2006.

Orłowicz, Mieczysław. *Ilustrowany przewodnik po Lwowie ze 102 ilustracjami i planem miasta*. Polska biblioteka turystyczna 13. Lviv; Warsaw: Atlas, 1925.

Osiecki, J. *Koleje żelazne w Galicji i stosunek tychże do kolei w Polsce i Rosji: z Mappą topograficzną kolei europejskich*. Vienna: Zamarski, Dittmarz i spółka, 1858.

Osterhammel, Jürgen. *The Transformation of the World: A Global History of the Nineteenth Century*. Princeton, NJ: Princeton University Press, 2014.
Ostrovskii, Grigorii. *L'vov*. Leningrad: Iskusstvo, 1982.
Parisien, Stephen. *Station to Station*. London: Phaidon Press, 1997.
Pavlova, V.E., and M.M. Uzdina, eds. *Istoriia zheleznodorozhnogo transporta Rossii i Sovetskogo Soiuza*. Vol. 2, *1917–1945*. Saint Petersburg; Moscow, 1997.
Peters, Tom F. *Building the Nineteenth Century*. Cambridge, MA: MIT Press, 1996.
Piłka Nożna na Ziemi Lwowskiej 1894–1939. Warsaw: SPAR, 1996.
Piwowar, Mieczysław. *Wspomnienia lwowskiego chłopaka*. Opole; Warsaw: Warsgraf, 2004.
Pohl, Dieter. *Nationalsozialistische Judenverfolgung in Ostgalizien 1941–1944*. Studien zur Zeitgeschichte, Band 50. Munich: R. Oldenbourg, 1997.
Połoniecki, Bernard. *Dzienniki, pamiętniki i listy z lat 1880–1943*. Edited and introduction by Maria Konopka. Warsaw: Biblioteka Narodowa, 2006.
Porter-Szücs, Brian. *Faith and Fatherland: Catholicism, Modernity, and Poland*. Oxford: Oxford University Press, 2011.
Powszechny spis ludności z dnia 9.XII.1931.
Presner, Todd Samuel. *Mobile Modernity: Germans, Jews, Trains*. New York: Columbia University Press, 2007.
Pro zlochynstva nimtsiv na terytoriï L'vivs'koï oblasti: povidomlennia Nadzvychainoï Derzhavnoï Komisiï po vstanovlenniu i rozsliduvanniu zlochynstv nimets'ko-fashysts'kykh zaharbnykiv. Kyiv: Ukraïns'ke derzhavne vydavnytstvo, 1945.
Prokopovych, Markian. *Habsburg Lemberg: Architecture, Public Space, and Politics in the Galician Capital, 1772–1914*. West Lafayette, IN: Purdue University Press, 2009.
Purchla, Jacek. *Patterns of Influence: Lviv and Vienna in the Mirror of Architecture*. Cambridge, MA: Harvard Ukrainian Research Institute, 2000.
Ratyński, Władysław. *Lewica Związkowa w II Rzeczypospolitej*. Warsaw: PWN, 1976.
Reclus, Élisée. *The Earth and Its Inhabitants*. Vol. 3, *Europe*. New York: D. Appleton and Company, 1882.
Reed, John. *The War in Eastern Europe*. New York: Charles Scribner's Sons, 1916.
Reichman, Fr., ed. *Księga adresowa królewskiego stołecznego miasta Lwowa 1900*, r.4. Lviv: A. Stryjkowskiego, 1900.
Reichman, Franciszek, ed. *Księga adresowa król. stoł. miasta Lwowa: rocznik siedemnasty 1913*. Lviv: Narodowa, 1912.
Reichman, Henry F. *Railwaymen and Revolution: Russia, 1905*. Berkeley: University of California Press, 1987.
Richman, Leon. *Why? Extermination Camp Lwów (Lemberg) 134 Janowska Street, Poland: A Documentary by an Inmate*. New York: Vantage Press, 1975.

Risch, William Jay. *The Ukrainian West: Culture and the Fate of Empire in Soviet Lviv.* Cambridge, MA: Harvard University Press, 2011.

Romaniczówna, Zofia. *Dziennik lwowski 1842–1930.* 2 vols. Warsaw: Ancher, 2005.

[Romanov, Nikolai]. *Dnevniki imperatora Nikolaia II.* Moscow: Orbita, 1991.

Rudolf, Archduke, Crown Prince of Austria, ed. *Die Österreichisch-ungarische Monarchie in Wort und Bild.* Vol. 12, *Galizien.* Vienna: k.k. Hof- und Staatsdruckerei, 1898.

Ryklin, Mikhail. "'The Best in the World': The Discourse of the Moscow Metro in the 1930s." In *The Landscape of Stalinism: The Art and Ideology of Soviet Space,* edited by Evgenii Dobrenko and Eric Naiman, 261–76. Seattle: University of Washington Press, 2003.

Rymar, Marta. *Architektura dworców Kolei Karola Ludwika w Galicji w latach 1855–1910.* Warsaw: Neriton, 2009.

Ryszkowski, Władysław. *Wspomnienia lwowskie z lat 1895–1900.* t.2. BN, IV 10189.

Sayer, Derek. *The Coasts of Bohemia: A Czech History.* Princeton, NJ: Princeton University Press, 1998.

Sayer, Derek. "Review of *The Idea of Galicia: History and Fantasy in Habsburg Imperial Culture,* by Larry Wolff." *Common Knowledge* 19, no. 3 (2013): 568–70.

Sayer, Derek. *The Violence of Abstraction: The Analytical Foundation of Historical Materialism.* Oxford: Basil Blackwell, 1986.

Schenk, Frithjof Benjamin. *Russlands Fahrt in die Moderne: Mobilität und sozialer Raum im Eisenbahnzeitalter.* Stuttgart: Franz Steiner Verlag, 2014.

Schivelbusch, Wolfgang. *The Railway Journey: The Industrialization of Time and Space in the Nineteenth Century.* Berkeley; Los Angeles: University of California Press, 1987.

Schorske, Carl E. *Fin-de-Siècle Vienna.* New York: Random House, 1981.

Segev, Tom. *Simon Wiesenthal: The Life and Legends.* New York: Doubleday, 2010.

Serov, Ivan. *Zapiski iz chemodana: tainye dnevniki pervogo predsedatelia KGB, naidennye cherez 25 let posle ego smerti.* Moscow: Prosveshchenie, 2017.

Sewell Jr., William J. *Logics of History: Social Theory and Social Transformation.* Chicago: University of Chicago Press, 2005.

Shabalin, N. "V strok vosstanovim L'vovskii vokzal." *L'vovskii zheleznodorohnik,* no. 68, 2 June 1945.

Shakh, Stepan. *L'viv – misto moieï molodosty.* Pt. 3. *Spomyn prysviahcenyi Tiniam zabutykh L'vov'ian.* Munich: Khrystyians'kyi Holos, 1955.

Shedel, James. *Art and Society: The New Art Movement in Vienna, 1897–1914.* New York: Sposs, 1981.

Sheptyts'kyi, Andrei. *Ostoroha Ioho Eksts: vpreosviashchenoho Mytropolyta Kyr Andreia Sheptys'koho pered zahrozoiu komunizmu*. Biblioteka "Prominchyka sontsia liubovy." Ch. 1. Univ: Lavra Studyts'koho Ustavu v Unevi, 1936.

[Shevchuk, Mykola]. "Kak my obsluzhivaem passazhirov (Iz doklada dezhurnogo po vokzalu stantsii L'vov-passazhirskaia tov. N.K. Shevchuka)." *L'vovskii zheleznodorozhnik*, no. 139, 15 November 1949.

Shoenfeld, Joachim. *Holocaust Memoirs: Jews in the Lwów Ghetto, the Janowski Concentration Camp, and as Deportees in Siberia*. Hoboken, NJ: Kitav, 1985.

Shporliuk, Roman. "Try (?) nenapysani statti pro L'viv." In *Leopolis multiplex*, edited by Ihor Balyns'kyi and Bohdana Matiiash, 292–6. Kyiv: Hrani-T, 2008.

Siegelbaum, Lewis H. "Whither Soviet History? Some Reflections on Recent Anglophone Historiography." *Region: Regional Studies of Russia, Eastern Europe, and Central Asia* 1, no. 2 (2012): 213–30.

Simons, Jack. *St Pancras Station*. Revised ed. with a new chapter by Robert Thorne. Zaragoza: Historical Publications, 2003.

Skoryi, A., I. Alekseev, and N. L'vov. "Na vokzale stantsii L'vov-passazhirskii." *L'vovskii zhelznodorozhnik*, no. 79, 5 July 1952.

Skwarzyński, Józef. "Rozwój sieci kolejowej pod zaborem austrijackim." *Inżynier Kolejowy* 3, no. 24–25 (1926): 215–19.

Slipyi, Iosyf. *Spomyny*. Lviv; Rome: Vydavnytstvo Ukrains'koho Katolyts'koho Universytetu, 2014.

Slyvka, Iurii, ed. *Deportatsiï. Zakhidni zemli Ukraïny kintsia 30-kh - pochatku 50-kh rr.: Dokumenty, materialy, spohady*. Vol. 1. Lviv: Instytut uraïnoznavstva NANU, 1996.

Smirnow, Jurij. "Historia światyń rzymskokatolickich," *Kurjer Galicyjski*, no. 3, 14 February 2008, 15.

Smirnow, Jurji. "Świątynia-pomnik: kośćiół św. Elżbiety." *Kurier Galicyjski* 71, no. 19 (2008), 18–19.

Smith, Michael P. *The City and Social Theory*. New York: St Martin's Press, 1979.

Snyder, Timothy. *Bloodlands: Europe between Hitler and Stalin*. New York: Basic Books, 2010.

Soja, Edward W. *Postmodern Geographies: The Reassertion of Space in Critical Social Theory*. London; New York: Verso, 1989.

Soja, Edward W. "Writing the City Spatially," *City* 7, no. 3 (2003): 269–80.

Soviet Statements on Nazi Atrocities. London: Hutchinson, [1946].

Sprawozdanie komissii wyznaczonej przez Sejm to wypracowania projektu kolei żelaznej w Galicii, złożone Prześwietnym Sejmującym Stanom w miesiącu wrześniu roku 1842 (Lviv, 1842).

Stansky, Peter. *Redesigning the World: William Morris, the 1880s, and the Arts and Crafts*. Princeton, NJ: Princeton University Press, 1985.

Stapiński, Jan. *Pamiętnik*. Warsaw: Ludowa spółdzielnia wydawnicza, 1959.

Stauter-Halsted, Kelly. *The Devil's Chain: Prostitution and Social Control in Partitioned Poland*. Ithaca, NY: Cornell University Press, 2015.

Stauter-Halsted, Kelly. "Jews as Middleman Minorities in Rural Poland: Understanding the Galician Pogroms of 1898." In *Antisemitism and Its Responses,* edited by Robert Blobaum, 39–59. Ithaca, NY: Cornell University Press, 2005.

Steblii, Feodosii. "Sotsial'no-demohrafichnyi portret." In *Istoriia Lvova y triokh tomakh*. Vol.2, edited by Iaroslav Isaievych, Mykola Lytvyn, Feodosii Steblii, and Liudmyla Batrak, 28–30. Lviv: Tsentr Ievropy, 2007.

Steenson, Gary P. *After Marx, Before Lenin: Marxism and Socialist Working Class Parties in Europe, 1884–1914*. Pittsburgh: University of Pittsburgh Press, 1991.

Sternberg, Yitzhak. *Under Assumed Identity*. Israel: Hakibbutz Hameuchad and Ghetto Fighters' House, 1986.

Strach, Herman, ed. *Geschichte der Eisenbahnen der Österreichisch-Ungarischen Monarchie*. Band 6, *Das Eisenbahnwesen Österreichs in seiner allgemeinen und technischen Entwicklung, 1898–1908*, vol. 2. Vienna: Karl Prochaska, 1908.

Struve, Kai. *Deutsche Herrschaft, ukrainischer Nationalismus, antijüdische Gewalt: Der Sommer 1941 in der Westukraine*. Berlin: De Gruyter, 2015.

Studyns'kyi, Kyrylo. *Z pobutu na Radians'kii Ukraïni: na marginesi pravopysnoï konferentsiï*. Lviv: nakladom Knyharni NTSh, 1927.

Sudoł, Jan. *Moje wspomnienia z lat 1890–1945*. Kolbuszowa: Biblioteka Publiczna Miasta i Gminy, 1994.

Sura, Konrad. "Moja ulica Gródecka." *Cracovia-Leopolis* 17, no. 1 (1991): 19–20.

Szczepaniec, Witold. *Wspomnienia z Ostbahnu: Żurawcia Nord Zugabfertigung Mitte 1942–1944*. Szczecin: Arsoba, 2003.

Szczygielski, Zbigniew. *Członkowie KPP 1918–1939 w świetle badań ankietowych*. Warsaw: Książka i Wiedza, 1988.

Szelburg-Zarembina, Ewa. *Dzieła*. Vol. 4. Lublin: Wydawnictwo Lubelskie, 1971.

Szporluk, Roman. "The Strange Politics of Lviv: An Essay in Search of an Explanation." In *The Politics of Nationality and the Erosion of the USSR*, edited by Zvi Gitelman, 215–31. Basingstoke, UK: Palgrave Macmillan, 1992.

Szporluk, Roman. "West Ukraine and West Belorussia: Historical Tradition, Social Communication and Linguistic Assimilation." *Soviet Studies* 31, no. 1 (1979): 76–98.

Tąkiel, Alfons. "Pamiętnik." In *Lwów i lwowianie. Pamiętniki-Wspomnienia-Relacje*. Vol. 3, edited by Jerzy Kowalczuk, 149–61. Krakow, 2011.

Tarnavs'kyi, Ostap. *Literaturnyi L'viv, 1939–1944: Spomyny*. Lviv: Prosvita, 1995.

Tarnavs'kyi, Zenon. *Doroha na Vysokyi Zamok: noveli, opovidannia, narysy*. Toronto: Homin Ukrainy, 1964.

Taussig, Michael. *Walter Banjamin's Grave.* Chicago: University of Chicago Press, 2006.

Thompson, Edward Palmer. *Whigs and Hunters: The Origins of the Black Act.* New York: Pantheon Books, 1975.

Trusz, Stanisław. "Wspomnienia wojenne." In *Lwów i lwowianie: Pamiętniki-Wspomnienia-Relacje.* Vol. 3, edited by Jerzy Kowalczuk, 188–274. Krakow, 2011.

Tscherkes, Bohdan. "Stalinist Visions for the Urban Transformation of Lviv, 1939–1955." *Harvard Ukrainian Studies* 24 (2000): 205–22.

Unowski, Daniel L. *The Pomp and Politics of Patriotism: Imperial Celebrations in Habsburg Austria, 1848–1916.* West Lafayette, IN: Purdue University Press, 2006.

Varga-Harris, Christine. *Stories of House and Home: Soviet Apartment Life during the Khrushchev Years.* Ithaca, NY: Cornell University Press, 2015.

Verbovyi, D.D. "V robitnychomu seredovyshchi," *KPZU – orhanizator revoliutsiinoï borot'by: spohady kolyshnikh chleniv Komunistychnoï partiï Zakhidnoï Ukraïny.* Lviv: Knyzhkovo-zhurnal'ne vydavnytstvo, 1958.

Verdery, Katherine. *The Political Lives of Dead Bodies: Reburial and Postsocialist Change.* New York: Columbia University Press, 1999.

Vergo, Peter. *Art in Vienna, 1898–1918: Klimt, Kokoschka, Schiele and Their Contemporaries.* New York: Phaidon, 1975.

V'iatrovych, Volodymyr. ed., *Pol's'ko-Ukrains'ki stosunky v 1942–1947 rokakh u dokumentakh OUN ta UPA.* Vol. 1. Lviv: Tsentr doslidzhen' vyzvol'noho rukhu, 2011.

Vil'chur, Iatsek [Jacek Wilczur]. *Na nebo srazu ne popast': L'vov, 1941–1943.* Moscow: Regnum, 2012.

Volkov, Vadim. "The Concept of *Kul'turnost'*: Notes on the Stalinist Civilizing Process." In *Stalinism: New Directions,* edited by Sheila Fizpatrick, 210–30. New York: Routledge, 2000.

Vuitsyk, V., and R. Lypka. *Zustrich zi L'vovom: Putivnyk.* Lviv: Kameniar, 1987.

Washburn, Stanley. *Field Notes from the Russian Front.* London: Andrew Melrose, [1915?].

Wat, Aleksander [Aleksander Chwat]. *My Century: The Odyssey of a Polish Intellectual.* Berkeley: University of California Press, 1988.

Węgierski, Artur. *W lwowskiej Armii Krajowej.* Warsaw: PAX, 1989.

Wells, Leon Weliczker. *The Death Brigade (the Janowska Road).* New York: Holocaust Library, 1963.

Wereszycki, Henryk. *Niewygasła przeszłość.* Krakow: Znak, 1987.

Westwood, John N. *Soviet Railway Today.* London: Ian Allan, 1963.

Wieczffińska, Dyoniza."Wspomnienia." In *Lwów i lwowianie. Pamiętniki-Wspomnienia-Relacje.* Vol. 3, edited by Jerzy Kowalczuk, 106–22. Krakow, 2011.

Wiczkowski, Józef. *Lwów, jego rozwój i stan kulturalny oraz przewodnik po mieście.* Lviv: Wydział gospodarczy X zjazdu lekarzy i przyrodników polskich, oraz reprezentacyi m. Lwowa, 1907.

Wielki Lwów: Przewodnik i informator. Lviv: Komitet Wydawniczy, 1933.

Wierzbicki, Ludwik. "Bożnica w miasteczku Jabłonowie nad Prutem." In *Sprawozdanie komisyi do badania historyi sztuki w Polsce,* Vol. 4, no. 2. Krakow: Akademia Umiejętności, 1889.

Wierzbicki, Ludwig. "Rozwój sieci kolei żelaznych w Galicyi od roku 1847 włącznie do roku 1880." Pts. 1, 2, 3, and 4. *Czasopismo Techniczne* 21 (1907): 307–12; 21 (1907): 328–33; 21 (1907): 345–9; 21 (1907): 361–6.

Wierzbicki, Ludwig. *Wzory przemysłu domowego,* various subtitles. Titles and text in Polish, Ukrainian, French, and German. 10 Vols. Lviv, 1880–89.

Wiktor, Stanisław. "Stanisławska Dyrekscja Kolejowa w cyfrach." *Inżynier Kolejowy,* no. 3, 1 March 1931.

Wilson, Rosalyn A. *Transportation in America: Statistical Analysis of Transportation in the United States.* 18th ed. Washington, DC: Eno Transportation Foundation, 2001.

Wingfield, Nancy M. "Destination: Alexandria, Buenos Aires, Constantinople; 'White Slavers' in Late Imperial Austria." *Journal of the History of Sexuality* 20, no. 2 (2011): 291–311.

Wirzyński, Hieronim. "W bohaterskim Lwowie." *Tygodnik Ilustrowany,* no. 5, 1 Feburary 1919.

Wittlin, Józef. *Mój Lwów.* London: Poslka fundacja kulturalna, 1975.

Wittlin, Józef. *Sól ziemi. Powieść o cierpliwym piechurze.* Warsaw: Państwowy Instytut Wydawniczy, 1988.

Wityk, Semen. *Jak żyje 10.500 mieszkańców Lwowa.* Lviv: Semenr Wityk, 1903.

Wołczański, Józef. "Listy Anny z Działyńskich Potockiej do Arcybiskupa Józefa Bilczewskiego z lat 1901- ok. 1919." *Nasza Przeszłość* 90 (1998): 430–68.

Wołczański, Józef, ed. *Nieznana korespondencja metropolitów lwowskich Józefa Bilczewskiego z Andrzejem Szeptyckim w czasie wojny polsko-ukraińskiej 1918–1919.* Lviv; Krakow: Wydawnictwo bł. Jakuba Strzemię Archidiecezji Lwowskiej ob. Łac. Oddział w Krakowie, 1997.

Wolff, Larry. *The Idea of Galicia: History and Fantasy in Habsburg Imperial Culture.* Stanford, CA: Stanford University Press, 2010.

Wood, Nathan. *Becoming Metropolitan: Urban Selfhood and the Making of Modern Cracow.* DeKalb: Northern Illinois University Press, 2010.

Wysocki, Alfred. *Sprzed pół wieku.* Krakow: Wydawnictwo Literackie, 1974.

Yones. Eliyahu. *Smoke in the Sand: The Jews of Lvov in the War Years 1939–1944.* Jerusalem; New York: Gefen, 2004.

Zahra, Tara. "Travel Agents on Trial: Policing Mobility in Late Imperial Austria." *Past & Present* 223 (May 2014): 161–93.

Zakrewski, Leszek. "Stacja ropałowa w Nowym Sączu," *Zeszyty Naukowo-Techniczne Stowarzyszenia Inżynierów i Techników Komunikacji Rzeczypospolitej Polskiej. Oddział w Krakowie* 1, no. 108 (2016): 125–40.

Zaporozhtsev, G.P., and S.I. Iakushin. *Novye zheleznodorozhnye vokzaly.* Moscow: Gosudarstvennoe transportnoe zheleznodorzhnoe izdatelstvo, 1957.

Żarnowski, Janusz. "Strajk kolejarzy i strajk powszechny w lutym-marcu 1921 r." *Kwartalnik historyczny* 63, no. 1 (1956): 55–88.

Zhaloba, Ihor. *Infrastrukturna polityka avstriis'koho uriadu na pivnichnomu skhodi monarkhiï v ostannii chverti XVIII – 60-kh rokakh XIX st. (na prykladi shliakhiv spoluchennia).* Chernivtsi: Knyhy-XXI, 2004.

Zhernoklieiev, Oleh. *Natsional'ni sektsii avstriis'koi sotsial-demokratii v Halychyni j na Bukovyni (1890–1918 rr.).* Ivano-Frankivs'k: Vydavnycho-dyzainers'kyi viddil Tsentru informatsiinykh tekhnolohii, 2006.

Zhuk, Ihor. *L'viv Levyns'koho: misto i budivnychyi.* Lviv: Hrani, 2010.

Zhuk, Ihor. "'Teoriia arkhitekturnykh tsyvilizatsii': krytychni uvahy shchodo monohrafiï Markiiana Prokopovycha." *Ukraïna Moderna* 23 (2016): 216–71.

Zieliński. *Lwów po inwazyi rosyjskiej, wrzesień-grudzień 1914: Opowiadanie naocznego świadka.* Vienna: Z. Machnowski, 1915.

Zubkova, Elena, ed. *Sovetskaia zhizn': 1945–1953 gg.* Moscow: ROSSPEN, 2003.

Żuławski, Zygmunt. *Wspomnienia.* Warsaw: Niezależna Oficyna Wydawnicza, [1980].

Index

www.ingramcontent.com/pod-product-compliance
Lightning Source LLC
LaVergne TN
LVHW090147080826
844660LV00013B/701/J

* 9 7 8 1 4 8 7 5 0 5 1 9 6 *